Tackling Child Neglect

of related interest

Risk in Child Protection
Assessment Challenges and Frameworks for Practice
Martin C. Calder with Julie Archer
ISBN 978 1 84905 479 9
eISBN 978 0 85700 858 9

Safeguarding Black Children
Good Practice in Child Protection
Edited by Claudia Bernard and Perlita Harris
Foreword by June Thoburn
ISBN 978 1 84905 569 7
eISBN 978 1 78450 011 5

Learning from Baby P
The Politics of blame, fear and denial
Sharon Shoesmith
ISBN 978 1 78592 003 5
eISBN 978 1 78450 238 6

Practical Guide to Child Protection
The Challenges, Pitfalls and Practical Solutions
Joanna Nicolas
ISBN 978 1 84905 586 4
eISBN 978 1 78450 032 0

Challenging Child Protection
New Directions in Safeguarding Children
Edited by Lorraine Waterhouse and Janice McGhee
ISBN 978 1 84905 395 2
eISBN 978 0 85700 760 5

Eradicating Child Maltreatment
Evidence-Based Approaches to Prevention and Intervention Across Services
Edited by Arnon Bentovim and Jenny Gray
ISBN 978 1 84905 449 2
eISBN 978 0 85700 823 7

Recognizing and Helping the Neglected Child
Evidence-Based Practice for Assessment and Intervention
Brigid Daniel, Julie Taylor and Jane Scott with David Derbyshire and Deanna Neilson
Foreword by Enid Hendry
ISBN 978 1 84905 093 7
eISBN 978 0 85700 274 7

Caring for Abused and Neglected Children
Making the Right Decisions for Reunification or Long-Term Care
Jim Wade, Nina Biehal, Nicola Farrelly and Ian Sinclair
ISBN 978 1 84905 207 8
eISBN 978 0 85700 441 3

The Child's World
The Comprehensive Guide to Assessing Children in Need
Second Edition
Edited by Jan Horwath
ISBN 978 1 84310 568 8
eISBN 978 0 85700 183 2

Tackling
Child
Neglect

Research, Policy and Evidence-Based Practice

Edited by
RUTH GARDNER

Foreword by
DAVID HOWE

Jessica Kingsley *Publishers*
London and Philadelphia

Research Note on 'Preventing Dental Neglect' on pp.94–7 is reproduced with kind permission from Emily Keene.

Figure 8.4 'The Safety House tool' on p.253 is reproduced with kind permission from Sonja Parker.

Note on 'The UK evaluation of SafeCare®' on pp.302–4 is reproduced with kind permission from Gillian Churchill, NSPCC.

First published in 2016
by Jessica Kingsley Publishers
73 Collier Street
London N1 9BE, UK
and
400 Market Street, Suite 400
Philadelphia, PA 19106, USA

www.jkp.com

Library of Congress Cataloging in Publication Data
Names: Gardner, Ruth, 1950 January 21- editor.
Title: Tackling child neglect : research, policy and evidence-based practice
   / edited by Ruth Gardner.
Description: Philadelphia : Jessica Kingsley Publishers, 2016. | Includes
   bibliographical references and index.
Identifiers: LCCN 2016005399 | ISBN 9781849056625 (alk. paper)
Subjects: LCSH: Child abuse. | Child abuse--Prevention.
Classification: LCC HV6626.5 .T33 2016 | DDC 362.76--dc23 LC record available at
http://lccn.loc.gov/2016005399

British Library Cataloguing in Publication Data
A CIP catalogue record for this book is available from the British Library

ISBN 978 1 84905 662 5
eISBN 978 1 78450 165 5

Printed and bound in Great Britain

CONTENTS

PART 3: PREVENTING AND REVERSING
CHILD NEGLECT

FOREWORD
David Howe

For many years the neglect of children did not trigger the same sense of outrage as that caused when children were found to be victims of abuse. Neglect seemed to lack the drama and urgency of bruises and broken bones. But slowly, neglect's long term, insidious and damaging effects were recognised. The research findings of developmental psychologists proved particularly important in helping child and family workers across all disciplines understand why neglect had to be treated much more seriously. It became apparent that deprivation and neglect starved children not only of physical care and sustenance but also emotional, social and intellectual stimulation. The neglect of the mind turns out to be just as critical as neglect of the body.

Children only become psychologically competent, socially fluent and emotionally intelligent beings when they have been in relationship with others who are themselves psychologically, socially and emotionally attuned, sensitive, interested, responsive and empathic. And of course the most powerful and influential of these relationships is that which children have with their primary caregivers. Children who are deprived of these reflective, reciprocal and responsive relationships will fail to develop these self-same psychosocial skills. This puts them at a huge developmental and social disadvantage. Lacking these skills, neglected children are at increased risk of poor physical health, poor mental health, reduced resilience, low educational attainment, and problematic social relationships. Researchers have also taught us that most parents of neglected children suffered abuse and neglect, rejection or trauma when they were children. Lacking the psychosocial skills to understand, empathise and respond to other people's mental states they risk neglecting their own children's psychological, social and health needs, just as their own were neglected when they were growing up.

Today, therefore, we have a reasonably good understanding of neglect, what causes it, and what the adverse effects are on young bodies and minds. We also know that there are huge costs to society when neglect is ignored. The price tag for dealing with the long-term consequences of neglect including increased risks of poor physical health, psychopathology, unemployment, substance abuse, and problematic parenting is very high. However, even when neglect is recognised, we are only just beginning to develop reliable ways of assessing its presence, character and extent. And perhaps least developed of all is how to prevent it in the first place, and if it is occurring, what to do about it. But there is progress and the current book reports the work of a number of pioneering, cutting edge specialists who are teaching us how to assess and treat cases of neglect in ways both creative and efficacious.

Stress, of course, runs as a corrosive thread through all cases of neglect. Stressed minds find it difficult to think about, or indeed care about others. And minds become stressed if they live in poverty, poor housing and communities of violence. It behoves practitioners always to start with the obvious. Help families deal with their material and nutritional needs whenever possible.

But minds that find it difficult to fathom other minds because they lack the mentalising skills that make relationships and social life intelligible also find interpersonal life stressful. Other people are a puzzle and strain. A vicious circle sets in. Stress further decreases the ability to empathise and see the world from other people's point of view. Relationships become more difficult. It all becomes too hard – thinking, planning, feeling, relating, deciding, caring, coping, hoping. Drink and drugs might dampen some of the pain. Switching off, sleeping, and withdrawing might solve the problem of how tough it is to make sense of and deal with others, particularly those who make demands on you, especially children. It is all very depressing. The parent who feels stressed, helpless and disconnected is no longer available, emotionally or psychologically, for the child who in turn feels abandoned and alone, unloved and frightened. The child, too, begins to experience stress and distress and so, like the parent, they have to develop ways of surviving, physically, emotionally and psychologically. These survival strategies, although they make sense in the context of the dysfunctional parent–child relationship, rarely help the child cope with the outside world. Their attempts to survive and stay safe are therefore relationship-specific but in the broader scheme of things, ultimately maladaptive.

In this excellent book, Ruth Gardner has brought together a number of leading international experts in the business of recognising and understanding, assessing and dealing with neglect. We hear of the latest research on what causes and sustains neglect. We are introduced to some imaginative and engaging ways of assessing neglect that actively and therapeutically involve the parents themselves. Profiles and ratings of current parenting practices are generated in collaboration with mothers, fathers and children. The ratings are then used to determine and discuss with the parents how they think they might move from a poor score to a better score, always building on whatever positives, however few and fleeting, might be present. And perhaps even more fittingly, several authors make the compelling case that the most powerful accounts of what it feels like to be neglected come from the children themselves. Whenever age allows, children need to be involved in helping professionals understand and assess what it feels like to be on the receiving end of care that is neglectful – the shame, the hunger, the smell, the loneliness, the bullying, the fear, the pain, the strain, the sadness.

And finally, based on our current best understanding of neglect, and that it is always wise to collaborate with the parents and children themselves in formulating assessments, the book describes a number of original and inspired interventions. If neglectful parents are to recognise and become interested in their children's bodies and minds, thoughts and feelings, responses and reflections, hopes and wishes, then practitioners have to become interested in the bodies and minds, thoughts and feelings, responses and reflections, hopes and wishes of the parents. Underpinning all successful interventions is the creation of a good worker–family relationship in which trust, interest, belief, and above all, hope are present. We are shown a variety of ways in which these things can be done – by building on whatever positives might be seen even in the thinnest of parent–child relationships – using video interaction guidance techniques; offering support, skills acquisition, guidance and behavioural training; and building on the familys' strengths, resources, networks. Change has to be seen as an endeavour that is purposeful, collaborative and shared.

This is a book full of sound thinking and original ideas. I defy anyone who reads this compilation not to come away feeling even more inspired, enthused and, yes, even optimistic as they work with both the parents who neglect and the children who are neglected.

David Howe
Emeritus Professor of Social Work
University of East Anglia
Norwich

INTRODUCTION
Ruth Gardner

Tackling child neglect

The prevention and treatment of child neglect present huge challenges for all those who care for and work with children. Arising from new research and practice there are now fresh opportunities for the lives of children and families to improve by changing the family dynamics and the circumstances that could otherwise lead to neglectful parenting for the next generation. This book explores current challenges and opportunities in research, policy and practice relating to neglect.

Content of the book

Eighteen contributors, based on three continents, introduce a wide span of international literature and professional knowledge on neglect, drawing on the experiences and views of children, parents and practitioners. The first section reviews the evidence about how neglect affects children in their early years (Chapter 1); in their development of speech, language and communication (Chapter 2) and in their everyday experiences (Chapter 3) and these chapters also consider responses to mitigate the negative effects of neglect. The second section takes four different perspectives on neglect. It starts with a broad research review (Chapter 4); goes on to tell us what children and young people have to say (Chapter 5); details the experiences of medical practitioners in the community (Chapter 6), and brings together learning from the most serious and closely examined cases of neglect (Chapter 7). The final section of the book examines the latest evidence on practice that is now being tested internationally in situations of child neglect. This includes Signs of Safety (Chapter 8); evidence-based parent support, including SafeCare® (Chapter 9); and finally Video Interaction Guidance (Chapter 10). In these chapters the voices of parents and practitioners can be heard. In the Conclusion, I explore some of the issues and questions arising from the evidence collected here and the idea that to address child neglect in a systematic way, requires whole families to be able to draw on physical, emotional and learning resources within their communities.

While the chapters follow a similar format, the contributors' different approaches to their subjects, and their individual styles, offer variety. Some chapters (for example 1, 2, 4 and 9) review a wide body of literature; others (Chapter 3, and the final section of the book) describe ways of working with children and families, and the evidence base for them. Yet others (Chapters 5, 6 and 7) examine original research in depth. Chapters start with a summary and introduction to the topic, followed by an account of any relevant research and evaluation methods, the learning being drawn on with illustrations or examples, and the most interesting and important findings. Each chapter concludes with implications for practice, policy and research, key messages and some questions for readers to research further themselves or to reflect on. The book offers readers who are in practice (or training for practice) with children and families, who are involved in policy or research affecting their lives, or who are simply curious to find out more about a subject that is yet to be fully mapped and understood, overviews of relevant work as well as opportunities to immerse in the fine detail of practice and research.

What is child neglect?

Child neglect is widely recognised nationally and internationally (for instance by the World Health Organization (WHO 2006)) as a form of child maltreatment with serious and potentially fatal consequences. Official definitions in public law and in guidance are for childcare professionals who work with families on a voluntary or compulsory basis. Child neglect can be encountered by anyone who works with children, including volunteers, family support workers, teachers and doctors. In the UK, when neglect constitutes a child protection concern, it is usually dealt with by qualified social workers working in local Children's Social Care Departments or their equivalents (sometimes referred to as 'social services'). Definitions are related to particular jurisdictions and are interpreted according to local thresholds for action and expectations of parenting. However, there are some common elements; they frequently refer to types of neglect (neglect of the child's health, safety and security) as well as to a child's basic needs (for food and shelter, emotional care, social and educational input); and they refer to the cause of neglect as a failure of care to meet those needs on the part of an adult (usually a parent). They refer to the harmful effects of neglect, as well as sometimes to contributory factors, such as parental substance misuse, hardship or domestic violence. There are variations; for instance within the UK, an updated definition in Wales (see Chapter 4) omits the term 'persistent' that is used in English public law, recognising that (as with other forms of maltreatment) neglect does not necessarily need to persist to cause damage. Similarly, in England, the National Institute for Health and Clinical Excellence (NICE) (2008) refers to neglect as sometimes 'occasional and unpredictable' adding that it is a 'process involving accumulating risk to the child'. The definition of neglect in criminal law (in England) is included in older legislation that deals with child cruelty. The threshold for criminal prosecution is higher, requiring intentional or wilful harm (rather than 'failure of care') to be proven. The advantages and limitations of these ways of thinking about neglect are explored further below and throughout the book, alongside other perceptions, for example, personal accounts of neglect. These are often more telling than any definition;

> Over the weeks I spent alone, with myself and a woman who only got up to buy some more beer and drink herself back into a coma that would last from one to three days, I did realise that something was wrong with her. I also realised that there was nothing I could do. So I did what I could for myself. I got drinks by climbing onto the kitchen table and pouring the contents of a bottle into a dirty glass, which I used repeatedly... I would wait for my mother to resurface... (Girl aged 16, quoted in Harris 2008, p.16)

See also chapters 3, 5, 6, 9 and 10.

> to this day, I think they are lost because they were left with their mother who, for no fault of her own and because of her own, you know, all of her background and things, really wasn't capable of providing good enough parenting for them. I mean, they're here, they're alive, but you know – and that was an – I think it's been terrible neglect really. (General medical practitioner quoted by Woodman in Chapter 6)

For the adult who has been without emotional support and lacks self-belief, any positive reaction may be rejected, but if trust has been established with a practitioner, this can be a turning point:

> On one occasion I said 'well done, that was really good' about something little that she had done. She looked at me and her face lit up; 'no-one has ever said well done before'. This was such an important step for this young mother. (Family Nurse Practitioner quoted in Beesley 2011, p.116)

See also Chapter 10.

The official definitions, in attempting to set a bar on unacceptable behaviour to children, combine two ideas that are conveyed by these quotations: the act of neglecting *and* the neglect suffered by a child. The failure of parental responsibility (e.g. not taking a child to health appointments) is set alongside the observed harm to a child who is uncared for physically and/or emotionally (in the case of missed appointments, the result for the child could be an accelerating health problem). Both 'failure' and 'harm' are hard ideas to take on board, and can easily alienate families already under stress. It may be more helpful to observe and describe the child's developmental needs with the parent, and tools such as The Horwath Model (Chapter 3), the Graded Care Profile (GCP 2) (Johnson and Cotmore 2015; Johnson, Smith and Fisher 2015; Chapter 3), The North Carolina Family Assessment Scale (Kirk and Reed-Ashcraft 2004) and Signs of Safety (Chapter 9) are extremely helpful here in measuring and evidencing progress over time, framing and informing the difficult conversations that need to be held, and also in highlighting the resources that can be deployed and what is working well, which parents say they find encouraging.

There is evidence here on all these aspects: on how neglect harms children and young people; on the care that children at various developmental stages need in order to get a good start, or to get back on track; on work with parents to help them offer this care; and how this work is being tested to an unprecedented extent.

The extent and cost of child neglect and its impact on children and young people

In terms of prevalence (frequency of occurrence in the population) neglect is the commonest form of maltreatment in many economically advanced as well as developing nations; and in many of them neglect is also the highest proportion of child protection cases. Jonson-Reid *et al.* (2009) write that in the US:

> each year, about six million children are reported to child protective services…while some are reported only once, others become involved with the system repeatedly. Neglect cases make up the majority of maltreatment reports nationwide. In addition, re-reports are most likely to fall into the category of neglect, regardless of whether the initial report was for physical or sexual abuse.

In Chapter 9, Rostad *et al.* point out that a similar picture has persisted across English speaking nations and that 'while recent decades have seen a decline in the rates of physical and sexual abuse, rates of child neglect have remained relatively stable' (see also Finkelhor and Jones 2006).

Despite the continuing high prevalence and incidence of neglect, as Allnock writes in Chapter 4, a lack of basic data on neglect impedes understanding of 'the scale and scope of a problem…that is critical for determining the nature and size of the response that is required'. Without there being a commitment to collect the necessary data, neglect is too amorphous to be addressed in a coherent way. This 'wallpaper effect' means that policy-makers know neglect is there, but without more evidence it is easy to ignore its salience. For example, government-funded family projects target children receiving protection services but do not always require projects to understand the precise profile of harm those services address. An exception is Wales, where a project is underway to create a national strategy to address child neglect based on improved data (Stevens and Laing 2015).

Given its wide range of demonstrable impacts on learning and earning potential, on health and mental health, and on social and parenting skills, it is not surprising that the costs of neglect in terms of personal and social wellbeing, family stability and economic productivity are enormous (Gilbert *et al.* 2009). Costs associated with families who chronically neglect their children have been determined to be seven times those associated with non-chronic families (Loman and Siegal 2004 quoted by Kaplan *et al.* 2009).

The robust evidence of the seriousness of neglect in terms of its impact is a thread throughout the book, from the life-threatening examples discussed in Chapter 7 to the impacts discussed in earlier chapters. Gilbert *et al.* (2009) comment that 'studies show post-traumatic stress disorder to be as frequently the result of neglect as of any other form of harm'. Particularly strong evidence comes from research across generations such as the Minnesota Study (Sroufe *et al.* 2005). This demonstrates that a parent's emotional unavailability (coldness or aversion) to a child is a devastating form of abuse, whether or not accompanied by poverty or deprivation. It causes specific damage to social and learning capacity that can last into adulthood and risk compromising their future social adjustment and parenting. Growing evidence on the cumulative effect on adult health status of multiple forms of adverse childhood experiences (MACEs), including neglect, is emerging (e.g. Felitti and Anda 2009, and systematic reviews such as Kalamakis and Chandler's (2015) (see Chapter 4). Most recently, Geoffroy et al. 2016 present research on a large British population cohort with important new findings , including 'a strong association of child neglect with cognitive deficits throughout life...an association was evident by age 7 or 11 in childhood and then appeared to persist to ages 16 and 50'. They conclude that this 'has implications for policy, practice and future research. Primary prevention of child neglect is paramount to avoid a lifelong cognitive burden and poorer educational outcomes'. They argue that 'remediation of long-term effects of child neglect' (p.39) is also realistic, given that 'although there is stability of cognition, there is also malleability, as other compensatory factors are experienced'.

The failure of prevention

'Recurrence' of neglect is the number of repeat incidents that have been substantiated within a given period. Fluke and colleagues found in the US that recurrence was more likely for neglect than any other form of harm, and worryingly, that the likelihood of another incident of neglect was greater after each subsequent event (Fluke, Yuan and Edwards 1999). This led them to conclude that within the US child protection system there was 'a group of chronically maltreated children' who repeatedly suffered neglect. Farmer and Lutman (2010) also found in the UK that children within the child protection and care systems continued to suffer parental neglect. There was a 'wait and see' attitude; the systems seemed to be offered as protection by themselves without proactive decision-making or intervention to address the risks these children faced. This was increasingly the case after children reached age six, and where it was endemic it could be described as systemic neglect.

The issues in dealing with neglect appear to be the same across jurisdictions; assessments of need and risk tend to take account only of abusive incidents, rather than detailing and measuring cumulative harm. As a result they may exclude all but the most severe 'immediate risk' cases of neglect. Hester (2009) makes a similar point about the police assessment of domestic violence cases, describing their practice 'moving from a merely incident-based to a more contextualised/pattern-based approach' (p 7). With neglect, many decisions are pragmatic rather than child-focused. These cases may be 'logged' administratively but fail to reach the threshold for either early help or protective intervention. In England, inspectors report that 'the failure of assessments to effectively identify and analyse the level of risk and the impact of neglect on children has a serious and detrimental effect on short- and long-term planning for some children' (Ofsted 2014). Caren Kaplan *et al.* (2009; emphasis added) emphasise the importance of a preventive and proactive stance with neglect; 'it is imperative that focused and coordinated efforts be initiated that offer assistance the *first time* families are identified with neglect concerns (thereby preventing chronic neglect)'. A practitioner describes applying this lesson to the use of Signs of Safety in Chapter 9.

This kind of evidence on successful interventions in child neglect is slowly accumulating. Examples are, first, research by Keene *et al.* (2015) summarised at the end of Chapter 3, which shows that children suffering unnecessarily from dental neglect, who were previously thought 'hard to reach', can receive treatment if they are helped to do so; second, findings that children referred for neglect who suffer burns have more lasting and serious physical injuries than those not referred for neglect (Chester *et al.* 2006) (see also Chapters 7 and 9). Finally, a study comparing children and a review of the Home Start early education service in the US noted that 'early care and education made little practical difference on language development outcomes for children referred for other types of maltreatment, but for the third of the sample referred to Children's Welfare Services for supervisory neglect, it had an incredibly salient positive impact' (Merritt and Klein 2015). The crucial importance of nurturing aspects of communication is covered in fascinating detail in the first two chapters of this book. Such important evidence can sometimes appear in research whose primary focus is not neglect, and it needs to be made more accessible not only for research but for service development.

While methods of identifying children at risk of neglect improve, we still cannot know which children will actually go on to experience it. These chapters offer evidence, first on how to identify parents of children at risk quickly and accurately, and second on how to engage them in acceptable and effective help. They demonstrate that leadership and conviction are needed to build on these encouraging findings, to seek out data profiling the extent and nature of child neglect in greater detail and depth, and to ensure that it is used to make child neglect less common in our societies.

Note: Unless otherwise stated, the views and recommendations expressed in this book are those of the authors and not of any organisation.

References

Beesley, P. (2011) *Identifying Neglect.* London: British Association of Fostering and Adoption (BAAF).

Chester, D.L., Jose, R.M., Aldyami, E., King, H. and Moieman, N.S. (2006) 'Non-accidental burns in children – are we neglecting neglect?' *Burns 32,* 2, 222–228.

Farmer, E. and Lutman, E. (2010) *Case Management and Outcomes for Neglected Children Returned to Their Parents: A Five Year Follow-up Study.* Bristol: School for Policy Studies, University of Bristol.

Felitti, V. and Anda, R. (2009) 'The Relationship of Adverse Childhood Experiences to Adult Health, Well-being, Social Function and Health Care.' In R. Lanius and E. Vermetten (eds) *The Hidden Epidemic: The Impact of Early Life Trauma on Health and Disease.* Cambridge: Cambridge University Press.

Finkelhor, D. and Jones, L. (2006) 'Why have child maltreatment and child victimisation declined?' *Journal of Social Issues 62,* 5, 685–716.

Fluke, J., Yuan, Y-Y.T. and Edwards, M. (1999) 'Recurrence of maltreatment: an application of the National Child Abuse and Neglect Data System (NCANDS).' *Child Abuse & Neglect 23,* 7, 633–650.

Geoffroy, M.C., Pereira, S.P., Li, L. and Power, C. (2016) 'Child neglect and maltreatment and childhood-to-adulthood cognition and mental health in a prospective birth cohort.' *Journal of the American Academy of Child and Adolescent Psychiatry* 55, 33–40.

Gilbert R., Spatz Widom, C., Browne, K., Fergusson, D., Webb, E. and Janson, S. (2009) 'Burden and consequences of child maltreatment in high income countries.' *The Lancet 373*, 68–81.

Harris, P. (ed.) (2008) *The Colours in Me: Writing and Poetry by Adopted Children and Young People.* London: BAAF.

Hester , M. (2009) 'Who does what to whom? Gender and domestic violence perpetrators'. *Domestic Abuse Quarterly, Summer 2009*, 4–7.

Johnson, R. and Cotmore, R. (2015) *National Evaluation of the Graded Care Profile.* London: NSPCC. Available at www.nspcc.org.uk/services-and-resources/services-for-children-and-families/graded-care-profile/graded-care-profile-evidence-impact-and-evaluation, accessed on 11 July 2016.

Johnson, R., Smith, E. and Fisher, H. (2015) *Testing the Reliability and Validity of the Graded Care Profile 2 (GCP2).* London: NSPCC.

Jonson-Reid, M., Swarnes, A., Wilson, B., Stahlschmidt, M. and Drake, B. (2009) 'Building healthy families: an innovative approach to working with families affected by chronic neglect.' *Protecting Children 24*, 1, 57–66.

Kalamakis, K. and Chandler, G. (2015) 'Health consequences of adverse childhood experiences: a systematic review.' *Journal of the American Association of Nurse Practitioners 27*, 8, 457–465.

Kaplan, C., Schene, P., De Panfilis, D. and Gilmore, D. (2009) 'Introduction: Shining light on chronic neglect.' *Protecting Children 24*, 1, 2–8.

Kirk, S.K. and Reed-Ashcraft K. (2004) *NCFAS: North Carolina Family Assessment Scale: Research Report.* Buhl, ID: National Family Preservation Network. Available at www.nfpn.org/Portals/0/Documents/ncfas_research_report.pdf, accessed on 15 January 2016.

Keene, E.J., Skelton, R., Day, P.F., Munyombwe, T. and Balmer, R.C. (2015) 'The dental health of children subject to a child protection plan.' *International Journal of Paediatric Dentistry 25*, 428–435.

Loman, L.A. and Siegel, G.L (2004) *Differential Response in Missouri after Five Years: Final Report.* St Louis, MO: Institute of Applied Research.

Merritt, D.H. and Klein, S. (2015) 'Do early care and education services improve language development for maltreated children? Evidence from a national child welfare sample.' *Child Abuse & Neglect 39*, 185–196.

National Institute for Health and Clinical Excellence (NICE) (2008) *When to Suspect Child Maltreatment.* London: NICE.

Ofsted (Office for Standards in Education, Children's Services and Skills) (2014) *In the Child's Time: Professional Responses to Neglect.* Manchester: Ofsted.

Sroufe, A., Egeland, B., Carlson, E.A. and Collins, W.A. (2005) *The Development of the Person: The Minnesota Study of Risk and Adaptation from Birth to Adulthood.* New York: The Guildford Press.

Stevens R. and Laing V. (2015) *Summary Report of Year Two of the Welsh Neglect Project 2014/15*, Cardiff, Action for Children Wales, NSPCC Wales, Welsh Government.

World Health Organization (2006) *Preventing Child Maltreatment: A Guide to Taking Action and Generating Evidence.* Geneva, Switzerland: WHO and International Society for Prevention of Child Abuse and Neglect.

1

THE EFFECTS OF CHILD NEGLECT

Understanding and responding

1

THE EFFECTS OF EMOTIONAL NEGLECT DURING THE FIRST TWO YEARS OF LIFE

Jane Barlow

Introduction

Neglect refers to the failure to provide a child with the type of care that has been identified as being necessary for them to achieve the development that is commensurate with their personal potential (WHO 1999). Emotional neglect refers explicitly to parenting that is emotionally or psychologically unavailable in terms of responding to the child's needs. Emotional neglect is typically the result of omission in which the parent fails to respond to the child's emotional needs (i.e. ignores a child who is distressed). In addition, young children may be exposed to acts of commission (i.e. emotional abuse rather than neglect), in which the parent responds in highly inappropriate ways, for example by frightening a child who is seeking comfort. During the early years, emotional neglect and abuse can co-occur, with parents alternating between being helpless and hostile (Lyons-Ruth *et al.* 2005) (see below). Both emotional neglect and abuse are of particular importance during the first two years of life because since the discovery of attachment in the 1960s, we have become aware of the importance for the child's later attachment security of appropriate emotional responses to infant cues (DeWolf 1997). This research has in turn enabled us to begin to recognise the characteristics of parenting that can be defined as emotionally neglectful or abusive in terms of its role in the development of adverse outcomes.

This chapter will examine the ways in which parenting that is either emotionally neglectful or abusive in the early years has been studied in terms of the main methods and approaches that have been used.

The key findings of this research are presented in terms of what is now known about the impact of early emotional neglect or abuse on the child's long-term development. The chapter will conclude by describing the implications of these findings for future research, policy and practice.

Methods and approaches to the study of emotional neglect in the early years

Two key approaches can be identified to the study of emotional abuse and neglect in the early years. First, *epidemiological studies*, that examine the nature, causes and consequences of particular [health] problems, and that focus on:

- the impact over time of attachment security or insecurity

- the impact of different types of early parenting during the first two years, and

- the factors that can affect the ability of the parent to provide care (e.g. substance dependency and mental health problems).

Second, *intervention studies* that examine the impacts and benefits of improving parenting during this period, in terms of children's long-term development. It should be noted that most of this research focuses on mothers, and only recently has research begun to examine the impact of parenting provided by fathers.

Epidemiological studies: The impact over time of attachment security or insecurity

Most of the epidemiological research consists of prospective longitudinal studies (i.e. that look forward over time) to examine the importance of the early years for later development. These studies consist of research that has focused on Bowlby's (1973, 1982) concept of attachment, and has followed children from infancy to adulthood. The studies have enabled us to identify the importance of secure attachment in early childhood – i.e. at one year of age – in terms of a range of aspects of children's later development. Secure attachment means that children are able to be comforted when they are distressed and to use their caregiver as a secure base from which to explore the world. In insecure attachment the child has difficulty obtaining comfort from their caregiver, showing signs of either avoidance or ambivalence when the attachment system is activated, and is also less able to use the parent as a secure base.

The Minnesota study, which began in 1975 and followed around 267 children from birth to age 40 years, showed poorer outcomes across key domains in childhood and early adolescence for infants who were independently observed to be insecurely attached. These domains included self-reliance; emotional regulation; and social competence (Sroufe 2005). This study found that insecurely attached children were more reliant on teachers and were also rated as highly dependent by the teachers through early childhood and into adolescence. They showed less positive affective expression, coped less well with social problems showing more frustration behaviour, aggression or resignation, and had more negative responses to the overtures of others including whining, fussing and frustration. Insecure children also had less overall social competence. They were less active in their peer group and more frequently isolated; in pre-school they showed less empathy; in middle school they had fewer reciprocated close friendships; and in adolescence they were less effective in their peer group. This study showed that in conjunction with a number of other variables, attachment accounted for as much as 50 per cent of the variance in children's outcomes. It also showed that emotional unavailability on the part of a caregiver was one of the most serious forms of abuse because of its profound consequences in terms of the child's long-term development.

A number of reviews have systematically collated evidence from studies that have examined the association between insecure attachment (described above) and disorganised attachment (i.e. in which the child shows contradictory behaviours, including both approaching and avoiding the caregiver when the attachment system is activated) and later psychopathology.

These studies show that insecure and disorganised attachment are significant predictors of later psychopathology (Green and Goldwyn 2002; van Ijzendoorn, Schuengel and Bakermans-Kranenberg 1999); of externalising disorders such as conduct and behaviour problems (Fearon *et al.* 2010); and of personality disorder, defined as mental health problems characterised by enduring maladaptive patterns of emotional regulation, relating and behaviour (Steele and Siever 2010).

Individual empirical studies have also found an association between disorganised attachment and later mental health problems such as dissociation or detachment from physical and emotional experiences (Dutra and Lyons-Ruth 2005); post-traumatic stress disorder (PTSD) (MacDonald *et al.* 2008); and an increased likelihood of children experiencing symptoms that meet clinical criteria (Borelli *et al.* 2010).

In addition to prospective longitudinal studies, a number of retrospective studies (i.e. that look back in time) have examined the factors associated with long-term mental health problems in both children and adults. For example, a review of 13 studies that examined the attachment classification of patients diagnosed with borderline personality disorder (BPD), found that the attachment patterns most characteristic of such patients were *unresolved, preoccupied* and *fearful,* corresponding with insecure and disorganised types of attachment in childhood. This is suggested to explain the disturbed interpersonal relationships of patients with BPD (Agrawal *et al.* 2004).

Although a number of reviews of retrospective studies have examined the impact of child maltreatment and neglect on the developing brain (e.g. Grassi-Oliveira, Ashy and Stein 2008; Twardosz and Lutzker 2010), these have not separated out the results in terms of the specific impact of early neglect. The best evidence about the impact of early severe neglect on the brain is derived from prospective studies of children raised in institutional care, the evidence from which is set out below.

Epidemiological studies: The impact of different types of parenting during the early years

In addition to the above studies that have focused explicitly on the *consequences for the child* of different types of attachment in terms of their capacity for emotional regulation, there is now a large body of research that has examined the *type of parenting* that is needed during the first two years of life to promote the child's capacity for affect or emotional regulation.

Residential institutions such as orphanages have allowed psychologists a number of opportunities to study directly the impact of the early environment on children's emotional development. One of the key features characterising these institutions was a very low staff-to-baby ratio, resulting in these infants sadly experiencing what has now been described as 'global early deprivation' or 'pervasive neglect' (Rutter *et al.* 1998), meaning neglect of virtually all aspects of the child's development other than their basic physical needs. Psychologists were able to examine the long-term impact on these children of being raised in an environment characterised by such neglect, and also to examine the consequences of removing children from these environments and placing them in foster care where they received individual care and attention.

These empirical studies showed that children raised in institutions for extensive periods, beginning during the immediate postnatal period and with little or no individual care, experienced a range of later problems across all aspects of their functioning. For example, studies show that such institutional care increased the likelihood of reactive attachment disorder (the inability to establish attachments with parents or caregivers) (Zeanah *et al.* 2005); psychiatric disorders (Zeanah *et al.* 2009); a range of neurological and behavioural problems (Zeanah *et al.* 2003); and deficits in memory and executive function (Bos *et al.* 2009). Importantly, these studies also showed that early removal from this environment could compensate for some of these early deficits (Zeanah *et al.* 2009).

In addition to research examining the impact of extreme neglect during the early years, there is also a body of research that has examined the impact of early emotional maltreatment, including neglect within families. The Minnesota Study found that such abuse was associated with a range of problematic behaviours in childhood, for example non-compliance; negativistic, impulsive behaviour; high dependence on teachers; nervous signs; self-abusive behaviour and other problems (Egeland, Sroufe and Erickson 1983); and with mental illness by adolescence. A majority of these children had received at least one diagnosis of mental illness and 73 per cent were comorbid for two or more disorders (Egeland 2009). As described above, a caregiver's emotional unavailability or emotional neglect was found to have particularly serious long-term consequences for the child.

Prospective studies in the field of developmental psychology have also begun to examine the type of parenting that is associated with secure attachment. These studies provide another important source of information about the type of care that is necessary during the first two years of life, for optimal later development. For example, a systematic review examined the results of 21 prospective studies exploring the antecedents, or precursory conditions, for infant attachment security. Attachment security was measured at age 12 months using the Strange Situation Test, a laboratory-based assessment of the infant's response to the parent following a brief separation. This body of research found that parental sensitivity (i.e. the ability of the parent to respond both in a timely and appropriate way to the infant's distress) was an important but not exclusive condition of attachment security (De Wolff and van Ijzendoorn 1997).

Subsequent prospective studies sought to identify other factors that characterised the parenting of secure and insecurely attached infants, many of which focused on factors that appeared to compromise the ability of the parents to interact with their infant. For example, researchers in the United States (Beebe *et al.* 2010; Beebe and Lachman 2013) conducted detailed micro-analysis of mother–infant face-to-face communication in early infancy, around four months of age, to examine its impact on the later attachment status of the infant at 12 months of age. They identified the importance for infant attachment security of what is defined as 'mid-range contingency', referring to the ability of the parent to regulate flexibly both their own internal emotional states and the interaction with the baby. This flexible regulation is characterised by moments of synchrony or attunement between parent and child, followed by rupture and then by repair. This research found that interaction outside this mid-range was associated with later insecure or disorganised attachment in the infant. Such interaction resulted from the parent's preoccupation either with self-regulation (e.g. depressed parents) or with interactive regulation (e.g. anxious parents).

In addition to the above body of research that has focused on aspects of the parent's emotional functioning in terms of its impact on the parent–infant interaction, researchers have also conducted prospective studies examining the impact of the parent's cognitive mind on the interaction, and in particular the parent's capacity for reflective functioning and mind-mindedness. The term 'reflective function' (RF) refers to a parent's capacity to treat their infant as an intentional being, and to understand their behaviours in terms of the child's feelings, beliefs and intentions (Fonagy *et al.* 2002). It is suggested that parents who are low in RF are more likely to respond to their babies in terms of their concrete physical needs, rather than their emotional needs. The related concept of 'mind-mindedness' refers to the parent's ability to read or understand the child's mind (Meins *et al.* 2001). Reflective functioning is measured using the Parent Development Interview, and mind-mindedness is measured through the coding of videos of mothers and babies interacting to assess the extent to which the mother's comments accurately reflect the infant's state of mind. RF is strongly associated with positive maternal parenting behaviours such as flexibility and responsiveness, and use of the mother as a secure base on the part of the infant, while low RF has been found to be associated with emotionally unresponsive maternal behaviours such as withdrawal, hostility and intrusiveness (Grienenberger, Kelly and Slade 2005; Slade *et al.* 2005). 'Mind-mindedness', which is similar to RF in terms of its practical consequences, has also been found to be correlated with behavioural sensitivity and interactive synchrony (Meins *et al.* 2001), and to be a better predictor of attachment security of the child at age one year than maternal sensitivity (Lundy 2003; Meins *et al.* 2001). (See also Chapter 10.)

The findings of this research are consistent with a wider body of research that has examined the impact of parental mental health problems on the capacity of parents to provide emotionally responsive care. For example, prospective studies of clinically depressed mothers have found that they were less sensitively attuned to infants, less affirming and more negating of infant experience (Murray *et al.* 1996). Their infants engaged in less affective sharing, had lower rates of interactive behaviour, poorer concentration, increased negative responses with strangers and reduced secure attachment at 12 and 18 months (Murray and Cooper 1997; Stein *et al.* 1991; Tronick 2007).

Borderline personality disorder (BPD) has also been found to be associated with an increased prevalence of a range of interactional difficulties on the part of the parent (Laulik *et al.* 2013) including less structuring in their interaction with their infants, who were found to be less attentive, less interested and less eager to interact with their mother. The research also shows that these mothers were less satisfied, less competent and more distressed (Newman *et al.* 2007); that they showed evidence of disrupted communication, and frightened and disoriented behaviours (Hobson *et al.* 2009); impaired sensitivity (Crandell, Patrick and Hobson 2003); and increased intrusiveness (Hobson *et al.* 2005). Similarly, some studies of parents with schizophrenia have shown less responsive and sensitive, and more remote, intrusive and self-absorbed interaction with their child, as compared with parents experiencing affective disorders (Wan *et al.* 2007, 2008a, 2008b).

A review of over 30 studies that have examined the impact of substance abuse during pregnancy on parent–infant/toddler interaction, found reduced parental sensitivity (Hatzis *et al.* forthcoming). Research that has examined the impact of domestic violence has found a significant impact on the women's representations, or mental images, of themselves as a parent and their baby in pregnancy. These representations were significantly more likely be classified as 'disengaged' (i.e. less likely to involve the baby) or 'distorted' (i.e inclined to view the baby as an extension of themselves) (Huth-Bocks *et al.* 2004). Infants of women who are experiencing domestic violence have been found to be significantly less likely to be securely attached at 12 and 18 months (Levendosky, Bogat and Huth-Bocks 2011), and also to show signs of increased distress reactions to conflict (DeJonghe *et al.* 2005) and trauma symptoms (Bogat *et al.* 2006).

Intervention studies examining the impact of improving parenting during the early years

Studies examining the benefits of improving parenting during the early years have provided another source of evidence regarding the impact of the early environment on later outcomes. They show that improved child outcomes can be achieved by reducing early emotionally neglectful and/or abusive parenting.

Possibly one of the best evaluated methods of working with parents and young children during the postnatal period are known as 'attachment-based' interventions. These are 'dyadic' interventions undertaken with both the parent (usually the mother) and baby/toddler together, where the dyad is experiencing a range of problems. They are primarily aimed at improving the sensitivity of the parent in order to increase the likelihood of the infant being securely attached. A systematic review of 70 studies of attachment-based interventions (not all of which used randomised controlled trials) found that these interventions were effective in changing insensitive parenting and infant attachment insecurity (Bakermans-Kranenburg, van Ijzendoorn and Juffer 2003). This large-scale review concluded that the most effective interventions in terms of improving child attachment were those that improved parental sensitivity. This body of evidence confirms earlier findings from epidemiological studies regarding the importance of early sensitive parenting in terms of children's long-term development.

What do we know about emotional neglect in the early years?

This chapter has defined emotional neglect as including parenting behaviours that are emotionally neglectful by virtue of ignoring or avoiding the infant's needs (i.e. omission) or abusive in terms of highly inappropriate responses (i.e. commission). During the early years the two types of parenting behaviour can often co-occur. The above research has enabled us to understand more precisely the nature of parenting that constitutes emotional neglect at this crucial time in a child's life, and the long-term consequences for the child.

What is emotional neglect in the early years?

The research has clearly identified the key factors that are associated with optimal infant development in terms not only of babies' ability to regulate themselves emotionally, but also their rapidly developing neurological system (e.g. Schore 2000). This suggests that optimal child development is achieved as a result of the type of parental behaviours and interactions with the infant that will result in a secure attachment. This body of research has also helped us to begin to identify the type of interaction that is sufficiently suboptimal for it to be defined as emotionally neglectful. A range of 'atypical' or 'anomalous' parent–infant interactions have been identified. These have been characterised as *Fr-behaviours*, that is, the behaviours of parents who are either frightened and/or frightening (Jacobvitz, Hazen and Riggs 1997; Main and Hesse 1990) or who are hostile and helpless (Lyons-Ruth *et al.* 2005). 'Fr-behaviours' have been described as being subtle (e.g. periods of being dazed and unresponsive) or more overt (deliberately frightening children) (ibid.).

Research has also found that 'atypical' or 'anomalous' parenting behaviours consist of:

- *parental withdrawing responses*: maternal behaviours that are rejecting of the infant

- *negative–intrusive responses*: where the mother is mocking or pulls at part of the infant's body

- *role-confused responses*: where the mother seeks attention from the infant to meet her own emotional needs

- *disoriented responses*: where the mother adopts a frightened expression or has a sudden complete loss of affect, and

- *affective communication errors*: in which the mother might be positive while the infant is distressed (ibid.).

How extensive is such emotional neglect?

Prevalence data in the United Kingdom suggests that emotional neglect and abuse in the early years is a significant problem. Infants under one represent over a tenth (i.e. 11%) of children who are the subject of a child protection plan in England (Department for Education 2014), with neglect (49%) and emotional abuse (25%) accounting for nearly three-quarters of these (ibid.). Research suggests that these figures significantly underestimate the full extent of the problem (Sidebotham 2000).

What are the consequences of such neglect?

The research strongly suggests that one of the key consequences of emotional neglect or abuse is a disorganised attachment. For example, a recent meta-analysis based on the findings of 12 prospective studies found a strong association between the type of atypical or anomalous parent–infant interactions at 12 and 18 months described above, and disorganised attachment (Madigan *et al.* 2006). Disorganised attachment in infancy has been found to be associated with many later types of psychopathology, ranging from externalising behaviour problems through to personality disorder (see the section on epidemiological studies above). Later in life, this may have adverse effects on the child's own parenting (see Introduction p.16).

Which parents are most at risk of emotional neglect in the early years?

As we have seen, studies examining the impact of parenting indicate that parents experiencing many problems, ranging from postnatal depression through to domestic abuse and substance dependency, have been found to have less than optimal interactions with their infants. While some of these types of interaction are not optimal for the infant and may result in the child's insecure attachment, they are not sufficiently suboptimal to be defined as emotional neglect, although if the child's behaviour or presentation suggests that the parenting or wider environment is contributing to their experiencing significant harm, this would need to be investigated.

In this chapter, emotional neglect and abuse have been described in terms of a range of atypical and anomalous interactions with the infant that can result in the child's disorganised attachment. Parents who are most at risk of providing emotionally neglectful or abusive care during the first two years of life are very often 'unresolved' with regard to trauma that they have experienced themselves during childhood (Jacobvitz *et al.* 1997). They may have ongoing problems in terms of issues such as substance dependency and exposure to domestic violence. As a result these parents are more likely to have had a 'fearful' (i.e. disorganised) attachment themselves and to have low reflective functioning, poor affect regulation and little ability to identify with or understand the needs of infants. There may also be an unconscious need to repeat the trauma that they experienced (see Lieberman *et al.* 2005a). A range of other social problems, such as poverty and single parenthood (Lieberman and Osofsky 2009) will add greatly to the stress of caring for a baby.

What works to improve emotional neglect in the early years?

Interventions that are aimed at preventing or reversing emotional neglect in the early years have targeted parents experiencing a range of problems that place them at risk of such neglect, including substance dependency. A review of innovative and evidence-based approaches to safeguarding children from emotional maltreatment (Barlow and Schrader-McMillan 2010) identified a number of parent-, and parent-and-child-focused, methods of working. Innovative dyadic methods of working, focusing on the parent and infant/toddler together, include video feedback, parent–infant psychotherapy, and a number of home visiting programmes promoting the parent's mentalization, such as Minding the Baby (Sadler *et al.* 2013) and the Mothers and Toddlers Program (Suchman *et al.* 2011) (see also Chapter 9).

Video feedback

This involves the use of brief videotaped periods of interaction between the primary caregiver and child, which are examined by the practitioner to identify moments of sensitive interaction. The video is then watched jointly by the guider and parent to discuss the positive interaction, and to help the parent to think about the baby/toddler as an intentional being. Video feedback is currently being used within a range of standardised programmes including Video Interaction Guidance (VIG) (see Chapter 10); Video Interaction to Promote Positive Parenting (VIPP) (Kalinauskiene *et al.* 2009; Velderman *et al.* 2006); Circle of Security (Cassidy *et al.* 2011; Hoffman *et al.* 2006) and Parents under Pressure (Dawe and Harnett 2007). It is also used in broader service settings such as the Family Drug and Alcohol Court (FDAC), involving work with substance dependent parents of young children (Harwin *et al.* 2011), as well as in residential mother and baby units where it is being used effectively with mothers experiencing serious mental health problems (Kenny *et al.* 2013; Pawlby *et al.* 2005). A systematic review of video feedback with parents and children under five years of age showed that it was effective in improving a range of parenting behaviours and child outcomes (Fukkink 2008).

Parent–infant/child psychotherapy

A therapist works with the parent–child dyad, observing and discussing the interaction with the parents. The aim is to understand better what the parent–child interaction conveys about the parent's internal 'working models' (these are internal maps about self and other built up from their own early relationships) and their representations or mental images of their child, which result from their own experiences of being parented. This method has been used with a range of vulnerable women, including those in prison, and typically involves the delivery of between 5 and 20 sessions. Evaluations of such therapy with parents of infants (Barlow *et al.* 2015a) and with parents of young children (Lieberman, Ghosh Ippen and Van Horn 2006; Lieberman, Van Horn and Ghosh Ippen 2005b), show evidence of benefits across a range of outcomes, including improvements in the children's insecure and disorganised attachment.

Home visiting programmes

Minding the Baby is an intensive home visiting programme that begins in pregnancy and continues into the postnatal period, and is delivered by a health and a social care practitioner as part of a multidisciplinary team. The programme targets vulnerable parents, most of whom are from ethnic minority groups (in the United States, Latino and Black) and who are single and living in poverty. There are child protection concerns about approximately 7 per cent of the parents. There is some evidence that the programme is effective in improving the attachment security of children in the intervention group at 12 months (Sadler *et al.* 2013).

The Mothers and Toddlers Program provides 12 weeks of individual therapy as an adjunct to standard outpatient substance abuse treatment programmes, and aims to improve negative maternal representations and capacity for reflective functioning, as well as to increase maternal capacity for sensitivity and responsiveness to a toddler's emotional cues (Suchman *et al.* 2011). Early evaluation shows improved reflective functioning, representational coherence and sensitivity, and caregiving behaviour (ibid.).

Innovative methods of working with vulnerable parents of young babies (i.e. as opposed to explicitly targeting the parent–infant/toddler dyad) include the Parents under Pressure programme, which works with vulnerable parents who may be substance dependent or experiencing mental health problems, and consists of 12 modules that are delivered flexibly over 20 weeks in the home (Dawe and Harnett 2007). Although this intervention has only been trialled to date with parents of older children (ibid.), it is currently being evaluated with parents of children under two years of age (Barlow *et al.* 2013).

Implications for future research, policy and practice

The extensive body of research summarised in this chapter indicates that emotional neglect in the early years has a high prevalence, in addition to a range of serious long-term consequences, and points to the importance of working effectively to support parents and where necessary to protect children who may be at risk. Although this chapter has examined only the evidence relating to the postnatal period, parenting begins before the baby is born, with the parent undertaking a range of health behaviours that are designed to protect the baby in utero, in addition to their developing a bond with the unborn baby. The factors that place infants at risk of emotional abuse and neglect – including, for example, parental substance dependency (Advisory Council on the Misuse of Drugs 2003) and domestic abuse (Department of Health 2010) – are very often present before the baby is born, and pose significant risks to the foetus (e.g. Riley, Infante and Warren 2011).

This suggests that pregnancy is an important window of opportunity in terms of the protection of infants from actual or potential emotional abuse or neglect, and that we should begin proactively during this period with the identification and support of women who are vulnerable and high risk, including, for example, women who have significant mental health problems, substance or alcohol dependency, who experience domestic violence, or who have experienced the previous removal of a child. Midwives and other professionals working with pregnant women should identify individuals who could benefit from support at booking in and during subsequent contact with them, and refer them as appropriate to adult services, family support and children's social services.

The provision of perinatal support by a specialist team of social and family support workers has been successfully trialled in a local authority within the UK. This model of working involves the provision of intensive assessment and intervention by a small team of case carrying practitioners following referral by midwives of high-risk pregnant women between 12 and 18 weeks of gestation. The model involves the use of a range of standardised tools as part of an assessment of capacity to change. The assessment is repeated at a number of time-points following the delivery of intensive, therapeutic working with the pregnant woman, using the Parents under Pressure (PUP) programme, which 'combines psychological principles relating to parenting, child behaviour and parental emotion regulation within a case management model'[1] (Dawe and Harnett 2007).

The pilot evaluation of this model of working (Barlow *et al.* 2015b) was positive. The model appeared to be effective in supporting families in a way that was valued by the recipients; all assessments were conducted within the specified timeframe; the courts required no further information to make a decision other than that provided as part of the assessment process by the team; and there were significant cost savings across a small number of cases. The evaluation also found that this model of working was effective in identifying those babies where the ongoing risk was sufficiently high to justify early removal (i.e. before seven months of age). This is particularly important, given what we now know about the trauma that is caused through emotional abuse or neglect during this period (see the section on the impact of parenting during the early years). The National Society for the Prevention of Cruelty to Children (NSPCC forthcoming) have a very similar prenatal assessment model in development, and further research is needed to compare the long-term outcomes for children and families who receive such specialist assessment and care, compared with standard services.

In addition to such specialist perinatal teams, there is also a need for social work and other practitioners working with vulnerable women during the postnatal period to have the necessary skills to deliver some of the evidence-based methods of working described above. Research shows that the additional investment needed to achieve this is justified because the cost-benefits of early intervention range from about $1400 per child to nearly $240,000 per child, particularly in the case of disadvantaged children.[2]

There is a need for further research to identify which of these methods work best with which groups of parents, but the evidence base is now sufficiently strong to justify ensuring that all social workers know how to use methods such as video feedback. There is also a need for staff in adult services who work with parents who have mental health problems, substance dependency or face domestic abuse,

---

1   www.pupprogram.net.au
2   www.rand.org/pubs/research_briefs/RB9145.html

to be aware of the importance of parenting during this period, and for effective communication and information sharing across sectors. Examples of innovative working across sectors in the UK include a range of integrated models of working such as the multi-agency safeguarding hub (MASH) (2011) and co-located early help services such as Team Around the Child Models (Oliver, Mooney and Statham 2010).

Conclusions

Research from a number of disciplines and utilising a range of methodologies (i.e. both prospective and retrospective, epidemiological and intervention) has provided an extensive and robust body of evidence. First, this charts the importance of the first two years of life in terms of the individual's later ability to regulate their emotional states, and second the type of environment in terms of parenting that is necessary to facilitate optimal emotional development of the child during this period as a basis for future development.

Third, research has also increased our understanding about what constitutes emotional neglect during the first two years of life in terms of the long-term consequences, and finally it has helped to identify methods of working with vulnerable and high risk families to improve outcomes for the child. Further research is still needed, particularly in terms of the identification of effective methods of working with high risk families and those who do not readily engage with services.

The body of research discussed in this chapter highlights the importance first of policy guidance and resources to support the delivery of early intervention, and second of key groups of practitioners having the necessary skills to work effectively with parents during pregnancy and the first two years of life.

Key learning points

-   The first two years of life are extremely important in terms of parental emotional responsiveness, and emotional neglect that occurs during this period therefore has significant long-term consequences for a range of aspects of the child's later development.

- The prevention of emotional neglect should begin in pregnancy and involve the provision of intensive assessment and support to high risk women.

- Core groups of practitioners such as social workers should be skilled in using techniques that have been demonstrated to improve outcomes for high risk women including, for example, video feedback.

Questions for reflection

- Which constellations of factors in pregnancy is the best predictor of parents who may be at risk of emotional neglect and abuse of their child or children in the postnatal period?

- What services should be provided for parents and children aged 0 to two years in addition to some of the evidence-based therapeutic methods of working described in this paper?

- What service delivery approaches are most helpful?

- Might some of the techniques identified in this paper be useful with parents and older children who have experienced emotional neglect?

References

Advisory Council on the Misuse of Drugs (2003) *Hidden Harm: Responding to the Needs of Children of Problem Drug Users. The report of an Inquiry by the Advisory Council on the Misuse of Drugs.* London: Home Office.

Agrawal, H.R., Gunderson, J., Holmes, B.M. and Lyons-Ruth, K. (2004) 'Attachment studies with borderline patients: a review.' *Harvard Review of Psychiatry 12*, 2, 94–104.

Bakermans-Kranenburg, M.J., van Ijzendoorn, M.H. and Juffer, F. (2003) 'Less is more: meta-analyses of sensitivity and attachment interventions in early childhood.' *Psychological Bulletin 129*, 2, 195–215.

Barlow, J. and Schrader-McMillan, A. (2010) *Safeguarding Children from Emotional Abuse: What Works.* London: Jessica Kingsley Publishers.

Barlow, J., Bennett, C., Midgley, N., Larkin, S.K. and Wei, Y. (2015a) 'Parent-infant psychotherapy for improving parental and infant mental health.' Cochrane Database of Systematic Reviews, Issue 1. Art. No.: CD010534. DOI: 10.1002/14651858. CD010534.pub2.

Barlow, J., Dawe, S., Coe, C. and Harnett P. (2015b) 'An evidence-based, pre-birth assessment pathway for vulnerable, pregnant women.' *British Journal of Social Work.* DOI: 10.1093/bjsw/bcu150 1–14.

Barlow, J., Sembi, S., Gardner, F., Macdonald, G., *et al.* (2013) 'An evaluation of the parents under pressure programme: a study protocol for an RCT into its clinical and cost effectiveness.' *Trials 14*, 1745–6215.

Beebe, B., Jaffe, J., Markese, S., Buck, K., *et al.* (2010) 'The origins of 12-month attachment: a microanalysis of 4-month mother-infant interaction.' *Attachment & Human Development 12*, 1–2, 6–141.

Beebe, B. and Lachman, F. (2013) *Infant Research and Adult Treatment: Co-Constructing Interactions.* London: Routledge.

Bogat, G.A., DeJonghe, E., Levendosky, A.A., von Eye, A. and Davidson, W.S. (2006) 'Trauma symptoms in infants who witness violence towards their mothers.' *Child Abuse & Neglect 30*, 2, 109–125.

Borelli, J.L., David, D.H., Crowley, M.J. and Mayes, L.C. (2010) 'Links between disorganised attachment classification and clinical symptoms in school-aged children.' *Journal of Child and Family Studies 19*, 3, 243–256.

Bos, K.J., Fox, N., Zeanah, C.H. and Nelson, C.A. (2009) 'Effects of early psychosocial deprivation on the development of memory and executive function.' *Frontiers in Behavioral Neuroscience 3*, 1–7.

Bowlby, J. (1973) *Attachment and Loss: Vol. 2. Separation.* New York: Basic Books.

Bowlby, J. (1982) *Attachment and Loss: Vol. 1. Attachment.* New York: Basic Books.

Cassidy, J., Woodhouse, S., Sherman, L., Stupica, B. and Lejuez, C. (2011) 'Enhancing infant attachment security: an examination of treatment efficacy and differential susceptibility.' *Journal of Development and Psychopathology 23*, 131–148.

Crandell, L.E., Patrick, P.H.P. and Hobson, R.P. (2003) 'Still-face interactions between mother with borderline personality disorder and their 2-month old infants.' *British Journal of Psychiatry 183*, 239–247.

Dawe. S. and Harnett, P.H. (2007) 'Reducing potential for child abuse in methadone maintained parents: Results from a randomised controlled trial.' *Journal of Substance Abuse Treatment 32*, 381–390.

De Wolff, M.S. and van Ijzendoorn, M.H. (1997) 'Sensitivity and attachment: a meta-analysis on parental antecedents of infant attachment security.' *Child Development 68*, 604–609.

DeJonghe, E.S., Bogat, G.A., Levendosky, A.A., von Eye, A. and Davidson, W.S. (2005) 'Infant exposure to domestic violence predicts heightened sensitivity to adult verbal conflict.' *Infant Mental Health Journal 26*, 268–281.

Department for Education (2014) *Characteristics of Children in Need in England: 2013 to 2014.* London: Department for Education. Available at: www.gov.uk/government/uploads/system/uploads/attachment_data/file/367877/SFR43_2014_Main_Text.pdf, accessed June 2015.

Department of Health (2010) *The Report from the Taskforce on the Health Aspects of Violence against Women and Children.* London: Department of Health.

Dutra, L. and Lyons-Ruth, K. (2005) 'Maltreatment, maternal and child psychopathology, and quality of early care as predictors of adolescent dissociation.' Presented at the Biennial Meeting of the Society for Research in Child Development, Atlanta, GA.

Egeland, B. (2009) 'Taking stock: childhood emotional maltreatment and developmental psychopathology.' *Child Abuse & Neglect 33*, 22–36.

Egeland, B., Sroufe, L. and Erickson, M. (1983) 'The developmental consequence of different patterns of maltreatment.' *Child Abuse & Neglect 7*, 4, 459–469.

Fearon, R.P., Bakermans-Kranenburg, M.J., van Ijzendoorn, M.H., Lapsley, A.M. and Roisman, G.I. (2010) 'The significance of insecure attachment and disorganization in the development of children's externalizing behavior: a meta-analytic study. *Child Development 81*, 2, 435–456.

Fonagy, P., Gergely, G., Jurist, E. and Target, M. (2002) *Affect Regulation, Mentalization and the Development of the Self.* New York: Other Press.

Fukkink, R.G. (2008) 'Video feedback in widescreen: a meta-analysis of family programs.' *Clinical Psychology Review 28*, 6, 904–916.

Grassi-Oliveira, R., Ashy, M. and Stein, L.M. (2008) 'Psychobiology of childhood maltreatment: effects of allostatic load?' *Revista Brasileira de Psiquiatria 30*, 1, 60–68.

Green, J. and Goldwyn, R. (2002) 'Attachment disorganisation and psychopathology: new findings in attachment research and their potential implications for developmental psychopathology in childhood.' *Journal of Child Psychology and Psychiatry 43*, 835–846.

Grienenberger, J., Kelly, K. and Slade, A. (2005) 'Maternal reflective functioning, mother-infant affective communication, and infant attachment: exploring the link between mental states and observed caregiving behavior in the intergenerational transmission of attachment.' *Attachment & Human Development 7*, 299–311.

Harwin, J., Ryan, M., Tunnard, J., Pokhrel, S., Alrouh, B., Matias, C. and Momenian-Schneider, I. (2011) *The Family Drug and Alcohol Court (FDAC): Evaluation Project.* London: Nuffield Foundation.

Hatzis, D.M., Dawe, S., Harnett, P. and Barlow J (forthcoming) *Quality of Caregiving in Substance-Misusing Mothers: A Systematic Review and Meta-Analysis.*

Hobson, P., Patrick M., Crandell L., Garcia-Perez R. and Lee A. (2005) 'Personal relatedness and attachment in infants of mothers with borderline personality disorder.' *Developmental Psychopathology 17*, 329–347.

Hobson, R.P., Patrick, M.P., Hobson, J.A., Crandell, L., Bronfman, E. and Lyons-Ruth, K. (2009) 'How mothers with borderline personality disorder relate to their year-old infants.' *British Journal of Psychiatry 195*, 4, 325–330.

Hoffman, K., Marin, R., Cooper, G. and Powell, B. (2006) 'Changing toddlers' and preschoolers' attachment classifications: the Circle of Security intervention.' *Journal of Consulting and Clinical Psychology 74*, 6, 1017–1026.

Huth-Bocks, A.C., Levendosky, A.A., Theran, S.A. and Bogat, G.A. (2004) 'The impact of domestic violence on mothers' prenatal representations of their infants.' *Infant Mental Health Journal 25*, 79–98.

Jacobvitz, D., Hazen, N.L. and Riggs, S. (1997) 'Disorganized mental processes in mothers, frightened/frightening behavior in caregivers, and disoriented, disorganized behavior in infancy.' Paper presented at the biennial meeting of the Society for Research in Child Development, Washington, DC.

Kalinauskiene, L., Cekuoliene, D., van Ijzendoorn, M.H., Bakermans-Kranenburg, M.J., Juffer, F. and Kusakovskaja, I. (2009) 'Supporting insensitive mothers: the Vilnius randomized control trial of video-feedback intervention to promote maternal sensitivity and infant attachment security.' *Child: Care, Health and Development 35*, 5, 613–623.

Kenny, M., Conroy, S., Pariante, C.M., Seneviratne, G. and Pawlby, S. (2013) 'Mother-infant interaction in mother and baby unit patients: before and after treatment.' *Journal of Psychiatric Research 47*, 9, 1192–1198.

Laulik, S., Chou, S., Browne, K.D. and Allam, J. (2013) 'The link between personality disorder and parenting behaviors: A systematic review.' *Aggression and Violent Behavior 18*, 6, 644–655.

Levendosky, A.A., Bogat, G.A. and Huth-Bocks, A.C. (2011) 'The influence of domestic violence on the development of the attachment relationship between mother and young child.' *Psychoanalytic Psychology 28*, 4, 512–527.

Lieberman, A.F., Ghosh Ippen, C. and Van Horn, P. (2006) 'Child-parent psychotherapy: 6-month follow-up of a randomized controlled trial.' *Journal of the American Academy of Child and Adolescent Pscyhiatry 45*, 8, 913–918.

Lieberman, A.F. and Osofsky, J.D. (2009) 'Poverty, trauma and infant mental health.' *Zero to Three*, November. Available at http://main.zerotothree.org/site/DocServer/30-2_Lieberman.pdf?docID=12481, accessed on 5 August 2015.

Lieberman, A.F., Padrón, E., Van Horn, P. and Harris, W.W. (2005a) 'Angels in the nursery: the intergenerational transmission of benevolent parental influences.' *Infant Mental Health Journal 26*, 504–520.

Lieberman, A.F., Van Horn, P. and Ghosh Ippen, C. (2005b) 'Toward evidence-based treatment: child-parent psychotherapy with preschoolers exposed to marital violence.' *Journal of the American Academy of Child and Adolescent Psychiatry 44*, 12, 1241–1248.

Lundy, B.L. (2003) 'Father- and mother-infant face-to-face interactions: differences in mind-related comments and infant attachment?' *Infant Behavior and Development 26*, 200–212.

Lyons-Ruth, K., Yellin, C., Melnick, S. and Atwood, G. (2005) 'Expanding the concept of unresolved mental states: hostile/helpless states of mind on the Adult Attachment Interview are associated with disrupted mother-infant communication and infant disorganization.' *Developmental Psychopathology 17*, 1–23.

MacDonald, H.Z., Beeghly, M., Grant-Knight, W., Augustyn, M., *et al.* (2008) 'Longitudinal association between infant disorganized attachment and childhood posttraumatic stress symptoms.' *Developmental Psychopathology 20*, 2, 493–508.

Madigan, S., Bakermans-Kranenburg, M.J., van Ijzendoorn, M.H., Moran, G., Pederson, D.R. and Benoit, D. (2006) 'Unresolved states of mind, anomalous parenting behaviour, and disorganized attachment: a review and meta-analysis of a transmission gap.' *Attachment and Human Development 8*, 2, 89–111.

Main, M. and Hesse, E. (1990) 'Parents' Unresolved Traumatic Experiences Are Related to Infant Disorganized Attachment Status: Is Frightened and/or Frightening Parental Behavior the Linking Mechanism?' In M.T. Greenberg, D. Cicchetti and E.M. Cummings (eds) *Attachment in the Preschool Years: Theory, Research, and Intervention.* Chicago: University of Chicago Press.

Meins, E., Fernyhough, C., Fradley, E. and Tuckey, M. (2001) 'Rethinking maternal sensitivity: Mothers' comments on infants' mental processes predict security of attachment at 12 months.' *Journal of Child Psychology and Psychiatry 42*, 637–648.

Multi-Agency Safeguarding Hub (MASH) (2011). Available at www.communitycare.co.uk/2011/06/03/multi-agency-safeguarding-centre-for-childrens-referrals, accessed 3 May 2016.

Murray, L. and Cooper, P.J. (1997) 'The effects of postnatal depression on infant development.' *Archives of Disease in Childhood 77*, 99–101.

Murray, L., Fiori-Cowley, A., Hooper, R. and Cooper, P.J. (1996) 'The impact of postnatal depression and associated adversity on early mother infant interactions and later infant outcome.' *Child Development 67*, 2512–2526.

Newman, L., Stevenson, C., Bergman, L.R. and Boyce, P. (2007) 'Borderline personality disorder, mother-infant interaction and parenting perceptions: Preliminary findings.' *Australian and New Zealand Journal of Psychiatry 41*, 7, 598–605.

NSPCC (forthcoming) *Risk Assessment Pre-birth: A Practice Model.*

Oliver, C., Mooney, A. and Statham, J. (2010) *Integrated Working: A Review of the Evidence.* Leeds: Children's Workforce Development Council.

Pawlby, S., Marks, M., Clarke, R., Best, E., Weir, D. and O'Keane, V. (2005) 'Mother-infant interaction in postpartum women with severe mental illness, before and after treatment.' *Archives of Women's Mental Health 8,* 120.

Riley, E.P., Infante, M.A. and Warren, K.R. (2011) 'Fetal alcohol spectrum disorders: an overview.' *Neuropsychology Review 21,* 73–80.

Rutter, M. and the English and Romanian Adoptees study team (1998) 'Developmental catch-up, and deficit, following adoption after severe global early privation.' *Journal of Child Psychology and Psychiatry 39,* 465–476.

Sadler, L.S., Slade, A., Close, N., Webb, D.L., *et al.* (2013) 'Minding the baby: enhancing reflectiveness to improve early health and relationship outcomes in an interdisciplinary home-visiting program.' *Infant Mental Health Journal 34,* 5, 391–405.

Schore, A.N. (2000) 'The Self-organization of the Right Brain and the Neurobiology of Emotional Development.' In M.D. Lewis and I. Granic (eds) *Emotion, Development, and Self-organization.* New York: Cambridge University Press.

Sidebotham, P.D. (2000) 'The ALSPAC study team. Patterns of child abuse in early childhood, a cohort study of the "Children of the Nineties".' *Child Abuse Review 9,* 311–320.

Slade, A., Grienenberger, J., Bernbach, E., Levy, D, and Locker, A. (2005) 'Maternal reflective functioning, attachment, and the transmission gap: a preliminary study.' *Attachment & Human Development 7,* 3, 283–298.

Sroufe, L.A. (2005) 'Attachment and development: a prospective, longitudinal study from birth to adulthood.' *Attachment & Human Development 7,* 4, 349–367.

Steele, H. and Siever, L. (2010) 'An attachment perspective on borderline personality disorder: advances in gene-environment considerations. *Current Psychiatry Reports 12,* 1, 61–67.

Stein, A., Gath, D.H., Bucher, J., Bond, A., Day, A. and Cooper, P.J. (1991) 'The relationship between postnatal depression and mother-child interaction.' *British Journal of Psychiatry 158,* 46–52.

Suchman, N.E., Decoste, C., Mcmahon, T.J., Rounsaville, B. and Mayes, L. (2011) 'The mothers and toddlers program, an attachment-based parenting intervention for substance-using women: Results at 6-week follow-up in a randomized clinical pilot.' *Infant Mental Health Journal 32,* 4, 427–449.

Twardosz, S. and Lutzker, J.R. (2010) 'Child maltreatment and the developing brain: a review of neuroscience perspectives.' *Aggression and Violent Behavior 15,* 1, 59–68.

Tronick, E.Z. (2007) *The Neurobehavioral and Social-Emotional Development of Infants and Children.* London: WW Norton.

van Ijzendoorn, M.H., Schuengel, C. and Bakermans-Kranenburg, M.J. (1999) 'Disorganized attachment in early childhood: meta-analysis of precursors, concomitants, and sequelae.' *Developmental Psychopathology 11,* 2, 225–249.

Velderman, K.M., Bakermans-Kranenburg, M.J., Juffer, F. and van Ijzendoorn, M.H. (2006) 'Effects of attachment-based interventions on maternal sensitivity and infant attachment: differential susciptibillity of highly reactive infants.' *Journal of Family Psychology 20,* 2, 266–274.

Wan, M.W., Salmon, M.P., Riordan, D., Appleby, L., Webb, R. and Abel, K.M. (2007) 'What predicts mother-infant interaction in schizophrenia?' *Psychological Medicine 37,* 537–538.

Wan, M.W., Penketh, V., Salmon, M.P. and Abel, K.M. (2008a) 'Content and style of speech from mothers with schizophrenia towards their infants.' *Psychiatry Research* *159*, 109–114.

Wan, M.W., Warren, K., Salmon, M.P. and Abel, K.M (2008b) 'Patterns of maternal responding in postpartum mothers with schizophrenia.' *Infant Behaviour and Development 31*, 532–538.

WHO (World Health Organization) (1999) *Report of the Consultation on Child Abuse Prevention, Geneva, 29–31March 1999.* Available at www.yesican.org/definitions/WHO.html, accessed on June 2015.

Zeanah, C.H., Egger. H.L., Smyke, A.T., Nelson, C.A., *et al.* (2009) 'Institutional rearing and psychiatric disorders in Romanian preschool children.' *American Journal of Psychiatry 166,* 777–785.

Zeanah, C.H., Nelson, C.A., Fox, N.A., Smyke, A.T., *et al.* (2003) 'Designing research to study the effects of institutionalization on brain and behavioral development: the Bucharest Early Intervention Project.' *Development and Psychopathology 15*, 4, 885–907.

Zeanah, C.H., Smyke, A.T., Koga, S.F., Carlson, E. and the BEIP Core Group (2005) 'Attachment in institutionalized and community children in Romania.' *Child Development 76*, 5, 1015–1028.

2

CHILD NEGLECT AND THE DEVELOPMENT OF COMMUNICATION

Jan McAllister and Wendy Lee

Introduction

This chapter explores the association between neglect of children and the development of their speech, language and communication abilities. We first explore the factors that drive typical communicative development, including the terminology that is used for describing it. We then outline the diagnostic framework which applies to atypical communicative development and give an example of communicative development in a child with a history of neglect. We summarise the evidence regarding the association between neglect and communicative development and the intervention approaches that have been used when communication difficulties arise. Finally we consider implications for research, policy and practice.

Why is communicative development so important?

Children who experience neglect are at risk of poorer communicative development. A person's speech, language and communication abilities affect almost every aspect of their life – for example, their access to information, their participation in activities that involve engagement with others, such as education, work, cultural activity, personal relationships and social interaction, and the impact that all of the foregoing have on their emotional wellbeing, quality of life and sense of identity. In today's society, communication skills are greatly valued, and those with a high level of communicative ability stand to gain, while those with significant communicative difficulties are likely to be disadvantaged (Ruben 2000). Communication difficulty is associated with various negative outcomes, including poor mental health (Cohen, Farnia and Im-Bolter 2013; Iverach and Rapee 2014) and involvement in the criminal justice system (Bryan 2004), all of which have substantial societal and economic costs (Hartshorne 2006).

Good oral language skills are crucial to a child's ability to progress in the educational system. The amount and quality of the language children experience at home is one of the best predictors of their academic attainment (Hart and Risely 1995; Roy, Chiat and Dodd 2014). Oral language is the medium through which classroom learning (questioning, answering, discussion, problem-solving, etc.) takes place. Furthermore, a child's oral language ability underpins their acquisition of both literacy and writing (Save The Children 2015; Shanahan 2006) and literacy is essential to achieving proficiency in academic subjects throughout their academic career.

Children with communication impairments are more likely than typically developing children to experience social, emotional and behavioural difficulties. These difficulties can be associated with various kinds of communication impairment (Clegg *et al.* 2014; Ketelaars *et al.* 2010; McAllister submitted).

Why should neglect affect children's communicative development?

Theories of communicative development differ fundamentally with regard to the relative importance that they assign to biological versus environmental drivers, or, to put it another way, their emphasis on nature versus nurture. Broadly speaking, three approaches can be identified. The 'nature' approach regards the *structure and function* of the child's brain, motor and sensory systems as having the pre-eminent role in language acquisition. The 'nurture' approach emphasises the importance of *environmental factors* such as social interaction with other humans, including caregivers; and the interactionist approach proposes that communicative development results from the *subtle and complex interplay* between the child's biological endowment and environmental factors.

Regardless of which theoretical approach is adopted, however, it would be predicted that being deprived of adequate supervision or care could have a negative impact on a child's communicative development. On the one hand, maltreatment such as neglect is known to have a detrimental effect on the neurobiology of the infant brain, perhaps via a mechanism involving chronic production of cortisol in response to the stressful experience of neglect, which would affect the development of systems underpinning learning, memory and language (Lum *et al.* 2015). On the other hand, successful communicative development is dependent on sustained, child-directed, face-to-face interaction with carers (Tomasello 2003), which is likely to be deficient or absent when the infant is neglected (see also Chapter 1).

Typical development of speech, language and communication

Part of the challenge for the child learning to speak his or her first language must lie in its complexity. To make the problem of analysing communication more tractable, specialists in this area find it helpful to identify a number of systems that contribute to spoken communication, which will be relevant to discussion later in this chapter (McAllister and Miller 2013). These systems are concerned with three aspects of communication: speech, language, and pragmatics or social communication.

Speech

This component of the system is concerned with the articulation of speech via the relevant neurological and motor systems. Impairments to this component can result in difficulties with producing appropriate pronunciations, or in fluency problems such as stuttering. It can take a child several years fully to master the pronunciation of sounds in their native language. Typically developing children produce speech that is relatively fluent in the sense that, although it will contain some non-fluencies, these are qualitatively and quantitatively different to the interruptions and timing difficulties that characterise a disorder of fluency such as stuttering.

Language

This system contains a number of components including vocabulary, phonology, morphology, syntax and semantics. Although the *phonology* component is concerned with speech, it deals with the structure of the speech sound system (e.g. the sequences of sounds that are permissible in a particular language), rather than the articulation or motor production of speech sounds alone; it is therefore included as a part of the language system along with other components that are also concerned with structure. *Morphology* is concerned with the internal structure of words, for example, how to form the plural or past tense. The *syntax* component contains the rules of sentence formation; because of the close relationship between morphology and syntax in many languages, the term *morpho-syntax* is used to refer to the interface between these systems. The *semantics* component contains knowledge about the meaning of words and sentences.

Pragmatics or the social use of language

This system contains information about the way that utterances are used, rather than their form or structure. It is concerned with, among other things, the knowledge that governs conversational interaction, for example, turn-taking, adapting language to take into account the needs of the listener, and topic management; the way that the 'same' utterance, such as 'I'm not going to tell you again', can be used with more than one communicative intention (statement, threat, etc.); use of indirect or non-literal language, for example, metaphor; use of humour and irony; and repair of inappropriate or ambiguous conversational contributions. An important aspect of pragmatic behaviour is *theory of mind* (Baron-Cohen 2001), which refers to the ability to attribute mental states (beliefs, intentions, etc.) that are different to one's own current mental state, to oneself and to others.

These systems can be used in both *expressive* communication (that is, when an utterance is being produced) and in *receptive* communication (when an utterance is being understood or interpreted). By the time they start school, typically developing children know several thousand words and have gained significant competence in the majority of the speech and language components; the period from birth to five is crucial for communicative development. However, all of the systems continue to develop as the child matures (Nippold 1998). Table 2.1 outlines typical communicative development up to age five years (for more detail, see The Communication Trust (2015).

Table 2.1 Stages in typical communicative development between birth and age five

Age	Typical communicative behaviour
By 6 months	– Makes sounds cooing, babbling, gurgling – Makes noises to attract caregiver's attention or when spoken to – Pays attention to others' speech and responds by vocalising or physical movement – Smiles and laughs in response to smiles and laughter from others
By 1 year	– Produces reduplicated babbling, with repetition of syllables such as 'ba-ba-ba' or 'ma-ma-ma-ma' – Uses babbling, takes turns in conversations – Points and makes eye contact to get caregiver's attention – Understands some words and gestures, e.g. 'bye-bye', 'up' – Knows the names of familiar objects, e.g. 'daddy', 'teddy', 'car' – May be starting to use first words and gestures
By 18 months	– Uses around 20 words, but these are pronounced in a 'baby' way so that strangers may not understand – Understands more words and some short phrases – Points to familiar objects when asked to do so – Takes part in games like 'peek-a-boo'
By 2 years	– Has an expressive vocabulary of around 50 words – Understands between 200 and 500 words – Begins to produce rudimentary sentences of two or three words – Understands simple questions and instructions – Enjoys pretend play
By 3 years	– Uses a wider variety of word categories – Produces sentences of four or five words – Has clearer speech, although still with some babyish pronunciation – Understands simple 'Who?' 'What?' and 'Where?' questions – Plays imaginative games that are longer or more complicated – Can have proper conversations – Can listen to and remember simple stories
By 4 years	– Asks lots of questions like 'What?' 'Where?' and 'Why?' – Answers questions about 'why' something has happened – Uses longer sentences and links sentences together – Describes events that have already happened – Likes simple jokes, though often their own jokes make little sense – Starts to be able to plan games with others

Age	Typical communicative behaviour
By 5 years	– Takes turns in much longer conversations – Uses well-formed sentences – Learns more words all the time and thinks more about what different words mean – Can re-tell short stories using appropriate language, like 'Once upon a time…' – Has fluent speech and uses most speech sounds, though may have difficulty with longer words and with certain sounds, e.g. 'r', 'th'

To explain the speed and accuracy of pre-school communicative development, some researchers hypothesise specialised mechanisms which are part of the child's innate psychobiological endowment (Pinker 1995). Yet if such mechanisms were a sufficient condition for the development of a child's communicative competence, this would emerge regardless of the features of child's environment, such as the availability of social interaction with other humans. To support this point, cases of children who grow up in extreme isolation and neglect, and fail to acquire full communicative competence are often used, but with certain exceptions (e.g. Fromkin *et al.* 1974; Kenneally *et al.* 1998). Such cases are often not well documented and there may be other developmental reasons for the children's impaired communication systems.

Nonetheless, it is clear that social interaction with caregivers has the potential to make an important contribution to the emerging communicative competence of typically developing children (Pruden, Hisch-Pasek and Golinkoff 2006). Even pre-verbal infants benefit from the conversational 'scaffolding' (Vygotsky 1978) provided by caregivers during everyday routines such as feeding and nappy-changing, as the following interaction between a three-month-old, Ann, and her mother illustrates (Snow 1977, p.12):

Ann: (smiles)

Mother: Oh, what a nice little smile. Yes, isn't that nice? There. There's a nice little smile.

Ann: (burps)

Mother: What a nice little wind as well. Yes, that's better, isn't it? Yes. Yes. Yes.

Ann: (vocalizes)

Mother: There's a nice noise.

Early 'proto-conversations' like this one are examples of 'serve and return' interactions which are believed to contribute to the development of brain architecture (Center on the Developing Child 2015). They may also provide the child with a training ground for how to engage in social interactions as well as encouraging the child to vocalise. Proto-conversations depend on the caregiver providing all of the meaningful conversational turns and timing these to fit with the child's contributions. As the infant develops, their contributions to interactions must gradually become more sophisticated, via ritualised exchanges such as those seen in games like 'peek-a-boo' and semi-structured interactions such as looking at a picture book, until true conversational interaction can be achieved (Pruden *et al.* 2006).

Beyond infancy, there is an association between the nature of caregivers' contributions to interactions and typical children's communicative development (Tamis-LeMonda and Rodrigues 2009). Most research has focused on mothers' interactions with their children. Maternal warmth, acceptance and responsiveness have been found to be positively correlated with communicative development in several studies (Baumwell, Tamis-LeMonda and Bornstein 1997; Fewell and Deutscher 2002; Gartstein, Crawford and Robertson 2008; Westerlund and Lagerberg 2007), a correlation potentially even more strong than with the mother's vocabulary (Bornstein, Tamis-LeMonda and Haynes 1999). Interestingly, children with the poorest receptive abilities make the greatest gains in receptive language ability when their mothers display a responsive interaction style (Baumwell *et al.* 1997).

Mothers who follow their child's lead in interactions (Bornstein *et al.* 1999; Fewell and Deutscher 2002; Hoff-Ginsberg 1991) and whose conversational contributions develop topics of shared interest (Baumwell *et al.* 1997) also have children with better communicative skills. Conversely, excessive use of interruption, commands and prohibition on the part of caregivers is associated with poorer communicative development (Baumwell *et al.*1997; Fewell and Deutscher 2002; Hart and Risley 1995). The linguistic structure of caregiver utterances may also be important for communicative development; Huttenlocher *et al.* (2002) found a positive correlation between the syntactic complexity of utterances of parents and those of their four-year-olds.

It must be noted that these findings all concern associations found in observational studies and that they do not conclusively demonstrate that adopting the more positive interaction styles causes improvements in communicative development. Although it is possible that caregivers' use of positive styles causes better communicative development in children, the opposite direction of causality is also possible, especially since there is evidence that parents do respond to changes in their children's perceived communicative abilities, particularly their receptive abilities (Andersen and Marinac 2007). These changes rather than (or as well as) parents' interaction styles might also lead to the association, or indeed another mediating variable may be involved. It would obviously be unethical to carry out the kind of experiment that would investigate causal relationships between these factors. The relationship between caregiver interaction style and children's communicative development is clearly a complex one. Nonetheless, the view that caregiver input has a critical role in communicative development is widely held among researchers and practitioners (Allen and Marshall 2011), alongside other features of the child's environment such as the availability of books in the home (Dickinson *et al.* 2012).

Atypical or non-typical development of speech, language and communication

Practitioners and researchers distinguish *delay*, where the child follows the same pattern of development as his or her peers (though at a slower rate), from *disorder*, referring to a pattern of development that differs from those of peers. Any of the three communication systems mentioned above (speech, language and social communication/ pragmatics), or indeed their components, can be delayed or disordered. Most research exploring the association between neglect and communication has focused on delay. Law *et al.* (2000) estimated the prevalence of speech and language delays and disorders at between 5 per cent and 12 per cent in pre-school children, making these among the most common forms of developmental difficulty. The prevalence is higher in socially disadvantaged areas (Law, McBean and Rush 2011). A substantial number of these children experience persistent rather than transient difficulties.

An internationally recognised framework for conceptualising types of impairment is the Diagnostic and Statistical Manual of Mental

Disorders (American Psychiatric Association 2013), which categorises communication difficulties as follows:

- *Speech sound disorder:* persistent difficulty with speech sound production that interferes with speech intelligibility or prevents verbal communication of messages.

- *Child-onset fluency disorder:* disturbances in the normal fluency and time patterning of speech, for example, stuttering.

- *Language disorder:* persistent difficulties in the acquisition and use of language across modalities (i.e. spoken, written, sign language or other) due to deficits in comprehension or production and language abilities that are substantially and quantifiably below age expectations. Practitioners still use the term specific language impairment (SLI) (Bishop 1997) to refer to this type of disorder, where the child has significant language difficulties despite having no other condition that could explain the difficulty, such as hearing impairment or general learning difficulty.

- *Social (pragmatic) communication disorder:* persistent difficulties in the social use of verbal and nonverbal communication. This includes difficulties with communication for social purposes, impairment in the ability to change communication to match the context or needs of the listener, and difficulty understanding what is not explicitly stated and non-literal or ambiguous meaning of language, in which *the symptoms are not attributable to low abilities in the domains of word structure or grammar or to another medical or neurological condition* (our italics).

The latter exclusion criterion (in italics above) means that people with autistic spectrum disorders (ASD) are not diagnosed with this form of communication impairment. Social (pragmatic) communication disorder is a new DSM category, created in response to research findings indicating that children could still experience difficulties in this aspect of communication while neither having significant difficulties with the form of language and speech, nor meeting diagnostic criteria for ASD. The introduction of this DSM category has been controversial because the categorical nature of the DSM system means that the label does not capture the status of this impairment on a continuum between specific language impairment (SLI) and high functioning autism (Gibson *et al.* 2013). Practitioners currently use the term pragmatic language impairment (Bishop 2000) to refer to these difficulties.

The scenario below gives an example of a child with atypical speech and language development in the context of neglect, illustrating the presenting issues. This is not an actual case.

SCENARIO ILLUSTRATING THE IMPACT OF NEGLECT ON COMMUNICATIVE DEVELOPMENT

Jake was first picked up by his health visitor at 18 months of age. He was small for his age; his mum was dependent on alcohol and was clearly struggling to meet his needs. She was persuaded to attend the local Sure Start centre, where she attended afternoon sessions on a semi-regular basis. Jake was seen by a speech and language therapist (SLT) as part of a 'Talking Toddlers' group, where it was quickly apparent that he was very delayed in his understanding of language.

His attention and listening skills were poor and his play underdeveloped; he didn't engage with toys without support and he wasn't using any words. He needed encouragement to engage with group activities such as singing and his attention was limited. He made his needs known mainly by pointing, though he was generally passive.

To support his language development, a home worker, under guidance from the SLT, supported the family at home. They worked with mum and Jake, building attention and listening skills alongside early receptive language skills. Simple 'ready, steady, go' games, rhymes and early book sharing were encouraged, alongside simple language to link with everyday routines: 'bath time', 'dinner time', 'find your shoes', 'we're going out', 'where's teddy?' 'it's bed time', etc.

Mum was suspicious of professionals, so alongside these activities, she joined a group of young mums who were working with a local community volunteer who was well regarded in the community and volunteered in the Sure Start centre where she worked with some of the younger mums. The volunteer had training in supporting early language development and had a positive view of parents as ' the best toy in the toy box' in this respect.

A combination of support to mum through the volunteer programme and home worker support, combined with ongoing input from the speech and language therapist through the

Talking Toddlers group, impacted positively on Jake's language and interaction skills. He made good progress in his receptive language, and expressive language skills were developing. By age three, his language skills were almost age-appropriate, though his speech sound system was delayed and he continued to struggle at times with his social interaction skills. Ongoing input was needed to support these crucial skills.

The association between neglect and communication difficulty

Several reviews of the literature have explored the development of communication in maltreated children, for example Core Info Cardiff University 2012, 2013, 2014; Hwa-Froelich 2012; Law and Conway 1992; Naughton *et al.* 2013; and Veltman and Browne 2001.

One meta-analysis (Lum *et al.* 2015) includes only studies that matched socio-economic status of maltreated children with that of children in control groups. These sources included literature addressing abuse as well as neglect and all of them concluded that there was evidence linking both kinds of maltreatment with poorer development of various aspects of communication: speech, language and pragmatics/social communication.

Unfortunately, in the source literature, it is sometimes difficult to distinguish results relating to neglect from those relating to abuse, as researchers frequently combine the two categories on the basis of non-significant differences between these two types of maltreatment in preliminary analyses (see Chapter 5). However, where it is possible to determine the effect of neglect on language development, findings often suggest that its impact is greater than that of abuse, or of abuse and neglect combined (Law and Conway 1992; Merritt and Klein 2015). Not all studies have reported this finding (Stacks *et al.* 2011), but this may be because of methodological factors (Merritt and Klein 2015).

Sylvestre and Mérette (2010), who explored the factors associated with language delay in 68 severely neglected children under three years old, found that 35 per cent of this sample experienced language delay, which is more than twice the level in the general population of children in this age group. The likelihood of language delay in severely neglected children increased in proportion to the cumulative count of risk factors, but was particularly associated with the following variables:

- poorer cognitive development in the child

- the mother's own experience of physical and emotional abuse as a child

- maternal depression, and

- the mother's level of acceptance of the child.

Allen and Oliver (1982) reported that, while physically abused and non-maltreated pre-schoolers did not differ from each other in terms of receptive and expressive language, neglected pre-schoolers scored lower than the other two groups on both kinds of language measure. Culp *et al.* (1991) also found that neglect alone had a more detrimental effect than abuse on the expressive and receptive language development of pre-schoolers: those who experienced neglect alone (n=41) showed language delay of 6–9 months, while the delay was 4–8 months for those who experienced both abuse and neglect (n=13) and 0–2 months in those who experienced abuse alone. They speculated that the reason that neglect rather than abuse was associated with poorer communicative development than abuse could be that the public regard abuse as a more serious form of maltreatment than neglect, and therefore are likely to report it more quickly, so that the duration of the maltreatment may be longer in the case of neglect. A similar explanation is proposed by Roulstone *et al.* (2011) who suggest that children who are abused are more likely to be removed from the family home and may possibly encounter a richer verbal environment, while those who are neglected are more likely to stay in the home where language stimulation is poor.

To our knowledge, no study to date has identified an association between maltreatment and disorders of fluency such as stuttering, but language, other aspects of speech, and social communication/ pragmatics have all been the subject of maltreatment research.

The impact of neglect on language

The impact of neglect experienced in the pre-school years may be evident in later performance on measures of language ability

(English *et al.* 2005). The most commonly studied aspect of language development in maltreated children is receptive vocabulary. This is typically assessed using a picture-selection task such as the Peabody Picture Vocabulary Test (Dunn and Dunn 1981), in which the examiner says a word and the child has to point to the target picture in a set of several alternatives. In their meta-analysis, Lum *et al.* (2015) found that on average, maltreated children performed more poorly than controls on such tests. De Bellis *et al.* (2009) specifically compared neglected children with non-neglected controls. They found poorer receptive vocabulary abilities (i.e. the ability to understand or interpret words) in the neglected group, and this effect remained significant with a moderate effect size even after controlling for intellectual ability.

Not all studies have found a statistically significant difference between neglected children and controls in terms of receptive vocabulary (Coster *et al.* 1989; Valentino *et al.* 2008). In their meta-analysis, Lum *et al.* (2015) were only able to identify two studies which had looked at the association between maltreatment and expressive vocabulary development, which reported only small, non-significant differences between maltreated children and controls, and they did not report results for neglect separately.

Neglect has a negative impact on other aspects of language beyond vocabulary. Various studies have shown that, compared with children suffering other kinds of maltreatment as well as compared with non-maltreated controls, neglected children have significantly poorer expressive and receptive morpho-syntax (Allen and Oliver 1982; Culp *et al.* 1991; De Bellis *et al.* 2009; Eigsti and Cicchetti 2004; Fox, Long and Langlois 1988).

The impact of neglect on speech

The impact of neglect on speech development has received less in-depth attention than other aspects of communication. Culp *et al.* (1991) found that the three groups of pre-schoolers they studied (neglected, abused, and neglected and abused) performed below average on the Goldman-Fristoe Test of Articulation (Goldman and Fristoe 2000), but found no significant difference between the groups.

Windsor *et al.* (2007) found that children raised in orphanages in Romania had poorer speech development and were less intelligible at 30 months old compared with children raised in the family environment. Because of the unfavourable child-to-caregiver ratio, children raised in such orphanages are more likely than those raised in family settings to experience extreme neglect (Tizard *et al.* 1972; see also Chapter 1).

The impact of neglect on social communication/pragmatics

There is reason to predict impairments in social communication in neglected children (Hwa-Froelich 2012). As noted above, pragmatic aspects of communication involve skills such as tailoring one's conversational contributions to the needs of the listener or (for example) using humour and irony. In a review of the effects of maltreatment, including neglect, Schore (2001) reported that these include a detrimental impact on the development of the right hemisphere of the brain, which subserves social communication, and that as a result maltreated children could potentially be deficient in understanding the perspectives of others, a crucial ability in successful social use of communication.

Understanding the perspectives of others depends on the development of theory of mind, the ability to infer alternative mental states (Baron-Cohen 2001). A widely recognised measure of theory of mind development is 'false belief understanding'. This is measured by having children carry out tasks in which they observe and comment on scenarios in which participants develop 'false beliefs' when they are only given partial information. Cicchetti *et al.* (2003) measured the development of false belief understanding in 203 children who had experienced maltreatment; the majority had experienced neglect. Maltreated children had significantly poorer understanding of false beliefs, compared with the control group who had not experienced maltreatment. Impairment of theory of mind was particularly associated with maltreatment which occurred when the children were toddlers rather than infants.

Interestingly, children who had experienced abuse performed more poorly on this measure of development than those who had experienced neglect, the reverse of the finding for language measures in other studies. Poorer theory of mind performance was also found for children in Turkey who were raised in orphanages compared with those raised in family homes (Yagmurlu, Berument and Celimli 2005);

as noted earlier, neglect is more likely in the former setting because of the more unfavourable caregiver-to-child ratio.

Neglect is associated with particular features of caregiver-child interaction (Core Info Cardiff University 2012, 2013, 2014). Neglectful parents typically do not adopt the responsive 'serve and return' style of interaction with their infants. As the child matures, their interactions with parents are briefer, and characterised by various negative features.

Naughton *et al.* (2013) reviewed the features indicative of neglect or emotional abuse in preschool children. They identified the communicative aspects of neglected children and caregivers alongside other developmental signs. From three years old, children displayed delays in complex language. Caregivers used more restricted language patterns and gave less positive feedback. The authors emphasised the importance of such signs as a means of early identification leading to early intervention, which is as important for communicative development as for dealing with the other consequences of neglect. See also Bercow (2008).

Interventions for children with speech, language and communication needs

The Bercow review (Bercow 2008) of services for children and young people with speech, language and communication needs (SLCN) drew attention to deficiencies in provision for SLCN, lack of awareness of SLCN among policymakers, the importance of early intervention, and the need for coordinated, community-wide, multiagency commissioning of services. Within education, the term SLCN is narrowly applied to those with primary special educational needs relating to speech, language and communication, but researchers and speech and language therapists apply the term more broadly (Dockrell *et al.* 2014).

In the United Kingdom, specialist intervention for children with SLCN is provided by speech and language therapists (SLTs). Referrals to speech and language therapy services can be made by parents themselves or by a wide range of professionals including general practitioners, district nurses, health visitors, teachers and nursery staff. Like all health and education professionals, SLTs have to follow robust procedures when they suspect that children or other vulnerable people are at risk of harm, including neglect. SLTs working with children who have experienced neglect will often be working as part of a wider multidisciplinary team to ensure that agencies and practitioners work together efficiently and effectively to enable the best outcomes. In this context, SLTs aim to consider the child, family and other practitioners working directly with the child in a holistic way to determine the most appropriate support. They support practitioners and parents to know more about how communication develops and the adult's role in this process, they implement strategies to support the child in everyday activities and they provide more targeted intervention.

There are numerous approaches to intervention for communication difficulties. SLTs aim to take an evidence-based approach to identifying particular interventions that would be most appropriate for the children they are working with. Where strong evidence is lacking, they may use a dynamic assessment approach (an interactive approach which involves identifying the child's strengths and learning potential), or/and they gather evidence from smaller studies or professional consensus to support clinical decision-making. Two searchable online resources can be used to identify what interventions are available for particular kinds of difficulty and what level of evidence exists regarding their efficacy: the SpeechBITE database and the What Works website.[1]

In addition, several reviews and meta-analyses of speech and language therapy approaches targeting particular areas have appeared in recent years.

Many interventions for pre-school children have been shown to be effective. Law, Garrett and Nye (2004) carried out a meta-analysis of the efficacy of interventions for communication difficulties. Only 13 studies were suitable for inclusion in the analysis, covering expressive and receptive phonology, vocabulary and syntax, and the majority focused on pre-school children. The analysis found evidence in favour of interventions for phonology and expressive vocabulary, but the evidence for expressive syntax interventions was mixed, and the number of studies available for the other areas was too small to provide conclusive results. The authors drew attention to the paucity of studies of interventions for receptive abilities. Some interventions could be successfully delivered by trained parents as well as clinicians. The efficacy of parent-delivered interventions addressing stuttering, articulation, and expressive and receptive language was also supported in a meta-analysis by Lawler,

---

1   http://speechbite.com and www.thecommunicationtrust.org.uk/whatworks

Taylor and Shields (2013), and a review by Wallace *et al.* (2015) also found evidence in favour of this mode of delivery.

Ebbels (2014) reviewed around 30 studies that targeted various aspects of expressive and receptive morpho-syntax in school-aged children. The interventions adopted a wide variety of techniques and some could be delivered by teachers, parents and others as well as speech and language therapists, or could be carried out online. A substantial number of interventions were able to provide evidence of efficacy, as well as maintenance of improvement at follow-up and generalisation to new situations and items. Like earlier reviewers, Ebbels noted that there were relatively few studies that targeted receptive grammar abilities in this age group, and called for more research in this area.

Most reviews of interventions targeting social communication focus on children with, or at risk of, autism. A review by Gerber *et al.* (2012) focused instead on school-aged children without sensory or neurodevelopmental disorders, brain damage or intellectual disability, but with pragmatic language impairment. They found preliminary evidence in support of interventions that improved topic management, conversational repair and narrative formation.

These reviews and meta-analyses provide evidence for the efficacy of interventions to address a wide range of communicative difficulties in children who have not necessarily experienced neglect; however, Naughton *et al.* (2013) emphasise the importance of early intervention in the case of abused and neglected children. It seems likely that communicative interventions that are effective in the general population of children with communication impairments may also prove effective for neglected children, but there has been relatively little research into this.

Merritt and Klein (2015) carried out one such study. They evaluated the effectiveness of early care and education programmes in the United States, such as Head Start (similar to Sure Start in the UK) or attendance at preschool provision, with regard to communicative development in maltreated pre-schoolers. They used data from 1652 children in the US child welfare system taken from the National Survey of Child and Adolescent Well-Being II (US Department of Health & Human Services 2013) and compared scores on the Preschool Language Scale (PLS-3) over an 18-month period. At baseline, PLS-3 scores for all maltreatment groups indicated mild language delay.

For children who had been referred for supervisory neglect, who comprised around one third of the sample, early care and education were extremely beneficial: after 18 months those who had received this intervention had PLS-3 scores that were on average within normal limits, while all other groups (those with other forms of maltreatment, or who had not received the intervention) continued to display mild delay. It is not clear whether children in this study received targeted interventions to address their communicative needs specifically; it may be that the improvements that were seen resulted simply from an increase in positive verbal interactions with staff and other children as part of the day-to-day activities in the programmes. More work is needed to examine the need for and efficacy of interventions that target specific communicative needs of neglected children. Such research has been carried out with abused children (Moreno Manso *et al.* 2012), and has reported positive results.

Implications for research, policy and practice

Research gaps

Communication difficulties are common among children, and if untreated can lead to negative consequences for the child, the family and society. Neglected children have been shown to be more vulnerable than non-maltreated children to language impairments, especially vocabulary and morpho-syntax, and some studies have also found that they are more vulnerable to communicative difficulties than children who experience other forms of maltreatment. To date there has been little or no research exploring the development of neglected children in the other communicative domains: speech, dysfluency and pragmatics/social communication. These are important aspects of communicative development and more research should be focused on them.

Early intervention is known to be important both for neglected children and for those with communication difficulties to mitigate the long-term effects of both conditions, and is likely to be especially important for those who are disadvantaged with respect to both. Well-evidenced interventions are available to address a wide range of communication difficulty and some can be delivered by parents as well as health and education professionals. The communicative competence of neglected children has been shown to respond well to generalised interventions such as Head Start and attendance at other pre-school care and education programmes (Merritt and Klein 2015), placing their post-intervention performance within normal limits on a standardised measure of communication development.

It is unclear which children failed to reap the communicative benefits of these early education and care programmes, and research needs to be directed at this question, as well as the effectiveness for such children of more targeted speech and language therapy which specifically addresses communication problems.

Early identification of communication problems is key

Early identification (both in terms of the child's age and the stage of the difficulty) is the *sine qua non* of early intervention. Neglected children and their caregivers display communicative characteristics which, when taken alongside other indicators, should alert practitioners to a potential problem. Gardner (2008) and Naughton *et al.* (2013) reported that practitioners lacked confidence in recognising the signs of neglect. The diverse workforce who may come into contact with these children need to develop awareness of the relevant features during training, and also of the interventions that are available to address communication problems and appropriate referral routes.

Cooperation within multidisciplinary teams in identifying signs of neglect is essential if long-term outcomes for the child are to be ameliorated (Gardner 2008; Hwa-Froelich 2012).

The role of speech and language specialists in public health policy

The speech and language therapy profession is one practitioner group with in-depth specialist expertise relevant to communication as a consequence of neglect. Yet despite the demonstrable association between neglect and communication impairment, historically SLTs have not occupied positions of influence in the arena of public health policy-making, even in affluent 'first world' countries like the UK (Snow 2009). Public affairs work is now a priority to organisations such as the Royal College of Speech and Language Therapists as well as for national charities such as The Communication Trust, which aim to raise the profile of the issue with national and local policy makers – but there is still much to be done. The importance of such influence is also something that needs to be part of the pre-registration training of SLTs.

Improving public understanding of the impact of child neglect

As we have seen, the evidence shows that neglected children display poorer communication abilities (even than children who have experienced other forms of maltreatment). Researchers have hypothesised that one reason could be that members of the public view neglect as a less serious problem than abuse, and therefore are slower to bring it to the attention of the authorities. Yet several studies have shown that with regard to some aspects of communication, neglected children are more at risk than other maltreated groups. The public as well as professionals would benefit from information campaigns and public health education to correct the impression that neglect is a less serious form of maltreatment.

Key learning points

– Communicative development involves the evolution of three systems dealing with speech, language and communication.

– Existing evidence indicates that childhood neglect is associated with poorer language development, particularly vocabulary and morpho-syntax, but less is known about the effect of neglect on speech or social communication and what would help these children. More research is needed.

– Early identification of communication problems is key to an early response, as is better general awareness of the impact of child neglect on communicative development.

Questions for reflection

– What mechanisms could be put in place to encourage researchers from different backgrounds (e.g. child protection, speech and language therapy, neuroscience) to reach a shared perspective on the impact of neglect on communicative development?

- What mechanisms could promote early identification and early intervention?

- How can awareness be raised among the public about the negative impact of neglect on communicative development?

References

Allen, J. and Marshall, C. (2011) 'Parent-Child Interaction Therapy (PCIT) in school-aged children with specific language impairment.' *International Journal of Language and Communication Disorders 46*, 397–410.

Allen, R.E. and Oliver, J.M. (1982) 'The effects of child maltreatment on language development.' *Child Abuse & Neglect 6*, 299–305.

American Psychiatric Association (2013) *Diagnostic and Statistical Manual of Mental Disorders* (5th ed.). Arlington, VA: American Psychiatric Publishing.

Andersen, C.E. and Marinac, J.V. (2007) 'Using an observational framework to investigate adult language input to young children in a naturalistic environment.' *Child Language Teaching and Therapy 23*, 307–324.

Baron-Cohen, S. (2001) 'Theory of mind in normal development and autism.' *Prisme 34*, 174–183.

Baumwell, L., Tamis-LeMonda, C.S. and Bornstein, M.H. (1997) 'Maternal verbal sensitivity and child language comprehension.' *Infant Behavior and Development 20*, 2, 247–258.

Bercow, J. (2008) *The Bercow Report: A Review of Services for Children and Young People (0–19) with Speech, Language and Communication Needs*. London: Department for Children, Schools and Families.

Bishop, D.V.M. (1997) *Uncommon Understanding: Development and Disorders of Language Comprehension in Children*. Hove: Psychology Press.

Bishop, D.V.M. (2000) 'Pragmatic Language Impairment: A Correlate of SLI, a Distinct Subgroup, or Part of the Autistic Continuum?' In D.V.M. Bishop and L.B. Leonard (eds) *Speech and Language Impairments in Children: Causes, Characteristics, Intervention and Outcome*. Hove: Psychology Press.

Bornstein, M.H., Tamis-LeMonda, C.S. and Haynes, O.M. (1999) 'First word in the second year: continuity, stability, and models of concurrent and predictive correspondence in vocabulary and verbal responsiveness across age and context.' *Infant Behavior and Development 22*, 1, 65–85.

Bryan, K. (2004) 'Prevalence of speech and language difficulties in young offenders.' *International Journal of Language and Communication Disorders 39*, 391–400.

Center on The Developing Child, Harvard University (2015) *Serve and Return*. Available at http://developingchild.harvard.edu/key_concepts/serve_and_return, accessed on 29 October 2015.

Cicchetti, D., Rogosch, F.A., Maughan, A., Toth, S.L., and Bruce, J. (2003) 'False belief understanding in maltreated children.' *Development and Psychopathology 15*, 1067–1091.

Clegg, J., Law, J., Rush, R., Peters, T.J. and Roulstone, S. (2014) 'The contribution of early language development to children's emotional and behavioural functioning at 6 years: an analysis of data from the Children in Focus sample from the ALSPAC birth cohort.' *Journal of Child Psychology and Psychiatry 56*, 1, 67–75.

Cohen, N., Farnia, F. and Im-Bolter, N. (2013) 'Higher order language competence and adolescent mental health.' *Journal of Child Psychology and Psychiatry 54*, 733–744.

Core Info Cardiff University (2012) 'Emotional neglect and emotional abuse in pre-school children.' Available at www.core-info.cardiff.ac.uk/publications/emotional-neglect, accessed on 29 October 2015.

Core Info Cardiff University (2013) 'Neglect or emotional abuse in teenagers aged 13–18.' Available at www.core-info.cardiff.ac.uk/publications/teenage-neglect-em, accessed on 29 October 2015.

Core Info Cardiff University (2014) 'Neglect or emotional abuse in children aged 5 to 14.' Available at www.core-info.cardiff.ac.uk/publications/school-aged-neglect, accessed on 29 October 2015.

Coster, W.J., Gersten, M.S., Beeghly, M., and Cicchetti, D. (1989) 'Communicative functioning in maltreated toddlers.' *Developmental Psychology 25*, 1020–1029.

Culp, R.E., Watkins, R.V., Lawrence, H., Letts, D., Kelly, D.J. and Rice, M. (1991) 'Maltreated children's language and speech development: abused, neglected, and abused and neglected.' *First Language 11*, 377–389.

De Bellis, M.D., Hooper, S.R., Spratt, E.G. and Woolley, D.P. (2009) 'Neuropsychological findings in childhood neglect and their relationships to pediatric PTSD.' *Journal of the International Neuropsychological Society 15*, 868–878.

Dickinson, D., Griffith, J., Golinkoff, R.M. and Hirsh-Pasek, K. (2012) 'How reading books fosters language development around the world.' *Child Development Research 2012*, 1–15.

Dockrell, J., Lindsay, G., Law, J. and Roulstone, S. (2014) 'Supporting children with speech, language and communication needs: an overview of the results of the Better Communication Research Programme.' *International Journal of Language & Communication Disorders 49*, 543–557.

Dunn, L. and Dunn, L. (1981) *The Peabody Picture Vocabulary Test – Revised.* Circle Pines, MN: American Guidance Service.

Ebbels, S. (2014) 'Effectiveness of intervention for grammar in school-aged children with primary language impairments: a review of the evidence.' *Child Language Teaching and Therapy 30*, 7–40.

Eigsti, I. and Cicchetti, D. (2004) 'The impact of child maltreatment on expressive syntax at 60 months.' *Developmental Science 7*, 1, 88–102.

English D., Thompson, R., Graham J. and Briggs E. (2005) 'Toward a definition of neglect in young children.' *Child Maltreatment 10*, 2, 190–206.

Fewell, R.R. and Deutscher, B. (2002) 'Contributions of receptive vocabulary and maternal style: variables to later verbal ability and reading in low-birthweight children.' *Topics in Early Childhood Special Education 22*, 181–190.

Fox, L., Long, S.H. and Langlois, A. (1988) 'Patterns of language comprehension deficit in abused and neglected children.' *Journal of Speech and Hearing Disorders 53*, 239–244.

Fromkin, V., Krashen, S., Curtiss, S., Rigler, D. and Rigler, M. (1974) 'The development of language in genie: a case of language acquisition beyond the "critical period".' *Brain and Language, 1*, 81–107.

Gardner, R. (2008) *Developing an Effective Response to Neglect and Emotional Harm to Children.* Available at www.nspcc.org.uk/globalassets/documents/research-reports/developing-effective-response-neglect-emotional-harm-children.pdf, accessed on 29 October 2015.

Gartstein, M.A., Crawford, J. and Robertson, C.D. (2008) 'Early markers of language and attention: mutual contributions and the impact of parent–child interactions.' *Child Psychiatry Human Development 39*, 9–26.

Gerber, S., Brice, A., Capone, N., Fujiki, M. and Timler, G. (2012) 'Language use in social interactions of school-age children with language impairments: an evidence-based systematic review of treatment.' *Language, Speech and Hearing Services in Schools 43*, 2, 235–249.

Gibson, J., Adams, C., Lockton, E. and Green, J. (2013) 'Social communication disorder outside autism? A diagnostic classification approach to delineating pragmatic language impairment, high functioning autism and specific language impairment.' *Journal of Child Psychology and Psychiatry 54*, 1186–1197.

Goldman, R. and Fristoe, M. (2000) *Goldman-Fristoe Test of Articulation*. Minneapolis, MN: Pearson Assessments.

Hart, B. and Risley, T.R. (1995) *Meaningful Differences in the Everyday Experience of Young American Children*. Baltimore, MD: Paul H. Brookes.

Hartshorne M. (2006) *The Cost to the Nation of Children's Poor Communication*. London: ICAN.

Hoff-Ginsberg, E. (1991) 'Mother–child conversation in different social classes and communicative settings.' *Child Development 62*, 782–796.

Huttenlocher, J., Vasilyeva, M., Cymerman, E. and Levine, S. (2002) 'Language input and child syntax.' *Cognitive Psychology 45*, 337–374.

Hwa-Froelich, D. (2012) 'Childhood maltreatment and communication development.' *Perspectives on School-Based Issues 13*, 2, 43–53.

Iverach, L. and Rapee, R.M. (2014) 'Social anxiety disorder and stuttering: current status and future directions.' *Journal of Fluency Disorders 40*, 69–82.

Kenneally, S.M., Bruck, G.E., Frank, E.M. and Nalty, L. (1998) 'Language intervention after thirty years of isolation: a case study of a feral child.' *Education and Training in Mental Retardation and Developmental Disabilities 33*, 13–23.

Ketelaars, M.P., Cuperus, J., Jansonius, K. and Verhoeven, L. (2010) 'Pragmatic language impairment and associated behavioural problems.' *International Journal of Language & Communication Disorders 45*, 204–214.

Law, J. and Conway, J. (1992) 'Effect of abuse and neglect on the development of children's speech and language.' *Developmental Medicine & Child Neurology 34*, 943–948.

Law, J., Boyle, J., Harris, F., Harkness, A. and Nye, C. (2000) 'Prevalence and natural history of primary speech and language delay: findings from a systematic review of the literature.' *International Journal of Language & Communication Disorders 35*, 2, 165–188.

Law, J., Garrett, Z. and Nye, C. (2004) 'The efficacy of treatment for children with developmental speech and language delay/disorder: a meta-analysis.' *Journal of Speech, Language and Hearing Research 47*, 924–943.

Law, J., McBean, K. and Rush, R. (2011) 'Communication skills in a population of primary school-aged children raised in an area of pronounced social disadvantage.' *International Journal of Language & Communication Disorders 46*, 657–664.

Lawler, K., Taylor, N. and Shields, N. (2013) 'Outcomes after caregiver-provided speech and language or other allied health therapy: a systematic review.' *Archives of Physical Medicine and Rehabilitation 94*, 1139–1160.

Lum, J.A., Powell, M., Timms, L. and Snow P. (2015) 'A meta-analysis of cross sectional studies investigating language in maltreated children.' *Journal of Speech, Language and Hearing Research 58*, 961–976.

McAllister, J. (submitted) 'Behavioural, emotional and social development of children who stutter.'

McAllister, J. and Miller, J. (2013) *Introductory Linguistics for Speech and Language Therapy Practice.* Chichester: Wiley-Blackwell.

Merritt, D. and Klein, S. (2015) 'Do early care and education services improve language development for maltreated children? Evidence from a national child welfare sample.' *Child Abuse & Neglect 39,* 185–196.

Moreno Manso, J., García-Baamonde Sánchez, M., Blázquez Alonso, M. and Pozueco Romero, J. (2012) 'Pragmatic-communicative intervention strategies for victims of child abuse.' *Children and Youth Services Review 34,* 1729–1734.

Naughton, A., Maguire, S., Mann, M., Lumb, R., Tempest, V., Gracias, S., *et al.* (2013) 'Emotional, behavioural, and developmental features indicative of neglect or emotional abuse in preschool children: a systematic review.' *JAMA Pediatrics 167,* 8, 769–775.

Nippold, M.A. (1998) *Later Language Development: The School-age and Adolescent Years* (2nd ed.). Austin, TX: Pro-Ed.

Pinker, S. (1995) *The Language Instinct.* New York, NY: Harper Perennial Modern Classics.

Pruden, S., Hisch-Pasek, K. and Golinkoff, R. (2006) 'The Social Dimension in Language Development: A Rich History and a New Frontier.' In P.J. Marshall and N.A. Fox (eds) *The Development of Social Engagement: Neurobiological Perspectives.* Oxford: Oxford University Press.

Roulstone, S., Law, J., Rush, R., Clegg, J. and Peters, T. (2011) *Investigating the Role of Language in Children's Early Educational Outcomes.* DfE Research Report DFE-RR134. Bristol: University of the West of England.

Roy, P., Chiat, S. and Dodd, B. (2014) *Language and Socioeconomic Disadvantage: From Research to Practice.* London: City University London.

Ruben, R.J. (2000) 'Redefining the survival of the fittest: communication disorders in the 21st century.' *Laryngoscope 110,* 241–245.

Save The Children (2015) *Ready To Read: Closing the Gap in Early Language Skills so that Every Child in England Can Read Well.* Available at www.savethechildren.org.uk/resources/online-library/ready-read, accessed on 29 October 2015.

Schore, A.N. (2001) 'The effects of early relational trauma on right brain development, affect regulation, and infant mental health.' *Infant Mental Health Journal 22,* 1–2, 201–269.

Shahannan, T. (2006) 'Relations among Oral Language, Reading and Writing Development.' In C. Macarthur, S. Graham and J. Fitzgerald (eds) *Handbook of Writing Research.* New York, NY: Guildford.

Snow, C.E. (1977) 'The development of conversation between mothers and babies.' *Journal of Child Language 4,* 1–22.

Snow, P. (2009) 'Child maltreatment, mental health and oral language competence: inviting speech-language pathology to the prevention table.' *International Journal of Speech-Language Pathology 11,* 2, 95–103.

Stacks, A., Beeghly, M., Partridge, T. and Dexter, C. (2011) 'Effects of placement type on the language developmental trajectories of maltreated children from infancy to early childhood.' *Child Maltreatment 16,* 4, 287–299.

Sylvestre, A. and Mérette, C. (2010) 'Language delay in severely neglected children: a cumulative or specific effect of risk factors?' *Child Abuse & Neglect 34,* 6, 414–428.

Tamis-LeMonda, C.S. and Rodriguez, E.T. (2009) 'Parent's role in fostering young children's learning and language development.' *Encyclopedia on Early Childhood Development.* Montreal, Quebec: Centre of Excellence for Early Childhood Development. Available at www.child-encyclopedia.com/en-ca/language-development-literacy/according-to-experts/tamis-lemonda-rodriguez.html, accessed on 29 October 2015.

The Communication Trust (2015) *Universally Speaking – Ages and Stages of Children's Communication Development.* London: The Communication Trust. Available at www.thecommunicationtrust.org.uk/resources/resources/resources-for-practitioners/universally-speaking.aspx, accessed on 29 October 2015.

Tizard, B., Cooperman, O., Joseph, A. and Tizard, J. (1972) 'Environmental effects on language development: a study of young children in long-stay residential nurseries.' *Child Development 43,* 337–358.

Tomasello, M. (2003) *Constructing a Language: A Usage-based Theory of Language.* London: Harvard University Press.

US Department of Health & Human Services (2013) *National Survey of Child and Adolescent Well-Being.* Available at www.acf.hhs.gov/programs/opre/resource/national-survey-of-child-and-adolescent-well-being-nscaw-ii-wave-2-child, accessed on 29 October 2015.

Valentino, K., Cicchetti, D., Rogosch, F.A. and Toth, S.L. (2008) 'Memory, maternal representations, and internalizing symptomatology among abused, neglected, and nonmaltreated children.' *Child Development 79,* 705–719.

Veltman, M.W.M. and Browne, K.D. (2001) 'Three decades of child maltreatment research: Implications for the school years.' *Trauma, Violence, & Abuse 2,* 215–239.

Vygotsky, L. (1978) *Mind in Society: The Development of Higher Psychological Processes.* Cambridge, MA: Harvard University Press.

Wallace, I., Berkman, N., Watson, L., Coyne-Beasley, *et al.* (2015) 'Screening for speech and language delay in children 5 years old and younger: a systematic review.' *Pediatrics 136,* e448–462.

Westerlund, M. and Lagerberg, D. (2007) 'Expressive vocabulary in 18-month-old children in relation to demographic factors, mother and child characteristics, communication style and shared reading.' *Child: Care, Health and Development 34,* 257–266.

Windsor, J., Glaze, L.E., Koga, S.F. and the Bucharest Early Intervention Project Core Group (2007) 'Language acquisition with limited input: Romanian institution and foster care.' *Journal of Speech, Language, and Hearing Research 50,* 1365–1381.

Yagmurlu, B., Berument, S.K. and Celimli, S. (2005) 'The role of institution and home contexts in theory of mind development.' *Applied Developmental Psychology 26,* 521–537.

3

MAKING A DIFFERENCE TO THE NEGLECTED CHILD'S LIVED EXPERIENCE

Jan Horwath

Introduction

'No one asked me what was going on. I felt worthless and alone. Nothing was working in my life' (ChildLine 2015). This was the experience of 11-year-old Leanne who was suffering neglect. She was known to social services and also attended school. She eventually ran away from home and contacted ChildLine, a children's help line. How is it, when there is so much emphasis on child-centred practice in the United Kingdom, that a young person such as Leanne is made to feel that no one is concerned about her and that she is invisible and alone?

Over a quarter of a century ago, Butler-Sloss (1988, p.245), in her inquiry report into child abuse in Cleveland, expressed disquiet that children were seen by practitioners only as 'objects of concern'. The workers failed to recognise children as agents who should have a voice. The 1989 United Nations Convention on the Rights of the Child (UNCRC) Article 12 made clear that children have the right to participate fully in family, cultural and social life and freely express their views on all matters relating to them (United Nations 1989). In England and Wales, Article 12 is embedded in the Children Act 1989 as well as in the Children Act 2004. These rights are also enshrined in similar acts in Northern Ireland, Scotland and other nation states. According to those Acts, local authorities have a duty to ascertain the wishes and feelings of a child and to give them due consideration when making decisions during the child protection process. In England it is not only legislation but also accompanying guidance, such as the *Framework for the Assessment of Children in Need and Their Families*

(Department of Health, Home Office *et al.* 2000) and *Working Together to Safeguard Children: A Guide to Inter-agency Working to Safeguard and Promote the Welfare of Children* (HM Government 2015), that places emphasis on the importance of child-centred professional practice.

What do we mean by 'the principle of child-centred practice'? It does not necessarily mean inevitably acting on the young person's wishes and feelings or always allowing young people to determine what happens to them. Rather, it means keeping a focus on the individual child and their needs throughout the assessment and in subsequent interventions. Workers should observe children in different settings, particularly the interactions between the child and their main carers; listen to the child; and draw on their professional knowledge and skills to appreciate the impact of parenting behaviours and issues on the lives of children. Maintaining a focus on the individual child is particularly important in cases of child neglect because neglect has a cumulative effect. Moreover, seemingly identical behaviours on the part of the carer may affect individual children in the family differently (Daniel *et al.* 2011; Dickens 2007).

Fully to appreciate the impact of neglect on the child one needs to know not only the child's wishes and feelings, but also how they are experiencing the neglect: in other words, *how is it affecting their daily lived experience?* Take the case of 11-year-old Ian (examples in this chapter are modified in order to ensure anonymity). Ian is a middle child in a family of five. He lives with his mother Jane, and Rob her boyfriend of two years who is violent towards Jane. Jane drinks heavily and leaves the children to their own devices. The three-bedroomed house that they rent is dirty, cold and sparsely furnished; the kitchen cupboards are usually empty. Ian shares a room with his 14-year-old brother Nathan and the two boys sleep on the floor on a double mattress that is soiled, with no sheets and one filthy duvet with no cover.

This is how the social worker describes the impact of neglect on Ian:

> Ian's school attendance is erratic and he has not settled in well at his new secondary school. His year tutor believes he is bullied because of his generally unkempt appearance and clumsiness. He has been assessed as having dyspraxia (a developmental coordination disorder, which can affect basic motor skills such as walking and balancing, as well as finer motor skills like writing and drawing). At school Ian is 'a bit of a loner'; he is small for his age; he is very quiet and

withdrawn; and he only has one friend who comes from a family similar to his own.

Contrast this with what Ian has to say about his life:

I hate my life, no one cares about me. If I was dead I don't think anyone would notice. I share a room with Nathan – he spends less and less time at home and is only bothered about the girls when he's here because he thinks I can care for myself. Our room is shit. Some of my friends have computers and TVs in their rooms – that's a laugh, all I've got is a stinking old mattress and some dirty covers. The walls are all black with mould Mum calls it, and you can't stick anything on the walls because of it. The room is freezing, the radiator hasn't worked for years and I hate getting up in the mornings. If I leave my clothes in the room they smell and get damp. It's really hard keeping anything clean here so none of us bother anymore. If I get up in time I think about going to school. At least at school you get something to eat and there's never much to eat in the house in the mornings. I hate walking to school. There is a gang of boys who bully me and laugh at me saying I stink and look like a tramp. The problem is they are right.

I've only got one friend at school, Tim. He's a bit like me; his mum does not care about him as she's a bit mad and sometimes has to be taken to hospital. Tim is the only one who has been to my house and he did not laugh or anything when he saw my room. Tim and I have started bunking off during the day. We stay for dinner and then go and hang around in the park. We have a really good laugh. Tim always goes home at the end of school time as he gets worried about his mum. I sometimes hang around on my own after he's gone as I hate going home.

When I get home I never know what is going to happen. Usually no one notices me or says hello so I go into the kitchen to find some food. There is not much there: a few biscuits and crisps or the remains of the take-out Rob and Mum have had the night before – if I'm lucky. When Mum gets her money she'll send me to buy everyone chips for tea: that is my best day. If there is no food I'll take one or two of Mum's cans. The drink makes me feels warm and sleepy and then I don't feel too hungry and then I'm not particularly bothered about anything. I hate it if Rob is around as he bosses me about and makes me put the girls to bed. Their room is as bad as mine and they often cry because they are cold and hungry. If I tell Mum, Rob usually shouts at us that we should toughen up. I like it when Rob is out as I sit with Mum and we cuddle up on the settee. That is just the best time. Only sometimes Mum cries and says she wishes she was a better mum. I try and tell her everything will be alright but I can't see how it ever will be. If we know Rob is not coming back I'll sleep on the settee as it is nice and warm downstairs.

This account by Ian provides practitioners with much clearer insight into Ian's needs than the practitioner's assessment alone. Whilst, as can be seen from the above, obtaining such an account is valuable, it is not easy. In this chapter I consider the challenges practitioners encounter when assessing child neglect and how these challenges can lead to practice that marginalises the impact of neglect on children. I then describe a model – the Horwath Model – that I have developed in collaboration with practitioners. The Model seeks to enable workers both to be more child-focused in their practice and to hear directly what young people say about their experiences of neglect. The value of the Model is considered through the findings of a qualitative study of its use in practice. I use anonymised quotes from practitioners and families who participated in the study to illustrate the points made. The chapter concludes with practical suggestions as to how practitioners, irrespective of their discipline and jurisdiction, can use the Model to be child-centred, act as change agents and engage meaningfully with families.

Seeing the neglected child: the challenges

Assessment of child neglect

It is not standard practice to secure an appreciation of the lived experience of neglected children, whether they require early help or child protection interventions (Daniel *et al.* 2011; Davies and Ward 2012). The reasons for this are considered below.

In order to establish whether a child is being neglected, practitioners should complete a multidisciplinary assessment. When doing this it is all too easy to focus on parenting issues and behaviour, ignoring the specific *impact* of these behaviours on individual children – for example, how parental drug misuse is affecting each child in the family. A report into the arrangements for safeguarding neglected children from England's Office for Standards in Education, Children's Services and Skills (Ofsted) found that half the assessments of neglectful parenting in the 124 cases they looked at did not consider the impact of the neglect on the child. In some assessments, practitioners had not considered how the parents' behaviour was affecting individual children (Ofsted 2014).

One contributory factor to this situation may be the definition of child neglect that is used to establish whether a child is suffering significant harm. The definition in England, for example, like that in other UK countries, centres on practitioners demonstrating a failure on the part of the carer to provide specific aspects of care such as 'food, clothing and shelter', 'ensuring supervision', 'protecting a child from physical and emotional danger' and 'ensuring access to appropriate medical care or treatment'. (HM Government 2015, p.93). If parental failure is the focus of assessment, it encourages practitioners to gather evidence about signs of parental neglect. This can result in 'the construction of a "neglected child" as little more than a collection of indicators of neglect' (Horwath and Tarr 2015, p.139). This process was highlighted in a study I completed with Sukey Tarr (for more detail see Horwath and Tarr 2015). The study included an analysis of 21 case files, focus groups attended by 34 practitioners, telephone interviews with six conference chairs and 12 social workers, as well as completion of a questionnaire by 162 practitioners from a range of disciplines.

We found that, in contrast to the way in which practitioners identified specific parental behaviours, their assessments of children's developmental needs were generalised. They often just echoed concerns about parenting behaviour and issues without describing how these affected the child. For example, under the heading 'parenting capacity', statements such as 'the parents do not provide clear boundaries' were common. In terms of the child's developmental needs this was then described as 'child does not have clear age appropriate boundaries'. This description provides little information as to the *impact* of the lack of boundaries on the individual child. Ofsted, in their review of child neglect cases, also found a lack of attention by practitioners to the impact of neglect on a child. When professionals did try to consider this impact, they often only had partial knowledge. For example, the teacher would know about the impact of neglect on the child whilst the child is at school but might not know what life is like for the child out of school.

If one is to really appreciate the lived experience of children, one needs a sense of who they are and how they see themselves – in other words, their sense of identity. Arguably, one of the most striking findings from the study described above was the lack of attention given to the identity of individual children. The child's identity was usually described in assessments in terms of ethnicity, language and religion, using standard phrases that are repeated in numerous assessments such as 'white, English speaking'. Yet neglect has a significant impact on other aspects of children's identity, such as their social lives. For example, in the study we found that the neglected children were often loners, experienced bullying, acted as young carers, or lived with chronic health conditions, which were not considered to be affecting their identity.

Regulations in England (HM Government 2015) and Wales (Welsh Assembly Government 2006) mean that assessments for child protection case conferences are required within 15 working days of the decision to proceed with child protection enquires. These conferences are where decisions are made as to whether the child has or is likely to suffer from significant harm and if so, whether a multiagency child protection plan is needed. The schedule is challenging if practitioners wish to ensure that their assessments are child-centred. In the limited time available, those practitioners who do not have established relationships with the family need to familiarise themselves with the case; to read lengthy case files and establish the past history and patterns of engagement; as well as meet and develop a rapport with family members, including the children.

These tasks can be made even more complex in cases of possible chronic neglect, where the parents may have completed numerous assessments. In these situations, parents are often able to deflect professionals' attention away from the neglect to other issues and concerns (Horwath 2007). This pressure to meet deadlines is likely to contribute to practitioners focusing on presenting problems, practical issues and parents' needs rather than the lived experience of the child. Moreover, as practitioners have little time to establish relationships with children, any engagement with them is likely to be superficial and focused on generalised wishes and feelings.

Child protection conferences

Moving on to the child protection conference, researchers have found the content is often driven by professionals' own concerns and anxieties (Keddell 2011; Vis, Holtan and Thomas 2012). Conference members can become so focused on the effects of parenting issues on parenting capacity that they do not consider the specific impact on each child and the differing needs of siblings. The more obvious needs of children who act out and exhibit challenging behaviour can result in the needs of quieter, more withdrawn siblings being ignored or minimised at the conference and in plans (Horwath 2013).

Davies and Ward (2012) found that there is very limited time spent at conference on action planning. This usually takes place only after a lengthy and often stressful discussion of the information obtained by participants. This means that professionals and family are developing the outline plan together at the end of a lengthy conference when concentration is often waning. Plans can be developed speedily using professional jargon and shorthand. For example, professionals may suggest local projects and programmes by name, not explaining to families what the project is for and why parents should attend. This can leave families confused regarding what needs to change, the rationale behind actions, and the intended benefits for the child and the family.

Children do not often attend conference or indeed core groups (Office of the Children's Commissioner 2010). The participants in the Horwath and Tarr study reflected on the reasons why this occurs in cases of neglect. They concluded that the child or young person may be overwhelmed by having to listen to difficult content and so chose not to attend; that venues, set-up and timing of conferences, core groups and reviews are not child-friendly; and finally that professionals may feel intimidated by children and young people being present and therefore do not encourage them to attend. If children and young people do not participate directly in the conference, they depend on professionals or family members to present their views – if they are given a voice at all (Woolfson *et al.* 2010). As a consequence, conference members have little idea as to whether planned interventions have prioritised what the children and young people themselves consider important. For example, a young woman I met recently described how her child protection plan centred on getting her to school on time. The view at conference had been that her parents were not supporting her to get ready for school, which, she acknowledged, they were not doing.

However, no one had asked her *why* she was late for school. She told me that she was quite capable of getting herself up and ready in the morning but deliberately set off late to avoid some boys from a neighbouring school who were bullying her, an insight which would have informed her protection plan.

Sustaining change

If the focus at child protection conferences is mainly or solely on neglectful parental behaviours, it is not surprising that the focus of interventions centres on parents completing tasks to improve these behaviours. The kind of parental tasks often included in child protection plans are: attending parenting programmes, cleaning the house, getting up in the morning and taking the children to school and ensuring the children have a meal in the evening. Whilst these are all likely to be appropriate actions, completing the tasks alone does not necessarily mean that the quality of life for the child will improve. Ofsted (2014), in their review of child neglect cases, found there was evidence of good short-term support meeting the needs of the family. However, there was little evidence of more long-term support ensuring that positive changes are having a sustained impact on children.

An alternative approach: Making the child visible

If practitioners are to have a positive impact on the lives of neglected children then, as discussed above, it is necessary for them to make sense of the daily lived experience of the child. Capturing this experience should inform the assessment of the developmental needs of the child. Hence any assessment should start with establishing, from a variety of sources, what life is like for the child as the baseline for action. Clearly, the child or young person in the majority of cases is the best source of information. However, practitioners involved with the family and family members are also able to provide some insight, particularly regarding babies and pre-verbal children. Ofsted (2014) noted that many practitioners have limited insights into the life of the child but that, if these insights are pooled together with the child and family's perspectives, it is possible to build up a clear picture of the developmental needs of the child and whether they are or are not being met.

Take as an example the case of nine-year-old Karlie who lives with her mother who is a lone parent (this case is fictitious but not unusual):

> Karlie suffers from poor dental hygiene. She has tooth decay and has constant infections as a result of this. (School nurse)

As practitioners find out about Karlie's day by talking to her and drawing on their knowledge of her, they learn about her specific experience of toothache.

> She describes sleepless nights because she is in pain. She rarely eats as it hurts so she tends to live on fizzy drinks at home and if she's at school she cannot eat her school dinner and is hungry. She often does not go to school as she frequently gets infections and feels ill or her toothache means she finally falls asleep in the early hours and therefore does not wake up in time for school. If she stays at home she tries to sleep on the sofa during the day. As she is irritable she annoys her mum and they end up arguing. When that happens, Karlie will go and sit in the park for a bit. If she does go to school she is usually late, really tired due to lack of sleep and therefore lacks ability to concentrate, she feels miserable, is irritable and gets into fights easily. Also, her breath smells and other children tease or bully her. She finds the pain is worse in the evenings and is increasingly helping herself to mum's paracetamol as she's learnt this numbs the pain for a bit and helps her sleep.

Drawing on the above, it becomes apparent that most aspects of Karlie's health and development are being affected by dental neglect. Thus, practitioners are able to provide a more specific account as to how just one aspect of neglect is impacting on her whole life.

> Her general health is clearly affected and her usage of paracetamol may be causing harm to her liver.

> Her educational needs are not being met as her school attendance is poor and her ability to learn when at school means she is falling behind.

> Her social presentation is affected as her teeth look unpleasant and she smells.

> Her self-esteem is low, particularly as others tease or bully her.

> Her behaviour is erratic; she is aggressive because of the pain she is in.

Her relationships with her peers are also affected as a result of her irritability and she argues with her mother.

Working collaboratively with practitioners from a range of disciplines I have developed the Horwath Model as a way of capturing the lived experience of children. The Model has three functions:

- to ensure practitioners capture the daily lived experience of the child and draw on this when assessing and intervening in neglect cases

- to provide a vehicle for understanding how the parent's lived experience impacts on the child's experience, and

- to enable practitioners to measure change to parenting behaviour in terms of the quality of the child's daily experience.

The Model was piloted in practice with 15 chronic neglect cases in three different locations in England, and the experiences of practitioners and family members who used the Model was evaluated. Helen Richardson-Foster carried out interviews with conference chairs (n=5) and 12 social workers who had acted as key workers. In addition, case discussions with 16 practitioners from different disciplines involved in the cases were held. The views of six parents and three children were also sought (Horwath and Richardson-Foster, forthcoming). The Model is described below alongside feedback from respondents in the study regarding their experiences of using it.

The practitioners involved in the cases captured information about the daily lived experience of the child using 24-hour 'clocks' or 'circles', as shown in Figure 3.1. They captured the child's experience by summarising it in the centre circle, and did the same for the perspective of the parent(s) in the middle circle. They summarised what professionals know about various parts of the child's day in the outer circle. A clock or circle was completed for each child in the family. In two of the three pilot areas, the information obtained was used at child protection conferences to establish whether the child was suffering or was likely to suffer significant harm. The information from the clocks/circles was also used in all three pilot areas to inform the content of child protection plans and follow-up case reviews.

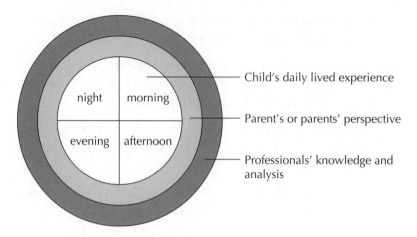

*Figure 3.1 The clocks/circles: Capturing perceptions
of the daily lived experience of the child*

The following comments provide a flavour of what a number of children and young people said when this Model was used to ask them about their daily lived experiences:

> Mum or dad don't cuddle or talk to me when I get home.
>
> I like school and have nice friends.
>
> I am embarrassed when my friends say my stuff has come off the tip.
>
> I am only really happy in school because I feel safe there.
>
> Sometimes I wake up crying, and Nan says mum should keep the light on.
>
> I fall asleep on the couch because I'm scared of monsters in my room.
>
> Sometimes we watch films. I wish someone would play Connect 4 with me.
>
> At 2.30pm a taxi takes me home; I can go home early from school depending on the activity. Someone will knock for me and I'll go out and have spliff.

Significantly, in the case of pre-verbal children or where the child was not forthcoming, workers still established a day in the life of the child, by gaining information from family members and other professionals as in the following example:

Mum makes tea at 4.30 p.m. [Child's name] has a limited range of food she enjoys. She enjoys fruit and pasta.

There is a choice of food with dad. [Child's name] may choose not to eat as he is a picky eater.

[Child's name] wakes up at 1 or 2 p.m. Once he slept through the entire day and he was shocked. Sometimes he goes to bed at 1 a.m.

In cases where the child lived with carers other than their parents, the child's lived experience in the different settings was captured. This enabled both parents and practitioners to compare and contrast the quality of the child's life with different carers.

Using the Model has a number of benefits that were highlighted by practitioners. These included:

- *Ensuring that practice was child-centred* and went beyond identifying generalised feelings to establish what was important for the child and what they would like to see change. In other words it gave the child or young person a voice, for example:

  Things that bothered them were the fact there wasn't credit on their mobile phones, the fact they didn't have a Facebook account and couldn't talk to friends like a lot of the others that they knew. That's what made them feel different. (Conference chair)

- *Enabling practitioners to step 'into the child's shoes'* and gain a deeper understanding about the impact of neglect on life for each child in the family:

  You know, 24 hours in his life, it does highlight that it is pretty poor. And I have used that now when I've thought of babies, you know, when babies are left in cots and stuff like that. (Social worker)

Practitioners are able to draw on the information within the clocks/ circles to compare and contrast what it is that parents say they do with the child's experience and professionals' knowledge. This facilitates discussion with parents about what is 'good enough' parenting and how their behaviours can be adapted to ensure the needs of the child are met:

Mother states that breakfast is at 7 a.m. followed by getting dressed, having a play, snack, watching TV, and having a nap at 11 a.m. This, however, is not what was observed on my unannounced morning visits. The mother knew what she should do, so this was used as a basis to identify how to do it. (Social worker)

- *Promoting a holistic perspective on family life.* This was particularly important for practitioners, such as those in adult services or those with a specific brief, who were helped by the Model to appreciate the impact of parenting behaviours on the children.

From our perspective only visiting for a short space of time once a week it [the Model] gave a great insight into what actually goes on around the dynamics of the household. Maybe for somebody that has a lot more involvement within the house it might not have been quite as beneficial. But because we're only there for that short period of time, we only really see a very, very short snapshot of what goes on in the house. We're just in, we pick him up and we're out again, and then [we hear] whatever he may divulge to us when we're out. So from my perspective to be able [to] pass that [insight] on to [workers] to help them support [the child], it was very beneficial. (Family Support Manager)

- *Ensuring marginalised children are made more visible.* One of the most striking findings from the study was that the quiet withdrawn children became more visible. Practitioners tend to focus their attention on the children who are clearly affected by neglect and demonstrating this with challenging behaviours (Horwath 2013).

[Child 2] had been so high profile that [Child 1] had sort of been a bit in the background. (Conference chair)

All too often, particularly with large families, it is too easy to provide generalised interventions designed to meet the needs of all the children. When this occurs the specific needs of some children can be sidelined. The practitioners found that the clocks/circles enabled the differing needs of siblings to be identified and addressed.

[Child 1]'s clock/circle indicated she was completely oblivious to what was going on with everybody else within the household, and that for her everything was fine and dandy. So [Child 1] was completely unaffected, [Child 2] was affected a little bit, so she'd got some of those issues around for example 'if [Child 3] doesn't have to go to school why do I?' and [Child 3] was worst affected.

So what the Model did show very clearly was the different impacts of long-term neglect on each of the children. (Conference chair)

- *Facilitating family engagement* by being specific, with clear examples of concerns and strengths. The clocks/circles also present the information more visually, in a way which is easier to understand than lengthy reports written in professional jargon.

Because normally, you see, you get the social worker and every report and then you go to the family to say is there anything that you want to say, anything that you want to add or amend. It puts a lot of pressure on them in a room full of people. But when they're going through the clock it's easier for them, I think. (Conference chair)

- *Increasing understanding of the impact on children of parenting behaviours.* The parents are made aware of the impact of their behaviour on each child, in a very clear, specific manner:

I think this is great to highlight negatives and for the child to say, 'Yeah I woke up this morning for breakfast and Mummy didn't have any milk in', which is the situation still with this family. 'You know, Mummy didn't have any milk and I couldn't have breakfast. I went to school and I was hungry and school had to feed me.' (Social worker)

- *Providing a vehicle for measuring progress.*

So, when you come to do the review, so, you could look at that [the clocks] and then do the reviews with him [the child] there, focus on what was different; what had moved on and what was better for him and what needed to continue. (Social worker)

The interplay between the child's and the parent's lived experience

A key lesson learnt from the Horwath and Richardson-Foster study was that practitioners need to understand the parents' lived experience as well as that of the child or children. Only by appreciating the lives of both the parent or parents and each individual child in a family can one begin to understand why the specific needs of the child are not being met. Practitioners can also be clearer as to what should change in order for those needs to be met.

This will be explained by returning to the fictitious case of Karlie, her mother Sam and the dental neglect. Drawing on the information obtained about Karlie's experience it would make sense if an action in the outline plan was: 'Sam is to take Karlie to the dentist and ensure a daily teeth-cleaning regime.'

However, this is what practitioners have learnt about Sam's lived experience:

> Sam knows the flat is a mess and she never gets round to cleaning up or washing, etc. She struggles to get up in the morning as she is on anti-depressants and has often been up in the night to look after her four-month old baby. By the time she does get up it is mid-morning so she never knows if Karlie has gone to school or not, what she is wearing and whether she has washed or eaten something. If she hasn't gone to school she has not got the energy to argue with her and just lets her be.
>
> By the time she's got herself up and sorted out the baby it's usually one-ish and she is exhausted. She rarely bothers to get dressed and has no appetite. If she has money she gives Karlie some, to get Sam's vodka and food for herself, but she has little idea what Karlie buys. She spends the afternoon in front of the TV and has usually had a couple of vodkas so she's able to have a snooze. She finds Karlie is always moaning and irritable and gets really cross if she asks her to mind the baby. She knows that Karlie has toothache and that she should sort it out, but the days just seem to fly past and she never gets round to making an appointment for her at the dentist. (Social worker's report)

By gaining this insight into life for Sam, one can begin to appreciate that there would be little point in just saying to Sam that she needs to take Karlie to the dentist and ensure she brushes her teeth. The issues impacting on her parenting capacity would need to be addressed first. By clearly establishing what daily life is like for the parent, practitioners can identify behaviours that may be risky or harmful to the child and that need to change, but also positive aspects of parenting.

Improving the quality of the child and parent's lived experience

Using the Horwath Model to draw on information of this kind that is gathered about the daily lived experience of family members, professionals can begin to explore with the family which of the needs of each child are and are not being met. In the Horwath and Richardson-Foster study (forthcoming), this level of clarity was achieved using a variety of visual methods at conferences, core groups and reviews. For example, at one pilot site the conference chair drew a set of traffic lights and at another a windscreen divided into three sections: red, amber and green. Participants at the conference and review considered the information captured on the clocks (see Figure 3.1); they mapped out what they now knew about the developmental needs of each child and indicated their level of concern to parents as follows:

- Red means we are really worried about this and you will need to work with us as part of a child protection plan to prevent this happening again to your child.

- Orange means that this is not great but we will work on the red problems first.

- Green is good practice and should continue.

Parents found this approach useful:

> that was useful because I had it bullet-pointed exactly what they thought I needed to do, so I could deal with it and get off the 'red' and into the 'ambers' and 'greens'. It was good. It was very clear on what was expected and what was needed. (Mother A)

This approach also enabled conference members, including the family, to discuss the concerns and which thresholds the concerns reached:

> It can provoke reaction, thoughts, from parents and from other professionals and you enter into a debate, argument, discussion – however you want to put it. (Social worker)

I'm quite confident to say I that think we've missed this off, or... you know, if something had been put in red or amber or green and I think – well actually don't you think that should go [somewhere else]? (Social worker)

Yeah I think there were a few [issues]. While we were talking about it they ended up in red or amber, and then when we went round to review things we sort of said, that needs to move into the other [level of concern] really. (Family support worker)

You could see visually what was going on, what needs to be done, and obviously yeah they'd get the concerns although there's some of it, half and half – half of it I don't agree. (Mother B)

Where a parent had difficulties with written information, use of the traffic lights or windscreen was an effective way to convey the risk factors and strengths in the situation:

I think as well for her, as she's got limited writing and reading skills, that it is quite good for her as well; because it breaks it down doesn't it, a bit more easily. (Social worker)

How the Horwath Model fits with other assessments

The Model complements Signs of Safety, an assessment approach used at many child protection conferences and reviews in the UK (see Chapter 8). Andrew Turnell, who developed Signs of Safety with colleagues in Australia, recognises the importance of understanding 'the typically messy lived experience' of families and indeed of practitioners (Turnell 2012, p.10). The Signs of Safety approach requires an assessment of harm, danger, complicating factors, strengths, existing and required safety, built on both the family's and the professionals' knowledge and experience. Based on this information a judgement is made as to what is necessary to keep the child safe. Using the Horwath Model to focus on the lived experience of the child(ren) and parent(s), and combining it with key elements of Signs of Safety, practitioners are able to be very specific about their risks and worries about the child and what is happening to the child on a daily basis, the complicating factors and the strengths and safety factors. The Model can also be used alongside the Graded Care Profile (Johnson and Cotmore 2015;

Srivastava and Polnay 1997). This gives specific evidence to grade the quality of care provided by parents as part of an initial assessment and through the course of intervention.

It is notoriously difficult to bring about change in cases of chronic neglect (Farmer and Lutman 2010). All too often the priority, as described at the beginning of this chapter, is the completion of tasks rather than outcomes for children. By highlighting the need to improve the lived experience of children and their parents, all those involved can focus more readily on achieving concrete, observable improvements to identified outcomes for children. Actions included in child protection plans can enable parents and practitioners to be specific and identify not only what needs to change in the daily life of the child but also the incremental steps that need to be taken.

Consider the example of Karlie and Sam. The desired final outcome would be for Karlie and her sibling to have their developmental needs met. At present it is most urgent that Karlie receives dental treatment. However, bearing in mind what is now known about Sam, it might be more appropriate for a family member or a family support worker to ensure that this takes place, for example going with Sam and Karlie to appointments. At the same time, Sam needs to access and engage in treatment for her depression and alcohol use and to have support in her care of the baby. Her parenting capacity is unlikely to improve without the underlying parenting issues being addressed and she is unlikely to become the perfect parent overnight. Therefore, practitioners can work with her on incremental steps to change. Parents in the Horwath and Richardson-Foster study (forthcoming) found that the use of the traffic lights/windscreen, drawing on evidence of changes to the lived experience of the child, enabled them to measure and to see their progress in a meaningful way.

> That was bad in the red and then, the orange was a bit better and the green was fantastic. It's everything, you could see the change going from red to green. (Mother C)

> I found it quite useful because instead of just telling you, you could actually see it, some things moved onto the amber and nearly everything is in green now. (Mother A)

The clocks/circles, combined with the traffic lights/windscreen, also provide practitioners with evidence as to whether parents are engaging in the plan in a meaningful way. The aim of the plan is to see improvements in the quality of the lived experience of the child. If there is a lack of change, then it would appear that parents are merely going through the motions and superficially complying with plans. Alternatively, they may not have the ability or motivation required to make the changes and it may be necessary to consider court proceedings. If this is the case, practitioners will already have child-centred evidence of the parent's inability to meet the needs of the child, despite professional interventions.

Table 3.1 below is an anonymised example of a child protection plan. It highlights the detail that needs to be included in a plan by members of the core group and how outcomes focus on changes to the quality of life for the child.

Applying the Model to practice: Lessons learnt

The lessons learnt are arguably best expressed in the words of a young person who participated in a child protection conference in the piloting of the Horwath Model:

> The [clocks] were like pinned up on the wall so everyone could see them...I didn't feel annoyed that they were up there, I felt annoyed at some of the things that were on there. But as it sort of went on I thought it was better that it happened, if you get me, so that everyone then knew what they needed to do.

This chapter draws on a small-scale pilot study completed in three locations in England, the findings of which indicate that child-centred outcomes are more likely to be achieved by drawing directly on the daily lived experience of children, young people and parents. At the time of writing, this Model is being tested further in a variety of different contexts. Early indications are that it is a valuable tool. It can be used by practitioners irrespective of jurisdiction: for assessing the needs of children not only experiencing neglect, but also for those who are suffering maltreatment from emotional harm, physical or sexual abuse; and for a variety of other purposes. To date it has been used to understand the lived experiences of groups of vulnerable children being assessed for early help services; living with chronic health conditions; and in out-of-home care.

For practitioners wishing to incorporate the Model into their practice there are some points that are worth considering.

Table 3.1: An example of a partially completed child protection plan for Nathan age five

RED What current aspects of the daily lived experience of the child are worrying professionals as being unsafe or causing harm?	FROM RED TO GREEN How will the daily lived experience of the child be different at the point where the child is safe from harm and we can consider ending the child protection plan?	What aspects of the daily lived experience of the parent(s), parenting issues, family and environmental factors may positively and negatively influence the ability and motivation of the parent(s) to meet the needs of the child?	What will the parent(s) need to do differently to ensure the child is protected from harm and the child's lived experience improves?	How can we achieve this? What are the first steps? Who needs to do what? To what timescales?
Nathan is bullied at school for being dirty and smelly and wearing torn, shabby clothing. Because of this he has no friends, has become withdrawn and does not engage in interactive activities.	There will be evidence from school that Nathan is arriving clean and tidy with clothing appropriate for school every day. Nathan should be indicating, and school acknowledging, that he is now beginning to make friends and interacting more with children in his class.	Mum is committed to working with professionals. Drawing on her own childhood experiences she realises how Nathan's life is being affected by poor physical care. The family are on benefits and mum has a considerable amount of debt, so buying clothes and toiletries is a problem. She is also not confident she knows how to use her washing machine properly and often puts clothes away damp. Mum's parents both had learning difficulties and did not teach her about the importance of regular washing. As a result, she struggles with her own personal hygiene and does not realise the importance of regular washing and dental hygiene.	Mum to ensure that she has washing products at home and check daily whether she needs to do a wash to ensure Nathan has clean clothes each day that are suitable for the weather. Mum to use her washing machine routinely and dry clothes properly. Mum to watch Nathan to make sure he has a wash before going to school and his hair and teeth are clean. She is to establish a bedtime routine. Wash his hair and make sure he has a bath at least twice a week.	Family support worker to ensure mum knows how to use the washing machine and how to dry the clothes. (1 month) Family support worker to help mum identify where to buy cheap washing products and discuss what products are essential. Also, how to buy children's clothes cheaply from charity shops, etc. (2 weeks) School to get Nathan a uniform voucher. (1 month) Mum to be demonstrating she is using the washing machine routinely and economically and that she completes a morning and evening washing routine. This is evidenced by Nathan going to school every day in clean and tidy clothes. (3-month review)

First, tools for collecting information about the daily lived experience of the child and their family should be adapted for their age and ability. For example, whilst primary school-age children may enjoy going through a 'clock', older children might wish to use a timeline or strip cartoon and pre-school children or those with a learning disability may benefit from talking through their day using pictures and symbols. In addition, information should be obtained from parents in a manner that does not make them feel patronised.

Second, it is important that children and young people do not become bored by completing clocks/circles routinely, and therefore find the process tedious. This can be avoided by using a variety of methods such as picture diaries and drawings to collect information about their daily lived experience.

Third, the clocks/circles should be completed periodically, for example at three-monthly intervals. If it is done too often it might become yet another hoop the family needs to jump through and is done mechanistically without real interest.

Fourth, when eliciting information it is important not to take anything for granted and ask open questions. For example, 'When do you get up in the morning?' presumes that the family member does actually get up in the morning, which may not be the case, so 'When do you tend to get up?' is more appropriate. One cannot presume any kind of routine, such as having meals, washing, etc. It is therefore important to ask questions such as, 'Once you are up, what happens next?'

Fifth, both parents and children may be guarded in their responses and reluctant to provide insights into the day, perhaps because of fear of the consequences. One method for handling this is to reflect on some of the concerns identified by practitioners, and ask the family member to consider why this may be happening during the course of the day. For example, in one case known to the author, a mother, when initially asked about her day, emphasised how she provided a meal for her children every evening. This did not fit with the children always being hungry at school and telling the teacher they had little to eat after school. By asking the mother how this could be it became clear that the 'meal' was toast and orange squash.

Finally, the Model, when used in some cases of chronic neglect, may not only highlight concerns about the parenting capacity but also limited parenting strengths. This can be very demoralising for parents. As one father in the study put it:

I find they tend to concentrate on the negatives more sometimes and are very reluctant to give any credit when it's deserved.

It is important, therefore, when making sense of the clocks/circles and completing the traffic lights/windscreens, that practitioners do not to minimise or marginalise indicators of good enough parenting.

Key learning points

In cases of child neglect, practitioners cannot improve outcomes for children and young people if they do not understand how the neglect is affecting the daily lives of the child or young person.

- Children experiencing similar forms of neglect may be affected differently. Therefore, it is essential that practitioners ensure they capture the daily lived experience of each child in the family, rather than assume they will all experience neglect in similar ways.

- It is also important to understand the daily lives of the each parent, in order to gain insights as to why they are not meeting the needs of the child.

- Meaningful outcomes should focus on positive change to the quality of the lived experience of the child rather than simply on actions or tasks to be completed by parents (such as attending a parenting programme).

- Child-focused outcomes will only be achieved by working with parents to ensure they understand the effect of their daily behaviours on their child, and have the ability and motivation to change those behaviours in order to meet the needs of the child.

Questions for reflection

- Are you interested to try out the clock/circle to see whether it helps in your work? What would help you to do so?

- How do you currently find out and record how a child's needs are being met? What are the benefits and challenges of that approach?

References

Butler-Sloss, E. (1988) *Report of the Inquiry into Child Abuse in Cleveland 1987*. London: HMSO.

ChildLine (2015) *Leanne – My experience of Neglect*. Available at www.childline.org.uk/ Play/GetInvolved/Pages/Leanne-my-experience-of-neglect.aspx, accessed on 3 July 2015.

Daniel, B., Taylor, J. and Scott J. with Derbyshire, D. and Neilson, D. (2011) *Recognizing and Helping the Neglected Child: Evidence-Based Practice for Assessment and Intervention*. London: Jessica Kingsley Publishers.

Davies, C. and Ward H. (2012) *Safeguarding Children across Services: Messages from Research on Identifying and Responding to Maltreatment*. London: Jessica Kingsley Publishers.

Department of Health, Department for Education and Employment and Home Office (2000) *Framework for the Assessment of Children in Need and their Families*. London: The Stationery Office.

Dickens, J. (2007) 'Child neglect and the law: catapults, thresholds and delay.' *Child Abuse Review 16*, 77–92.

Farmer, E. and Lutman, E. (2010) *Case Management and Outcomes for Neglected Children Returned to Their Parents: A Five Year Follow-up Study*. Bristol: School for Policy Studies, University of Bristol.

HM Government (2015) *Working Together to Safeguard Children: A Guide to Inter-agency Working to Safeguard and Promote the Welfare of Children*. London: DfE. Available at www.gov.uk/government/publications/working-together-to-safeguard-children--2, accessed on 25 August 2015.

Horwath, J. (2007) *The Neglected Child: Identification and Assessment*. London: Palgrave.

Horwath, J. (2013) *Child Neglect: Planning and Intervention*. Basingstoke: Palgrave Macmillan.

Horwath, J. and Richardson-Foster, H. (forthcoming) *Making Sense of The Daily Lived Experience of The Neglected Child: Planning and Intervening In Cases of Child Neglect*.

Horwath, J. and Tarr, S. (2015) 'Child visibility in cases of chronic neglect: implications for social work practice.' *British Journal of Social Work 45*, 1395–1432.

Johnson, R. and Cotmore, R. (2015) *National evaluation of the graded care profile*. Available at www.nspcc.org.uk/globalassets/documents/research-reports/graded-care-profile-evaluation-report-large-text.pdf, accessed 28/8/2015.

Keddell, E. (2011) 'Reasoning processes in child protection decison making: negotiating moral minefields and risky relationships.' *British Journal of Social Work 41*, 1251–1270.

Office of the Children's Commissioner (2010) *Family Perspectives on Safeguarding and on Relationships with Children's Services*. London: Office of the Children's Commissioner.

Office of Standards in Education, Children's Services and Skills (Ofsted) (2014) *In the Child's Time: Professional Responses to Neglect*. Manchester: Ofsted.

Srivastava, O.P. and Polnay, L. (1997) 'Field trial of Graded Care Profile (GCP) scale: A new measure of care.' *Archives of Disease in Childhood 76*, 4, 337–340.

Turnell, A. (2012) *The Signs of Safety: Comprehensive Briefing Paper*. Available at www.aascf.com/pdf/Signs%20of%20Safety%20Breifing%20paper%20April%202012.pdf, accessed on 14 April 2015.

United Nations (1989) *United Nations Convention on the Rights of the Child (UNCRC)*. Geneva: United Nations.

Vis, S.A., Holtan, A. and Thomas, N. (2012) 'Obstacles for child participation in care and protection cases – why Norwegian social workers find it difficult.' *Child Abuse Review 21*, 7–23.

Welsh Assembly Government (2006) *Safeguarding Children: Working Together under the Children Act 2004.* Cardiff: The Welsh Assembly Government.

Woolfson, R.C., Heffernan, E., Paul, M. and Brown, M. (2010) 'Young people's views of the child protection system in Scotland.' *British Journal of Social Work 40,* 2069–2085.

RESEARCH NOTE
Preventing dental neglect

Emily Keene
Specialist in Paediatric Dentistry

Background

This note summarises a recent research study completed in Bradford, a city in the UK, conducted to investigate whether children subject to child protection plans had different dental health to children without child protection plans (Keene *et al.* 2015).

Dental caries is the commonest oral disease in children. It may occur in isolation but there is increasing acceptance that it may be a sign of a wider picture of abuse or neglect (Balmer, Gibson and Harris 2010; Harris, Balmer and Sidebotham 2009). Dental neglect has been defined as 'the persistent failure to meet a child's basic oral health needs, likely to result in the serious impairment of a child's oral or general health or development' (Harris *et al.* 2009). It may be one sign of many which, taking all factors into account, could lead to a diagnosis of general abuse or neglect. Dental neglect can lead to dental caries, serious infection and loss of function. These in turn can cause pain, irritability and loss of sleep; problems eating and resulting in poor nutrition and weight loss; time off school; and interference with learning, playing and socialising. An example of the latter might be a child who is avoided (or even bullied) because of bad breath due to dental decay. Ultimately, hospital admission and emergency visits, along with repeated antibiotics may ne necessary. Long-standing disease can also lead to damage to permanent teeth.

Aims and methodology

The aims of the study were to compare the dental decay, dental access and oral hygiene habits of children subject to child protection plans (CPPs) as a result of child maltreatment, compared to controls. (For an explanation of CPPs, see Chapter 3.) The study included children who were subject to CCPs developed by Bradford Safeguarding Children Board. Control children were obtained from Orthopaedic and General Surgery Paediatric clinics. All children were aged between 2 and 11 years old, and were healthy or had mild systemic disease. They all received a standardised dental examination according to the British Association for the Study of Community Dentistry instructions using a light dental mirror and cotton wool rolls. A questionnaire was used to collect information about past dental access and experience, and oral hygiene habits.

Results

Seventy-nine children in each group were examined. The study group consisted of 39 per cent of children with CPPs for neglect, 33 per cent for emotional abuse, 19 per cent for physical abuse and 5 per cent for sexual abuse. The age, gender and race of children were similar for each group. The children with CPPs had a lower socio-economic status than the controls ($p = 0.001$, Mann Whitney U test). Children in the study group had more dental decay than the control group with their mean number of decayed missing and filled primary teeth being 3.82 and 2.03 respectively ($p = 0.002$), and their mean decayed missing and filled permanent teeth being 0.71 and 0.30 respectively ($p = 0.374$). There were more children who were free of dental decay (68%) in the control group compared with the study group, the latter having 42 per cent ($p = 0.001$). The care index is the proportion of decayed missing and filled teeth which have been filled – that is, how much restorative treatment has been carried out for the decay. The care index was much lower in the study group at 1.69 per cent compared with 6.02 per cent in the control group ($p = 0.008$) (i.e. the children on CPPs had had less professional help to deal with the decay). Children in the study group had their teeth brushed fewer times a day than the control group ($p = 0.015$) and their oral hygiene was worse with statistically more plaque ($p = 0.002$) and gingivitis (p = 0.046). Children with child protection plans had been to a dentist less frequently in the previous year (p = 0.000).

Discussion

These results showed increased dental decay in children subject to child protection plans. They reinforce the proposition that dental decay may be used as an indicator for possible general child maltreatment, although the indicator should not be used in isolation. Dental practitioners should be aware of this when treating children and act when there is an area for concern. Other professionals involved in assessing children for maltreatment may also consider checking their teeth or referring them for a dental assessment, both to alleviate any of symptoms described and also to note any concerns they raise.

More children had plaque and gingivitis present in the study group. This indicates that children with child protection plans (and their parents) may not be as motivated in oral hygiene practices as control children (and their parents). This was also highlighted in the results to the questionnaire about frequency of tooth brushing, with the study group brushing less frequently than the control group. The majority of the study group tended to brush 'never' or 'occasionally', compared to the majority of controls brushing the recommended twice per day. This poorer oral hygiene may be a causative factor in the higher decay levels of children with child protection plans.

Conclusions: Taking action to identify and remedy dental neglect

Children with child protection plans are already a vulnerable group. Their higher levels of untreated decay have the potential to have more negative impact on their dental and general health, since they accessed dental care less often than controls. *If access to dental care is difficult for children on CPPs or with other social issues, they should be identified as a priority group.*

An incidental finding in the study, but one that is also significant for remedial action, was the relatively high attendance (81%) of children with CPPs who were selected for the study group once appointments had been made made for them to receive a dental examination. This demonstrates that by working closely with colleagues and families, and by formally incorporating dental check-ups as part of the child protection plans, it is possible to achieve high levels of dental attendance in this group. *All children who have child protection plans developed should be asked if they have a dentist. If they do not, then these children should be referred by children's social care to an appropriate local dentist; and followed up if they do not attend.*

Dental prevention is of paramount importance to try to prevent the high levels of dental disease the researchers found in this group of children. These findings indicate that prevention and treatment of dental decay are possible with this group; prevention should be advised and reinforced by the full range of professionals in contact with the families (including health, education and adults' and children's social care as well as community organisations), and accessed in more depth by dental professionals.

References

Balmer, R., Gibson, E. and Harris, J. (2010) 'Understanding child neglect. Current perspectives in dentistry.' *Primary Dental Care 17*, 105–109.

Harris, J.C., Balmer, R.C. and Sidebotham, P.D. (2009) 'British Society of Paediatric Dentistry: a policy document of dental neglect in children.' *International Journal of Paediatric Dentistry.* DOI: 10.1111/j.1365-263X.2009.00996.x

Keene, E.J., Skelton, R., Day, P.F., Munyombwe, T. and Balmer, R.C. (2015) 'The dental health of children subject to a child protection plan.' *International Journal of Paediatric Dentistry 25*, 428–435.

2

PERSPECTIVES ON CHILD NEGLECT

4

CHILD NEGLECT
The research landscape
Debra Allnock

Introduction

The evidence shows that child neglect is a serious and pervasive form of child maltreatment. It has significant and far-reaching consequences for individuals across the life span (Brandon *et al.* 2014; Egeland and Sroufe 1981; Gilbert *et al.* 2009). It is recognised as a key risk for other forms of harm (Berelowitz *et al.* 2012) and it places considerable financial burdens on societies (Fang *et al.* 2012). We know from prevalence studies and child protection statistics in some parts of the world that it is one of the most common forms of maltreatment in the family (Finkelhor *et al.* 2014; Radford *et al.* 2013; Stoltenborgh, Bakermans-Kranenburg and van Ijzendoorn 2013). Child protection statistics show it is a relatively stable form of maltreatment, and is found to be the most likely form of maltreatment to recur (Hindley, Ramchandani and Jones 2006), indicating the complex and entrenched nature of neglect. Despite neglect being a common form of maltreatment however, it is comparatively under-researched (McSherry 2007; Stoltenborgh *et al.* 2015).

This chapter addresses the broad state of research on neglect and highlights key areas for debate required to move the evidence-base forward. Drawing on the existing literature to demonstrate the gaps, this chapter argues that neglect is under-researched compared with other forms of maltreatment, and considers the reasons why this may be so. Is neglect 'neglected' because researchers are simply uninterested in it? Or are there political and social challenges to researching neglect? Alternatively, are there particular research challenges that make some aspects of neglect difficult to research? Two key research issues are explored here, first the ongoing definitional problems that present challenges for researchers investigating neglect, and second the relative merits of researching neglect as a single issue, as against the study of neglect combined with other forms of harm and victimisation.

A 'neglect of neglect'?

Over the past two decades, commentators have frequently used that familiar phrase 'a neglect of neglect' to describe the state of knowledge and evidence in policy and practice (Hobbs and Wynne 2002; Stone 1998; Wald 2015) and within empirical research (Kaplan, Pelcovitz and Labruna 1999; Taylor, Daniel and Scott 2010). McSherry (2007) called it an 'absurd paradox' that, despite neglect being consistently shown to have a higher incidence rate than other forms of maltreatment, it remains under-studied and the least understood type of maltreatment, referring particularly to a review of the child maltreatment literature by Kaplan *et al.* (1999) which found that few studies had investigated neglect. More recently, commentators have pointed to advances in the field, citing increased publication of books, chapters, new research studies and training packages on neglect (Dubowitz 2007; Stevenson 2008; Taylor *et al.* 2010). Dubowitz (2007) also pointed to increased media attention to neglect, albeit attention that is typically focused on extreme cases. Despite the advances, however, most experts and commentators have been in agreement that not enough progress has been made in the field (Gilbert *et al.* 2009), that neglect gets the least attention from the public and policymakers (Lindland and Kendall-Taylor 2013) and that we have 'failed to grasp the nettle' in understanding and responding to neglect (Stevenson 2008).

Prevalence and incidence of neglect

Neglect is often identified as the most common form of maltreatment reported in child protection statistics and national self-report surveys in several countries where neglect is recorded and measured. For example, child protection statistics in the United Kingdom show neglect to be the most common reason for a child to be the subject of a child protection plan. In England, 43 per cent of all child protection plans in 2014 were made for the reason of neglect, while 33 per cent were made for emotional abuse, 10 per cent for physical abuse, 9 per cent for multiple reasons and 5 per cent for sexual abuse (see Jütte *et al.* 2015). In the other nations of the UK – Wales, Northern Ireland and Scotland – although trends show some differences, neglect also consistently remains the most common reason for a child to be the subject of a child protection plan (see Jütte *et al.* 2015).

Self-report studies often show far higher rates of maltreatment experiences than other studies (Gilbert *et al.* 2009; Sethi *et al.* 2013). According to the most recent general population study in the UK, neglect is identified as the most common form of maltreatment children experience within the family (Radford *et al.* 2011): 5 per cent of children under 11 (as reported by a parent or carer), 13.3 per cent of 11- to 17-year-old respondents, and 16 per cent of 18- to 24-year-old respondents were neglected at some point in their childhoods (Radford *et al.* 2013). These are the highest rates across all of the age groups in relation to all four forms of maltreatment (sexual, physical, emotional abuse and neglect). 'Severe' neglect was experienced by 3.7 per cent of children under 11, 9.8 per cent of 11- to 17-year-olds and 9 per cent of 18- to 24-year-olds at some time during childhood (Radford *et al.* 2011). 'Severe' neglect included serious emotional neglect, lack of supervision or physical care that would place a child or young person at risk of neglect that the young person defined as abusive or criminal (Radford *et al.* 2011).

A prevalence study of maltreatment in Germany found that severe emotional abuse in childhood and/or adolescence was reported by 1.6 per cent of respondents, severe physical abuse by 2.8 per cent of respondents and severe sexual abuse by 1.9 per cent of respondents. Severe emotional neglect was reported by 6.6 per cent of respondents and severe physical neglect by 10.8 per cent of respondents (see Sethi *et al.* 2013). A recent study of maltreatment prevalence in the Netherlands also reported emotional (19.8%) and physical (10.2%) neglect to be the most common form of maltreatment reported by professionals and child protective services. This was in comparison to reported sexual abuse at 0.8 per cent, physical abuse at 5.1 per cent and emotional abuse at 5.5 per cent (Euser *et al.* 2013). In the US, Finkelhor *et al.*'s (2014) most recent work on prevalence reported the lifetime rate of neglect to be 11.6 per cent, compared with 10.3 per cent for emotional abuse, 8.9 per cent for physical abuse and 0.7 per cent for sexual abuse. The past year rate of neglect was 4.7 per cent, with only emotional abuse revealing a higher past year rate at 5.6 per cent. Of those who reported that neglect had happened at some point in their childhood, 73 per cent said that it had happened more than once. Despite these findings that neglect is a common form of maltreatment in a number of countries, and despite emerging and new evidence about neglect, it still remains comparatively understudied.

One way of assessing the state of the evidence on a topic is through consideration of meta-analyses, which can act as a sort of 'barometer' or measure of the volume of studies devoted to a specific topic. These reviews and analyses clearly demonstrate that neglect is given relatively less attention than other forms of child maltreatment. A meta-analysis is a type of statistical technique that combines effect sizes from different studies researching the same question to get better estimates of the population effect sizes (Field 2009). However, in order to undertake a meta-analysis, enough studies researching the same question, using roughly comparable measures and using similar populations, must be available to analyse in this way. Systematic reviews can also provide a picture of the volume of studies related to specific topics, without the additional calculation of population effect size. This chapter examines several very recent meta-analyses and systematic reviews for findings related to child neglect.

The first example is a recent global meta-analysis of child maltreatment prevalence rates. This reveals that neglect is comparatively absent among studies of scale. Stoltenborgh and colleagues (2013, p.345–355) reviewed a series of meta-analyses of prevalence studies published between 1980 and 2008 and found a 'deplorable dearth' of studies on the prevalence of neglect, with especially large gaps in knowledge about this form of maltreatment in low resource settings. The analysis found only 13 studies that reported prevalence rates of emotional neglect (including ~60,000 participants) and 16 that reported prevalence rates of physical neglect (including ~60,000 participants). This stands in comparison with over 200 identified studies reporting the prevalence of sexual abuse (including over 400,000 participants).

Starkly, this meta-analysis of child maltreatment emphasises that our knowledge of the prevalence of neglect is restricted to a small number of countries covering approximately only 15 per cent of the world's population. Yet even in high-resource nations, the number of studies examining the prevalence of neglect is small (see, for example, Kloppen et al. 2015; Stoltenborgh et al. 2013). The dearth of studies on the prevalence of neglect is especially concerning, given that prevalence is a key measure of the scale and scope of a problem and provides basic information that is critical for determining the required nature and size of the response.

Other research

More evidence showing that 'neglect of neglect' is real is provided by a recent systematic review of population studies assessing child maltreatment and health outcomes (Hovdestad *et al.* 2015). The authors found 13 studies that assessed child neglect and health, compared with 15 studies that assessed emotional abuse, 18 studies that assessed family violence, 26 studies that assessed physical abuse and 48 studies that assessed sexual abuse. Half of the 54 studies reviewed by the authors examined a single type of abuse, almost always sexual abuse.

Studies examining the risk factors for child neglect appear to be in better supply than other subject areas. There are several reviews of risk factors for child neglect which are useful, but now dated. Schumacher, Smith-Slep and Heyman's (2001) review included 13 studies of risk factors for neglect while Connell-Carrick's (2003) included 24 studies. A meta-analysis of risk factors for child physical abuse and neglect was undertaken more recently by Stith and colleagues (2009), allowing the assessment of information on neglect as compared with physical abuse. They were able to assess 39 risk factors in relation to physical abuse but only 22 of these same risk factors could be assessed for child neglect. The authors found no studies on child neglect which addressed the remaining 17 factors analysed and they concluded that 'considerably more research has gone into understanding child physical abuse than in understanding child neglect' (Stith *et al.* 2009, p.25).

One possible explanation for the lack of attention to researching neglect may be that it is perceived as less serious than other forms of maltreatment. Neglect is an insidious form of maltreatment – one in which harm accumulates over time and may therefore not be immediately obvious. Dubowitz (2007) argued that because of these features, neglect is likely to continue to be viewed as subordinate to other forms of maltreatment – in particular, to sexual abuse which tends to provoke strong reactions among many in society who view it as morally reprehensible and repugnant. In practice, at least, this subordination seems to be the case. A study of referrals to children's social services in the UK revealed that concerns about neglect were given less priority than other forms of maltreatment: 61 per cent of referrals for neglect received no further action in comparison with 30 per cent of referrals for physical or sexual abuse (Wilding and Thoburn 1997). A more recent survey of 242 social workers in the UK found that 60 per cent said they felt pressure to downgrade neglect and emotional abuse cases and 59 per cent said that it was 'quite' or 'very' unlikely that children's social care would respond quickly to neglected children. Furthermore, 76 per cent were confident that timely action was taken in relation to physical abuse, 75 per cent in relation to sexual abuse and, in stark contrast, only 7 per cent were confident that timely action was being taken in response to neglect (Community Care 2013). Underpinning this may be a wider sense of fatalism amongst the public, as well as experts and professionals, that there are few solutions to neglect (Fond, Haydon and Kendall-Taylor 2015; Lindland and Kendall-Taylor 2013). Particularly in a period of financial austerity, cuts to services for children may disproportionately impact on cases of neglect, where the gathering of information is complex and it can take longer to demonstrate that it has been causing harm to the child (Community Care 2013; Stevenson 2008).

Historically, neglect has never really garnered the same kinds of political or social attention as have physical and sexual abuse. Cruelty to children has been recognised in both the US and the UK since the late nineteenth century, although it was specifically child physical abuse that was propelled into the public spotlight in the 1960s, instigating significant changes to child protection legislation and practice in the USA, soon thereafter influencing change in the UK. Public acknowledgement of child physical abuse in the USA emerged as a result of an influential publication by Kempe *et al.* (1962) describing what the authors called the 'battered baby syndrome'. Following this, physical abuse of children became a major social issue, with every state in the USA enacting mandatory reporting laws by 1967 (Corby, Shemmings and Wilkins 2012). In the UK, the term 'battered baby syndrome' was first used by Griffiths and Moynihan (1963, p.1558) – two orthopaedic surgeons – in an article in the *British Medical Journal*. The National Society for the Prevention of Cruelty to Children (NSPCC) (one of the largest children's charities in the UK) then took a lead in establishing a service devoted to families referred for child abuse and remained (and remains) influential in establishing public awareness of child abuse as a social problem (see Parton 1985).

By the 1980s, the long-standing taboos that had kept child sexual abuse (CSA) from public debate were being challenged from a number of different directions in the US, including the feminist movement, media coverage and public testimony from individual survivors of sexual abuse (Angelides 2005; Greer and McLaughlin 2013; Kitzinger 2001, 2004). Following this, a feminist analysis of sexual abuse emerging from the refuge/domestic violence movement (Dobash and Dobash 1992) and the anti-rape movement in Britain in the 1970s also began to develop (MacLeod and Saraga 1988). Child sexual abuse continued to receive considerable public attention after this in both the US and the UK (Kitzinger 1996; Parton 1991). In the UK, for example, Kitzinger (1996) examined news coverage of CSA by *The Times* and *The Sunday Times* between the years 1980 and 1994 and found a remarkable expansion of coverage (an increase of 300%) between 1985 and 1987, in response to the emergence of the national telephone hotline ChildLine.

Satanic ritual abuse became the centre of attention in the US in the 1980s, with awareness spreading to other parts of the world in the 1990s (Sakheim and Devine 1992), including the UK (Ashenden 2003; Kitzinger 1996, 2004; Parton 2006). In the UK, concerns with organisational and institutional sexual abuse dominated in the 1990s (Barter 1998; Critcher 2002; Kitzinger 1996; Silverman and Wilson 2002; Waterhouse 2012). By the second half of the 1990s, concern with institutional abuse focused almost entirely on sexual abuse and several 'abusive terrorists' in children's homes (Parton 2006). The increasing media coverage in these years illustrates that CSA was taking on a fully-fledged public character.

Globally, agendas concerning violence against women (VAW), violence against women and girls (VAWG) and gender based violence (GBV) have dominated debates, originating in 1993 with the United Nations (UN) General Assembly Declaration on the Elimination of Violence Against Women, which recognised sexual violence as a borderless issue. Related global problems such as trafficking and modern slavery have further emerged as key platforms for activism and debate. As new mediums for the perpetration of sexual abuse have begun to emerge and become more established as a focus for intervention, attention has turned to these separate issues such as online sexual abuse and exploitation (Davidson *et al.* 2011; UNICEF Innocenti Research Centre 2011). Offline sexual exploitation (previously referred to as 'child prostitution'), while not a new pattern of abuse, has also been 'discovered' (or rediscovered) as a key political and social phenomenon over the last 15 years in some countries (Jay 2014; Melrose 2013). Sexual exploitation is taking centre-stage in some nations; for example, sexual exploitation has become a national priority in England and is now framed as a form of serious and organised crime (Home Office 2015) and prioritised in policy and applied research (see, for example, Jago and Pearce 2008; Beckett *et al.* 2013; Berelowitz *et al.* 2013; Coy *et al.* 2013; with a national action plan on sexual exploitation produced in 2011 (Department for Education (DfE) 2011).

This highly focused attention on child sexual abuse may come at the expense of attention to other forms of maltreatment, particularly neglect. While there are national strategies for sexual violence in many countries now, including the UK, there are no national strategies to tackle child neglect specifically. In the UK, despite significant activism by national children's charities such as Action for Children and the NSPCC as well as clear attempts to develop frameworks for preventing and intervening early in neglect (Haynes *et al.* 2015), a national government-led strategy for addressing neglect remains elusive. Recently commissioned research by the Welsh Government has resulted in clear recommendations by the authors that a national strategy be developed and adopted, but at present remains a recommendation rather than an action (Stevenson and Laing 2015).

To summarise, the evidence described indicates that neglect is indeed a comparatively under-researched form of child maltreatment and lacks a high policy profile. As stated above, one possible contributory reason is that professionals and the public view neglect as a less serious form of child maltreatment. The political and social history of child maltreatment arguably demonstrates that, perhaps due to this perception, neglect has also failed to achieve recognition and media prominence in the same way that other forms of abuse have. The difficulties inherent in researching neglect may be another contributory reason. The remainder of this chapter will examine two particular issues, raising questions for future research into child neglect.

Navigating the challenges: Definition and meaning

The second half of this chapter considers two key aspects of child neglect with implications for future research. First, the ongoing problem of definitional challenges which present barriers to increasing our understanding of neglect; second, the new and emerging evidence of neglect as part of a range of other forms of harm and victimisation which children experience collectively. The chapter ends with a review of the relative merits of investigating neglect as a single issue or consistently researching child maltreatment with reference to other victimization experiences.

Defining neglect

Defining neglect is a crucial task for researchers investigating it, as it is for those developing and delivering services to address it. From a research perspective, clear definitions are important in the determination of incidence and prevalence of neglect and in understanding the impacts and consequences of neglect. Research definitions are, of necessity, inter-dependent with practice definitions, which determine whether or not services to maltreating families will be provided, and the types of services provided, including whether or not children will be removed from parental custody.

Child neglect can manifest in different ways and occurs in a wide range of contexts, and it has proven a real challenge to define it in a way that reliably generalises across all cases. While advances in conceptualisations and definitions are being made (see Dubowitz *et al.* 2005; English *et al.* 2005a), definitional challenges still remain. This in turn has important implications for the building of knowledge. Heterogeneity of definitions across studies, including evaluations of interventions, mean that classification and comparison of findings is not always possible or straightforward, and this may be precisely why so few meta-analyses of neglect have been undertaken in comparison to other forms of maltreatment (Taylor *et al.* 2010). Without a clear body of evidence, implementation and practice decisions are in turn difficult to make.

In considering definitions for research, a good place to start is with international and national definitions of neglect. How societies construct neglect has important implications for the way it is measured and analysed within research. While there is fair consensus internationally concerning what constitutes physical and sexual abuse, there is much less agreement about the definitions and thresholds for neglect, and additional confusion is added when considering the overlap between neglect and emotional abuse (Hibbard, Barlow and MacMillan 2012; Naughton *et al.* 2013; Ward, Brown and Westlake 2012).

What is not in dispute is that neglect is one of four recognised forms of maltreatment. Child maltreatment is defined as 'all forms of physical and/or emotional ill-treatment, sexual abuse, neglect or negligent treatment or commercial or other exploitation, resulting in actual or potential harm to the child's health, survival, development or dignity in the context of a relationship of responsibility, trust or power' (Krug *et al.* 2002; p.59). Internationally, child neglect is defined by the World Health Organization (WHO) in the following way:

> Neglect includes both isolated incidents, as well as a pattern of failure over time on the part of a parent or other family member to provide for the development and well-being of the child – where the parent is in a position to do so – in one or more of the following areas:
>
> - health;
> - education;
> - emotional development;
> - nutrition;
> - shelter and safe living conditions.
>
> The parents of neglected children are not necessarily poor. They may equally be financially well-off. (Butchart and Finney 2006 p.10)

National definitions often vary from this, however, and also vary cross-nationally. For example, the current definition of neglect in England as set out in the statutory guidance *Working Together to Safeguard Children* is:

> The persistent failure to meet a child's basic physical and/or psychological needs, likely to result in the serious impairment of the child's health or development. Neglect may occur during pregnancy as a result of maternal substance abuse. Once a child is born, neglect may involve a parent or carer failing to:

- provide adequate food, clothing and shelter (1 exclusion from home or abandonment);

- protect a child from physical and emotional harm or danger;

- ensure adequate supervision (including the use of inadequate care-givers); or

- ensure access to appropriate medical care or treatment.

It may also include neglect of, or unresponsiveness to, a child's basic emotional needs. (HM Government 2015, p.93)

The Welsh Government, however, recently removed the reference to 'persistence' within the Social Services and Well-being (Wales) Act 2014 and the definition applies to a 'person', which may include a child or an adult:

'neglect' ('esgeulustod') means a failure to meet a person's basic physical, emotional, social or psychological needs, which is likely to result in an impairment of the person's well-being (for example, an impairment of the person's health or, in the case of a child, an impairment of the child's development).

One noticeable difference between the English and Welsh definition is in the emphasis on persistence. The Welsh definition allows, like the international definition, for consideration of isolated incidents. The international definition also recognises the ability of parents to provide for the development and wellbeing of a child, which the English definition lacks. In reality, however, these definitions are not always helpful and are subjective in nature. It is not clear, for example, how the terms 'persistent' or indeed 'adequate' should be defined and interpreted. Neglect is often chronic, with harm being cumulative rather than the result of acute incidents (Stevenson 2008). It is more likely that there will be a series of concerns over a period of time that, taken together, demonstrate that the child is in need or at risk. One-off incidents – for example, the failure to provide adequate clothing – would not necessarily qualify as neglect, but it can be difficult for practitioners to determine how many times this would have to happen, or under what circumstances it might harm a child, before intervention is required.

Despite these problems in defining neglect at international and national levels, national definitions do establish societally constructed

distinguishing neglect that has reached child
al thresholds from early indications of neglect. A
evalence studies of neglect have taken the approach
ner self-reported indicators of neglect meet civil or
ds, which has enabled researchers to establish severity
for example, Finkelhor *et al.* 2014; Radford *et al.* 2011).
Thei inherent challenges in doing this. For example, the UK
study of chnd abuse and neglect by Radford and colleagues (2011)
covered England, Wales, Northern Ireland and Scotland, all of which
have slight variations in national definitions of neglect. Similarly, in
the US, definitions of child neglect continue to vary from one state to
the next and reflect the diverse conceptualisations by professionals and
non-professionals as to what constitutes child neglect, making a 'one-
nation' definition impossible to obtain (Zuravin 1999).

There are a number of obstacles to the establishment of a useful
definition of neglect for researchers. These include: 1) thresholds; 2)
neglect as an omission of care; 3) neglect from a child's perspective;
and 4) considerations of responsibility and intention.

Thresholds

One obstacle is the problem of threshold, the crucial point in
establishing what may be considered minimally adequate levels of care
and when intervention is justified. This is important for prioritising
services, for applying sanctions in some cases and for collecting
evidence on the levels of need and risk. There is general agreement
about what constitutes inadequate care, such as a lack of food,
clothing, shelter, affection, and attention or supervision. However,
the threshold for minimal or 'good enough' care is far more elusive.
There have historically been disagreements between professionals and
minority ethnic groups about how to establish thresholds of minimal
care (McSherry 2007). Indeed, a key debate in the research literature
concerns the scope of what is considered to be neglect, including
whether or not potential harm should be included in addition to
actual harm (Zuravin 1999). The prevailing concept in the child
welfare system in the UK has concentrated on omissions in care by
parents or caregivers that result in actual and potential significant
harm (HM Government 2015). This is also the case at the federal level
in the US, although Zuravin (1999) found variations in state statutes.
Understanding civil and criminal definitions is of clear importance

to researchers, where those definitions are being used to distinguish statutory and criminal thresholds for neglect from other incidents or patterns of neglect.

Neglect as an omission of care

The conceptualisation of neglect as an omission of specific behaviours by caregivers in comparison to acts of commission (as is characteristic of other forms of maltreatment such as sexual and physical abuse) presents its own challenges (Connell-Carrick 2003). English *et al.* (2005a, p.191) state it more clearly: 'neglect is the absence of a desired set of conditions or behaviours as opposed to the presence of an undesirable set of behaviours'. Clearly, identifying what has not happened is more difficult than identifying what has happened (McSherry 2007). The Juvenile Victimization Questionnaire (JVQ-R2) provides one example of a measure of general absence of care, defined through the following screener question (Module B, Child Maltreatment, M3) (Finkelhor *et al.* 2014):

> When someone is neglected, it means that the grown-ups in their life didn't take care of them the way they should. They might not get them enough food, take them to the doctor when they are sick, or make sure they have a safe place to stay. At any time in your life, were you neglected?

Given the broad range of circumstances that can constitute neglect, this definition may well screen out a range of other forms of neglect such as supervisory or educational neglect. New supplemental neglect items have been added to the JVQ-R2 to measure neglect due to other reasons, such as parental incapacitation due to drugs or alcohol; neglect from parental absence; neglect from inappropriate adults in the home; neglect from unsafe environments; and neglect from lack of hygiene supervision (M5-M9). Finkelhor and colleagues (2014), however, acknowledge that neglect has many manifestations, all of which may be difficult to comprehensively capture in a survey with a relatively brief instrument. The implication of this, therefore, is that neglect is likely, in prevalence surveys such as this, to be under-reported.

From whose perspective should neglect be measured?

Further compounding the debates is the question of whether neglect should be viewed as occurring when a child's basic developmental and welfare needs are not met from the child's perspective, regardless of the contributory factors, such as poverty, or whether neglect should be viewed as occurring based on the more conventional focus on parental omissions in care (Dubowitz *et al.* 1993). An approach to defining neglect based on the child's needs delineates specific targets for change, such as increasing child-focused parental behaviours or/ and improving caregiver parenting practices (e.g. reducing aggressive disciplinary techniques). Some examples are provided here of how researchers have conceptualised neglect using developmental markers from the child's perspective.

English *et al.* (2005a) examined the relationship of child experiences from infancy to toddlerhood that were identified conceptually as neglectful, based on child developmental needs, (regardless of whether classified as neglect by child protective services systems). Child need was identified within categories of physical and psychological safety and security; for example, a lack of a safe, clean or stimulating home environment predicted impairments in language development and cognitive functioning for young children; multiple changes in residence and exposure to verbal aggression predicted child behaviour problems.

Dubowitz *et al.*'s (2005) study also examined a conceptual model of neglect based on children's developmental needs related to support, affection and safety. The relationship of these latent constructs of neglect to a child's functioning at age eight was then examined. Level of support from mothers, a child's experience of little early affection and exposure to family conflict were all associated with child social and behaviour problems. The conceptualisation studies of neglect indicate the potential for improvement in classification of maltreatment when utilising alternative conceptualisations independent of the current legal standard.

Responsibility and intention

There is some confusion and expert disagreement on the significance of parental responsibility and the carer's intention in relation to omission of care. One argument proposes that omission of care resulting from deliberate harm – or the malicious withholding of needs – is in fact abuse and should not be confused with neglect. Neglect instead, it is argued, results from and should be confined to, omissions resulting from parent/caregiver ignorance or competing carer priorities. This latter view asserts that, in cases of neglect, the carer is without a malicious motive and is usually unaware of the harm to the child (Golden, Samuels and Southall 2003). Another argument, however, proposes that neglectful carer or parental acts should be considered to be harmful and a matter of parental responsibility, irrespective of the reason why they have occurred. This argument warns against a preoccupation with determining carer intention, as it may overshadow concern about the impact on the child and also hinder working with parents (Dubowitz *et al.* 2005).

This section has considered the definitional challenges which still plague research on neglect. Advances in conceptualisation have been highlighted, such as the use of developmental indicators to measure neglect from the child's perspective, and the use of national definitions to establish civil and criminal thresholds of neglect have been described.

Research on neglect: A single issue or part of a range of harm and adversities?

Findings on neglect alone

Emerging evidence about multiple and overlapping forms of abuse, harm and other adversities provides fertile ground for debate over whether research should focus on 'single issues' (such as neglect) as it has done traditionally, or whether a new approach to understanding maltreatment, harm and victimisation is needed for a better understanding of children's experiences. There may be room for both approaches, as the evidence indicates that neglect is a particularly damaging form of maltreatment whether experienced on its own or with other harm or adversity.

To take the single-issue argument first, some commentators have argued that a better understanding of neglect in and of itself is needed. Taylor and colleagues (2010) particularly highlight the paucity of literature related to neglect and found, in their systematic review of professional responses to neglect, that many studies of child maltreatment fail to disentangle findings specific to neglect (for an example, see Sidebotham and Heron 2003). Neglect-specific studies have provided important insights into the knowledge-base in this area; we have seen that, despite the paucity of prevalence studies reporting rates of neglect, those that do exist show that neglect is a common form of maltreatment (Stoltenborgh *et al.* 2015). Additionally, studies of the risk factors and indicators specifically for neglect are in better supply, providing important pointers for recognising and identifying neglect (Connell-Carrick 2003; Naughton *et al.* 2013; Sidebotham, Golding and the ALSPAC Study Team 2001; Taylor *et al.* 2010). Observational studies of interactions between parents and children have similarly provided insights into the indicators of neglect (Crittenden 1992; Crittenden and DiLalla 1988; Pianta, Egeland and Erickson 1989).

Finally, there is increasing evidence that the consequences of childhood neglect alone can be as damaging, or even more so, than those of physical or sexual abuse because its impact is the most far-reaching and difficult to overcome (Gilbert *et al.* 2009). Although it can be difficult to disentangle the effects of neglect from other forms of maltreatment, as we shall see below, there is now a fair consensus based on a range of empirical studies that neglect has significant implications for a range of developmental dimensions, including health; speech, language and communication; education; identity; emotional and behavioural development; family and social relationships; social presentation; and self-care skills (Hildyard and Wolfe 2002; Norman *et al.* 2012; Tanner and Turney 2003).

Impact of neglect over time

Neglect is thought to be most detrimental in the first few years of life, but there is also evidence that it can compromise development in adolescence. Exposure to neglect is hypothesised to alter the development of the hypothalamic-pituitary-adrenal (HPA) axis stress response and change brain structure and function. Researchers believe that vulnerability becomes embedded in children, only emerging later in a range of mental and/or physical health problems (McCrory, De Brito and Viding 2010; McCrory, De Brito and Viding 2012). Evidence also suggests that neglect not only affects a wide range of developmental domains but is also cumulative in impact and, it is thought, the longer the exposure to neglect, the greater the harm. With neglect, declines have been observed in a range of functions among infants and toddlers including development scores (Naughton *et al.* 2013) and cognitive functioning (Strathearn *et al.* 2001); see also Chapters 1 and 2.

Research has also identified longer-term impacts. Childhood aggression has been linked with early neglect, which in turn has been associated with violence and delinquency in adolescence. Where this stretches into adulthood, it can increase risk for violent offences. Widom (1989) found that adults who were neglected in childhood were more likely than their peers to be arrested for violent offences. Neglect also increases risk for adolescent and adult mental health difficulties and physical difficulties (Anda *et al.* 2006; Widom 1989; Widom, DuMont and Czaja 2007). Findings from longitudinal cohort studies such as that in the US by a consortium for Longitudinal Studies of Child Abuse and Neglect (LONGSCAN) provide compelling evidence about the early impacts of neglect (Dubowitz *et al.* 2002) and long-term impacts such as the links between neglect and substance use (Besinger *et al.* 1999). However, longitudinal studies following child maltreatment are rare and we need to know far more about the long-term impact of all forms of neglect.

Research on neglect as part of a range of harm and adversities

An alternative view is that it is not fruitful, nor indeed possible, to fully extract outcomes of single forms of abuse or neglect from other forms of harm. Emerging findings from a range of studies examining multiple adverse childhood experiences (ACEs) appear to support cumulative risk theory (CRT), which posits that the number or amount of exposures a child has to risk factors over time determines outcomes in a 'dose-dependent manner' (O'Hara *et al.* 2015, p.2). In other words, CRT hypothesises that multiple maltreatment will lead to worse outcomes than a single form of maltreatment. Findings supportive of CRT emerge from studies of polyvictimisation, which focus on a range of different experiences of maltreatment and victimisation in different life domains (see, for example, Finkelhor, Ormrod and Turner 2007 and Radford *et al.* 2011). Findings supportive of CRT also emerge from 'multiple adversity' research, which examines not only maltreatment and victimisation experiences but other types of adversity such as 'household dysfunction'. This can include, for example, parental separation or divorce, parental mental illness, parental substance misuse, domestic violence and crime (see, for example, Dong *et al.* 2004). ACEs may differ among countries to reflect local context. For instance, in a South African study, ACEs did not include neglect as a form of maltreatment but did include 'orphanhood by AIDS', 'orphanhood by homicide', 'parental AIDS illness' and 'food insecurity' (Cluver *et al.* 2015).

There is sufficient international evidence that there are a subgroup of children who have experienced multiple – and different – forms of victimisation (polyvictimisation) in different areas of their lives (Aziz and Dawood 2015; Bashir and Dasti 2015; Finkelhor *et al.* 2007; Pereda, Abad and Guilera 2015; Radford *et al.* 2013). Experts have critiqued studies that fail to establish full victimisation profiles. Studies which fail to establish full profiles describing all forms of victimisation, it is argued, may be inaccurately associating impacts, effects and risk factors to the wrong experiences (Sabri *et al.* 2013). Finkelhor *et al.*'s (2007) study of polyvictimisation found that, of 71 per cent of children who reported any victimisation, 69 per cent reported at least one additional, different type of victimisation. In the same study, 51 per cent of children who reported experiencing neglect in the last year also reported four or more additional victimisations of different types: 15 per cent of these experienced 'low' polyvictimisation (between four and six different types) and 36 per cent experienced 'high' polyvictimisation (seven or more types). Polyvictimisation studies further reveal that those who experience a high number of different types of victimisation also report the highest trauma and victimisation scores, suggesting that it is the cumulative impact of harm through victimisation that underpins the most serious short- and long-term adversity (Radford *et al.* 2011).

Studies within the field of multiple adversities support findings from the polyvictimisation literature and CRT (see above) but with the added dimension of non-maltreatment related adversity. Dong *et al.*'s (2004) analysis of survey data from over 8000 participants in the US examined ten ACEs including emotional, sexual and physical abuse, neglect and household dysfunction. Those who reported neglect reported higher numbers of additional ACEs than participants who reported sexual or physical abuse, although a smaller percentage of participants reported physical (9.9%) or emotional (14.9%) neglect than those reporting sexual abuse (21%) or physical abuse (26.4%). Of those who reported having experienced emotional neglect in childhood, 19 per cent experienced more than six other childhood adversities. Of those who reported having experienced physical neglect in childhood, 24 per cent experienced more than six other childhood adversities. Only those who reported emotional abuse reported more

ACEs than those who reported neglect (25%). The authors state that the statistically significant relationships observed between ACEs, and the finding that none of the ACEs occurred independently of the others 'clearly indicates that these experiences should not be assumed to be isolated events in children's lives' (Dong *et al.* 2004, p.779). On the basis of their findings, the authors advise that where researchers are focusing on the consequences of a specific ACE they should be collecting information about exposure to other ACEs. Sabri *et al.* (2013) further notes that in the case of multiple maltreatment experiences, outcomes may differ depending upon which type of maltreatment occurred first.

Long-term consequences

Studies of multiple childhood adversities also draw attention to the long-term health and social consequences associated with them. Those who experience multiple adverse experiences in childhood tend to do more poorly on health and social related measurements (Davidson, Bunting and Webb 2012). Kalamakis and Chandler's (2015) systematic review of health impacts of ACEs reveal that ACEs are significantly associated with negative health consequences in adults. The review findings also support CRT theory in that there is a cumulative effect of ACEs on health. The studies included in the review measured ACEs inconsistently and did not always include measures of neglect (for example, see Afifi *et al.* 2008; Douglas *et al.* 2010). All studies reviewed, however, found that the more ACEs a person had experienced, the greater the effect on their physical and psychological health as well as on their behaviour. The authors found, however, that certain types of ACE have greater influence on certain types of health outcomes. Sexual abuse, for instance, had the strongest association with sexual risk behaviour, delinquency and suicidal behaviour in comparison to other combinations of ACEs. Physical and emotional abuse was significantly associated with all psychiatric outcomes, whereas parental divorce and imprisonment were associated with only one psychiatric outcome.

Where studies in Kalamkis and Chandler's review did include neglect, it was usually associated with other ACEs and predicted specific outcomes. For example, in LeardMann, Smith and Ryan's (2010) study of over 8000 Marine Corps recruits, physical neglect was most strongly associated with post-deployment post-traumatic stress disorder (PTSD). Neglect was also found to be significantly associated with schizotypal personality disorder in Lentz, Robinson and Bolton's (2010) analysis of over 34,000 people from the National Epidemiological Survey on Alcohol and Related Conditions.

Other areas of research also reveal links between neglect and other forms of harm. Research examining case reviews of child death and serious injuries in England[1] found that neglect is a background factor in a majority (60%) of serious case reviews (Brandon et al. 2013), despite neglect rarely being the immediate cause of death or serious injury. An analysis of data collected from over 800 children and young people aged 0 to 18 who were receiving a service for exposure to domestic abuse found significant overlaps in experiences of harm. The analysis showed that children exposed to severe domestic violence were more likely to experience neglect or physical harm, and that in these cases the harm was likely to be more severe (Co-ordinated Action Against Domestic Abuse 2014). Research into sexual exploitation in the UK also cites neglect as a key risk factor for this form of harm (Berelowitz et al. 2012). Young people may be at risk for sexual exploitation for a number of reasons, of which neglect may be one (Daniel, Taylor and Scott 2011; Hill et al. 2014). They may simply be vulnerable to exploitation through long-term impacts of neglect in adolescence, or they may be vulnerable through supervisory neglect. Indeed, a key risk indicator for child sexual exploitation is 'going missing' from home. Daniel et al.'s (2011) review of the literature on missing children found neglect to be a key push factor, which in turn may place them at greater risk of exploitation.

So, should neglect be studied as a single issue or as part of a continuum or cluster of harms? Recent analysis of the US prospective LONGSCAN data provides an argument that, as suggested above, both types of research are needed (O'Hara et al. 2015). The analysis compared 271 neglected-only children with 101 children who had

---

1   Throughout the four nations of the UK, the death of every child through abuse or neglect is subject to a local multiagency serious case review. In England the guidance for carrying out the review is enshrined in *Working Together to Safeguard Children* (HM Government 2015). The purpose of the review, in England, is to establish whether there are lessons to be learnt from the case about the way in which local professionals and organisations work individually and together to safeguard and promote the welfare of children.

been neglected and physically abused in childhood. The findings reveal that neglected-only children fare worse than children both neglected and physically abused on cognitive stimulation and language exchange (see also Chapter 2). Some findings challenge cumulative risk theory. The authors hypothesise that children are provided with less cognitive stimulation where there is neglect alone than where physical abuse occurs alongside neglect. The authors argue that the findings support earlier studies (e.g. Egeland and Sroufe 1981), which have shown that neglected children face greater risk for poor outcomes than those experiencing other forms of maltreatment. However, distinguishing findings on neglect which reveal important learning such as this would not be possible without attention to other forms of harm. As the authors themselves state, 'the complexities of factors that influence a child's intellectual development likely include the (whole) maltreatment profile' (O'Hara *et al.* 2015, p.6).

Conclusions

The significant costs to children and their futures, as well as the societal financial burden that neglect can incur, underline the importance of developing a better understanding of neglect and how it can be tackled. However, as demonstrated in this chapter, attention to neglect is often sidelined by attention to other forms of maltreatment. While the significant impacts of sexual abuse are now well recognised and are in the public eye, greater attention needs to be given to neglect, which may incur greater long-term costs to children.

First, more studies of prevalence are required to better understand the scale and nature of neglect, in both low- and high-resource settings. While there may remain challenges to defining neglect in practice and research which impact on the development of studies of prevalence, these challenges do not justify the lack of attention to a form of maltreatment that may have some of the most significant and far-reaching consequences for children across the lifespan.

Second, new approaches to measuring neglect are needed. Studies described here, which focus on measuring harm from a child's viewpoint, provide possible ways forward which may assist researchers in avoiding pitfalls such as heavy reliance on 'thresholds' and 'responsibility'. A 'child-centred' perspective on measurement is likely to increase the validity of findings concerning neglect and provide better opportunities for comparison of results across cultural boundaries. There are now a number of well-tested tools to measure scale and type of neglect and these merit further investigation and consideration for use in research and evaluation studies on neglect. See, for instance, Johnson and Cotmore (2015) for a link to the NSPCC's evaluation of the Graded Care Profile.

Third, studies on neglect as a single-issue are important for key insights into neglect which evidence suggests impact on children differently than other forms of maltreatment. However, neglect is often paired with other forms of harm, and this requires attention also. Studies examining different forms of maltreatment should, where possible, identify different forms of abuse and examine how they interact. Longitudinal studies are rare, but powerful in terms of highlighting the impacts and consequences of neglect in contrast to other forms of harm. However, such studies draw attention as well to important links between neglect and other victimisation and harm. While the current spotlight on sexual exploitation is important, given its lack of recognition in the recent past, research and practice should ultimately seek to address the early risks and adversities that underlie exploitation, of which neglect is one. Intervening early (both in terms of the child's development and in terms of cumulative harm) to protect children who may be experiencing neglect and building their resilience may be one of the most powerful preventive strategies that can be undertaken. A focus on sexual abuse, at the expense of neglect, ignores all of the evidence that early intervention is critical to improving children's outcomes and life chances as well as reducing the long-term burdens on society.

Questions for reflection

– Why may child neglect cost more to societies than other forms of maltreatment?

– Why is child neglect under-researched and how could this be rectified?

– What are the advantages and disadvantages of studying child neglect as a separate form of maltreatment or adverse childhood experience?

– Is child neglect a form of maltreatment that is often experienced with other ACEs?

References

Afifi, T., Enns, M., Cox, B., Asmundson, G., Stein, M. and Sareen, J. (2008) 'Population attributable fractions of psychiatric disorders and suicide ideation and attempts associated with adverse childhood experiences.' *American Journal of Public Health 98*, 5, 946–952.

Anda, R., Felitti, V., Bremner, J., Walker, J. *et al.* (2006) 'The enduring effects of abuse and related adverse experiences in childhood. A convergence of evidence from neurobiology and epidemiology.' *European Archives of Psychiatry and Clinical Neuroscience 256*, 3, 174–186.

Angelides, S. (2005) 'The emergence of the paedophile in the late twentieth century.' *Australian Historical Studies 36*, 126, 272–296.

Ashenden, S. (2003) *Governing Child Sexual Abuse: Negotiating the Boundaries of Public and Private, Law and Science.* London: Routledge.

Aziz, A. and Dawood, S. (2015) 'The epidemiology of poly-victimization in Pakistan.' *Journal of Behavioural Sciences 25*, 1, 108–119.

Barter, C. (1998) *Investigating Institutional Abuse of Children: An Exploration of the NSPCC Experience.* London: The NSPCC.

Bashir, Z. and Dasti, R. (2015) 'Demographic correlates of poly-victimization in Lahore City.' *Journal of the Indian Academy of Applied Psychology 41*, 3, 194–201.

Beckett, H., Brodie, I., Factor, F., Melrose, M., *et al.* (2013) *'It's wrong...but you get used to it.' A qualitative study of gang-associated sexual violence towards, and exploitation of, young people in England.* Luton: The University of Bedfordshire and the Office of the Children's Commissioner. Available at www.childrenscommissioner.gov.uk/publications/its-wrong-you-get-used-it-qualitative-study-gang-associated-sexual-violence-towards-and, accessed on 11 September 2015.

Berelowitz, S., Clifton, J., Firmin, C., Gulyurtlu, S. and Edwards, G. (2013) *'If only someone had listened.' Office of the Children's Commissioner's Inquiry into Child Sexual Exploitation in Gangs and Groups.* London: Office of the Children's Commissioner. Available at www.childrenscommissioner.gov.uk/publications/if-only-someone-had-listened-inquiry-child-sexual-exploitation-gangs-and-groups, accessed on 11 September 2015.

Berelowitz, S., Firmin, C., Edwards, G. and Gulyurtlu, S. (2012) *'I thought I was the only one. The only one in the world.' The Office of the Children's Commissioner Inquiry into Child Sexual Exploitation in Gangs and Groups. Interim report.* London: Office of the Children's Commissioner. Available at www.childrenscommissioner.gov.uk/sites/default/files/publications/I%20thought%20I%20was%20the%20only%20one%20in%20the%20world.pdf, accessed on 30 September 2015.

Besinger, B., Garland, A., Litrownik, A. and Landsverk, J. (1999) 'Caregiver substance abuse among maltreated children placed in out-of-home care.' *Child Welfare 78*, 2, 221–239.

Brandon, M., Bailey, S., Belderson, P. and Larsson, B. (2013) *Neglect and Serious case Reviews.* London: NSPCC. Available at www.nspcc.org.uk/globalassets/documents/research-reports/neglect-serious-case-reviews-report.pdf, accessed on 2 October 2015.

Brandon, M., Glaser, D., Maguire, S., McCrory, E., Lushey, C. and Ward, H. (2014) *Missed Opportunities: Indicators of Neglect – What Is Ignored, Why and What Can Be Done?* London: Department for Education. Available at www.gov.uk/government/uploads/system/uploads/attachment_data/file/379747/RR404_-_Indicators_of_neglect_missed_opportunities.pdf, accessed on 2 October 2015.

Butchart, A. and Finney, A. (2006) *Preventing Child Maltreatment: A Guide to Taking Action and Generating Evidence.* Geneva: World Health Organization and ISPCAN. Available at http://apps.who.int/iris/bitstream/10665/43499/1/9241594365_eng.pdf, accessed on 2 October 2015.

Cluver, L., Orkin, M., Boyes, M. and Sherr, L. (2015) 'Child and adolescent suicide attempts, suicidal behaviour and adverse childhood experiences in South Africa: a prospective study.' *Journal of Adolescent Health 57,* 1, 52–59.

Community Care (2013) 'Social workers unlikely to act quickly on neglect cases.' Available at www.communitycare.co.uk/2012/09/26/social-workers-unlikely-to-act-quickly-on-neglect-cases-2, accessed on 11 September 2015.

Connell-Carrick, K. (2003) 'A critical review of the empirical literature: identifying correlates of child neglect.' *Child and Adolescent Social Work Journal 20,* 5, 389–425.

Co-ordinated Action Against Domestic Abuse (2014) *In Plain Sight: Effective Help for Children Exposed to Domestic Abuse.* Bristol: CAADA. Available at www.torbay.gov.uk/helpchildrenexposedtodomesticabuse.pdf, accessed on 11 September 2015.

Corby, B., Shemmings, D. and Wilkins, D. (2012) *Child Abuse: An Evidence Base for Confident Practice* (4th ed.). Berkshire: Open University Press.

Coy, M., Kelly, L., Elvines, F., Garner, M. and Kanyeredzi, A. (2013) *'Sex without consent, I suppose that is rape': How young people in England understand sexual consent.* London: The OCC. Available at www.childrenscommissioner.gov.uk/publications/sex-without-consent-i-suppose-rape-how-young-people-england-understand-sexual-consent, accessed on 11 September 2015.

Critcher, C. (2002) 'Media, government and moral panic: the politics of paedophilia in Britain 2000–1.' *Journalism Studies 3,* 4, 521–535.

Crittenden P. (1992) 'Children's strategies for coping with adverse home environments: an interpretation using attachment theory.' *Child Abuse & Neglect 16,* 3, 329–343.

Crittenden, P. and DiLalla, D. (1988) 'Compulsive compliance: the development of an inhibitory coping strategy in infancy.' *Journal of Abnormal Child Psychology 16,* 5, 585–599.

Daniel, B., Taylor, J. and Scott, J. (2011) *Recognizing and Helping the Neglected Child: Evidence-based Practice for Assessment and Intervention.* London: Jessica Kingsley Publishers.

Davidson, G., Bunting, L. and Webb, M.A. (2012) *Families Experiencing Multiple Adversities: A Review of the International Literature.* Belfast: Barnardo's. Available at www.barnardos.org.uk/14796_ni_pp_briefing_paper_literature_review_lr.pdf, accessed on 2 October 2015.

Davidson, J., Grove-Hills, J., Bifulco, A., Gottschalk, P., *et al.* (2011) *Online Abuse: Literature Review and Policy Context.* London: European Commission Safer Internet Plus Programme. Available at www.europeanonlinegroomingproject.com/media/2080/eogp-literature-review.pdf, accessed on 11 September 2015.

Department for Education (2011) *Tackling Sexual Exploitation: Action Plan.* London: DfE. Available at www.gov.uk/government/publications/tackling-child-sexual-exploitation-action-plan, accessed on 2 October 2015.

Dobash, R. and Dobash, R. (1992). *Women, Violence and Social Change.* Routledge: New York.

Dong, M., Anda, R., Felitti, V., Dube, S. *et al.* (2004) 'The interrelatedness of multiple forms of childhood abuse, neglect and household dysfunction.' *Child Abuse & Neglect 28*, 7, 771–784.

Douglas, K., Chan, G., Gelernter, J., Arias, A., *et al.* (2010) 'Adverse childhood events as risk factors for substance dependence: Partial mediation by mood and anxiety disorders.' *Addictive Behaviors 35*, 1, 7–13.

Dubowitz, H. (2007) 'Understanding and addressing the "neglect of neglect": digging into the molehill.' *Child Abuse & Neglect 31*, 6, 603–606.

Dubowitz, H., Black, M., Starr, Jr., R. and Zuravin, S. (1993) 'A conceptual definition of child neglect.' *Criminal Justice and Behavior 20*, 1, 8–26.

Dubowitz, H., Newton, R., Litrownik, A., Lewis, T., *et al.* (2005) 'Examination of a Conceptual Model of Child Neglect.' *Child Maltreatment 10*, 2, 173–89.

Dubowitz, H., Papas, M., Black, M. and Starr, R., Jr. (2002) 'Child neglect: outcomes in high-risk urban preschoolers.' *Pediatrics 109*, 6, 1100–1107.

Egeland B. and Sroufe A. (1981) 'Developmental Sequelae of Maltreatment inInfancy.' In R. Rizley and D. Cicchetti (eds) *Developmental Perspectives in Child Maltreatment.* San Francisco, CA: Jossey Bass.

English, D., Thompson, R., Graham, J. and Briggs, E. (2005a) 'Towards a definition of neglect in young children.' *Child Maltreatment 10*, 2, 190–206.

English, D., Upadhyaya, M., Litrownik, A., Marshall, J. *et al.* (2005b) 'Maltreatment's wake: the relationship of maltreatment dimensions to child outcomes.' *Child Abuse & Neglect 29*, 5, 597–619.

Euser, S., Alink, L., Pannebakker, F., Vogels, T., Bakermans-Kranenburg, M. and van Ijzendoorn, M. (2013) 'The prevalence of child maltreatment in the Netherlands across a 5-year period.' *Child Abuse & Neglect 37*, 10, 841–851.

Fang, X., Brown, D., Florence, C. and Mercy, J. (2012) 'The economic burden of child maltreatment in the United States and implications for prevention.' *Child Abuse & Neglect 36*, 2, 156–165.

Field, A. (2009) *Discovering Statistics using SPSS.* London: Sage Publications.

Finkelhor, D., Ormrod, R. and Turner, H. (2007) 'Polyvictimization and trauma in a national longitudinal cohort.' *Development and Psychopathology 19*, 1, 149–166.

Finkelhor, D., Vanderminden, J., Turner, H., Hamby, S. and Shattuck, A. (2014) 'Child maltreatment rates assessed in a national household survey of caregivers and youth.' *Child Abuse & Neglect 38*, 9, 1421–1435.

Fond, M., Haydon, A. and Kendall-Taylor, N. (2015) *Communicating Connections: Framing the Relationship between Social Drivers, Early Adversity and Child Neglect.* Washington, D.C.: Frameworks Institute. Available at www.frameworksinstitute.org/assets/files/ECD/social_determinants_ecd_messagebrief_final.pdf, accessed on 13 November 2015.

Gilbert, R., Widom, C.S., Brown, K., Fergusson, D., Webb, F. and Johnson, S. (2009) 'Burden and consequences of maltreatment in high income countries.' *Lancet 373*, 9657, 68–81.

Golden, M., Samuels, M. and Southall, D. (2003) 'How to distinguish between neglect and deprivational abuse.' *Archives of Diseases in Childhood 88*, 2, 105–107.

Greer, C. and McLaughlin, E. (2013) 'The Sir Jimmy Savile scandal: child sexual abuse and institutional denial at the BBC.' *Crime, Media, Culture 9*, 3, 243–263.

Griffiths, D. and Moynihan, F. (1963) 'Multiple epiphysial injuries in babies (Battered baby syndrome).' *British Medical Journal 2*, 5372, 1558–1561.

Haynes, A., Cuthbert, C., Gardner, R., Telford, P. and Hodson, D. (2015) *Thriving Communities: A Framework for Preventing and Intervening Early in Child Neglect.* London: NSPCC. Available at: www.nspcc.org.uk/globalassets/documents/research-reports/thriving-communities-framework-neglect-report.pdf, accessed on 13 November 2015.

Hibbard, R., Barlow, J. and Macmillan, H. (2012) 'Clinical report: psychological maltreatment.' *Pediatrics 130*, 2, 372–768.

Hildyard, C. and Wolfe, D. (2002) 'Child neglect: developmental issues and outcomes.' *Child Abuse & Neglect 26*, 6–7, 679–695.

Hill, L., Taylor, J., Richards, F. and Reddington, S. (2014) '"No one runs away for no reason": understanding safeguarding issues when children and young people go missing from home.' *Child Abuse Review.* DOI: 10.1002/car.2322

Hindley, N., Ramchandani, P. and Jones, D. (2006) 'Risk factors for recurrence of maltreatment: a systematic review.' *Archives of Disability in Childhood, 9*1, 744–752.

HM Government (2015) *Working Together to Safeguard Children: A Guide to Inter-agency Working to Safeguard and Promote the Welfare of Children.* London: DfE. Available at www.gov.uk/government/publications/working-together-to-safeguard-children--2, accessed on 2 October 2015.

Hobbs, C. and Wynne, J. (2002) 'Neglect of neglect.' *Current Paediatrics 12*, 2, 144–150.

Home Office (2015) *Tackling Child Sexual Exploitation.* London: HM Government. Available at www.gov.uk/government/uploads/system/uploads/attachment_data/file/408604/2903652_RotherhamResponse_acc2.pdf, accessed on 13 November 2015.

Hovdestad, W., Campeau, A., Potter, D. and Tonmyr, L. (2015) 'A systematic review of childhood maltreatment assessments in population-representative surveys since 1990.' *PLoS One 10*, 5, e0123366.doi:10.1371/journal.pone.0123366.

Jago, S. and Pearce, J. (2008) *Gathering Evidence of the Sexual Exploitation of Children and Young People: A Scoping Exercise.* Luton: The University of Bedfordshire. Available at www.beds.ac.uk/__data/assets/pdf_file/0018/40824/Gathering_evidence_final_report_June_08.pdf, accessed on 2 October 2015.

Jay, A. (2014) *Independent Inquiry into Child Sexual Exploitation in Rotherham (1997–2013).* Rotherham: Rotherham Metropolitan Borough Council. Available at www.rotherham.gov.uk/downloads/file/1407/independent_inquiry_cse_in_rotherham, accessed on 11 September 2015.

Johnson, R. and Cotmore, R. (2015) *National Evaluation of the Graded Care Profile.* London: NSPCC. Available at www.nspcc.org.uk/globalassets/documents/research-reports/graded-care-profile-evaluation-report.pdf, accessed 4 June 2016.

Jütte, S., Bentley, H., Tallis, D., Mayes, J., *et al.* (2015) *How Safe Are Our Children? The Most Comprehensive Overview of Child Protection in the United Kingdom.* London: NSPCC. Available at www.nspcc.org.uk/globalassets/documents/research-reports/how-safe-children-2015-report.pdf, accessed on 2 October 2015.

Kalamakis, K. and Chandler, G. (2015) 'Health consequences of adverse childhood experiences: a systematic review.' *Journal of the American Association of Nurse Practitioners 27*, 8, 457–465.

Kaplan, S., Pelcovitz, D. and Labruna, V. (1999) 'Child and adolescent abuse and neglect research: a review of the past 10 years. Part 1: physical and emotional abuse and neglect.' *Journal of the American Academy of Child & Adolescent Psychiatry 38*, 10, 1214–1222.

Kempe, H., Silverman, F., Steele, B., Droegemueller, W. and Silver, H. (1962) 'The battered child syndrome.' *Child Abuse & Neglect 181*, 1, 17–24.

Kitzinger, J. (1996) 'Media representations of sexual abuse risks.' *Child Abuse Review 5*, 319–333.

Kitzinger, J. (2001) 'Transformations of public and private knowledge: audience reception, feminism and the experience of childhood sexual abuse.' *Feminist Media Studies 1*, 1, 91–104. DOI: 10.1080/14680770120042882

Kitzinger, J. (2004) *Framing Abuse: Media Influence and Public Understanding of Sexual Violence against Children.* London: Pluto.

Kloppen, K., Maehle, M., Kvello, O., Haugland, S. and Breivik, K. (2015) 'Prevalence of intra-familial child maltreatment in the Nordic countries: a review.' *Child Abuse Review 24*, 1, 51–66.

Krug, E., Dahlberg, L., Mercy, J., Zwi, A. and Lozano, R. (2002) *World Report on Violence and Health.* Geneva: World Health Organization. Available at http://apps.who.int/iris/bitstream/10665/42495/1/9241545615_eng.pdf, accessed on 11 September 2015.

LeardMann, C., Smith, B. and Ryan, M. (2010) 'Do adverse childhood experiences increase the risk of postdeployment posttraumatic stress disorder in US Marines?' *BioMed Central Public Health 10*, 437, 1–8.

Lentz, V., Robinson, J. and Bolton, J. (2010) 'Childhood adversity, mental disorder comorbidity and suicidal behaviour in schizotypal personality disorder.' *The Journal of Nervous and Mental Disease 198*, 11, 795–801.

Lindland, E. and Kendall-Taylor, N. (2013) *Mapping the Gaps between Expert and Public Understandings of Child Maltreatment in the UK.* Washington, DC: Frameworks Institute. Available at www.frameworksinstitute.org/pubs/mtg/childmaltreatment/toc.html, accessed on 13 November 2015.

MacLeod, M. and Saraga, E. (1988) 'Challenging the orthodoxy: towards a feminist theory and practice.' *Feminist Review 28*, 16–55.

McCrory, E., De Brito, S. and Viding, E. (2010) 'Research review: the neurobiological and genetic research of maltreatment and adversity.' *Journal of Child Psychology and Psychiatry 51*, 10, 1079–1095.

McCrory, E., De Brito, S. and Viding, E. (2012) 'The link between child abuse and psychopathology: a review of neurobiological and genetic research.' *Journal of the Royal Society of Medicine 105*, 151–156.

McSherry, D. (2007) 'Understanding and addressing the "neglect of neglect": why are we making a mole-hill out of a mountain?' *Child Abuse & Neglect 6*, 31, 607–614.

Melrose, M. (2013) 'Twenty-first century party people: young people and sexual exploitation in the new millennium.' *Child Abuse Review 22*, 3, 155–168.

Naughton, A., Maguire, S., Mann, M., Lumn, C., *et al.* (2013) 'Emotional, behavioural and developmental features indicative of neglect or emotional abuse in pre-school children: a systematic review.' *JAMA Pediatrics 167*, 8, 769–775.

Norman, R., Byambaa, M., De, R., Butchart, A., Scott, J. and Vos, T. (2012) 'The long-term health consequences of child physical abuse, emotional abuse, and neglect: a systematic review and meta-analysis.' *PLOS Medicine 9*, 1–31.

O'Hara, M., Legano, L., Homel, P., Walker-Descartes, I., Rojas, M. and Laraque, D. (2015) 'Children neglected: Where cumulative risk theory fails.' *Child Abuse & Neglect 45*, 1–8.

Parton, N. (1985) *The Politics of Child Abuse.* Basingstoke: Macmillan.

Parton, N. (1991) *Governing the Family: Child Care, Child Protection and the State.* Basingstoke: Palgrave McMillen Limited.

Parton, N. (2006) '"Every child matters": the shift to prevention whilst strengthening protection in children's services in England.' *Children and Youth Services Review 28*, 2, 976–992.

Pereda, N., Abad, J. and Guilera, G. (2015) 'Victimization and polyvictimization of Spanish youth involved in juvenile justice.' *Journal of Interpersonal Violence.* DOI:10.1177/0886260515597440

Pianta, R., Egeland, B. and Erickson, M. (1989) 'The Antecedents of Maltreatment: Results of the Mother-Child Interaction Research Project.' In D. Cicchetti and V. Carlson (eds) *Child Maltreatment: Theory and Research on the Causes and Consequences of Child Abuse and Neglect.* New York: Cambridge University Press.

Radford, L., Corral, S., Bradley, C. and Fisher, H. (2013) 'The prevalence and impact of child maltreatment and other types of victimization in the UK: Findings from a population survey of caregivers, children and young people and young adults.' *Child Abuse & Neglect 37*, 10, 801–813.

Radford, L., Corral, S., Bradley, C., Fisher, H., *et al.* (2011) *Child Abuse and Neglect in the UK Today.* London: NSPCC. Available at www.nspcc.org.uk/globalassets/documents/research-reports/child-abuse-neglect-uk-today-research-report.pdf, accessed on 11 September 2015.

Sabri, B., Hong, J., Campbell, J. and Cho, H. (2013) 'Understanding children and adolescents' victimizations at multiple levels: an ecological review of the literature.' *Journal of Social Service Research 39*, 3, 322–334.

Sakheim, D. and Devine, S. (1992) *Out of Darkness: Exploring Satanism and Ritual Abuse.* New York: Macmillan.

Schumacher, J., Smith-Slep, A. and Heyman, R. (2001) 'Risk factors for child neglect.' *Aggression and Violent Behavior 6*, 231–254.

Sethi, D., Bellis, M., Hughes, K., Gilbert, R., Mitis, F. and Galea, G. (2013) *European Report on Preventing Child Maltreatment.* Copenhagen: WHO. Available at www.euro.who.int/__data/assets/pdf_file/0019/217018/European-Report-on-Preventing-Child-Maltreatment.pdf, accessed on 11 September 2015.

Sidebotham, P. and Heron, J. (2003) 'Child maltreatment in the "children of the nineties": the role of the child.' *Child Abuse & Neglect 27*, 337–352.

Sidebotham, P., Golding, J. and the ALSPAC Study Team (2001) 'Child maltreatment in the "children of the nineties": a longitudinal study of parental risk factors.' *Child Abuse & Neglect 25*, 9, 1177–1200.

Silverman, J. and Wilson, D. (2002) *Innocence Betrayed: Paedophilia, the Media and Society.* Cambridge: Polity Press.

Social Services and Well-being (Wales) Act 2014. Available at www.legislation.gov.uk/anaw/2014/4/section/197/enacted, accessed on 11 September 2015.

Stevenson, O. (2008) *Neglected Children and Their Families.* New Jersey: Wiley Blackwell.

Stevenson, R. and Laing, V. (2015) *Summary Report of Year 2 of the Welsh Neglect Project 2014/2015.* (Unpublished report). London: Action for Children and the NSPCC.

Stith, S., Liu, T., Davies, L.C., Boykin, E., *et al.* (2009) 'Risk factors in child maltreatment: a meta-analytic review of the literature.' *Aggression and Violent Behavior 14*, 1, 13–29.

Stoltenborgh, M., Bakermans-Kranenburg, M. and van Ijzendoorn, M. (2013) 'The neglect of child neglect: a meta-analytic review of the prevalence of neglect.' *Social Psychiatry and Psychiatric Epidemiology 48*, 3, 345–355.

Stoltenborgh, M., Bakermans-Kranenburg, M., Alink, L. and van Ijzendoorn, M. (2015) 'The prevalence of child maltreatment across the globe: review of a series of meta-analyses.' *Child Abuse Review 24*, 1, 37–50.

Stone, B. (1998) 'Child neglect: practitioners' perspectives.' *Child Abuse Review 7*, 2, 87–96.

Strathearn, L., Gray, P., O'Callaghan, M. and Wood, D. (2001) 'Childhood neglect and cognitive development in extremely low birth weight infants: a prospective study.' *Pediatrics 108*, 1, 142–151.

Tanner K. and Turney D. (2003) 'What do we know about child neglect? A critical review of the literature and its application to social work practice.' *Child and Family Social Work 8*, 1, 25–34.

Taylor, J., Daniel, B. and Scott, J. (2010) 'Noticing and helping the neglected child: towards an international research agenda.' *Child & Family Social Work 17*, 4, 416–426.

UNICEF Innocenti Research Centre (2011) *Child Safety Online: Global Challenges and Strategies*. Florence: UNICEF. Available at www.unicef.org/pacificislands/ict_eng. pdf, accessed on 11 September 2015.

Wald, M. (2015) 'Beyond CPS: developing an effective system for helping children in "neglectful" families: policymakers have failed to address the neglect of neglect.' *Child Abuse & Neglect 41*, 49–66.

Ward, H., Brown, R. and Westlake, D. (2012) *Safeguarding Babies and Very Young Children from Abuse and Neglect*. London: Jessica Kingsley Publishers.

Waterhouse, S. (2012) *Lost in Care: Report of the Tribunal of Inquiry into the Abuse of Children in the Former County Council areas of Gwynedd and Clwyd since 1974*. London: The Stationery Office. Available at www.julyseventh.co.uk/pdf/Lost_In_Care_Report-Formatted.pdf, accessed on 11 September 2015.

Widom, C.S. (1989) 'The cycle of violence.' *Science 244*, 160–166.

Widom, C.S., DuMont, K. and Czaja, S. (2007) 'A prospective investigation of major depressive disorder and comorbidity in abused and neglected children grown up.' *Archives of General Psychiatry 64*, 1, 49–56.

Wilding J. and Thoburn J. (1997) 'Family support plans for neglected and emotionally maltreated children.' *Child Abuse Review 6*, 5, 343–356.

Zuravin, S. (1999) 'Child Neglect: A Review of Definitions and Measurement Research.' In H. Dubowitz (ed.) *Neglected Children: Research, Practice and Policy*. Thousand Oaks, CA: Sage Publications.

5

LEARNING FROM CHILDREN AND YOUNG PEOPLE ABOUT NEGLECT

Sarah Gorin

Introduction

This chapter will look at what we know about children and young people's understandings and experiences of neglect, its impact on them and what they have told us about the help they need. It will examine research undertaken both with children and young people who have direct experience of neglect and with those who do not, supplemented by messages from a broader range of studies on (for example) the child protection system. We will explore the following questions:

- How much do we know about how children and young people themselves define neglect, their awareness of neglect, the impact of neglect, their ability to disclose neglect and access help, and the kinds of help children and young people want?

- Where do the gaps in our knowledge lie?

- Can we see children and young people's understandings and experiences reflected in policy and practice over the last ten years?

- What needs to be done to develop more relevant policy and practice that involves children and young people and responds to their needs?

A central message here is the importance of practitioners actively involving children and young people in work on neglect, rather than, as is often the case, relying on adults to represent their views.

Why is learning from the views of children and young people relevant?

There is a pragmatic as well as a legal and ethical case for including children's views. The perspectives of children and young people have been found to be different from those of adults (Clifton 2014; Rees *et al.* 2011) and therefore potentially offer new insights. It is important to seek their views, understandings and experiences through research and evaluation as well as in social work practice and in service/policy development. The following quote, which includes the words of a young person, highlights this: '"Young people see things adults don't see"; so if only adults come up with the questions they may miss what really matters to young people' (Clifton 2014, p.2).

Why is there so little research with children about neglect?

Despite all the evidence that children experience neglect, there is a surprising lack of research, whether in the UK or elsewhere, that has explicitly set out to explore their understandings and experiences as research 'subjects', and there is even less research that has involved children and young people as more active participants. A systematic review of the recognition of neglect and early responses by Daniel, Taylor and Scott (2010, p.255) found that the biggest gap in evidence 'related to the views of parents and, even more, of children' and the authors conclude that 'attempts to develop a swifter response to neglect must be informed by the views of parents and children about what would help'.

The reasons for this lack of attention to children's views and experiences of neglect are unclear. They may include adults' conceptualisation of children as legally minors who are dependent and in need of protection (although children participate in research on many other aspects of their lives); their not seeing a benefit to involving children or being concerned that it might cause distress; their seeing neglect as more complicated than other forms of abuse (for instance, hard to define and quantify); or perhaps simply because research with children requires resources, time and effort.

There are practical constraints: research studies with children and young people who have experienced neglect or other forms of abuse have sometimes struggled to access, recruit and retain participants (Cleaver *et al.* 2006; Farmer and Lutman 2010; Leeson 2007; McLeod 2007); and all research is time consuming and can be costly. Without such studies we are missing a fundamental part of the jigsaw – how children themselves define and understand the experience of being neglected, what matters most to them, and how we can provide accessible, effective services to work with them and their families to influence change in their lives. The final report of the Munro Review of child protection in England continuously emphasised the importance of a child-centred approach to child protection:

> the child protection system should be child-centred, recognising children and young people as individuals with rights, including their right to participate in major decisions about them in line with their age and maturity. (Munro 2011, p.24)

But the report also expressed concern that child protection practice is not well informed by the most relevant perspective, that of children themselves:

> children and young people are a key source of information about their lives and the impact any problems are having on them in the specific culture and values of their family. It is therefore puzzling that the evidence shows that children are not being adequately included in child protection work. (Munro 2011, p.25)

One strong source of evidence is the largest-scale study in the UK to have asked young people themselves about the prevalence of neglect. This is the child safety and victimisation survey (Radford *et al.* 2011). A large group of young people (2275) between the ages of 11 and 17 years as well as 1761 young adults between the ages of 18 and 24 years were asked about their experiences of abuse and neglect. The study found that almost 10 per cent of the young people aged 11–17 said they had experienced severe neglect (with little variation across boys and girls). 'Severe' neglect included serious emotional neglect, lack of supervision or physical care that would place a child or young person at risk; or neglect that the young person defined as abusive or criminal (Radford *et al.* 2011). Miller and Brown (2014) found that disabled children and young people (whatever the disability) are at greater risk of all forms of abuse and neglect than non-disabled children and there can be significant barriers to safeguarding them.

They are also more likely to experience multiple kinds of abuse and multiple episodes of abuse (see also Chapter 4).

Children's rights: The law, policy and practice

In the field of children's social care in the UK, there has been a policy shift over the last 30 years seeking to increase the amount of direct participation of children and young people in decisions that affect them. This shift has been underpinned by the United Nations Convention on the Rights of the Child (UNCRC) 1989; the Human Rights Act 1998; the Equality Act, 2010; and the Children Act 1989, which applies to both England and Wales. (The equivalent legislation in Northern Ireland is the Children Order 1995). The UNCRC is an international agreement that was ratified by 194 countries in 2014 (with the United States of America and Somalia as the only exceptions) that protects the human rights of children under the age of 18. The most relevant Article in relation to listening to children about neglect is Article 12, which states that every child has the right to say what they think in all matters affecting them, with the views of the child being given due weight in accordance with their age and maturity (United Nations 1989).

GOVERNMENT GUIDANCE AND THE VIEW OF THE CHILD

In the UK the four nations (England, Northern Ireland, Scotland and Wales) each have their own child protection system, laws and framework of legislation and accompanying guidance. For a useful summary by nation see the NSPCC website (https://www.nspcc.org.uk/preventing-abuse/child-protection-system/). In England Guidance associated with the Children Act 1989 states that:

> Every assessment must be informed by the views of the child as well as the family. Children should, wherever possible, be seen alone and local authority children's social care has a duty to ascertain the child's wishes and feelings regarding the provision of services to be delivered. (Section 17 of the Children Act 1989, amended by Section 53 Children Act 2004) It is important to understand the resilience of the individual child when planning appropriate services. Every assessment

should reflect the unique characteristics of the child within their family and community context (HM Government 2015, p.23). In Wales the Social Services and Wellbeing (Wales) Act 2014 also places an emphasis on young people having a role to play in decision making (Welsh Government 2016).

Perceptions of children and children's rights

Whilst children's rights are established in legal terms, the extent to which children are actually consulted about 'matters affecting them' is extremely variable; and crucially there is very little practical recourse if they are not consulted. While children have historically been constituted as 'possessions' or 'subjects' (Lloyd-Smith and Tarr 2000 pp.62–64), current views of children and young people are frequently constructed in binary positions, either as 'innocent', 'vulnerable', 'incompetent' and 'powerless' or alternatively as 'deprived/disadvantaged', 'ignorant', 'excluded' or 'criminal' (Alderson 2005, p.30; Morrow 2005, pp.151–155), views that can alternate swiftly in the light of media depictions.

Munro (2011) has highlighted that practitioners have strong personal views about the age at which children should be consulted and that as a result there is evidence of polarised attitudes. She cites research on children and divorce that describes how:

adult constructions…become ensnared in…a simple…dichotomy, where children are classified as either subjects or objects, competent or incompetent, reliable or unreliable, harmed by decision-making or harmed by exclusion, wanting to participate or not wanting to participate. Practice then becomes founded upon certainties, the perfected (single) procedure, based on the single conception of the child. (Trinder 1997 quoted in Munro 2011, p.26)

There have long been debates about children's rights to protection versus their rights to participation. Cossar, Brandon and Jordan (2014) address this debate in an article about children's views on participation in the child protection system. They argue that there is a tension between children being seen, within literature on the sociology of childhood, as competent, autonomous and active agents in constructing their own lives; and on the other hand, in theory stemming from developmental psychology, as vulnerable and in need of protection. They conclude that a more sophisticated approach could combine notions of participation and protection.

Brownlie, Anderson and Ormston (2006) undertook a review to explore the challenges and opportunities of incorporating a 'children as researchers' perspective into the agenda of the government's social research in Scotland. They reviewed the participation agenda and found that whilst initially there had been an apparent assumption that involving children and young people was a 'good thing', more recently a more critical approach had evolved that continued to recognise benefits, but was aware that involvement was not an 'uncomplicated good'. The case for participation, they argue, tends to draw on arguments relating to 'efficiency' (that participation will produce better outcomes) and on 'empowerment' (that it will improve or change children and young people's lives). There are questions around what counts as participation; a danger of tokenism (i.e. including children and young people for the sake of it rather than genuine inclusiveness); and a need to build not just participatory practices but *organisational cultures* that consistently support participation.

Guidelines on how to involve children and young people in research are provided by, for example, the organisation INVOLVE (2012). See also Shaw, Brady and Davy (2011) and for ideas on good practice, visit the website for the Young People's Research Group at De Montfort University in Leicester.[1]

Munro (2011) states that although participation in social care practice can be empowering for children if it is undertaken well, practitioners may feel ill-equipped to communicate with and involve them at every stage of the child protection process. She cites Jones (2003) who stresses the importance of a number of core skills for adults' effective communication with children who have suffered adverse experiences; they include listening, being able to convey genuine interest, empathic concern, understanding, emotional warmth, respect for the child, and the capacity to reflect and to manage emotions.

What children and young people tell us about neglect

In order to think about the messages from children and young people about neglect we will draw on two main bodies of research. First,

---

1   Available at www.dmu.ac.uk/research/research-faculties-and-institutes/health-and-life-sciences/young-people/youth-community-and-education.aspx.

studies specifically undertaken to explore children and young people's views about neglect and/or their direct experiences of neglect. Second, research with children and young people about other child protection concerns, risks or safeguarding issues, likely to include children who have experienced neglect. The latter includes, for example, studies about other forms of child maltreatment, research on the child protection system, looked after children, parental problems such as alcohol and drug misuse or mental health problems, deprivation, running away, homelessness, suicide and those vulnerable to sexual exploitation.

There is only a small number of studies in the first group undertaken with children about neglect, but the second body of research also has important messages we can learn from. In these studies, neglect is often conflated with other forms of maltreatment so it can be difficult to disentangle messages that relate to neglect specifically. The majority of this work has been undertaken in the UK but has wider relevance wherever the UNCRC applies (see p.133).

How children and young people define and understand neglect

The four nations of the United Kingdom have slightly different operational definitions of neglect. In England, the government's statutory guidance *Working Together to Safeguard Children* (HM Government 2015) sets out the official definition of neglect:

> The persistent failure to meet a child's basic physical and/or psychological needs, likely to result in the serious impairment of the child's health or development. Neglect may occur during pregnancy as a result of maternal substance abuse. Once a child is born, neglect may involve a parent or carer failing to:
>
> - provide adequate food, clothing and shelter (including exclusion from home or abandonment);
>
> - protect a child from physical and emotional harm or danger;
>
> - ensure adequate supervision (including the use of inadequate care-givers); or
>
> - ensure access to appropriate medical care or treatment.

It may also include neglect of, or unresponsiveness to, a child's basic emotional needs. (HM Government 2015, p.93).

The use of terms such as 'persistent' (failure) and 'adequate' (food, clothing and shelter) mean that identifying what constitutes neglect of children can in practice be subjective and a matter of professional judgement (Ofsted 2014). Whilst there has been much debate amongst professionals about the definition of child neglect (see Rees *et al.* 2011 for a summary and Chapter 2) it is interesting to consider what children themselves understand by the term 'neglect'.

This chapter explores findings from an in-depth study in which the author was a member of the research team (Rees *et al.* 2011). This was undertaken in the UK – by the National Society for the Prevention of Cruelty to Children (NSPCC), The Children's Society and York University – with 51 young people (aged 12–24) and actively involved young people in the research, both as members of an advisory group and as co-researchers. Focus groups were used to explore with young people what 'neglect' meant to them. Some of the young people who participated in the research had experienced neglect or other forms of abuse whilst others had not. The study found that young people described many aspects of neglect that members of the public and professionals would also identify as neglectful, such as failure to provide adequate food and water, baths, clean/suitable clothes, shelter, a safe environment and also, importantly, affection and parental protection. Interestingly, some young people also provided descriptions of neglect relating to wider parental responsibilities including the absence of caring parental behaviours such as supervision, supporting school attendance, being involved in their children's education, attending events at school and ensuring young people received medical care if they needed it; 'basically if you had a burn and if they didn't do anything, if they didn't pay attention something bad could happen, that is serious neglect'. (Rees *et al.* 2011, p.59).

Young people's definitions were much broader than those employed by adults and perhaps more nuanced, encompassing details of care that adults might not attach the same significance to. This highlights that the priorities that children and young people have and the things they see as important to good parenting are not necessarily the same as those adults would identify. For example, some young people felt that a child was neglected if parents or foster and residential care workers did not provide them with a healthy diet, help prevent obesity, teach basic social skills, morals, manners and self-care/independence skills. These issues were particularly stressed by groups of young people leaving local authority care, who were being moved on to independence, and young people who had parents with substance misuse problems. These groups felt that as a result they were ill equipped to care for themselves into adulthood. These young people were often already experiencing difficulties in their young adult life that they saw as a direct result of being neglected. One young care leaver said of his peer group:

> When they're older they'll be sitting down 'Oh I don't know how to do that, I'm going to get someone else to do it'; 'I can't do cooking 'cos my mum didn't teach me. It's like a neglect because they're not shown the basics of life'. (Rees *et al.* 2011, p.60)

Other issues that were described as neglectful included parents 'leaving children out' – excluding them from activities or treats; favouring siblings; or prioritising new partners over the child; and also lack of involvement and support from an absent parent when children were living in single-parent households. Hooper *et al.* (2007), in their study with parents and children living on low incomes, found that the absence of a non-resident parent, and the unreliability and unavailability of some non-resident parents, could be akin to the withdrawal or withholding of care and affection that is present in definitions of emotional neglect and abuse. Research in Hong Kong by Chan, Lam and Shei (2011) considered Chinese primary school children's understandings of what constitutes abuse and neglect using vignettes. They found that, like adults, they did not have homogenous views and whilst some aspects of their understandings were the same as adults, there were also differences. These children were least likely to recognise neglect as abusive, compared to other forms of abuse.

Much of the academic literature on definitions of neglect discusses whether the category of neglect should only include acts of omission (things parents fail to do) or acts of commission (things they actively do) too. It is noticeable that young people's definitions of neglect in the study by Rees *et al.* (2011) often included what they saw as *deliberately punitive and active strategies* on the part of the parent or carer, for example making them do excessive chores or constantly care for younger siblings, or not allowing them to play. Viewing neglect narrowly as just including acts of omission does not recognise that young people see adults as having responsibility for their own behaviour (just as young people are encouraged to) and as a result, neglect includes active choices by the adult.

The same research found that children and young people often included aspects of physical, sexual and emotional abuse in their definitions of neglect. One young person said neglect was 'normally where you're either hurting the kids...that's the biggest neglect...or not feeding the kids.' (Rees *et al.* 2011, p.59). Others talked of neglect including emotional harm: 'mental abuse'; 'bullying'; 'lack of emotional security'; 'no love and affection'; 'no appreciation'; 'torment'; 'blamed for break up in relationships'; 'singled out by parents, emotional focus'. One young person said that neglect was 'being unaware of your child's feelings, for example depression' (Rees *et al.* 2011, p.59). It was unclear why children and young people drew fewer distinctions than professionals between types of maltreatment. It is possible they knew, from experience or otherwise, that different forms of harm may co-occur, or that they saw all harm (including sexual, physical and emotional abuse) as a neglectful experience for the child.

Children and young people's awareness and recognition of neglect

Cossar *et al.* (2013) undertook research on recognition and disclosure of maltreatment, using young people as co-researchers. The research included a literature review, analysis of an online peer-support website, interviews with 30 young people aged 11–20 and focus groups with children, parents and professionals. This multi-method study found that children reported a variety of problems under the category 'neglect' including physical, sexual and emotional abuse and domestic violence, and they suggest that (as for adults) this may reflect a lack of clarity surrounding what constitutes neglect as compared with other forms of maltreatment.

For those who have experienced neglect life may be messy, in every sense; and the harm children experience may be more important than the precise cause of it or the terminology used. Professionals use a language in which there are distinctions between forms of harm, as it provides a means of being more specific about the types of behaviours being described. The evidence shows that children and young people (and possibly other adults) may not have the same understandings of the language used. Their own terminology may be a closer approximation to their lived experience of neglect and therefore important to capture even if it is harder to categorise their views as a result.

As discussed above, Cossar *et al.* (2013) note that children (much like adults) are likely to find recognition of neglect a more complex process than with other forms of abuse, though research suggests that from the age of eight onwards, children in the general population become aware of the signs of neglect amongst children they are in contact with. Research with 8- to 12-year-olds in the general population about recognition of neglect found that 73 per cent of children and young people know a child who has shown signs of neglect – for example, a child who is often late or missing from school, or does not have friends to play with, or has parents who do not know where they are, or does not get meals at home – and three in ten have been worried about whether a child they know is being looked after properly (Burgess *et al.* 2014).

However, children who are being neglected themselves may find it harder to recognise their own experiences as 'neglect'. This is not surprising, as the situation may be habitual for them and there may not be any one specific behaviour or incident that occurs, but an accumulation of lack of care in various aspects of children's lives over time. Neglect can be episodic; there may be periods in a child's life when they experience positive care from a parent and times when due to the parent experiencing problems their care of the child deteriorates. In the research by Rees *et al.* one young person stated, 'children don't necessarily know what neglect is, they just think parents hate them' (2011, p.58).

Burgess *et al.* (2014) undertook an online survey with 1582 children aged 8 to 16 years and discussion groups with 40 children who were accessing services and had experience of neglect. One child said, 'some children don't know they are being neglected and not ever getting a hug is being neglected. If you've never had one, you just don't know' (p.19).

Children and young people may struggle to see their own experiences as abusive or neglectful. Important factors that hindered recognition included 'the young person feeling that they deserved it; a difficulty in acknowledging that a parent could be abusive; and a parent's unpredictability when abuse was episodic, and the relationship was sometimes good' (Cossar *et al.* 2013, p.iv).

Developmental changes in children's awareness of neglect

The same study suggests that, as they get older, children are more able to articulate that something is wrong, but that this may start with an emotional awareness that something is not right before they are able to articulate the problem to themselves or others. As one interviewee said, 'I think I was too young to realise, it was just I didn't like being there' (ibid., p.63). They found that as children got to the age of 11 or 12 they were increasingly able to compare their own experiences with those of their peers. Some young people talked about a situation which in hindsight they could see was abusive, but at the time they could not recognise or articulate this.

Allnock and Miller (2013) undertook in-depth interviews with over 60 young people aged 18 to 24 who had experienced maltreatment (often more than one type, but most had experienced sexual abuse) with similar findings. When the abuse started, many young people in this study were either developmentally unable to understand that abuse was wrong or they sensed that the abuse was wrong but lacked the vocabulary to describe or confirm their anxiety about it. Taylor *et al.* (2015), with six deaf and disabled children, found similar results with disclosure tending to happen in the teenage years. Cossar *et al.* (2013) warn that children can remain vulnerable even after they recognise the problem, as they may be unable to access help. These issues are explored further in the context of help-seeking.

The experience and effects of neglect: The views of children and young people

There are only a few studies that have set out to explore children's own views about the impact of neglect. Most studies about impact of neglect are based on adult perspectives. However, there are studies with children on problems such as parental substance misuse, parental mental health problems, young people who run away from home and 'young carers' that are likely to include children who have suffered neglect as a consequence of their parents' problems (see particularly the works cited below). This research helps to confirm the findings from neglect studies and provides additional insights into the lives of children who are vulnerable to neglect.

IMPACT ON CHILDREN'S PHYSICAL AND EMOTIONAL HEALTH AND WELLBEING

- Children report experiencing a potentially confusing mix of emotions, including fear, anxiety, sadness, anger, guilt and love, and loyalty for their parents.

- They describe how problems at home may lead to their lack of self-confidence and feelings of shame, guilt, confusion, rejection and a sense that they are somehow to blame.

- Children whose parents misuse substances or whose parents have mental health problems may have grave concerns about the health of their parents and worry about them dying.

- The losses that children report (particularly in research on parental substance misuse and parental mental health problems) can be very wide ranging, from losing parents (physically or emotionally) to feeling they have lost their childhood, their homes and possessions or that they have lost out on opportunities in later life because of the nature of their childhood.

- Children's accounts often talk about feeling as if parents are emotionally absent even when they are physically present and feeling as if parents are not 'there for them'.

- Children describe how neglect may lead to problems with friendships, feeling isolated, being bullied or bullying others.

- Accounts in neglect research and with children whose parents experience parental substance misuse/mental health problems show that problems at home may also lead to problems at school.

- At school, children may have poor attendance, lack concentration (through lack of sleep or worry), experience low achievement relative to their ability. Resulting behavioural problems may lead to difficulties and even school exclusion.

- Children describe how neglect may lead to mental health problems such as depression, self-harm and suicidal intentions or actions.

- Lack of supervision can mean that children are left at home alone for periods of time and this can expose them to physical dangers with the home (especially if there is substance misuse in the household) and worries about absent parents or whether parents will ever return.

- Children's accounts highlight that neglect can expose children to risks posed by inappropriate adults entering the household.

- Lack of supervision of children and young people may mean they are more vulnerable to getting involved in a range of risky behaviours such as alcohol and substance misuse, running away, crime, violence, under-age sex and sexual exploitation.

- Children may undertake inappropriate caring tasks for their age, such as looking after siblings, undertaking domestic chores or caring for parents.

Bancroft et al. 2004; Burgess et al. 2014; Cossar et al. 2013; Coy 2009; Gorin 2004; Peled and Cohavi 2009; Radford et al. 2011; Rees and Lee 2005; Rees et al. 2011; Safe on the Streets Research Team 1999; Smith, Ireland and Thornberry 2005; Taylor et al. 2015; Thrane et al. 2006.

In focus groups some young offenders talked about their own experiences of neglect (Rees et al. 2011). They discussed a range of physical and psychological impacts on them including feeling angry and punishing or 'taking it out on' others; having no visits whilst in jail; feeling unloved with no one to trust; and experiencing depression and suicidal thoughts. Depression, self-harm and suicide were mentioned by participants in four out of six of the focus groups, and bullying and being bullied were also seen as common problems. All the groups included older young people or those with direct experience of neglect. Bullying and isolation were also commonly identified concerns in research by Burgess et al. (2014).

Different experiences of neglect: Children with disabilities

Taylor *et al.* (2015) found that social isolation was a dominant feature of the childhoods of deaf and disabled children who had been maltreated. Isolation could restrict their access to peer conversations about acceptable and unacceptable adult behaviours, with the risk that they saw the abuse as 'normal'. Isolation (itself often a feature of neglect) could also reduce their opportunities to confide in trusted peers and adults, potentially damaging their self-esteem and making them question their right to freedom from abuse. Those who took part in the study lacked friends and had limited contact with their wider family and community. For these children, isolation was compounded by a lack of formal support from professional services and participants typically lacked choice of someone to confide in about concerns.

Developmentally different experiences of neglect

Neglect may impact upon children and young people in different ways as they get older; while babies and young children lack the ability to protect or remove themselves, it cannot be assumed that older children and young people are necessarily more resilient to the impact of neglect than younger children. As children become older, they are more vulnerable to a range of different risks (Gorin and Jobe 2013; Hanson and Holmes 2014; Jobe and Gorin 2013). These findings are supported by research on reviews of serious cases which stresses that neglect with the most serious outcomes is not just confined to the youngest children (Brandon *et al.* 2013; see also Chapter 7).

Recent research has been undertaken, using a nationally representative sample, on teenagers' experiences of parenting (Raws 2015). Older young people consistently reported less input from their parents than younger ones, with a marked decline in parental behaviour categorised as 'emotional support' relative to other types of parenting as they got older. Children aged 14–18 are thought to be particularly vulnerable to lack of emotional care, with those aged 16–18 also more likely to struggle to access any alternative support and protective services (House of Commons 2012).

Support: What helps

The importance of the individual child's or young person's views on parental care and the need for help

A literature review by Hanson and Holmes (2014) on developing an effective response to adolescents describes adolescence as a time of developing autonomy, and they highlight the variability in the speed at which individuals develop the propensities and skills involved in greater independence. Whether the young person feels that parental behaviour constitutes neglect or not will, in many cases, depend on that individual adolescent's developmental trajectory. They give the example that some 16-year-olds may desire and be skilled enough to live independently, whereas other 16-year-olds may not. A parent insisting that a child leaves home at 16 may be thought neglectful in the second instance, but not in the first. This highlights the vital importance of social workers and professionals developing close and trusting enough relationships with each child or young person for them to be able to express their *own* feelings and experiences and what behaviours they themselves feel are neglectful, as well as having their capacities assessed formally.

Accessing help as a neglected child or young person: Facilitators and barriers

We know very little about whether, how and how many children and young people who are experiencing neglect talk about it and whether they get access to the help that they need. It is important to recognise that many children and young people will never talk to anyone about problems they experience at home (see, for example, Gorin 2004). Research by Vincent and Daniel (2004) examined telephone calls over a period of a year to ChildLine – a free and confidential telephone helpline for children in the UK. This highlighted that disclosure was least likely where the form of maltreatment was neglect (for an update see also NSPCC 2015a).

Our inferences about disclosure of neglect come mainly from studies that have been undertaken with samples of children who have been in the child protection system or experienced other forms of maltreatment, some of whom are likely to have experienced neglect. Cossar *et al.* (2013) provide useful information about disclosure.

In their literature review they found that disclosure rates ranged from 11 per cent to 42 per cent and increased with age, with girls more likely to report abuse than boys. Studies have suggested that children and young people with disabilities are less likely to disclose abuse (Miller and Brown 2014; Stalker *et al.* 2010).

Studies have tended to find that children and young people are likely to seek help from informal sources of help first, such as friends, family, grandparents, siblings and wider family, but some may also seek the help of professionals who are known to them, who they trust and who are available. Teachers, youth workers and social workers were particularly identified by young people as sources of help (Cossar *et al.* 2013). Young people in Rees *et al.* (2011) often talked to peers about abuse before approaching a family member or professional; when professionals were approached, it was often on the advice of, or with the support of, the peers they had initially spoken to.

BARRIERS TO CHILDREN TALKING ABOUT ABUSE AND NEGLECT

Findings tend to be similar across studies (e.g. Allnock and Miller 2013; Burgess *et al.* 2014; Cossar *et al.* 2013; Jobe and Gorin 2013) and include:

- fear: of a parent; of being split up from parents and siblings; of the unknown; of the implications of reporting neglect for parents and other family members; and of not being believed

- stigma and shame: fear of being teased or bullied; fear of stigma surrounding disclosure of neglect may be more pronounced for some minority ethnic young people who may be concerned about preserving family honour

- feeling responsible or in some way to blame for the abuse

- being unsure whether an adult can be trusted to keep confidences and not tell other adults or the child's parents

- uncertainty about whether the adult has time to listen and what their reaction will be to what they are told

- fear of the story being 'twisted' in some way if relayed to others

- lack of trust that concerns will be acted upon or that, if they are acted upon, life may not be better; lack of control over decisions affecting their life

- failure to recognise neglectful behaviour or thinking it is not, or will not be seen as, problematic enough to talk about.

Previous research has found that disclosure of maltreatment is often not a one-off event but a lengthy process in which children reveal different experiences and events over time, and that it is closely linked to the confidence they have in their relationship with professionals (Allnock and Miller 2013; Baginsky 2001; Jobe and Gorin 2013; Taylor *et al.* 2015). Cossar *et al.* (2013) say that it is important for professionals to notice and respond sensitively to non-verbal (as well as verbal) signs and symptoms of children and young people's distress at any age, not relying only on the child or young person talking about their abuse. A significant risk of reliance on verbal telling is that a child's silence or denial means that abuse is not pursued: 'I think it's the adults who need to approach children if they think something's not right, it's not up to the children to approach them. It can be a big burden for a child to ask for help' (young person quoted in Action for Children 2014, p.2).

In another study on child protection (Jobe and Gorin 2013, p.433), Emma, aged 14, emphasised the importance of children and young people having the confidence to speak out:

Interviewer: So what do you think might help young people speak out?

Emma: Confidence and safety. That's the only reason why I didn't speak out for nine months because of low self-esteem and I was terrified. Have to have the confidence and they have to have a big safety net around them cos if kids don't feel safe they don't do anything.

Lack of confidence and not feeling safe may be reasons why disabled children and young people are more likely to delay disclosure than non-disabled children. The prolonged and heightened dependence of disabled children on their parents and carers may make them more susceptible to neglect, may mean they feel less able to report it and they may be less able to protect themselves:

> It's harder to make yourself heard at times. You can't communicate easily, because of whatever problem. And you also have to depend on other people. Even if you're able to verbalise what you want to say, you are always in a weaker position, as you need that help. (from Miller and Brown 2014, p.6)

Even if children and young people disclose experiences of neglect, there may still be barriers to receiving help. Disclosing abuse to family, friends and professionals should not always be assumed to be a positive experience and may not necessarily lead to action to protect the child. In Allnock and Miller's retrospective study (2013) they found that 48 of the 60 young people had attempted to disclose their abuse to at least one person before they were 18 years old and most young people had made more than one attempted disclosure. Of the 203 disclosures in childhood that were made, only 117 disclosures (58 per cent) were acted upon by recipients. This study highlighted how responses by friends to young people's disclosures, although largely positive and supportive, could also be negative, including disbelief that the abuse occurred. In some extreme situations, friends turned on the young people. The authors highlight the need for young people to be equipped with information on how to respond to a friend who is experiencing neglect. Their study also showed that more than half of the disclosures to mothers were seeking help to stop the abuse, but only nine mothers (30 per cent) took some action to do this and five mothers (17 per cent) ignored the disclosure or denied that the abuse occurred.

Children and young people, rather than explicitly disclosing abuse, most often come to the attention of services once their behaviour and demeanour has deteriorated (Cossar *et al.* 2013). Allnock and Miller (2013) found that those who could not disclose their abuse at the time wanted someone to notice and ask them about it. They believed that professionals should have asked more questions to uncover the nature of their depression and self-harming behaviours which stemmed directly from the abuse they were experiencing. With regard to neglect, this is supported by studies with children and young people who have contacted ChildLine. These show that neglect is frequently not raised as a primary issue when young people seek external help, despite the neglect being ongoing. The concern that they present (e.g. a parent's substance abuse) may be directly linked to the neglect (see Wales *et al.* 2009; NSPCC 2015). As stated above, this lack of recognition of underlying neglect may in part be the result of it being 'normalised' by the child as a way of life and its harm going unremarked upon by professionals in reports and conferences. Research by Turney *et al.* (2011) suggests that in cases of chronic neglect, professionals can over-identify with parents or become desensitised over a period of time to low levels of parental care; as a result, the children's difficulties are less likely to receive adequate attention.

Children's awareness of the help available and what different professionals do is variable; unsurprisingly, they are more likely to have a better understanding if they have already had contact with services. Rees *et al.* (2011) found that many young people did not understand distinctions between who would deal with them in which circumstances, even amongst a group of young offenders who had already had contact with a range of professionals. Many of the young people who participated in the research by Rees *et al.* (2011) struggled to think of any supportive services. Not all of the participants in focus groups referred to options such as helplines and no one talked about using new media options such as online counselling for support purposes.

In a study with young people who had been referred to children's social care (Jobe and Gorin 2013) many of the young people were unclear about the child protection processes or plans they had experienced, the roles of different professionals they had encountered, and some even had difficulty recollecting exactly what had happened when they were referred. With some cases this was due to the time lapse between the referral and the interview, but in others young people did not feel they had been informed sufficiently regarding what was happening and so felt unable to respond to questions about the process. The research by Rees *et al.* (2010) highlighted that children and young people are unlikely to know about routes to self-refer to children's services. Cossar *et al.* (2014) recommend encouraging children to self-refer and monitoring these self-referrals. Children who experience child protection services often also report lacking written knowledge about the process and what to expect. Ofsted (2012) found that many disabled children lacked information about child protection (see also Allard 2003; Cossar *et al.* 2014; Gorin 2004; Hooper *et al.* 2007; Rees *et al.* 2010).

The importance of supportive trusting relationships

There is now a considerable body of research with children and young people about the kinds of support they value. The messages from research about neglect with children and young people (e.g. Rees *et al.* 2010) are very similar to those from studies such as with children 'in need', 'in need of protection', 'looked after' or whose parents have substance misuse or mental health problems. There is a consensus across all this research that the most important feature of support for children and young people is developing a trusting and supportive relationship with an adult who listens to their views, keeps them informed about what is happening and acts upon their views where possible. (See for example Adamson and Templeton 2012; Buckley, Carr and Whelan 2011; Butler and Williamson 1994; Clifton 2014; Cossar *et al.* 2013; Freake, Barley and Kent 2007; Gorin 2004; Gorin and Jobe 2013; Hill 1999; McLeod 2007, 2010; Osbourne 2001; Taylor *et al.* 2015; Willow 2009; Woolfson *et al.* 2010).

A number of obstacles have been identified which may inhibit the building of positive relationships between young people and social workers. In Munro's research these included 'frequent changes of social worker, lack of effective voice at reviews, lack of confidentiality and, linked to this, lack of a confidante' (Munro 2001, p.129). Previous studies have highlighted that the often high turnover of staff in children's social care departments can mean that children (and parents) find themselves retelling their experiences to multiple social workers and this may cause them to disengage with workers altogether (Jobe and Gorin 2013).

Cossar *et al.* (2014) interviewed 26 children aged 6–17 with experience of the child protection system. Their research confirmed the importance of the relationship with a trusted adult, but they found that this could not be wholly delegated by their social worker to another worker; the young people recognised that their assigned social worker had the power to make decisions about them. A trusting relationship was found to offer opportunities to promote confidence, feelings of safety and self-efficacy; without this, some of the children and young people had no opportunity in which to express their opinions and feelings, let alone feel that those opinions had an impact on decision-making.

Findings of a consultation undertaken with young people by the Office of the Children's Commissioner (Clifton 2014) show that not only do children and young people want to have the opportunity to express their views, but they want to see actions after feedback has been given and they want to be kept informed about what happens as a result. If actions cannot be taken, they would like an explanation to help them understand why not.

WHAT CHILDREN SAYTHEY NEED FROM THE ADULTS RESPONSIBLE FOR THEIR WELFARE

- vigilance: to have adults notice when things are troubling them

- understanding and action: to understand what is happening; to be heard and understood; and to have that understanding acted upon

- stability: to be able to develop an ongoing, stable relationship of trust with those helping them

- respect: to be treated with the expectation that they are competent rather than not

- information and engagement: to be informed about and involved in procedures, decisions, concerns and plans

- explanation: to be informed of the outcome of assessments and about decisions and reasons when their views have not met with a positive response

- support: to be provided with support in their own right as well as a member of their family

- advocacy: to be provided with advocacy to assist them in putting forward their views.

(HM Government 2015, p.11)

Key findings

The following is a summary of key findings from the research with children and young people about neglect:

- Children and young people's definitions of neglect are broader than ours and include a wider spectrum of harm and adverse experiences. They also encompass aspects of care that adults might not attach the same significance to.

- Children and young people are less likely to draw distinctions between types of abuse and neglect than adults. This may be because they see all forms of abuse as including a neglectful experience for the child.

- For children and young people as for adults, recognition of neglect as a distinct form of maltreatment seems to be harder than it is with other forms of abuse.

- Recognition of neglect amongst peers seems likely to be increasingly possible from the age of eight onwards, but those experiencing neglect may find it hard to recognise in themselves. From the age of 11 or 12, children are increasingly able to compare their own experiences with those of their peers.

- Few studies have examined what children and young people themselves say about the impact of neglect and which aspects affect them most. Messages from studies with children whose parents misuse substances/have mental health problems, and studies with young runaways and young carers, some of whom may also have experienced neglect describe a range of emotional, social and physical impacts, some very serious (see also Chapter 7).

- The ways in which neglect impacts upon children vary according to their age. Babies and young children are clearly very vulnerable, but it should not be assumed that children become more resilient as they get older.

- Children often do not disclose neglect and are less likely to disclose neglect than other forms of abuse. Disabled children are particularly likely to find it difficult to recognise and disclose neglect.

- Research (mainly with children referred to children's social care services or who have experienced other forms of abuse) suggests that barriers to disclosure may differ depending on age/ability, but include fear, lack of confidence and concerns/ lack of control over what might happen next. Even when children and young people do disclose maltreatment, this may not always lead to help.

- Family and friends can play an important role in supporting children and young people to come forward when they are experiencing neglect. However, confiding in family and friends is not straightforward and young people's experiences may not always be positive.

- Neglect may be the root cause of young people displaying emotional or behavioural problems or anti-social behaviour so it is important that adults look beyond the immediately presenting behaviours to the experiences that may underlie them.

- Because they may not be able to come forward to talk to professionals about neglect, children and young people want caring adults to notice signs of neglect and take a more active interest in them.

- Children and young people want a supportive, trusting relationship with a safe and skilled adult (usually a social worker) who can help them through their experiences.

- Children and young people say they want information about neglect and about decisions that are being taken as they go through the child protection process.

Research gaps

The following summarise the key areas for further work:

- involving children themselves as researchers, as well as children being the 'subjects' of research by adults – involving children can make the research more authentic and the findings more relevant to them and their needs

- improving our understanding of how children define neglect would help improve communication between children and adults and ensure the use of a shared language

- understanding difficulties for children in recognising neglect, in order to help educate children and young people

- understanding why children and young people, including those with disabilities, are unlikely to disclose experiences of neglect and how they can be supported to disclose experiences

- research on children's views about the specific ways neglect can impact on children and young people and which parental behaviours or specific circumstances children think have the most negative impact in the short and long term

- understanding how age, gender, culture, disability and economic circumstances can influence children's experiences of neglect and short- and long-term outcomes

- longitudinal studies of cohorts of children and young people who have experienced neglect are needed in order to see what leads to positive outcomes in the long term (especially important with older children and children with disabilities)

- evaluating current practice and highlighting good practice examples of what works on how to involve children and young people who have experienced neglect more effectively in decisions regarding their care and protection.

Does policy reflect research with children and young people?

In recent years, there has undoubtedly been wider recognition of the potential impact of neglect on children and young people and there have been steps forward in relation to incorporating some of the above findings into safeguarding policy. For example, Children's Commissioners across the UK have undertaken work which has focused on promoting participation of children and young people, some of whom will have experienced neglect. For example, research undertaken by the Children's Commissioner for England as well as some of the work quoted above has been fed into the Munro Review of child protection, giving children a direct opportunity to be heard by Government (Munro 2011).

This review also reflected some of the findings from research that we have discussed above. Government guidance for all professionals who come into contact with children and young people (HM Government 2015, p.33) also draws on this work, stating that for services to be effective they should be based on a clear understanding of the needs and views of children:

> children want to be respected, their views to be heard, to have stable relationships with professionals built on trust and to have consistent support provided for their individual needs. This should guide the behaviour of professionals. Anyone working with children should see and speak to the child; listen to what they say; take their views seriously; and work with them collaboratively when deciding how to support their needs.

Children should be provided with 'honest and accurate information' about professional views of their current situation as well as about future possible plans and actions. However, guidance does not state that information in written or other media as appropriate should be provided to children; so its implementation may rely on the ability of individual professionals to be able to communicate complex information effectively to the child and the individual child's ability to retain it.

There has been an increasing policy focus over the last decade on the impact of maltreatment experienced in the early years following research findings about early brain development and the impact of neglect in the first three years of life (Allen 2011). With this focus on the early years has also come a drive to intervene early to support all ages of children to ensure that they have the best possible chance to fulfil their potential (see HM Government 2015).

Financial constraints in public sector work mean it is even tougher for social workers and other professionals to offer the direct work and other services needed by neglected children and their families. In 2012, 29 per cent of professionals surveyed felt spending cuts had made it more difficult to intervene in cases of child neglect. This increased to 35 per cent in 2013. They say that there is 'a sense among all professional groups surveyed that spending cuts will make it more difficult to intervene in the future' (Action for Children 2014, p.28).

One result of these pressures has been even less focus on the needs of adolescents (Gorin and Jobe 2013). The tensions have been recognised by the Children's Commissioner for England:

> claims for maximum effectiveness for early intervention can emphasise providing services at the earliest stages of life rather than for older children but there are powerful arguments for meeting the needs of older children at an earlier stage. Austerity measures and cuts to local authority and health budgets bring these areas of debate into sharp focus. (Cossar *et al.* 2013, p.i)

In 2012, a Government Education Select Committee undertook a review which focused on neglect and adolescents which recommended that 'the Government urgently review the support offered by the child protection system to older children and consult on proposals for re-shaping services to meet the needs of this very vulnerable group' (House of Commons 2012, p.86).

Does practice reflect these findings?

The last report of the Munro Review (2011) highlighted just how positive an impact professionals can have on children's lives when they can find time to spend with them and keep a clear focus on their needs. The Ofsted report (2012) with disabled children highlights the following example of good practice:

> One LSCB had consulted disabled children on their understanding of what safeguarding and child protection meant to them. From this it emerged that they did not know about sexual abuse and neglect and all had absolute trust in adults. This highlighted their vulnerability to abuse. This work informed the development of an intimate care policy and the children's views have been included in training on safeguarding disabled children. (p.21)

New methods of assessment such as Signs of Safety and the Graded Care Profile (the latter is designed to assess neglect – see NSPCC 2015b) are increasingly being tested and introduced in local authorities. These should mean that more neglected children are identified more swiftly, spoken to directly and involved in plans about their care. A report on the use of the Signs of Safety model in child protection (Bunn 2013) found that professionals thought that children and young people were being more involved in processes that affect them and that the use of this approach helped them to build the relationships which are so crucial to disclosure and safety. In particular the tools used with children in the Signs of Safety model have been found to be useful in giving children information about what has happened to them and why child protection services have been involved. They have helped family members communicate with each other, and created opportunities to ensure the child's voice has been heard (see Chapter 8).

Despite positive steps such as these, the Munro Review and Ofsted reports (2012 and 2014) concluded that individual professional practice remains too variable. Studies with children and young people who have experience of the child protection process consistently highlight low levels of participation in decisions about their care and the often difficult experiences of those who do participate (Buckley *et al.* 2011; Cossar, Brandon and Jordan 2011; Cossar *et al.* 2014; Woolfson *et al.* 2010). A review of how local authorities consult with children and young people found that all the participating authorities felt they needed to improve their understanding of children and young people's views and aspired to improving the way they reflected them in their practice (Godar 2013).

The Office of the Children's Commissioner (OCC) in England reported on research undertaken with children and young people with disabilities (OCC 2014b) that they find it hard to get their views heard and taken seriously and feel they have little autonomy over decisions that affect their lives. A scoping report by Stalker et al. (2010) found that disabled children were seldom involved in case conferences and there was little evidence of independent advocates being used to seek or represent children's views. They include in their report the following quote from an inspector who is reporting a social worker as stating: 'Well of course it wasn't really my job to make a relationship with [a disabled child]. I was only looking at the care plan so I didn't meet her because the adults thought everything was going ok' (Stalker *et al.* 2010, p.17).

Whilst some children may actively decide they do not wish to be involved in decision-making, those children who do are dependent upon the skills, commitment and real-time capacity of professionals involved to weigh up the extent to which they involve the child, how they involve the child and the weight they place on the child's view. Cossar *et al.* (2014) question what happens to the child if, for example, their views about what is in their best interests conflict with those of professionals' views? This highlights just how vital good quality relationships between social workers and children are in changing circumstances.

Raising awareness and understanding of neglect with children, families and professionals is a real priority. The House of Commons Education Select Committee report (2012) recognised 'considerable work to be done by central and local agencies in raising awareness amongst children of the nature of abuse and how it might affect them' (House of Commons 2012, p.5). More information for children and young people about neglect is needed on a wide scale and in a variety of formats and media (see websites for children's charities such as the NSPCC and Action for Children[2]). Information for professionals about neglect is also crucial, as is the time for them to be able to study it as part of their workload. Action for Children with Stirling University have produced a resource pack available on the Action for Children website (see Burgess *et al.* 2013) and multiagency training materials (Department for Education (DfE) 2012).

Practice, policy, research: Action needed
Practice implications

- All professionals working with children and young people need to be aware that neglect is more difficult for children to define, recognise in themselves and disclose to others than other forms of abuse. Practitioners need to be particularly aware of vigilance when working with disabled children and older children, as they may experience different barriers to recognition and disclosure than younger children.

- Hard copy information (not just on websites) needs to be available for young people who are suffering from neglect and also for peers who are trying to assist their friends with disclosure/talking about neglect.

- Local authorities need to develop systems for children to self-refer if they have concerns about neglect and abuse.

---

2   www.nspcc.org.uk; www.actionforchildren.org.uk

- All professionals, but especially social workers, need to receive training on communicating with all children and young people (including those with disabilities) and practical advice on developing relationships with them. A good-practice guide that gives examples of strategies to use with children and young people if they find them difficult to engage with would be useful.

- Social workers and other professionals working directly with children must be given the time and training to consider the messages from research with children and think about ways they can incorporate children's views into their work.

- A series of short evidence-based summaries of research that are aimed at social workers working with neglected children would be really helpful. These need to summarise the research findings and highlight how social workers can use the findings in their everyday work with families.

- All local authorities should develop a charter or pledge about children and young people's participation that sets out what children and young people can expect from social workers and other professionals and from their care plans, and is signed by the Director of Children's Services (see OCC 2014a).

- Local authorities should find ways to incorporate neglected children's views into all aspects of relevant work, for example, the development of strategy and planning of local services, especially in relevant services such as family support services, voluntary services working with vulnerable teenagers and advocacy.

- Schools have a vital role to play in helping to raise awareness of what neglect is, how to recognise it and who to talk to about it.

- National good practice guidance for professionals should be developed (in partnership with children) on involving neglected children and young people in their care, with examples of what works.

Policy implications

- Develop a national strategy on neglect in partnership with children and young people that uses the messages from research, such as incorporating children's definitions and understandings, and highlights the centrality of eliciting the child's views.

- Develop a national working group on neglect (that includes children and young people) to map and coordinate work on neglect and act as a central body for disseminating good practice and developing national information for children and young people. This should have a particular focus on ensuring that this information is accessible to all disabled children.

- Develop more detailed definitions and/or descriptors of neglect that recognise how neglect can affect children of different ages and abilities.

- Run a public awareness campaign to raise the awareness of adults and children about neglect, addressing what neglect is, how to recognise it and how/who to approach to disclose concerns.

- Act on the messages from the House of Commons' (2012) report that calls for a review of the support offered by the child protection system to older children and consult on proposals for reshaping services to meet their needs.

- Undertake a review on the neglect of children over age ten (research, policy and practice) and how it is best prevented and addressed.

- More research and evaluation of what works for neglected children needs to be undertaken urgently, including the use of different approaches with different age groups.

Conclusions

All too often, issues that affect children are defined solely by adults. This chapter has discussed evidence that children want a relationship of trust, on an individual basis, with a supportive and competent adult, and that this is likely to be hugely preventive and protective. The chapter also provides evidence that children and young people are more than capable of contributing their views in an insightful and clear way; that they can have different perspectives to those of adults; and that these can inform and improve practice, policy and research. These are all areas, we argue, that potentially are far more relevant and impactful with the systematic input of young service recipients' views. This potential merits being realised in service design and implementation by directly involving children and young people themselves.

Key learning points

- Children and young people experience a wide variety of neglectful parental behaviour and their priorities and concerns may not be the same as those of adults. It is important to talk directly to each individual child and to understand her or his particular views and experiences.

- There are many barriers to disclosure for children and young people; they differ according to the child's age, confidence, abilities and circumstances. All who work with children and young people need to actively and sensitively approach those about whom they have concerns, or seek advice, but not simply wait for them to disclose neglect.

- All neglected children and young people can benefit from developing a relationship of trust with an adult who has the skills to help support them; they should all have this opportunity.

Questions for reflection

- How could professionals and those working with children and young people involve them more directly in the work they do for and with them?

- What ways could be used to ask children and young people who may be neglected about their experiences and what affects them or matters most to them?

- What ideas or approaches might best help children and young people to recognise and/or talk about neglect?

References

Action for Children (2014) *Child Neglect: The Scandal That Never Breaks*. Watford: Action for Children.

Adamson, J. and Templeton, L. (2012) *Silent Voices. Supporting Children and Young People Affected by Parental Substance Misuse*. London: Office of the Children's Commissioner for England.

Alderson, P. (2005) 'Designing Ethical Research with Children.' In A. Farrall (ed.) *Ethical Research with Children*. Maidenhead: Open University Press.

Allard, A. (2003) *'The End of My Tether': The Unmet Support Needs of Families with Teenagers – A Scandalous Gap in Provision*. London: Action for Children.

Allen, G. (2011) *Early Intervention: The Next Steps*. London: HM Government.

Allnock, D. and Miller, P. (2013) *No One Noticed, No One Heard: A Study of Disclosures of Child Abuse*. London: NSPCC.

Baginsky, M. (2001) (ed.) *Counselling and Support Services for Young People Aged 12–16 Who Have Experienced Sexual Abuse*. London: NSPCC.

Bancroft, A., Wilson, S., Cunningham-Burley, S., Backett-Milburn, K. and Masters, H. (2004) *Parental Drug and Alcohol Misuse. Resilience and Transition among Young People*. York: Joseph Rowntree Foundation.

Brandon, M., Bailey, S., Belderson, P. and Larsson, B. (2013) *Neglect and Serious Case Reviews. A Report from the University of East Anglia Commissioned by the NSPCC*. London: NSPCC.

Brownlie, J., Anderson, S. and Ormston, R. (2006) *Children as Researchers*. Edinburgh: Scottish Executive Social Research.

Buckley, H., Carr, N. and Whelan, S. (2011) '"Like walking on eggshells": services user views and expectations of the child protection system.' *Child and Family Social Work* 16, 101–110.

Bunn, A. (2013) *Signs of Safety in England. An NSPCC Commissioned Report on the Signs of Safety Model in Child Protection*. London: NSPCC.

Burgess, C., Daniel, B., Scott, J., Dobbin, H., Mulley, K. and Whitfield, E. (2014) *Preventing Child Neglect in the UK: What Makes Services Accessible to Children and Families? An Annual Review by Action for Children in Partnership with the University of Stirling*. Watford: Action for Children.

Burgess, C., Daniel, B., Whitfield, E., Derbyshire, D. and Taylor, J. (2013) *Action on Neglect: A Resource Pack*. University of Stirling, Action for Children and University of Dundee.

Butler, I. and Williamson, H. (1994) *Children Speak: Children, Trauma and Social Work*. Essex: Longman.

Chan, Y., Lam, G. and Shae, W. (2011) 'Children's views on child abuse and neglect: findings from an exploratory study with Chinese children in Hong Kong.' *Child Abuse & Neglect 35*, 162–172.

Cleaver, H., Nicholson, D., Tarr, S. and Cleaver, D. (2006) *The Response of Child Protection Practices and Procedures to Children Exposed to Domestic Violence or Parental Substance Misuse: Executive Summary*. London: Department for Education and Skills.

Clifton, J. (2014) *Children and Young People Giving Feedback on Services for Children in Need: Ideas from a Participation Programme*. London: The Office of the Children's Commissioner for England.

Cossar, J., Brandon, M., Bailey, S., Belderson, P., Biggart, L. and Sharpe, D. (2013) *'It Takes a Lot to Build Trust.' Recognition and Telling: Developing Earlier Routes to Help for Children and Young People.* London: Office of the Children's Commissioner.

Cossar, J., Brandon, M. and Jordan, P. (2011) *'Don't Make Assumptions': Children and Young People's Views of the Child Protection System and Messages for Change.* University of East Anglia with Office of the Children's Commissioner.

Cossar, J., Brandon, M. and Jordan, P. (2014) '"You've got to trust her and she's got to trust you": children's views on participation in the child protection system.' *Child & Family Social Work 21,* 1, 103–112. DOI: 10.1111/cfs.12115

Coy, M. (2009) '"Moved around like bags of rubbish nobody wants": how multiple placement moves can make young women vulnerable to sexual exploitation.' *Child Abuse Review 18,* 4, 254–266.

Daniel, B., Taylor, J. and Scott, J. (2010) 'Recognition of neglect and early response: overview of a systematic review of the literature.' *Child and Family Social Work 1,* 2, 248–257.

Department for Education (2012) *Childhood Neglect: Training Resources.* London: DfE. Available at www.gov.uk/government/collections/childhood-neglect-training-resources, accessed on 18 May 2016.

Farmer, E. and Lutman, E. (2010) *Case Management and Outcomes for Neglected Children Returned to Their Parents: A Five Year Follow-up Study.* Bristol: School for Policy Studies, University of Bristol.

Freake, H., Barley, V. and Kent, G. (2007) 'Adolescents' view of helping professionals: a review of the literature.' *Journal of Adolescence 30,* 639–653.

Godar, R. (2013) 'Understanding Performance in Child Protection: How Local Authorities Are Responding to the Munro Review. A Summary for Policymakers.' Based on a dissertation submitted as part of an MSc in Policy Research at the University of Bristol.

Gorin, S. (2004) *Understanding What Children Say: Children's Experiences of Domestic Violence, Parental Substance Misuse and Parental Health Problems.* London: National Children's Bureau for the Joseph Rowntree Foundation.

Gorin, S. and Jobe, A. (2013) 'Young people who have been maltreated – different needs: different responses?' *British Journal of Social Work 43,* 7, 1330–1346.

Hanson, E. and Holmes, D. (2014) *That Difficult Age: Developing a More Effective Response to Risks in Adolescence.* Totnes: Research in Practice.

Hill, M. (1999) 'What's the problem? Who can help? The perspectives of children and young people on their well-being and on helping professionals.' *Journal of Social Work Practice 13,* 2, 136–145.

HM Government (2015) *Working Together to Safeguard Children. A Guide to Inter-agency Working to Safeguard and Promote the Welfare of Children.* London: DfE. Available at www.gov.uk/government/publications/working-together-to-safeguard-children--2, accessed on 2 October 2015.

Holland, S. and Scourfield, J. (2004) 'Liberty and respect in child protection.' *British Journal of Social Work 34,* 21–36.

Hooper, C.A., Gorin, S., Cabral, C. and Dyson, C. (2007) *Living with Hardship 24/7: The Diverse Experiences of Families in Poverty in England.* London: The Frank Buttle Trust.

House of Commons Education Committee (2012) *Children First: The Child Protection System in England. Fourth Report of Session 2012–2013.* London: The Stationery Office.

INVOLVE (2012) *Briefing Notes for Researchers: Involving the Public in NHS, Public Health and Social Care Research.* Eastleigh: INVOLVE.

Jobe, A. and Gorin, S. (2013) "'If kids don't feel safe they don't do anything": young people's views on being referred to children's social care services in England.' *Child and Family Social Work 18*, 429–438.

Jones, D.P.H. (2003) *Communicating with Vulnerable Children. A Guide for Practitioners.* London: Gaskell.

Leeson, C. (2007) 'My life in care: experiences of non-participation in decision-making processes.' *Child and Family Social Work 12*, 268–277.

Lloyd-Smith, M. and Tarr, J. (2000) 'Researching Children's Perspectives: A Sociological Dimension.' In A. Lewis and G. Lindsay (eds) *Researching Children's Perspectives.* Buckingham: Open University Press.

McLeod, A. (2007) 'Whose agenda? Issues of power and relationship when listening to looked-after young people.' *Child & Family Social Work 12*, 278–286.

McLeod, A. (2010) '"A friend and an equal": do young people in care seek the impossible from their social workers?' *British Journal of Social Work 40*, 772–788.

Miller, D. and Brown, J. (2014) *'We Have the Right to Be Safe': Protecting Disabled Children from Abuse.* London: NSPCC.

Morrow, V. (2005) 'Ethical Issues in Collaborative Research with Children.' In A. Farrall (ed.) *Ethical Research with Children.* Maidenhead: Open University Press.

Munro, E. (2001) 'Empowering looked after children.' *Child and Family Social Work 6*, 129–138.

Munro, E. (2011) *The Munro Review of Child Protection: Final Report. A Child-centred System.* London: Department for Education.

NSPCC (2015a) *Hurting Inside: NSPCC Report on the Learning from the NSPCC Helpline and ChildLine on Neglect.* London: NSPCC. Available at www.nspcc.org.uk/globalassets/ documents/research-reports/hurting-inside-helpline-childline-neglect.pdf, accessed on 5 June 2015.

NSPCC (2015b) Evaluation of the Graded Care Profile. London: NSPCC. Available at www.nspcc.org.uk/services-and-resources/services-for-children-and-families/ graded-care-profile/graded-care-profile-evidence-impact-and-evaluation, accessed on 5 June 2016.

Office of the Children's Commissioner (2014a) *Participation Strategy. June 2014–May 2015.* London: Office of the Children's Commissioner.

Office of the Children's Commissioner (2014b) *'They Still Need to Listen More': A Report about Disabled Children and Young People's Rights in England.* London: Office of the Children's Commissioner.

Ofsted (Office of Standards in Education, Children's Services and Skills) (2012) *Protecting Disabled Children* (120122). Manchester: Ofsted.

Ofsted (Office of Standards in Education, Children's Services and Skills) (2014) *In the Child's Time: Professional Response to Neglect.* Manchester: Ofsted.

Osbourne, D. (2001) 'Abused young people's views of adult intervention: an Irish study.' *Social Work in Europe 8*, 1, 11–21.

Peled, E. and Cohavi, A, (2009) 'The meaning of running away for girls.' *Child Abuse & Neglect 33*, 10, 739–749.

Radford, L., Corral, S., Bradley, C., Fisher, H., *et al.* (2011) *Child Abuse and Neglect in the UK today.* London: NSPCC.

Raws, P. (2015) 'Neglect of Adolescents at Home: Some New Research.' In *The Children's Society Too Old, Too Young?* London: The Children's Society.

Rees, G. and Lee, J. (2005) *Still Running 2: Findings from the Second National Survey of Young Runaways.* London: The Children's Society.

Rees, G., Gorin, S., Jobe, A., Stein, M., Medforth, R. and Goswami, H. (2010) *Safeguarding Young People: Responding to Young People aged 11 to 17 Who Are Maltreated.* London: The Children's Society.

Rees, G., Stein, M., Hicks, L. and Gorin, S. (2011) *Adolescent Neglect. Research, Policy and Practice.* London: Jessica Kingsley Publishers.

Safe on the Streets Research Team (1999) *Still Running. Children on the Streets in the UK.* London: The Children's Society.

Shaw, C., Brady, L-M. and Davey, C. (2011) *Guidelines for Research with Children and Young People.* London: National Children's Bureau.

Smith, C.A., Ireland, T.O. and Thornberry, T.P. (2005) 'Adolescent maltreatment and its impact on young adult antisocial behaviour.' *Child Abuse & Neglect 29,* 10, 1099– 1119.

Stalker, K., Green Lister, P., Lerpiniere, J. and McArthur, K. (2010) *Child Protection and the Needs and Rights of Disabled Children and Young People: A Scoping Study.* University of Strathclyde.

Taylor, J., Cameron, A., Jones, C., Franklin, A., Stalker, K. and Fry, D. (2015) *Deaf and Disabled Children Talking about Child Protection.* University of Edinburgh/NSPCC Child Protection Research Centre.

Thrane, L.E., Hoyt, D.R., Whitbeck, L.B. and Yoder, K.A. (2006) 'Impact of family abuse on running away, deviance, and street victimization amongst homeless rural and urban youth.' *Child Abuse & Neglect 30,* 10, 1117–1128.

Trinder, L. (1997) 'Competing constructions of childhood: children's rights and wishes in divorce.' *Journal of Social Welfare and Family Law 19,* 291–305.

Turney, D., Platt, D., Selwyn, J. and Farmer, E. (2011) *Social Work Assessment of Children in Need: What Do We Know? Messages from Research.* DFE-RBX-10-08. London: Department for Education.

United Nations (1989) *United Nations Convention on the Rights of the Child (UNCRC).* Geneva: United Nations.

Vincent, S. and Daniel, B. (2004) 'An analysis of children and young people's calls to ChildLine about abuse and neglect: a study for the Scottish Child Protection Review.' *Child Abuse Review 13,* 2, 158.

Wales, A., Gillian, E., Hill, L. and Robertson, F. (2009) *Untold Damage: Children's Accounts of Living with Harmful Parental Drinking.* Edinburgh: Scottish Health Action on Alcohol Problems.

Welsh Government (2016) *Care and support in Wales is changing: the Social Services and Well-being (Wales) Act gives you more say in your services: I am a young person, what does this mean for me?* http://gov.wales/docs/dhss/publications/160330younginfoen.pdf, accessed 30 May 2016.

Willow, C. (2009) 'Putting Children and Their Rights at the Heart of the Safeguarding Process.' In H. Cleaver, P. Cawson, S. Gorin and S. Walker, (eds) (2009) *Safeguarding Children: A Shared Responsibility.* Chichester, West Sussex: Wiley.

Woolfson, R.C., Heffernan, E., Paul, M. and Brown, M. (2010) 'Young people's views of the child protection system in Scotland.' *British Journal of Social Work 40,* 2069–2085.

6

GENERAL PRACTITIONERS' RESPONSES TO CHILD NEGLECT

The facilitating role of healthcare needs

Jenny Woodman

Introduction

This chapter addresses the actual and potential role of general practitioners (GPs) in relation to neglected children and young people and their families. It is based on a study of 14 GPs and a further four primary healthcare professionals from four sites in England who were interviewed in 2011 about their experiences of families which prompted 'maltreatment-related concerns'. Interviewees were asked to choose up to three families with whom they had been involved and tell the story of the concern and their professional involvement. A total of 37 families were discussed by the 18 professionals. The narratives of GPs' concerns about the families were remarkably consistent across the interviews, with four types of story emerging, described in detail below with examples. Overwhelmingly, the concerns were about child neglect.

The chapter reports how the GPs described the families and the characteristics of neglect which appeared to motivate them to act on their concerns. Neglected children and young people and families with high health need who visited the GP practice prompted GPs to remain involved and offered the greatest opportunities for GPs to build trust, reciprocal relationships and engagement with the parents, which in turn allowed the GPs to offer a range of supportive responses directly to these families. These supportive responses included proactively monitoring parents, coaching parents to change their perspective and behaviour, advocating for families by helping them navigate other public services and providing opportune healthcare to children.

In this chapter, these responses are referred to as 'direct' responses to children, young people and families.

Based on this small and in-depth qualitative study, neglectful families with high health need and help-seeking behaviour might be one particular group for whom GPs have an appropriate ongoing therapeutic role involving direct responses to children and young people and, perhaps most commonly, to their parents. This group may include children and young people judged to be 'in need', those receiving child protection services and those assessed to be below the threshold for services from children's social care. These hypotheses raise many questions, not least about the effectiveness and safety of the direct responses that the GPs described, how GPs might work jointly with children's services if and when they respond directly to families who prompt concerns about neglect, and how the answers to these questions vary according to the severity of welfare problems and current level of need in the family. Further research is needed but is only likely to be funded when policy-makers fully recognise that direct responses by GPs might be appropriate for some children, young people and families who prompt concerns about maltreatment. A good place to start further exploration of direct responses by GPs might be in relation to a subset of neglectful families with high health need and health-seeking behaviour.

Overview of general practice and GPs in England

For most people in England, the GP practice is the first place to go with a health problem. Like all National Health Service (NHS) services it is free at the point of use, meaning patients do not have to pay to see their GP. GP practices in England have large numbers of registered patients, with an average of approximately 7000 registered patients of all ages and approximately 1600 registered children and young people under 19 years old (Health and Social Care Information Centre 2015). A full-time GP sees on average approximately a hundred patients a week, the large majority in face-to-face consultations but with increasing numbers of telephone consultations and a very small number of home visits (The Information Centre for Health and Social Care 2007). On average, face-to-face consultations last just over ten minutes and telephone consultations about seven minutes (The Information Centre for Health and Social Care 2007).

It is widely accepted that general practice in England is under great pressure from falling funding, workforce problems, and the growing needs and rising expectations of an older, sicker population as well as increasing expectations about its remit (Dayan *et al.* 2014). These problems manifest as closures of GP practices, difficulties for patients in getting timely appointments and/or seeing the GP they prefer, and GP burn-out and desire to leave the profession (Dayan *et al.* 2014).

Despite these problems and a history of being described as disengaged from child protection (Woodman *et al.* 2014b), GPs have the potential to play an important role for neglected children, young people and their families. We know from research that GPs are already aware of very large numbers of children and young people with maltreatment-related problems. In a study using a large representative sample of electronic GP records from the UK, we found that 0.8 per cent of children and young people had a maltreatment-related code entered into their record in 2010 (Woodman *et al.* 2012b). A look at the community incidence of maltreatment tells us that identification and recording can undoubtedly be improved: there is a big gap between the 0.8 per cent of children and young people with a maltreatment-related code in their record and the 4–10 per cent of children and young people each year who are suffering maltreatment from parents or carers, based on studies using self-reports and parent reports (Gilbert *et al.* 2009a; Radford *et al.* 2011). Some of these children and young people will not come into contact with a GP over the course of a year. In other cases, the large gap will be explained by a combination of GPs failing to identify the problems and/or not coding them in the child's record (Woodman *et al.* 2012a).

Extrapolating from the study of recording in GP records (Woodman *et al.* 2012b), there are a minimum of 90,000 children and young people with maltreatment-related problems known to GP practices in England. There is clear potential for GPs to use their routine and repeated contact with children and their parents and other family members to respond to the large numbers of children whose problems are already known to them. If GP identification of problems relating to child maltreatment is improved, the number of children and young people to whom GPs can respond will be even greater. There are no estimates of how often GPs identify and respond to different types of maltreatment, such as neglect.

How should GPs be responding to neglected children, young people and their families?

English policy and practice guidance

Like all professionals within the health, education and justice systems, GPs have a professional duty to identify neglect, make referrals to children's social care, share information with children's social care and contribute to enquiries, processes and procedures initiated by children's social care (Children Act 1989; Children Act 2004; General Medical Council 2012; HM Government 2015; NICE 2009; RCGP and NSPCC 2014). Referrals to children's social care should be made when a professional is concerned that a child may have complex needs and require extra services to meet their full potential (a 'child in need') or when they are suffering 'significant harm' due to abuse or neglect (HM Government 2015). A child may be in need due to maltreatment, including neglect, or for other reasons such as disability. Of the 397,630 children in England who were receiving child in need services at 31 March 2014, 47 per cent were receiving these services due to 'abuse and neglect', compared to 13 per cent who were in need due to their own or parental disability (Department for Education 2014). The concept of 'significant harm' revolves around establishing whether the child's health or development has been impaired or is likely to be impaired due to abuse or neglect, compared to what might reasonably be expected of another similar child (HM Government 2015). Establishing the threshold for significant harm in individual cases depends to some extent on professional judgement. Statutory guidance for professionals states that such judgements should take into account the nature and severity of abuse, premeditation, impact on the child's health and development, parental capacity to meet the child's needs and the child's wider social environment (HM Government 2015). A child judged to be suffering or at risk of suffering significant harm will receive child protection services from children's social care (HM Government 2015). GPs are required to share information about a child or young person with children's social care and other agencies, including without consent from that young person or parent, where there are concerns about significant harm (HM Government 2015).

Like other professionals who come into contact with children, such as teachers, early years workers or health visitors, GPs also have a role to play in making sure children get early preventive help before they reach thresholds for child in need or child protection interventions. The policy concepts of early help, child in need and child protection are designed to allow services to respond to the spectrum of need in children, young people and families and adopt a preventive as well as reactive approach to all forms of child maltreatment (HM Government 2015). GPs are specifically named as professionals who can take on a 'lead professional' role for children needing early help from multiple agencies (HM Government 2015). The lead professional role for children needing early help is only briefly defined in policy; it consists of undertaking an early help needs assessment, and going on to 'provide support to the child and family, act as an advocate on their behalf and coordinate the delivery of support services' (HM Government 2015, p.14). Professionals can undertake early help assessments using, for example, the Common Assessment Framework (HM Government 2013). As Eileen Munro points out in her Review of Child Protection in England (Munro 2011), the phrase 'the Common Assessment Framework' is used to describe both the policy of encouraging integrated professional work to provide early help and the form that has been developed by government to help professionals conduct a holistic needs assessment.

As well as restating expectations laid out in policy documents, professional practice guidance for GPs published by medical governing bodies, councils and royal colleges provide more detailed guidance on the GP's role for maltreated children, young people and families. Practice guidance encourages all health professionals, including GPs, who see adult patients to enquire about children and consider the impact of the problems they are treating (e.g. mental health problems) on their patient's capacity to parent and on the child (General Medical Council 2012; NICE 2014; RCPCH 2014; RCGP and NSPCC 2014). It envisages an ongoing role of proactive review and follow-up (monitoring) of children and young people with known concerns about maltreatment or risk factors such as parental substance misuse (Royal College of General Practitioners et al. 2014) or those who miss important appointments (Royal College of Paediatrics and Child Health 2014), including those who do not meet thresholds for referral to children's social care (NICE 2009; RCGP and NSPCC 2014). The National Institute for Health and Clinical Excellence (NICE) acknowledges the high thresholds for referral to children's social care and provides advice for all health professionals on when to 'consider' maltreatment, requiring recording, information gathering, discussion with colleagues and follow-up, and when to 'suspect' maltreatment, requiring referral to children's social care (NICE 2009). An update to the NICE guidance is due to be published in 2017. GPs are also expected to monitor and follow up referrals they make to children's social care (General Medical Council 2012).

It is well established now that all health professionals, including GPs, should also record concerns about maltreatment, including minor ones, in order that they can build up a cumulative picture and have information readily available to share with other agencies (General Medical Council 2012; NICE 2009; RCGP and NSPCC 2014). This is especially important for GPs who hold the health record for the child, which should act as a repository of all health-related information.

In more recent guidance, there is evidence of a shift in practice guidance towards all health professionals taking an ongoing and therapeutic role directly with vulnerable and maltreated children, young people and families (General Medical Council 2012; NICE 2014). This role is most clearly laid out by the Royal College of GPs (RCGP) which has specifically highlighted the potential for GPs to take on this type of role for *neglected* children and young people and their families (RCGP and NSPCC 2014). The RCGP describes this role as managing and treating parental mental health conditions, addictions or chronic ill health with the consequence of improving circumstances for a neglected child, and recommends that GPs consider measures to enhance parental competence and social support for parents (RCGP and NSPCC 2014, p.33).

The focus on GPs' potential to intervene directly with *neglect* (rather than other forms of abuse) is likely to be explained by three factors. First, GPs might be seeing more neglect than other forms of abuse because it is more common in the general population (Gilbert *et al.* 2009b; Radford *et al.* 2011).[1] Second, it is widely reported that children and young people suffering neglect are less likely to get an urgent or proportional response from children's social care than

---

1   The relative frequency of physical, sexual and emotional abuse and neglect depends on the measurement used. Although self and parent report studies largely report neglect as most common, studies relying on the Juvenile Victimisation Questionnaire report neglect to be less common than both emotional and physical abuse. See, for example: Finkelhor, Ormrod and Turner (2009a, 2009b) Radford *et al.* (2011).

children who are (also) suffering physical or sexual abuse (Daniel, Taylor and Scott 2011). For example, in a 2012 survey of 242 social workers, 60 per cent said they felt pressure to 'downgrade' neglect and emotional abuse cases to child in need cases. Fifty-nine per cent said that it was 'quite' or 'very' unlikely that children's social care would respond swiftly to children suffering neglect whilst only 4 per cent said the same about physical abuse (Community Care 2012). A 2013 survey of 600 social workers and managers suggests that thresholds for all child protection responses are rising but particularly so for cases of neglect (Pemberton 2013). A review of 47 cases of child death or serious injury following maltreatment between 2003 and 2005 in England concluded that cases of long-standing neglect rarely met child protection thresholds and, as child in need cases were subject to long waits and de-prioritisation, this could have disastrous consequences (Brandon *et al.* 2008a). This means that universal services such as GPs and teachers are more commonly left to respond to neglected children and those at risk of neglect without input from children's social care. Our research suggests a third possible reason: there are specific characteristics of neglect, especially in relation to a subset of families with high health needs and health-seeking behaviour, who come into contact with GPs and for whom GPs feel motivated and able to respond in an ongoing and therapeutic way. Describing why GPs might feel willing and able to take on this role for this subset of neglected children, young people and their families is the main focus of this chapter. The reasons relate to the (perceived) high thresholds for social care action, the framing of neglect as a 'medical' problem by GPs, the sympathetic way that GPs talked about neglectful mothers and the opportunities provided when parents came to the GP frequently for their own health problems.

In summary, GPs have a professional duty to refer children and young people to children's social care, share information (including breaching patient confidentiality) when thresholds of significant harm are met, and participate in enquiries, interventions and processes led by children's social care as well as record all maltreatment-related concerns in health records. There is also an expectation that GPs should have an ongoing monitoring role for children, young people and families who prompt concerns, and a recent and growing acknowledgement that GPs may have an ongoing and therapeutic role to play in terms of treating parental health conditions that might impact on parenting as well as supporting better parenting generally, especially for neglected children.

An in-depth review of the GP's role as laid out in policy and practice guidance is available in our report, jointly published with the NSPCC, Royal College of GPs and other academic partners (Woodman *et al.* 2014b).

Research

There is relatively little research in a UK setting available to tell us what GPs should do or actually do when they are worried a child may be abused or neglected or at risk of abuse or neglect. Historically, studies have focused on GPs' participation in children's social care processes and (to a lesser extent) participation in multidisciplinary teams to provide children with early help. This research suggests that GPs frequently do not fulfil their referral or cooperation role in relation to child protection and are disengaged from social care processes for early help. A study using 200 consecutive case conferences that took place in 1990 reported that only 11 per cent of invited GPs attended the conference and a similar proportion submitted a written report (Simpson *et al.* 1994). Although GPs have commonly cited lack of notice as a reason for not attending (Polnay 2000), the study did not find any difference in attendance rates when stratified by length of notice given to the GP by children's social care (Simpson *et al.* 1994). Similarly, more recent qualitative studies report that in the eyes of both GPs and other professionals GPs are disengaged from local systems for early identification and prevention of social welfare problems in children (Easton *et al.* 2014). In his evidence to the House of Commons Select Committee, Dr Quirk (a GP) commented that 'the majority of GPs in England would not know what CAF [Common Assessment Framework] stood for and do not use it (House of Commons Education Committee 2012).

We do not know how often GPs in England 'consider' or 'suspect' child maltreatment (see above for explanation of terms) or how often they refer children to children's social care for this reason. Routine data on referrals to children's social care in England are not published with details of referral source and there is an absence of any other data to answer this question.

One further study tells us about how GPs and other professionals in England perceive the GP's role in relation to child protection (Tompsett *et al.* 2010). Between 2006 and 2007, Tompsett and colleagues used a survey, interviews, focus groups and expert consensus to identify four (not mutually exclusive) roles that GPs could adopt in responding to maltreated children:

1. *The case holder.* The GP has an ongoing relationship with the family before, during and after referral to children's social care. This role builds on voluntary disclosure and establishing trust over time with the parents. The role was clearly identified by GPs but not recognised so much by the stakeholders.

2. *The sentinel.* The GP identifies child maltreatment and refers the concern to children's social care or other health services.

3. *The gatekeeper.* The GP provides information to other agencies so that those agencies can make decisions about access to services.

4. *Multiagency team player.* The GP has continued engagement with other professionals outside the practice. This role is fulfilled when the GP contributes actively to children's social care child protection processes.

The concept of the case holder in this study overlaps with expectations of GPs responding directly and therapeutically with neglectful families as laid out in guidance from the RCGP (2014), described above. The other three roles overlap with expectations that a GP should refer, share information where appropriate and working in multiagency teams. These roles are consistently explained in policy and practice guidance, as described above.

The Tompsett study also identified exemplars of good practice following safeguarding concerns. These included involving parents in safeguarding decisions and taking time to make those decisions; being clear with parents about limits of confidentiality; encouraging consultative and reflective practice; sharing information with other professionals; arranging for follow-up of a child when there were ongoing concerns; ensuring that parent and child had a separate GP where there were conflicts of interest; recording concerns; and taking a long-term view. Many of these good-practice recommendations overlap with policy recommendations (see above on the GP's role in policy and practice guidance). The study did not provide detail or context for implementation of these recommendations.

In summary, policy, practice guidance and research all support the expectation that the GP should not only refer concerns about child maltreatment or risk of maltreatment, share information, cooperate with children's social care and work jointly with children's social care and other agencies, but also take on some kind of therapeutic support role for vulnerable families. In policy this support role is envisaged as a 'lead professional' role for children and young people judged to need early help, largely focusing on coordination of services. In practice guidance from the RCGP, it is envisaged as a therapeutic role involving direct responses to *neglectful* families, focusing on improving parenting and managing parental health problems and their impact on children. In Tompsett's study, the support role is seen as 'case-holding', with the focus on relationships with parents and a long-term approach. However, there is little to guide GPs about how exactly they could put into practice any of these supportive roles or any detail about the types of families for whom it might be most appropriate or feasible.

Our study of current practice

In this context, we conducted an interview study with 18 primary healthcare professionals in England, asking them about their current practice. The results from this study provided a more detailed picture of the ways in which GPs might respond directly and therapeutically to children, young people and their parents and identified one group of children and young people for whom these types of responses might be most appropriate and feasible. These are children and young people suffering neglect or at risk of suffering neglect in families with very high parental health need. We describe the methods and results of this study in the following sections.

Methods

One researcher conducted in-depth individual interviews with 14 GPs, two practice nurses and two health visitors from four GP practices in England (18 primary healthcare professionals in total). The practices were recruited from a larger convenience sample of practices already known to the research team (Woodman *et al.* 2012a). Eight of the participants were 'experts', defined as those who held RCGP posts connected to child protection, were named doctors, delivered child protection training, contributed to policy in the area or considered themselves to have a specialist interest in child protection, and there was at least one expert GP in each of the four practices. The participants tended to be experienced health professionals and to have worked for an extended period with their current team: almost two thirds (n=11) reported being qualified for 20 years or more (range 1-40y) and n=10 had worked in their current team for at least ten years (range 6m to 20y). Just over half the respondents were female (n=10) The experience and specialist interest of many of the participants resulted in very rich stories about how they had responded to concerns about abuse and neglect but limited generalisability of results to the 'average' GP in England. The small sample size, while appropriate for in-depth qualitative research, also limits generalisability: the conclusions that we drew from this study were hypotheses that need further testing and exploration.

The interviews took place in 2010–2011 and the researcher elicited narratives by asking participants to choose two or three 'children, young people or families who had prompted maltreatment-related concerns' and describe their concerns and involvement. On average, interviews lasted 50 minutes and consisted of free-ranging discussion. We used thematic analysis with an inductive and interpretive approach (Braun and Clarke 2006; Green and Thorogood 2009). The detailed methods for this study are available elsewhere (Woodman *et al.* 2013; Woodman 2014).

In the 18 interviews, participants discussed a total of 37 families and the 14 GPs spoke about a total of 27 families. This chapter focuses on data from the interviews with the GPs.

The GP interviews were rich in detail and most participants had several cases in mind for the interview. Participants spoke about children and young people, ranging from unborn children to those who were 18 years old. However, only a minority of children discussed were at either end of the age spectrum.

Findings

Types of professional response

There were four types of response described by GPs, which represented specific actions and approaches GPs might use when adopting a therapeutic and supportive role with children and young people who are maltreated or at risk of maltreatment and their families. These are summarised below and described in more detail with quotations (which have been modified to preserve anonymity) in Table 6.1. The GPs described a further three actions: referral to children's social care, recording concerns and multidisciplinary working. As the focus of this chapter is on direct responses to families rather than interactions between GPs and other professionals or record keeping, these are not presented here but can be found in previous publications (see Woodman *et al.* 2013).

MONITORING

Monitoring was described by GPs as keeping a 'watchful eye on families' and being 'a bit more vigilant'. This was achieved through routine contact with children (e.g. at six-week baby checks); by ascertaining information from parents or grandparents when they came in for their own health needs; from the child or parent's health records; or by gathering wider information from colleagues through meetings. Some GPs and both health visitors interviewed thought that the effective monitoring role of the GP could be jeopardised when GPs only had access to health-related information and not to wider information about a family, and there was heavy reliance on health visitors to tell GPs what social workers were thinking or had decided. Not having the whole picture could potentially result in GPs being falsely reassured about a family and underestimating the risk to the child.

ADVOCATING

This was described by GPs as 'making a case' to other agencies on behalf of a child or young person and their family. Examples were writing letters to support claims for benefits; or strongly making the case to the local authority for rehousing the family; or making a case for more/less intervention from children's social care; or trying to improve the relationship between social care and the family. Advocacy was used, for example, where GPs felt that an improved quality of life (relating to housing or poverty) could directly impact on parenting and therefore on child welfare; where GPs felt that children's social care were either not taking the case seriously enough, or were too heavy handed with the family; or where families needed support and encouragement to cooperate with social workers.

COACHING

This was described by GPs as motivating parents by attempting to shift their mindset, encourage parents to take responsibility for their problems and, eventually, to change their behaviours. This was all done through repeated conversations with parents when they came to see GPs, usually for their own health needs. Coaching, as described by the GPs in this sample, incorporates elements common to self-management of chronic disease and motivational interviewing. In both these ways, professionals attempt to motivate patients by encouraging them to take responsibility for their own health. Motivational interviewing has been described as a way of 'chipping away' at the problems which prevent patients taking responsibility for their health and welfare (or their children's) and which act as barriers to behaviour change (Watt 2011). The GPs in our study described how difficult this was, and how they attempted but often failed at achieving improvement for children and young people through coaching parents, although they also described the occasional success.

PROVIDING OPPORTUNE HEALTHCARE

Two GPs spoke of how they undertook 'opportune healthcare' for children when their parents came in about something else. This opportune healthcare was in place of missed routine checks or preventive care, such as developmental checks, well-baby checks or immunisations. The GPs acknowledged that care had to be offered then and there as these families could not be relied on to come back at a later date. The GPs felt this was made easier to achieve when they had something to offer the parent in return, such as help with benefits letters or ability to meet parental health need (see Table 6.1 for more details).

Table 6.1 Summary of 'direct' GP responses to concerns about neglectful families, as described by GPs (adapted from Woodman et al. 2013)

What	How	Why	Context
1. Monitoring: Keeping a 'watchful eye' on families and being 'a bit more vigilant'	– Using routine health checks in children and consultations for health problems by parents to assess wellbeing of children and coping/risk factors in parents (quote A) – Receiving information about parenting from other family members (quote B) – Checking the electronic health records for subsequent presentations to colleagues – Interpreting missed appointments as a possible sign of escalating problems – Using practice meetings about vulnerable families to gather wider information, anticipate stressful or important points in a family's life, such as the birth of a new baby or to gather wider information. Health visitors were essential for meetings to facilitate monitoring	To ascertain whether or not there was relevant information that needed to be passed onto children's social care (in the form of a referral) and whether GPs should enact other strategies – e.g. coaching (see below) Missed appointments could result in a phone call from the GP and, if necessary, a letter and/or discussion in the vulnerable families meeting	When confident that the family would seek help and disclose honest information, GPs felt comfortable with monitoring and risk assessment in 'stable at this point' families Disclosure and help-seeking behaviour in families relied on the GP being seen as a trusted ally (quote C) Some GPs and the two health visitors recognised that GP monitoring was limited due to a lack of information beyond 'health'. GPs relied heavily on health visitors for monitoring

Illustrative quotes from interviews:

A. 'Every time I'd seen them, it's been on my mind and obviously when I did the six-week check on the little baby, we had a good look at him but he… he seemed absolutely fine.' (Participant 5, GP; Family 14; three children, 5 months–3 years)

B. Respondent: 'And the mother just goes off at night, got to go, I got a call from my boyfriend, I'm going clubbing. She'll leave the child.' Interviewer: And how do you know about this? Respondent: Yeah, from the great grandmother. Always great grandmother comes.' (Participant 15, GP; Family 35; 2-year-old child)

C. 'I can keep a watchful eye on the older two girls because I think they will bring them into see me now [now that trust has been established] too.' (Participant 0, GP; Family 3; 4-year-old child with older siblings)

What	How	Why	Context
2. Advocating: 'You've got to stand up and shout for people' (making a case to other agencies on the patient's behalf)	– Supporting requests for improved housing or benefits – Interceding with children's social care to make this agency recognise the seriousness of the family's problems and offer what they considered to be a more appropriate level of service (usually child protection services; quote D) – For other families, interceding with social care to reduce an unnecessarily heavy-handed or insensitive approach and encouraging these families to demonstrate cooperation with children's social care (Quote E)	Improving quality of life (housing, poverty) was perceived as directly impacting on parenting and therefore on child welfare By encouraging compliance, GPs aimed to prevent deterioration in the relationship between the family and social care and help the family access voluntary supportive services	The need to intercede with children's social care was seen as greatest in families whose children have suffered 'terrible neglect' over years but where maltreatment did not pose an immediate threat to the child's physical safety and/or was not as 'barn door' (obvious) as some of the other types of abuse

Illustrative quotes from interviews:

D. 'you always get the feeling the social services are overwhelmed and they have a lot of cases to deal with. And, you know, to a certain extent, if no one is batting on their door and the case is just left in a file until they get picked up again or until somebody starts shouting about them, you know, another one will always take precedence. And I think, you know, you've got to stand up and shout for people, because sadly, in some ways, that's the way they actually begin to take more notice.' (Participant 10, GP; Family 26; 16-year-old child with two younger siblings)

E. '…just trying to encourage her [the mum] that she needed to…just to be open with everybody and keep engaged in the process or it would become even more difficult and just trying to sup…support her to keep in there with the social workers and not…try not to get too cross with them. Um, and I think I managed to do that, um, and in the end they did go to a…some kind of hearing […] They did manage to engage with the social workers and I think I was trying to help them do that really.' (Participant 8, GP; Family 20; 8-year-old)

| 3. Coaching: Motivating and 'activating' of parents by attempting to shift mindset, encourage parents to take responsibility for their problems, and eventually change their behaviours | – Talking to parents, usually the mother, to encourage them to 'look at different ways of thinking about things', such as realising 'that there was actually a problem with the children' or that 'stopping drinking was a good thing'
– Talking to parents, usually the mother, to encourage them to 'change their life' or 'change her behaviours' (Quote F) | A parent's willingness or ability to recognise that there was a problem (in the GP's eyes) seemed to make the difference between situation perceived as hopeful and one perceived as hopeless for the family. Parental (maternal) recognition of the problem was seen as the first step in intervening to improve the child's situation (Quote G) | This was described as a difficult task that was often attempted but infrequently achieved (Quotes H, I and J)
In order to have a hope of changing parental mindset (and eventually behaviour), GPs saw that the parents needed to be engaged with primary care and to see the GP as a trusted ally |

Illustrative quotes from interviews:

F. I was mainly supporting, trying to urge her to change behaviours or look at different ways of thinking about things.' (Participant 2, GP; Family 7; two children aged 2 and 3 years)

G. 'but it does seem that she's beginning to get to the stage now where she appreciates herself that she needs some help [with her drinking], which is, you know, I was quite pleased when that happened because I thought that was a major advance really. And I think we actually might get somewhere in terms of making her better.' (Participant 15, GP; Family 31, children 3 and 7 years)

H. 'I would have liked to have seen them realising that their ability to parent children was not enough to cope with the children that they had. So they kept having children even though they were unable to raise properly the children that – the existing children that they had.' (Participant 4, GP; Family 13; four children, 3–13 years, and six older siblings)

I. 'And actually I'm aware that this family illustrates that not everybody gets better with caring doctor's supporting involvement.' (Participant 4, GP; Family 12; 2.5-years)

J. 'I think for her it's a matter of trying to persuade her that stopping drinking is a good idea…erm, and…and…and I really don't know how you do that, because at the moment she doesn't seem to believe me.' (Participant 12, GP; Family 30; two children aged 6 and 12 years)

What	How	Why	Context
4. Opportune healthcare: Providing (missed) routine and preventive healthcare for children during consultations for other reasons	– Meeting preventive healthcare needs of the children during parent/child consultations for other reasons (e.g. overdue immunisations or developmental checks) – This had to be done immediately as the parents could not be relied on to come back at a later date (Quote K)	To meet the healthcare needs of children and young people	Facilitated by being able to offer something that the family wanted (leverage) and easy access to a health visitor (Quotes K and L)

Illustrative quotes from interviews:

K. 'So I ended up saying where did she go to get the baby weighed and the baby's six weeks old and she never had the baby weighed before in the baby clinic. So we went along and met the health visitor and got the baby weighed and got the baby weighed and stuff, [...] so I have other mothers who forget their books [Personal Child Health Record], so fair enough, you know, bring it…pop it in another time, or…or getting your baby weighed and go along to the health visitor. I knew with her it would have to be a question of saying, 'Let's get you along to the health visitor; here's the health visitor [...] in case she said, 'Oh, I'm off, I'm going to go home' or felt that she was…and felt bad about not getting the baby weighed. There's so many reasons why she might not have wanted to get the baby weighed, so I thought it was an opportunity.' (Participant 5, GP; Family 15; 15-year-old girl with a baby, from a family of five)

L. 'Oh by the way, you want that sick note, I'll just immunize your child.' (Participant 0, GP; Family 1; 1-year-old child with older sibling)

The importance of parental engagement and trust

The four responses all rely on the family's engagement with their GPs. This includes help-seeking behaviour from young people, parents and wider family members as well as honest disclosure of problems from family members who see the GP. Without developing this mutual trust, GPs believed that they had no hope of successfully improving a child or young person's situation through the four direct and potentially therapeutic responses described here. The GPs thought that repeated contact with family members facilitated relationship building.

In their therapeutic approach and in the emphasis on building cooperative relationships with parents, these four responses fit within the 'case-holder' approach described by the GPs in the study by Tompsett *et al.* (2010). They also serve to give us a better idea of how exactly GPs might intervene directly with children, young people and their families as the RCGP and, to a lesser extent, other agencies are beginning to envisage. It is worth noting that in the Tompsett study (2010), the case-holder role for GPs was more commonly described by GPs *themselves* than by other professionals and this was echoed in our study. Unlike the GPs we interviewed, the two health visitors who participated did *not* see GPs as having an ongoing or therapeutic role for vulnerable or maltreated children (Woodman *et al.* 2013). And it is the RCGP, the body made up of and representing GPs, which most strongly put forward a case-holder type role for GPs in child safeguarding.

Potential challenges and benefits of direct responses by GPs

Although these are the most detailed descriptions available of direct therapeutic responses by GPs to vulnerable and maltreated children, young people and their families, the four responses described in this chapter only scratch the surface of what we want to know about how GPs might best intervene directly with families. First, they are probably not exhaustive; more research may find other types of direct and potentially therapeutic responses. Second, we do not know whether these responses work, or whether GPs make things worse for some children and young people when they try to respond in these direct ways. For example, there is a danger that building relationships with parents to facilitate coaching can become an 'accommodative strategy' (Strong 2001) towards the parent that ends up affirming patterns of 'bad' behaviour (Chew-Graham, May and Roland 2004).

Such a strategy could encourage professionals to focus on parents and overlook the needs of children, resulting in inadequately protecting them from abuse or neglect. On the other hand, developing a trusting relationship with parents can also be seen as a 'containment' strategy, which, alongside close monitoring of children's health and wellbeing, has been put forward as an appropriate approach within social work for keeping children safe (Howe 2010). As Brigid Daniel argues in her review of the evidence about professional responses to child neglect, relationships between parents and professionals need to be supportive yet challenging (Daniel, Taylor and Scott 2011).

Many would argue that GPs do not have the inclination, time or expertise to maintain this kind of supportive yet challenging relationship with parents, and are limited by not having access to the whole picture of a child or family's life. Even GPs themselves question whether they have time to address child maltreatment in a ten-minute consultation, whether they are still family doctors who know their patients and can offer continuity of care, and whether they see maltreatment frequently enough to give it a primary focus (Fitzpatrick 2011; Masters 2012). Coaching parents relies on repeated contact between the parents and a specific GP, and monitoring is much more difficult if patients cannot get appointments easily. Repeated contact between a GP and a parent was seen as a key facilitator of direct responses by GPs to neglectful families; the implications of this are discussed at length later in the chapter. On the other side of the argument, GPs maintain that child safeguarding and building relationships with challenging families encapsulates the nature of general practice as a holistic service and is an integral part of GP work (Allister 2011; Ford 2011). From this perspective, continuity of care and patient access are still possible in general practice but cannot be taken for granted; GPs and practices need to work a bit harder to ensure they happen (Freeman and Hughes 2010).

In addition, if these strategies by GPs do indeed work to help children and young people and it is possible for GPs to deliver them in the current system, this is unlikely to be the case universally. We need to know for whom they work and in which contexts. The next section of this chapter presents a possible answer to the 'for whom' question. Based on this small and in-depth qualitative study, *neglected children and young people, and their families with high health need* might be one particular group for whom GPs have an appropriate ongoing therapeutic role involving direct responses. A look at characteristics of this group explains why GPs might feel both motivated and able to respond to this particular group.

High health need in families of neglected children and young people

GPs overwhelmingly focused on their role for (possibly) neglectful families

This study started off as one about child maltreatment and ended up being about child neglect. The interviews we conducted with GPs suggested that the four direct responses of monitoring, advocating, coaching and providing opportune healthcare were being used for cases of (possible) child neglect and emotional abuse rather than (possible) physical or sexual abuse. The 14 GPs we interviewed spoke overwhelmingly about child neglect when we asked them to select families who had prompted maltreatment-related concerns.

The GPs described a range of neglectful situations, which included physical, medical, supervisory and emotional neglect and which covered all dimensions of parenting capacity related to neglect as described by Horwath (2013), reproduced below with illustrative quotes from our interviews with GPs. As the quotes make clear, many of the dimensions of neglectful parenting overlap and GPs described children who seemed to be experiencing multiple forms of neglect simultaneously.

- *Lack of basic care*: failure to provide appropriate diet, warmth, shelter, clothing, dress or hygiene or failure to access appropriate medical care for the child or meet the child's health needs

  > Neglect really. I think with chaotic lifestyles that the child may become…well just not be cared for adequately. […] Parents who become impoverished because of their drugs using behaviour are at just that much more risk of physical neglect of not feeding the child, not caring for the child, not changing its nappy, of not…and to an extent emotional neglect as well, just that there's not enough parenting input. (Participant 14, GP; Family 34; seven-month-old baby)

- *Failure to ensuring safety*: failure to ensure that the child is supervised properly and they were allowed to run round unsupervised. (Participant 4, GP; Family 13; four children 3–13 years and six older siblings)

- *Lack of emotional warmth*: failure to meet the child's emotional needs, including developing their sense of a positive self

    So she used to be a very bright little young thing. But I think the last three years she's just become that sort of disaffected teenager I suppose who has had a pretty rough time [...] And still, to this day, I think they are lost because they were left with their mother who, for no fault of her own and because of her own, you know, all of her background and things, really wasn't capable of providing good enough parenting for them. I mean, they're here, they're alive, but you know – and that was an – I think it's been terrible neglect really. (Participant 10, GP; Family 26; 16-year-old child with two younger siblings)

- *Lack of stimulation:* failure to provide opportunities for learning and development, including school attendance

    They [the parents] are both functioning at quite a low level. I don't think that the child is going to be beaten up, I do think that she, when she goes to nursery her speech, her speech isn't going to be good, she will be behind developmentally, that she is missing out on a crucial period of her development. (Participant 0, GP; Family 1; one-year-old child with older sibling)

- *Lack of guidance and boundaries:* failure to demonstrate appropriate emotion and interaction with others or provide guidance to enable appropriate social behaviours

    Clearly this girl, at 13, was out...that's probably 15 miles away, at two or three in the morning, getting drunk, you know, so that starts to feel quite neglectful. [...] I think probably she hasn't had boundaries. I think she probably is more out of control than ever comes to my attention, because your average parent of a 13-year-old who isn't at home at three o'clock in the morning, you know, would have the police out looking for them and all that kind of thing. I don't think that happened, which suggests that probably that's not the first time that she's gone missing, that that is a pattern that we didn't know about. (Participant 7, GP; Family 13; 13-year-old with two younger siblings)

- *Lack of stability:* failure to provide a sufficiently stable home life or to ensure secure attachment to the caregiver

    There's been suggestions that [...] maybe other people who come and go through the house, deal in drugs and that the children had been exposed to that. (Participant 7, GP; Family 13; 13-year-old with two younger siblings)

In contrast, the two health visitors we interviewed did not see that GPs had an ongoing role for neglected children such as these. They saw the role of the GP forensically, as one concerned with establishing whether or not a symptom or injury was the result of abuse or neglect. These results are not presented in full due to the disclosive nature of the small sample of health visitors.

GPs described using direct responses specifically in relation to child neglect

In our analysis, we classified the narratives that the GPs gave about their patients into four types, the three most common of which concerned possibly neglectful parenting. The four types of narrative about families are significant because how the GP saw the 'story' of the family seemed to influence how motivated and able they were to respond to the family in a supportive and ongoing capacity. The narratives tell us about how the GPs saw their patients and should not be relied on to provide accurate data about what was actually happening or how the children were experiencing life at home. The four categories were named using quotes from the collated interview data. The categories are summarised briefly below and presented in more detail in Table 6.2.

1. *'Stable at this point in time but it's a never-ending story':* these were narratives describing families with previous very serious maltreatment-related concerns, who had since achieved a fragile stability that GPs felt required extra vigilance. The main concern was usually about possible neglect and emotional abuse.

2. *'On the edge'*: these narratives described families who were barely coping and liable to tip over the edge at any moment. The main concern was usually about possible neglect and, in some cases, emotional abuse.

3. *'Was it, wasn't it (physical or sexual abuse)?'*: these were narratives describing situations where participants had a high degree of uncertainty as to whether physical or sexual abuse had taken place, and much time was spent trying to establish whether the suspected abuse was likely to have occurred. In all of these cases, the GPs ended up ruling out physical and sexual abuse in conjunction with children's social care but concerns about neglect remained.

4. *'Fairly straightforward'*: these were brief narratives in which there was high certainty about physical abuse and decisive onwards referrals. (The term 'straightforward', which was used by all three GPs describing these families, characterised how the GPs felt about their own response, rather than how they understood the child's or their family's situation.)

Table 6.2 Summary of narratives about families given by interview participants (adapted from Woodman et al. 2013)

'Stable at this point in time but it's a never-ending story'	'On the edge'	'Was it, wasn't it?'	'Fairly straightforward'
Most common narrative N=16/37	Second most common narrative N=12/37	Third most common narrative N=9/37	Least common narrative N=3/37
– Very serious and long-term parent drug/alcohol use, mental health problems and domestic violence – Extensive contact with child protection services, police, and drugs and alcohol services – Siblings taken into care or died – Concerns about physical, medical and emotional neglect – Circumstances seen to have recently improved for children – Participants felt hopeful about capacity to parent in the future – But new stability was seen as fragile and optimism about future was cautious and uneasy – Perceived need for continued vigilance to spot relapses (further neglect/emotional abuse) and prevent poor child outcomes	– Lack of boundaries for children; poor school attendance, missed medical appointments, concerns about nutrition and clothing Families experienced: poor housing; unemployment; poverty; parental alcohol use or mental health problems; and child health and behavioural problems – Concerns about physical, medical and emotional neglect – Families came often to the GP for problems (help-seeking) – Accounts of intermittent and inadequate involvement from child protection services – Children described as 'vulnerable' and as currently involved with child in need services – Worry about families 'tipping over the edge' at any moment	– Concerns focused on possible physical or sexual abuse – Participants were very uncertain whether suspicions 'amounted to anything or not' and believed that physical or sexual abuse was a possible but unlikely differential diagnosis – They described having just enough concern to take further action – After varying amounts of time (from a few days to over a year), participants reached the decision, usually in conjunction with children's social care, that the child was not likely to have been physically or sexually abused – However, in the four stories of injured children, participants described ongoing concerns about supervision (i.e. supervisory neglect)	– These narratives were characterised by concerns about maltreatment described as 'obvious' or 'barn door' with a high level of suspicion from participants and decisive referrals to social care or secondary healthcare – Concerned physical abuse and domestic violence – Narratives were characterised by participants believing that referral to social care or other agencies would result in appropriate and timely services – These cases were only mentioned in passing and usually as a contrast to one of the other family types, about whom participants talked in detail and at length

There were also seven descriptions of families (six families described by seven participants) where the stories did not fall into the four types of narrative that were generated from the rest of the data and where the characteristics were not similar enough to each other to generate a cohesive new category. Two cases did not concern children at risk of abuse from carers: a mother of an infant who committed suicide and a case of school bullying. Three narratives were brief with insufficient detail to characterise in the analysis. Two stories focused on families about to go through care proceedings, where there was no longer hope for parental capacity to look after the child. A handful of families are counted in more than one column in this table because their 'story' changed over time, in the eyes of the interviewee.

In the box below is a detailed description of the four narrative types described above in the participants' own words. GPs could see the short-, medium- and long-term impacts of neglect for these children, demonstrating a long-term view and appreciation that their health and wellbeing included social and economic aspects as well as physical and cognitive ones. These GPs were not thinking purely within the biomedical model.

FOUR NARRATIVE TYPES IN PARTICIPANTS' OWN WORDS

Some potentially identifying features of the family have been altered or omitted.

'Stable at this point'

The concerns that we've had with this child throughout her life is really firstly her mum was a known drug user throughout her pregnancy [...] Then when she was eight weeks old, it was reported to the police that there had been a domestic violence incident at the home, and the baby was in the home [and in danger]. And the first time I saw her bring her in on her own was when her skin was very, very infected. [...] And I was alerted to the fact that really she had let her skin get in a very poor condition before she had done anything about it [...] two to three weeks later she presented again in the same condition [...] So, really, things progressed on throughout her short life, er young life, of really neglect, really within the home. Her mum wasn't using drugs anymore, but she was drinking and there was an increasing amount of violence occurring in the home. Eventually, we had an incident where [...] not only had [the father seriously injured] the mum, but [threatened the children and the police had to intervene]. [...] So, again, social services were very heavily involved with both children again, because they were at risk in the family home. [...But now] Her mum is working, and we've had much – although she's still a child of concern, we've had much less worry about her of late. Because, in actual fact, on this last altercation with her partner, [the father] did get a custodial sentence. So for the last sort of six months things have been going much better for this particular child, and her mum has been doing much better. And even though we are concerned, things have been going much better.

So I feel that her life has improved [...] But she is obviously still a concern, because, you know, at any point her father who is going to be released could have contact with her again. (Participant 9, practice nurse; Family 23; two-year-old child a with older sibling)

'On the edge'

Interviewer: Are these medical problems?
Respondent: Medical problems...medical and behavioural problems, that kind of thing, mental health problems.

This other [family]...is a vulnerable family, I think we recognise them as a vulnerable family. It's complex, um, and this is a little boy who is, um, really could have picked several of the children really, ah, but this little boy is four and, ah, he's in a family in which there are, I think, um...one, two...there's two brothers, older brothers, I think there's an older sister, there's a very much older sister who's just had a baby, they all live in the same house with their mum and dad [...]. He's got, ah...I think he has problems with bed wetting and soiling actually and, um, he's also got a squint which, um...which isn't bad but the mother's repeatedly failing to get him along to appointments and that kind of stuff and, ah, he's kind of like...they're...they're...they're known to social services now, a child in need...he's a child...child in need, um, but they're... they're very difficult because they seem...the magnitude of their problem as a family can seem overwhelming really. Um, just every one of the children has a problem which of its own in a family would be a problem, and yet, they seem to have them all in...under one roof. [...] The older sister is 16, she's now got her own baby and they've...they'd have to have a room in the house, so I think he shares with two other siblings and the brothers are in another room [...] I mean, all of the kids have got problems of some sort or another and the parents have their own problems. The mother's had a stroke and the father's had a heart attack and [...] Unless something is done soon [about the squint] he's going to go blind [...] we're not talking about surgery or anything, we're just talking about patches and covering and making sure he uses the eye and that kind of stuff. (Participant 5, GP; Family 15; five children aged 4–16 years)

'Was it, wasn't it?'

Yeah. The first family…um…a mother with two little…actually, no, thinking about it…three little boys and ongoing concerns with them. Um, one is a baby, he's about five months, one little boy is about two, and the other one is three, um, and, um, there's a dad as well who is around […] and they've been a family of concern because, um, when the…before the baby was born, there was a child who…one of the boys was under one, and the other was under two and [the health visitor] was concerned about the fact that every time she saw the…the one who was about one, he always seemed to have quite a few bruises, not…ah, none of the bruises were of themselves suspicious. They were all in places where you might expect to see bruises but she just was concerned that every time she saw this little one, he had bruises and, um, she was uncertain, really, whether it amounted to anything or not and, um…and I think one of the difficult things was that when I then saw this baby…uh…probably just…just a bit more than one, he was at an age where he was ambulatory so it wasn't surprising to have bruises. He just seemed to have quite a lot of bruises and we had to make a difficult decision at that time to actually refer him into social services […] The mother said it was rough play. These two were always…and they were fairly boisterous in the consulting room, but, um, we decided to refer them into social services and the mother was obviously very unhappy at the time.

So, um, it was all pretty fraught really, and, um, they went up to the hospital escorted by the social worker [to see] the designated consultant for child protection and she had a look and, um, she was concerned about the extent of the bruising, because it was either…it's either a non-accidental injury and I think we all had agreed in the end it wasn't but there were issues around supervision of the children. (Participant 5, GP; Family 14; three children 5 months–3 years)

'Fairly straightforward'

When I see something that's obvious, I saw a child recently with what appeared to be a new fracture and referred it, you know, kind of, do not pass go, straight to A&E, and you know, and…and then it moves on, you know, and then you know, that the right things have happening…happened, and in a way that kind of seems fairly straightforward. (Participant 7, GP; Family 38; no details of age given)

Table 6.2 shows how GPs used different responses according to how they saw the family at any given time. GPs described using direct responses when they saw family narratives as 'stable at this point', 'on the edge' or 'was it, wasn't it?' The responses that GPs talked about for these families were often intensive and/or occurred over a very long period of time, often with the family moving in and out of thresholds for action from children's social care. In contrast, for families considered to need only a 'straightforward' response, GPs described how they were happy to refer onto children's social care or the police and seemed to feel that their role stopped with the referral. In one case, the GP even relied on the parents to make the referral themselves:

> When I see something that's obvious, I saw a child recently with what appeared to be a new fracture and referred it, you know, kind of, 'do not pass go, straight to Accident & Emergency...and...and then it moves on, you know, and then you know, that the right things have happening...happened, and in a way that kind of seems fairly straightforward. (Participant 7, GP; Family 38; no details of age given)

> Well, there's one that's fairly straightforward. I did the...you know... the...the parent...the mother, um, disclosed some domestic violence and so I...it just happened yesterday and so it was just about making sure she contacted the police and that they go through child protection in that way. I don't think there was that much to it, actually. (Participant 8, GP; Family 21; no details of age given)

Characteristics of neglectful families that may elicit direct responses

Table 6.2 prompts the question: why did GPs describe using direct responses (and a fuller range of these responses) for some families and not others? Or to put it another way: why were GPs apparently happy to refer on those they saw as 'straightforward' families whilst perceiving a much more involved and case-holding/advocacy role for themselves when they saw family narratives as 'on the edge, 'was it, wasn't it?' and, to a lesser extent, 'stable at this point'?

Some characteristics of these neglectful families, including high health need, seemed to facilitate direct GP responses. As we relied uniquely on GP accounts in this study, it is not clear how far children in the 'straightforward' families were also experiencing neglect or whether family members also had high health needs. It is possible that neglectful behaviour in these families was not recognised or described by the GPs, and/or that family members had high levels of unmet health need not known to the GPs because the families were disengaged from primary care and/or health services more generally.

Bearing in mind these caveats, a hypothesis arose from the study: that *GPs felt most motivated and able to offer a therapeutic and ongoing 'direct' response to neglectful families with high health needs.* This may have been the case for five reasons. The first two relate to neglect: 1) GPs described how, in their view, 'on the edge' and 'was it, wasn't it?' families were not receiving a proportional or timely response from children's social care; and 2) GPs described how they saw neglectful mothers more sympathetically than other maltreating parents, motivating them to get involved and attempt to help the family.

The remaining three reasons relate to a subset of neglectful families, those with high healthcare needs. This group 3) offered GPs an opportunity for identifying problems and enacting direct responses; 4) provided a legitimate and obvious reason for GP involvement; and 5) allowed GPs to build up reciprocal relationships with parents, something seen by the GPs as a prerequisite for monitoring, coaching and advocating.

These five drivers of ongoing therapeutic GP involvement with neglectful families are detailed below with examples from the interviews.

SCEPTICISM ABOUT THE APPROPRIATENESS OF
RESPONSES FROM OTHER AGENCIES

As described in the opening to this chapter, there is widespread recognition that neglect more rarely meets thresholds for services from children's social care, compared to physical and sexual abuse. Reflecting this, in the narratives about 'on the edge' and 'was it, wasn't it?' families, GPs thought that children's social care did not provide the help that the families needed. It was this that motivated GPs to take on an advocating role for the family (see Table 6.3).

> You always get the feeling the social services are overwhelmed and they have a lot of cases to deal with. And, you know, to a certain

extent, if no one is batting on their door and the case is just left in a file until they get picked up again or until somebody starts shouting about them, you know, another one will always take precedence. And I think, you know, you've got to stand up and shout for people, because sadly, in some ways, that's the way they actually begin to take more notice. (Participant 10, GP; Family 26; 16-year-old child with two younger siblings)

In the narratives about 'was it, wasn't it?' families, other services were portrayed as inappropriately heavy-handed. This was because the GP did not in fact believe sexual or physical abuse had taken place, although they could not rule it out definitively at that time:

Then I got a call from a doctor at…up at the Child Development Centre, to say they discussed my letter and they thought that I should refer her straight to social services, um, which was rather different from the approach that I'd wanted to take which was rather gentler because actually at the end of the day I really wasn't…I didn't have a high level of concern that C was being abused. […] The whole thing was rather getting…felt as though it was getting out of hand a bit. (Participant 8, GP; Family 20; eight-year-old child)

We had to make a difficult decision at that time to actually refer him into social services, um, and I think the difficulty was, with these things, they're like all-or-nothing responses, aren't they? They're like someone coming in with chest pain and you either decide it could be just a bit of indigestion and you give them a bit of Gaviscon or he could be having a heart attack, get a 999 ambulance. It isn't the sort of halfway house. (Participant 5, GP; Family 14; three children five months to three years old)

In contrast, GPs thought that children's social care and secondary healthcare services were depicted as having an adequate and appropriate role with families perceived as 'stable at this point' or 'straightforward':

Well their [children's social care's] response was…was quite good and quite quick, it […] I made the phone call and everything happened from there… (Participant 12, GP; Family 30; two children aged 6 and 12 years)

It was this (perceived) systematic bias in system responses to different types of child maltreatment that seemed to motivate GPs to take on professional responsibility and adopt a case-holder type role for neglect cases rather than physical and sexual abuses cases. When interpreting these comments, we must bear in mind that child and family social workers will have had far more extensive child protection experience than GPs in this area. It is entirely possible that social workers were in fact delivering the most appropriate response to families based on a fuller picture of the family and a higher level of child safeguarding expertise.

A SYMPATHETIC VIEW OF NEGLECTFUL MOTHERS

Participants described feelings sympathetic towards 'on the edge' and 'stable at this point' families, which seemed to arise from a feeling that in their cases, poor parenting could be explained or justified:

> I thought they [the parents] had some sort of excuse, I was sympathetic to them. (Participant 0, GP; Family 3; four-year-old child with two older siblings; participant describing how she suspected that two drug-using parents were self-medicating for bi-polar disorder)

The GPs' exoneration of poor parenting tended to be rooted in descriptions of the parent's own background. In the context of their own difficult childhoods, mothers were described as child-like, as needing 'parenting' themselves, and as being 'incapable' of better parenting through 'no fault of [their] own' (participants 2 and 10).

The sympathetic attitude to these families was also evident in GPs' descriptions of the mothers as 'loving' (participant 2, GP; Family 2; children aged two and three years); 'caring' (participant 12, GP; Family 31; two children aged three and seven years); and 'a good mum' (participant 7, GP; Family 18; 13-year-old child).

Mothers were described in these terms despite the serious consequences of child neglect outlined in their narratives. This sympathetic view of mothers appeared to be directly connected to participants' motivation to remain involved, rather than (as with other types of cases) to pass all responsibility to another professional or agency:

> I could've easily just said, 'Oh, I'll see your own doctor to contact CAMHS [Child and Adolescent Mental Health Services] or whatever,' but I just did it for her because I actually believe her story if you like and I was sympathetic to what she was saying. So that's why I did it for her. (Participant 11, GP; Family 11, teenage daughter)

Participant 2 was explicit about how it was necessary to cultivate this sympathetic view of some parents *deliberately*:

> What you've got to do with people whose behaviours aren't helping themselves, I think, is you've got to look beyond and try and find something you like about the person to work with it to try and help them. (Participant 2, GP; Family 7; two children aged two and three years and mother pregnant)

A sympathetic view of parents as 'loving' but incompetent was more compatible with neglect than with physical and sexual abuse:

> *Respondent:* So neglect is often a – is sometimes – is often not malicious. It's usually due to poor functioning parents, whereas malicious wounding of a child I think – I find more difficult personally because my own emotions start to take hold.

> *Interviewer:* And what emotions are they?

> *Respondent:* Well, disgust and I just find it difficult to be sympathetic towards a parent that can do that with their child really. And I – working with them it would – I would be slightly more arms-length with them I think. (Participant 2, GP; Family 7; two children aged two and three years and mother pregnant)

In summary, GPs depicted neglectful mothers as vulnerable and to some extent exonerated them, which facilitated ongoing engagement with the maltreatment-related concerns in these families and may explain the reason for the dominance of neglect in the stories about how GPs worked with vulnerable and maltreating families.

Opportunities for identifying problems and enacting direct responses

Ill health among parents and other adult family members offered GPs both an opportunity and a reason to worry about a child's welfare. As shown in Table 6.3, visits to the GP by parents or other adult family members for their own health problems were the most frequent trigger for concern about the children in the family in our interview data.

Table 6.3 What type of contact triggered maltreatment-related concerns among GPs?

How did GPs' current concern arise?	N of families*	Additional information
Child visit (for child's health issue)	8	In five cases, the children visited the GP for their own health problems and, in younger children, parents always accompanied the children to the GP. In these cases children and/or parents talked about child symptoms that directly prompted the maltreatment-related concerns (e.g. teenage pregnancy or failure to thrive). In the remaining three cases, the reason for consultation was unconnected to the concerns (e.g. chest infection or gastroenteritis). In these cases, the consultation gave an opportunity for the GP to observe the child and/or parent and collect wider information, giving rise to concerns. All eight cases had a history of previous GP concern.
Parent visit (for parental health issue)	12	In three cases, the mother disclosed domestic violence to the GP during a consultation about a related medical problem (e.g. depression). In seven cases, consultations with the mother prompted concerns from the GP about the mother's capacity to parent (e.g. a home visit for 'flu' which revealed alcohol misuse). Finally, in two cases, the parent came to see the GP because they were worried about their child's mental health (e.g. self-harming) or about their own capacity to parent.
Information from other professional	6	In two cases the child was referred from the health visitor or practice nurse to the GP for a second opinion about injuries and in a further case social care had referred the child to the GP due to behavioural problems. In one case, we inferred that the referral had come from social care as it concerned a very serious and possibly non-accidental injury in a young baby. In the remaining two cases, concerns arose following letters received from other healthcare services. The GPs interpreted these letters in the context of wider and/or historic information about the family. Most but not all of this information resulted in a consultation between the GP and the child.

*This table is based on the 26 families discussed in the 14 interviews with GPs. In many cases the families had a long history of professional concern and it was not clear from the interviews how the families first prompted maltreatment-related concerns from the GP. The data in this table are based on what the GPs reported as the most recent contact or an event which prompted renewed concern. A large amount of judgement was used in classifying how concerns arose.

GPs highlighted how health problems in adult family members, usually in the mother, resulted in regular contact with the family. This in turn allowed maltreatment-related concerns to emerge over time. GP concerns arose from their understanding of the parental health condition or the patient's ability (or inability) to manage it. In the majority of these cases, the reason for the parental visit to the GP only *indirectly* prompted concern for a child or children in the family. This necessitated skilled observation, drawing of inferences and response from the GPs. For example, after several consultations, one GP saw that a mother's poor compliance with treatment for her own chronic health problem was indicative of her chaotic lifestyle and a symptom of her alcohol misuse and this then raised questions about her parenting capacity and, as a result, about the children's welfare.

GPs also described how mothers gradually disclosed information to the GP when they were consulting repeatedly for their own health needs:

And then it became apparent that there were a lot of problems within the marriage. And this all culminated in a lot of domestic violence. (Participant 10, GP; Family 26; three children 9–16 years)

…what came out of the conversations was that there was some problem with the relationship with her husband which was occasionally abusive in that – verbally at least. (Participant 2, GP; Family 7; two children aged two and three years)

I'd been seeing her for the last six months [for mental health problems], that is the first time after six months she opened her mouth, this [domestic violence] is happening. (Participant 15, GP; Family 36; children aged 9 and 11 years)

Once a GP was concerned about child neglect, repeated parental consultations for parental health needs provided opportunities for direct responses to families as well as opportunities for identification of child welfare problems.

The GPs saw general practice as a reactive system. They felt that they could mainly respond to families who asked for help, either with specific requests or by dint of coming to an appointment. They described how they found it more difficult to initiate an intervention for families who were registered but did not actively seek help from the GP for health and/or related problems. This was the case even where there were known problems with child welfare in the family:

I think a lot of it is reactive. It's people asking us for information and us providing it, and it might be the patient wanting a letter to transport their...their...their house move or...or any number of things we write letters for, rather than us being able to say, 'I think we should be doing this, that and the other.' Don't...we don't seem to have the space to be able to think like that or act like that. (Participant 5, GP; Family 15; four-year-old child with four siblings)

The way general practice is set up is, is that we respond to people who decide that they want our help. [...] You know what's come to you, but you don't know what's out there that isn't coming to you, that isn't choosing to come through the door, for whatever reason. (Participant 7, GP; Family 19; two children aged six and ten years)

In light of this, it makes sense that the GPs we interviewed felt they could do most for those families who engage with and rely on general practice, and who come in to surgeries or health centres frequently for both routine child health checks and to manage the complex health needs of multiple family members. It was parents' (and other adult family members') health problems which provided opportunities and justification for GPs to adopt direct responses (monitoring, advocating and coaching) for families. In descriptions by GP interviewees, high adult health need and help-seeking behaviour were seen in chaotic and neglectful families. They had a host of physical and mental health problems and moved between social care thresholds for children in need and child protection over time (see Figure 6.1, 'on the edge' families).

The most worrying families may be those who simply do not engage with universal services and we certainly need to find ways of ensuring the health needs of these vulnerable children are met as well. However, there may be a subset of neglectful families who already are engaged with general practice and who repeatedly seek help from GPs, such as the families described by the GPs we interviewed as 'on the edge'. Our hypothesis is that this subset of families may be the starting point for exploring how GPs might (if possible) best use direct responses to families to help vulnerable children.

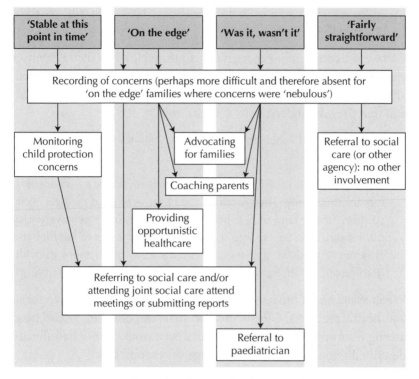

Figure 6.1 Relationships between family types and actions as described by GPs (adapted from Woodman et al. 2013)

LEGITIMATE AND OBVIOUS REASON FOR GPs INTERVENTION

The extent that GPs should take on an ongoing case-holder or advocacy role for families remained thorny, highly contentious and uncertain for GP participants. As one GP indicated, the contention can be thought of in terms of GPs stepping outside of their professional domain:

I am the person to whom they turn at every small opportunity with, you know, benefits problems, psychological problems, physical problems, housing problems [...] maybe we should just be saying, well, I'm sorry, but there's nothing I can do or, you know, I am the GP, I'm not the social worker. If she's not going to school, you know, you'll have to phone social services or somebody else who can do this, because that's not my job. And maybe we sort of just blurred boundaries too much by taking on work that possibly isn't really appropriate for us to do. (Participant 10, GP; Family 26; three children 9–16 years)

GPs were, as one might expect, more comfortable when their responses were framed in terms of meeting 'medical' rather than 'social' need, although they saw that the boundary between the two was blurred, and that they did indeed have a 'social' role:

Interviewer: And what do you think is your role as a GP for...for them?

Respondent: Well, I...I...I think that we'll always have a very medical role for this family. They're very...they have very great medical needs so they...that's kind of...although it's difficult, is the relatively easy bit. I mean, how we tap into the sort of welfare issues of families and children, I think is, um, much more difficult, much more difficult. (Participant 5, GP; Family 15; four-year-old child with four siblings)

When asked about proactive responses to families with multiple social and health problems, GPs focused on their responses to *medical* need arising from episodes of *medical* neglect, even when the GP had already described responding to a wider range of responses:

Interviewer: And can you think of an example where you've perceived an increased need in the family and tell me what you've done to try and meet those needs?

Respondent: Yes, I think the best example of that is where T [the child] has gone through a really bad phase with infected eczema, with her skin problem getting worse and reaching crisis point [because her parents were not giving her the regular treatment]. And so [...] we've been able to step up the frequency with which we see them. (Participant 4, GP; Family 13; four children 3–13 years and six older siblings)

So I actually got a letter from the optician recently and it said this girl's vision in this eye is getting worse and worse. Unless something is done soon she's going to lose her eye [because the parents are not complying with treatment or taking her to appointments]. So I actually rang the mother up. (Participant 5, GP; Family 15; four-year-old child with four siblings)

Here the GPs describe initiating a series of frequent child visits for eczema, and calling the mother after missed hospital appointments to impress on her the importance of complying with hospital care for her child's sight problems, participants 4 and 5 respectively (quoted above). In the proactive responses they depict, these quotes are in contrast to the descriptions of general practice as a reactive system, one of which was by the same GP (participant 5). Perhaps there are expectations that GPs will respond proactively to need that is so clearly 'medical' and have systems to facilitate this. GPs may also find that these more proactive expectations and systems can be put into play for wider safeguarding concerns and responses when the problem and response are framed in terms of medical neglect and medical need.

On the whole, neglect was understood and framed by participants as in many ways a medical problem and therefore one which was justifiably within their professional domain:

> I think [these cases] reflect first of all the great prevalence of neglect as a problem – as a social problem, but partly as a medical problem as well. (Participant 4, GP; Family 12; two-year-old child)

The framing of neglect as a medical problem seemed to give GPs permission to respond directly and in some cases proactively to these families, although the direct responses GPs used were far from limited to a narrow biomedical model of health.

BUILDING RECIPROCAL RELATIONSHIPS WITH PARENTS

GPs described using high healthcare need to position themselves as trusted professionals in the parents' lives and to build a reciprocal relationship with parents, through whom direct responses were enacted. One GP described a situation where healthcare provision gave something to 'trade' with the family in order to be able to persuade them to accept help for the child:

> because we can actually give them what they think they want but there may be a trade-off. 'I can get what I want, if I accept this.' As a trade-off. You trade, you know. 'You do this for me and I'll do this for you.' (Participant 0, GP; Family 1; 13-month-old child)

The same participant explained how leverage gained from the GP meeting health needs or assisting with social welfare need (e.g. benefit claims) could be used, for example, to encourage parents to accept help with parenting, or to allow delivery of preventive healthcare for the child, such as overdue developmental checks and immunisations, or to encourage further presentations which would, in turn, allow ongoing monitoring and intervention. This participant was very clear that the mother in her narrative was actively and consciously participating in this strategic 'trading': 'Oh, she *knew*' (original emphasis). Given the complicity of the trade-off, it might also be conceived of as 'game-playing' between the doctor and parent; this was a comment made by another GP in their feedback on preliminary results. Although only one GP spoke explicitly of creating leverage as part of their response to child neglect, the 'trade-off' theme ran implicitly through many interviews with GPs as they described how they went out of their way to be seen by parents as 'helpful' and as 'someone who gets things done'.

To recap, we have explored examples of the five drivers of GPs adopting an ongoing and therapeutic role with neglectful families with high health need and health-seeking behaviour. These were: 1) their scepticism about responses from other agencies in cases of neglect; 2) a sympathetic view of neglectful mothers compared to other maltreating parents; 3) frequent contact with parents that provided opportunities for identification and response to child welfare problems; 4) using healthcare provision as something to 'trade' with parents; and 5) building a trusting relationship with parents.

These five drivers carry risks as well as potential benefit. Analyses of serious case reviews (cases of children who have died or been seriously injured following maltreatment) warn that it can be very dangerous for children if professionals discount the possibility or impact of violence in the home because they think of the family as a 'neglect case' (Brandon *et al.* 2014). It is easy to see how viewing neglectful mothers sympathetically may lead to unintentional collusion with parents, at the cost of overlooking the child's perspective and hiding the extent of risk faced by the child. It is not clear whether or how far the focus on neglect and on a subset of neglectful parents by the GPs in our sample is an (unsafe) strategy designed to facilitate their ability and desire to work with parents, and how far it represents the problems that children and young people experience in their families. Additionally, the focus on neglectful families with high health need and help-seeking behaviour may divert attention away from other vulnerable children whose parents come less regularly to the GP or who do not fit the profile of parents that GPs think they can help. Authorising such an approach may allow GPs to pick and choose whom they work with, which is in direct contrast to law and policy guidance and perhaps also raises ethical questions.

Summary of findings

When 14 GPs from four practices in England were asked to describe families with maltreatment-related concerns with whom they had been involved, they:

- overwhelmingly described concerns about physical, medical and emotional neglect

- described direct responses: monitoring, coaching, advocating and providing opportune healthcare (coaching and advocating were strategies aimed at parents and monitoring was often enacted through adult family members)

- were motivated to remain involved with families in which there was child neglect rather than other forms of maltreatment, due to their scepticism about some responses from other agencies and a sympathetic view of neglectful mothers

- revealed that high healthcare need in adult family members acted as a further facilitator of direct responses, because it offered an opportunity to identify and respond to child welfare problems, justified ongoing GP involvement with child welfare concerns and allowed GPs to build reciprocal relationships with parents.

Our study begins the task of understanding exactly how GPs might be able to deliver the therapeutic ('lead professional') support role envisaged in English policy and professional guidance from healthcare bodies. There remain many unanswered questions. We do not know whether there are other direct responses that GPs can and do provide to vulnerable and maltreating families, whether the direct responses we identified are already happening widely, or whether they are feasible for the average GP. There are risks in the direct responses we identified and in the ways that GPs constructed neglect and identified families with whom they could work. We know little about the balance of potential harms and benefits of the direct responses we identified.

Interpretation of findings in light of what we already know

In this section, the findings are briefly contextualised in existing literature. A much fuller contextualisation can be found elsewhere (Woodman 2014).

Types of families

In keeping with our findings, other qualitative studies based on English and Danish GPs consistently report that in Europe, GPs focus on *parents* for identification of, and responses to, social welfare concerns about children, including concerns about child abuse or neglect (Hølge-Hazelton and Tulinius 2010; Lykke, Christensen and Reventlow 2008; Lykke, Christensen and Reventlow 2011; Tompsett *et al.* 2010). In many cases the GP had not recently been in contact with the child (Hølge-Hazelton *et al.* 2010).

Parents of 'on the edge' families in this study shared many characteristics with a wider population of adult patients with social problems, who may or may not have children. The impact of both types of patient (neglectful families and those with similarly entrenched social problems but not necessarily resulting in child neglect) is to make the listener feel overwhelmed (Brandon *et al.* 2008b; Frank 1998; O'Dowd 1988; Butler and Evans 1999). When seen in the context of other patients presenting to primary care, maltreatment-related concerns discussed by the GPs in this sample seem to be part of a bigger group of challenging patients with multifaceted, chronic and potentially overwhelming problems. On one hand this affirms the argument that direct responses, which are also used for adults with chronic conditions and entrenched problems (Woodman *et al.* 2013), are core GP work which they already have some expertise to enact. On the other hand, it reinforces the need for professional support and reflective practice for GPs, for which we cannot assume there is time and space with the current demands of general medical practice.

Concerns about neglect

Like the Tompsett study described in the Research section of this chapter, the findings of this study suggest that the GP's role for some types of neglectful family is under-recognised and therefore not supported by other professionals, even within healthcare. The most detailed guidance on the ongoing therapeutic role that GPs can play for maltreating families, and specifically for neglectful families, is from the RCGP (representing GPs) rather than bodies representing a wider range of healthcare professionals.

Direct responses

The direct responses described by GPs represent core skills and activities of general practice that are used for other patient groups (Woodman et al. 2013). Although our findings are based on only 14 GPs, all of whom worked in a practice with one expert in child protection, it is probable that many GPs are using their core skills such as monitoring, coaching and advocating to respond to child neglect, even if they do not think of this activity as safeguarding or responses to maltreatment. In a recent survey of 46 GPs by the UK children's charity the NSPCC, 67 per cent reported that they would offer 'practical and emotional support' to parents where they were concerned about child neglect, while 39 per cent said they would do the same for the children themselves; and in the same study, 47 per cent of the GP respondents said they would monitor families who prompted concerns about neglect (Haynes 2015).

There is a worrying lack of evidence to tell us whether or not direct responses to child neglect by GPs improve things for children and families. As described in the findings section of this chapter, GPs in our sample saw that things did not always seem to get better for children when they tried to work with the parents. Our previous review of the evidence found three randomised controlled trials which were indirectly relevant and which suggested that motivational interviewing (combining characteristics of the coaching and advocacy roles described in this chapter) is a promising avenue for exploration (Woodman et al. 2014b). It is particularly important that we establish the safety as well as the effectiveness of GP's direct responses to families, especially given that they may well be widespread in current general practice. As described earlier, they offer opportunity for risks as well as benefit. Direct GP responses to concerns about neglect or other forms of child maltreatment are not acknowledged or recognised in policy and only briefly mentioned in practice guidance for GPs (Woodman et al. 2014b).

Implications for policy, practice and research

- Direct responses from GPs to neglectful families are probably widespread in England but are not explicitly supported by evidence, policy or other professional groups. More research is needed to explore how far direct responses by GPs are effective for vulnerable and maltreated children, for which children and young people in particular and in which contexts. We suggest that a good starting point would be to explore the role of direct responses by GPs for neglectful families with high health need and help-seeking behaviour.

- Given the lack of research evidence about direct responses, it is common sense to recommend that if they are indeed already happening, they do so in the context of joint working, especially with children's social care and in an environment where peer support and reflective practice is possible. It is especially important that GPs do not single-handedly hold complex cases, especially those which meet thresholds of significant harm. Social workers are likely to have the bigger picture about a family and more expertise in cases of maltreatment.

- Direct responses to vulnerable families should not replace intervention by children's social care. It is possible that GPs can deliver direct responses before, alongside or after interventions from other agencies, where these are taking place. The RCGP recommends that GP practices hold regular meetings to discuss vulnerable families (RCGP *et al.* 2014). These meetings may be an opportunity for peer support, incorporating information from children's social care into decision-making within general practice, and encouraging reflective practice as well as information sharing with the primary healthcare team (Woodman *et al.* 2014a).

- The direct responses identified here may be one way that GPs can adopt a 'lead professional' role for families needing early help, a role that GPs have been slow to take on despite policy guidance. Even for children judged to be at the early help end of the child welfare spectrum, it is likely that GPs will need to be supported in this role.

Questions for reflection

- How can we find out more about effective and safe GP responses to neglectful families?

- What does best practice with neglect look like for a GP and primary care team?

- How can those working with families where there are concerns about neglect better support one another to deliver a high quality response, perhaps including direct responses from GPs?

- Are there differences or similarities in the way that GPs (should) use their core skills to respond to neglectful families, compared to other patients such as the elderly or those with chronic conditions? How can we use current practice for other groups of patients to develop best practice for neglectful families, both from GPs and across the safeguarding system?

- Can we learn from best practice either from within the UK or internationally?

- Can similar GP responses work across all types of maltreatment concern?

References

Allister, J. (2011) 'How to protect general practice from child protection.' *British Journal of General Practice 61*, 586, 326.

Brandon, M., Bailey, S., Belderson, P. and Larsson, B. (2014) 'The role of neglect in child fatality and serious injury.' *Child Abuse Review 23*, 235–245.

Brandon, M., Belderson, P., Warren, C., Gardner, R., *et al.* (2008a) 'The preoccupation with thresholds in cases of child death or serious injury through abuse and neglect.' *Child Abuse Review 17*, 5, 313–330.

Brandon, M., Belderson, P., Warren, C., Howe, D., *et al.* (2008b) *Analysing Child Deaths and Serious Injury through Abuse and Neglect: What Can We Learn? A Biennial Analysis of Serious Case Reviews 2003–2005.* London: DCSF.

Braun, V. and Clarke, V. (2006) 'Using thematic analysis in psychology.' *Qualitative Research in Psychology 3*, 2, 77–101.

Butler, C.C. and Evans, M. (1999) 'The 'heartsink' patient revisited. The Welsh Philosophy and General Practice Discussion Group.' *British Journal of General Practice 49*, 440, 230–233.

Chew-Graham, C.A., May, C.R. and Roland, M.O. (2004) 'The harmful consequences of elevating the doctor-patient relationship to be a primary goal of the general practice consultation.' *Family Practice 21*, 3, 229–231.

Children Act 1989, Chapter 41. London: The Stationery Office.

Children Act 2004, Chapter 31. London: The Stationery Office.

Community Care (2012) 'Social workers unlikely to act quickly on neglect cases.' *Community Care*, 26 September. Available at www.communitycare.co.uk/articles/27/09/2012/118548/social-workers-unlikely-to-act-quickly-on-neglect-cases.htm, accessed on 5 December 2012.

Daniel, B., Taylor, J. and Scott, J. (2011) *Recognizing and Helping the Neglected Child: Evidence-based Practice for Assessment and Intervention.* London: Jessica Kingsley Publishers.

Dayan, M., Arora, S., Rosen, R. and Curry, N. (2014) *Is General Practice in Crisis?* London: Nuffield Trust.

Department for Education (2014) *Characteristics of Children in Need: 2013 to 2014.* London: DfE. Available at www.gov.uk/government/statistics/characteristics-of-children-in-need-2013-to-2014, accessed on 12 May 2015.

Easton, C., Lamont, E., Smith, R. and Aston, H. (2014) *'We Should Have Been Helped from Day One': A Unique Perspective from Children, Families and Practitioners.* Slough: NFER.

Finkelhor, D., Ormrod, R.K. and Turner, H.A. (2009a) 'Lifetime assessment of poly-victimization in a national sample of children and youth.' *Child Abuse & Neglect 33*, 7, 403–411.

Finkelhor, D., Turner, H., Ormrod, R. and Hamby, S. L. (2009b) 'Violence, abuse, and crime exposure in a national sample of children and youth.' *Pediatrics 124*, 5, 1411–1423.

Fitzpatrick, M. (2011) 'How to protect general practice from child protection.' *British Journal of General Practice 61*, 588, 436.

Ford, S. (2011) Letter – Response to 'How to protect general practice from child protection.' *British Journal of General Practice 18*, 18.

Frank, A.W. (1998) 'Just listening: narrative and deep illness.' *Families, Systems, & Health 16*, 3, 197–212.

Freeman, G. and Hughes, J. (2010) *Continuity of Care and the Patient Experience.* London: The King's Fund.

General Medical Council (2012) *Protecting Children and Young People: The Responsibilities of All Doctors.* London: GMC.

Gilbert, R., Kemp, A., Thoburn, J., Sidebotham, P., *et al.* (2009a) 'Recognising and responding to child maltreatment.' *Lancet 373*, 9658, 167–180.

Gilbert, R., Widom, C.S., Browne, K., Fergusson, D., *et al.* (2009b) 'Burden and consequences of child maltreatment in high-income countries.' *Lancet 373*, 9657, 68–81.

Green, J. and Thorogood, N. (2009) *Qualitative Methods for Health Research.* London: Sage.

Haynes, A. (2015) *Realising the Potential. Tackling Child Neglect in Universal Services.* London: NSPCC. Available at www.nspcc.org.uk/globalassets/documents/research-reports/realising-potential-tackling-neglect-universal-services-report.pdf, accessed on 6 June 2016.

HSCIC (Health & Social Care Information Centre) (2015) *Numbers of Patients Registered at a GP Practice – April 2015.* Leeds: HSCIC. Available at www.hscic.gov.uk/searchcatalogue?productid=17788&topics=1%2fPrimary+care+services%2fGeneral+practice&sort=Most+recent&size=10&page=1#top, accessed on 11 May 2015.

HM Government (2013) *Working Together to Safeguard Children: A Guide to Inter-agency Working to Safeguard and Promote the Welfare of Children.* London: DfE.

HM Government (2015) *Working Together to Safeguard Children: A Guide to Inter-agency Working to Safeguard and Promote the Welfare of Children.* London: DfE.

Hølge-Hazelton, B. and Tulinius, C. (2010) 'Beyond the specific child: what is "a child's case" in general practice?' *British Journal of General Practice 60*, 570, e4–9.

Horwath, J. (2013) *Child Neglect: Planning and Intervention.* Basingstoke: Palgrave Macmillan.

House of Commons Education Committee (2012) *Children First: The Child Protection System in England. Fourth Report of Session 2012–2013.* London: The Stationery Office.

Howe, D. (2010) 'The safety of children and the parent-worker relationship in cases of child abuse and neglect.' *Child Abuse Review 19*, 5, 330–341.

Information Centre for Health and Social Care (2007) *2006/07 UK General Practice Workload Survey.* London: Information Centre.

Lykke, K., Christensen, P. and Reventlow, S. (2008) '"This is not normal…" – Signs that make the GP question the child's well-being.' *Family Practice 25*, 3, 146–153.

Lykke, K., Christensen, P. and Reventlow, S. (2011) 'The consultation as an interpretive dialogue about the child's health needs.' *Family Practice 28*, 4, 430–436.

Masters, N.J. (2012) 'What is the role of GPs in safeguarding children?' *BMJ 344*, e4123. DOI: 4110.1136/bmj.e4123

Munro, E. (2011) *The Munro Review of Child Protection: Final Report: A Child-Centred System.* London: The Stationery Office.

NICE (National Institute for Health and Care Excellence) (2014) *Domestic Violence and Abuse: Multi-agency Working.* London: NICE.

NICE (National Institute for Health and Clinical Excellence) (2009) *When to Suspect Child Maltreatment.* London: NICE.

O'Dowd, T.C. (1988) 'Five years of heartsink patients in general practice.' *BMJ 297*, 6647, 528–530.

Pemberton, C. (2013) 'Community Care survey exposes how rising thresholds are leaving children in danger.' *Community Care*, 19 November. Available at www.communitycare. co.uk/2013/11/19/community-care-survey-exposes-rising-thresholds-leaving-children-danger/#.UqL4-fRdXA0, accessed on 9 December 2013.

Polnay, J.C. (2000) 'General practitioners and child protection case conference participation: reasons for non-attendance and proposals for a way forward.' *Child Abuse Review 9*, 2, 108–123.

Radford, L., Corral, S., Bradley, C., Fisher, H., *et al.* (2011) *Child Abuse and Neglect in the UK Today.* London: NSPCC.

RCGP and NSPCC (Royal College of General Practitioners and National Society for the Prevention of Cruelty to Children) (2014) *Safeguarding Children and Young People: The RCGP/NSPCC Safeguarding Children Toolkit for General Practice.* London: RCGP.

RCPCH (Royal College of Paediatrics and Child Health) (2014) *Safeguarding Children and Young People: Roles and Competences for Health Care Staff. Intercollegiate Document.* 3rd edition. London: RCPCH.

Simpson, C.M., Simpson, R.J., Power, K.G., Salter, A. and Williams, G.J. (1994) 'GPs' and health visitors' participation in child protection case conferences.' *Child Abuse Review 3*, 3, 211–230.

Strong, P.M. (2001) *The Ceremonial Order of the Clinic: Parents, Doctors and Medical Bureaucracies.* London: Routledge & Kegan Paul.

Tompsett, H., Ashworth, M., Atkins, C., Bell, L., *et al.* (2010) *The Child, the Family and the GP: Tensions and Conflicts of Interest in Safeguarding Children May 2006–October 2008. Final Report February 2010.* London: Kingston University.

Watt, G. (2011) 'Patient encounters in very deprived areas.' *British Journal of General Practice 61*, 583, 146–146.

Woodman, J. (2014) 'The Role of the GP for Children with (Possible) Abuse and Neglect: a Mixed Methods Study in England' Thesis, University College London. Available at http://discovery.ucl.ac.uk/1452201/, accessed 20 July 2016.

Woodman, J., Allister, J., Rafi, I., de Lusignan, S., *et al.* (2012a) 'Simple approaches to improve recording of concerns about child maltreatment in primary care records: developing a quality improvement intervention.' *British Journal of General Practice 62*, 600, e478–e486(479).

Woodman, J., Freemantle, N., Allister, J., de Lusignan, S., *et al.* (2012b) 'Variation in recorded child maltreatment concerns in UK primary care records: a cohort study using The Health Improvement Network (THIN) database.' *PLOS ONE 7*, 11, 1–9.

Woodman, J., Gilbert, R., Allister, J., Glaser, D. and Brandon, M. (2013) 'Responses to concerns about child maltreatment: a qualitative study of GPs in England.' *BMJ Open 3*, 12, e003894. DOI: 003810.001136/bmjopen-002013-003894

Woodman, J., Gilbert, R., Glaser, D., Allister, J. and Brandon, M. (2014a) 'Vulnerable family meetings: a way of promoting team working in GPs' everyday responses to child maltreatment?' *Social Sciences 3*, 341–358.

Woodman, J., Woolley, A., Gilbert, R., Rafi, I., *et al.* (2014b) *The GP's Role in Responding to Child Maltreatment: Time for a Rethink?* London: NSPCC.

7

RESPONDING TO CHILD NEGLECT

Learning from serious case reviews

Marian Brandon and Pippa Belderson

Introduction

Although neglect and its harmful consequences are increasingly being brought into public consciousness in the UK, practitioners still appear to be slow to recognise and respond when they confront neglect according to inspection reports (Office of Standards in Education, Children's Services and Skills (Ofsted) 2014). A survey undertaken by *Community Care* in 2013 also suggested that social workers thought that their managers downgraded neglect (Community Care 2013). Factors like these are not likely to foster confident, competent practice in this area. The case reviews of high profile child deaths in the UK (like those of Peter Connelly, Daniel Pelka and others) illustrate the ways in which practitioners struggle to understand and then act in a timely way when neglect is part of a child's life. One example of this is the gap in practitioners' grasp of what life was like, especially at home, for each of these two children. This suggests that more attention should be focused on ways of getting to know and understand neglected children, and their interactions with their parents and caregivers (Brandon *et al.* 2014a, 2014b). See particularly Chapters 3 and 10 for approaches to this challenge.

This chapter is based on cumulative learning about neglect from serious case reviews (SCRs) in England. SCRs are local reviews, required by statutory regulation to be carried out when a child has died or been seriously harmed, and maltreatment is known or suspected. The purpose of these reviews is to identify any improvements that are needed and to consolidate good practice. A key finding from the ongoing national analysis of these reviews is that neglect needs to be treated with as much urgency as any other type of maltreatment. Although this chapter considers reviews in England, these issues are not confined to England and there is concern to learn from child death reviews to improve practice throughout many of the world's economically advanced nations. Some findings cross continents. A group analysis of ten neglect-related child deaths in Victoria, Australia had some findings that chimed with our analysis here (Victorian Child Death Review Committee 2006). In this Australian analysis, the need to understand developmental histories of children and parents was highlighted as important for working with neglect effectively. The chapter discusses the findings from the series of four national biennial reviews of these cases (over 800) from 2003 to 2011 commissioned by the English Government (Brandon *et al.* 2008, 2009, 2010, 2012). The aim of these regular national analyses of SCRs is to distil learning for national policy and practice.

After a brief literature review considering what is known about neglect in cases of serious child maltreatment, and the effects of neglect on the developing child, this chapter will focus on the evidence within SCRs of interacting risk factors presented by the children and their families, and the learning to be gained from the ways in which professionals responded to the family and to each other as part of their multiagency involvement. Better professional responses are suggested, which take into account both the child's emotional development and her or his physical safety.

There is increasing recognition in the UK and internationally of the long-term harm that stems from living with neglect during childhood (Daniel, Taylor and Scott 2010; Davies and Ward 2012; Gilbert *et al.* 2009). Neglect is the most common form of maltreatment in England and almost half of all child protection plans (43%) are made in response to neglect (Department for Education (DfE) 2013). We are starting to understand that child neglect can also be life-threatening, and we now know that that it features in over 60 per cent of serious case reviews which are effectively worst outcome cases (Brandon *et al.* 2012).

There are limits to the learning about neglect from SCRs, not least because they are worst outcome cases and are not representative of all children who have experienced neglect. That said, these reviews do offer transferable learning because, discounting the death or serious harm, the range of circumstances of children and families at the centre of a review are very similar to those a practitioner will confront on a daily basis. In addition, our findings from SCRs chime with findings from national studies of neglect across a more representative sample of cases (Ofsted 2014). Finally, only one in ten children at the centre of an SCR had been the subject of a child protection plan at the time of their death or suffered serious harm (and this figure is dropping over time); so there is other important transferable learning from SCR cases not in the child protection system. Furthermore, within the 800-plus SCRs, half of the children were not even known to social services at the time of the incident which prompted the review. This emphasises the importance of universal services being sensitised to the presence of neglect and aware of neglect as a risk factor alongside others. For instance, see Chapter 6 for a description of GP responses to child neglect.

Neglect and child death

Although severe physical assault is the most common cause of death and serious injury for children at the centre of an SCR, we found that many of these children had also been living with neglectful care. It had not previously been known that in England more children who died from assault were the subject of a child protection plan for reasons of neglect rather than for physical abuse (Brandon *et al.* 2013). This might suggest that in these cases where neglect was considered to be the key cause of harm, the possibility of harm from physical abuse had been overlooked or discounted. Death arising directly from extreme neglect, for example starvation, is very rare indeed with about one such case arising in England each year (Sidebotham *et al.* 2011). Neglect is most often to the fore in those serious case reviews where maltreatment is a contributory rather than a direct factor in the child's death or injury. This does not, however, mean that the contributory maltreatment is not serious, rather that it cannot be directly linked to the death. The types of cases where neglect contributes to the child's death include sudden unexpected death in infancy (SUDI), young suicide and other deaths that are accidental or of unknown cause and in which neglect is believed to have played a part. The cases of young suicide demonstrate the long-term consequences that can arise for children who have suffered neglectful care in childhood.

Tensions in defining neglect

It has been argued that the lack of shared definitions and thresholds for neglect lead to problems in understanding the causes and pathways to different types of neglect and result in delay about key decisions (Gardner 2008; Horwath 2007). When neglect is separated out from the wider term 'maltreatment' there are a number of ways of defining and understanding what it means (see also Chapter 4). This presents similar challenges in our studies of serious case reviews as it does in day-to-day practice. Different subtypes of neglect can be distinguished, for example, physical, emotional, educational and medical (Dubowitz 1999; Horwath 2007; Howe 2006) and these can be experienced by a child separately or in combination. In our re-analysis of neglect in SCR cases in 2013, we identified a six-fold typology of circumstances we found to be linked to the most serious neglect. These were:

- severe deprivation

- medical neglect

- accidents with some elements of forewarning

- sudden unexpected deaths in infancy

- neglect in combination with physical abuse, and

- suicide among young people.

Later in this chapter we give examples of some of these circumstances. Details of cases are modified to ensure anonymity.

Neglect can be defined from the perspective of a child's right not to be subject to inhuman or degrading treatment (European Convention on Human Rights 1950, Article 3). It has been argued that this focuses, unhelpfully, on parental intentions, when one of the distinguishing features of neglect is the omission of specific behaviours rather than the deliberate commission of abusive acts (Connell-Carrick 2003; see also Chapter 4). Defining neglect in terms of the impact on the child (i.e. the likelihood of significant harm or impairment to the child's development) puts the emphasis, instead, on whether a child's needs are being met, regardless of parental culpability, and is the approach adopted in England. See pp.8–9 for the UK definition of child neglect.

The UK children's charity Action for Children notes that it takes extraordinary levels of organisation and determination to parent effectively in situations of poor housing, meagre income, lack of local resources and limited educational and employment prospects (Burgess *et al.* 2014). However, the reference to 'persistent failure to meet the child's physical and/or psychological needs' in the *Working Together* guidance (HM Government 2015, p.93) puts the emphasis on the frequency, enormity and pervasiveness of the behaviours that would identify them as abusive. This offers a potential benchmark for neglect as maltreatment, particularly since there is no definition of neglect in the relevant legislation, the Children Act 1989.

Understanding neglect and children's development from an ecological–transactional perspective

If neglect is understood more widely from an ecological perspective (Bronfenbrenner 1979) it meshes together the development of the child with their experience of care at home (and/or elsewhere) and their experiences in the wider environment. If neglect is further understood transactionally, there is an additional emphasis on the way that relationships and experiences shape the child's development over time (Cicchetti and Valentino 2005; Howe 2005;).

The ecological–transactional perspective aims to shed light on the dynamics of interactions between children, carers and agencies and the way that different risks of harm combine and interact to influence children's development and their safety. Parents' and carers' capacity to nurture their child safely is understood primarily in terms of their psychological sensitivity and availability to that child (see Chapters 1 and 10). A major predictor of poor parenting, including child neglect, is a lack of understanding of the psychological complexity of children, including babies. The ecological–transactional perspective also acknowledges that parents' resources and ability to keep children safe and nurtured are challenged by social and economic factors like poverty, poor housing and community violence, and other adversities like parental mental ill health, which will affect their capacity to be attuned and sensitive to their developing children.

As well as the economic environment, the work setting has to be taken into account; the capacity of foster carers, residential workers and other practitioners to offer sensitive care to young people is also affected by personal and work-related stress (Glisson and Hemmelgarn 1998). This ecological–transactional perspective was used as a theoretical base for each of the four biennial reviews of serious case reviews (Brandon *et al.* 2008, 2009; 2010; 2012) and is used again here.

Interacting and cumulative adversities

Cumulative adversities are potentially related to poor child development and it may be the interaction of multiple adversities, including neglect, that has the biggest impact on a child's development (Margolin and Gordis 2000). The broad social, physical and emotional context within which children are nurtured has an important impact on their development. A child's healthy development is reliant on good nutrition, maintaining good health, hygiene, economic security, a safe and secure physical environment, as well as opportunities for social interaction and play. Healthy development also relies on aspects of parenting such as stability, availability, affection and setting boundaries.

It is recognised that some disabled children may be at higher risk of being maltreated (Goldson 1998; Stalker and McArthur 2012; Sullivan and Knutson 2000). The prolonged and heightened dependence of disabled children on their parents and carers may make them more susceptible to neglect, and may also increase the stress on parents as triggers for physical and emotional abuse (Goldson 1998; Murray and Osborne 2009). Disabled children, particularly those with language disability, may be less able to express any maltreatment they are experiencing. It is important, however, to recognise that disabled children do not form a heterogeneous group, either in severity or type of disability, so an understanding of the particular nature of any underlying disability and how the child's development is affected is essential to appreciating the nature and impact of any maltreatment a child may be experiencing.

Neglect and the developing child at different ages

The evidence from our research into serious case reviews indicates that there are two age-related peaks of potentially life-threatening vulnerability to neglect, which accord more widely with vulnerabilities in children's development. These peaks are first, for the youngest children (infants and pre-schoolers) and second, for those in adolescence. Children in their middle years (aged six to ten years) feature much less often in SCRs (this age range normally accounts for no more than one in ten cases). The cluster of ages of children living with neglect that has severe or fatal consequences may reflect the specific vulnerabilities that children bring to and take from their physical and caregiving environments. Although there is emphasis in the literature on the deleterious effects of neglect on the youngest children and their developing brains (see Chapter 1) the age group where neglect is most prominent in serious case reviews is among young people aged 11–15 (Brandon *et al.* 2012).

Everyday childhood involves the child as an active, changing (growing and developing) individual, interacting with his or her world where the child both influences and is influenced by his or her environment (Aldgate *et al.* 2006; Margolin and Gordis 2000). Key developmental stages can be identified which have implications for understanding maltreatment and neglect in particular. In the first year of life, the child is particularly vulnerable to both physical abuse and neglect, because of rapidly developing skills in all areas, the formation of multiple neural connections in the brain, the importance of perceptual input and the development of attachment relationships (Finkelhor 1995, 2008; Harden 2004).

In the earliest months and years, a child's rapidly developing brain organises to reflect that child's environment. In this way neurons, neural systems and the brain change in a 'use-dependent' way. A lack of, or inappropriate, stimulation during this vital phase lays patterns that may affect the acquisition of future developmental milestones (Cicchetti and Howes 1991; Hildyard and Wolfe 2002). Failure to develop appropriate language skills due to neglect in this stage may lead on to wider cognitive and social impairments (see Chapter 2), whilst disorders of attachment can give rise to future emotional and social difficulties (see Chapter 1). During the pre-school years, there is a strong emphasis on social development. Early maltreatment may lead to difficulties in emotion regulation, initiating social interactions and learning to respond appropriately to others (Cicchetti and Howes 1991).

During the school years, the effects of early adversity may be seen in poorer academic achievement and further social difficulties, whilst early attachment disorders can result in persistent negative concepts of self and others (Cicchetti and Howes 1991; Harden 2004). Although the primary school period is one in which there are relatively fewer cases subject to SCRs, this a vital time for preventative help. If risks are not picked up and contained at this age, cumulative harm from neglect can lead to serious damage by the teenage years.

Adolescents carry with them the legacy of early experiences and nurture. The impact of missed opportunities to identify neglect and respond to unmet developmental needs in earlier years will also be carried forward. These experiences lay the foundation of adolescents' capacity to cope with or withstand the stresses that come from outside influences and internal pressures. Young people with experiences of neglect and the rejection this entails will be vulnerable to other types of maltreatment too, and there is increasing evidence of links between neglect and child sexual exploitation (Jay 2014). Over time there is a moderate to strong link between maltreatment and attempted suicide, especially when the harm is cumulative, including neglect (Gilbert *et al.* 2009).

Overall, the impact of neglect (among other harms) on adolescent development very often presents as conduct disorder, alcohol misuse, drug misuse, risk-taking behaviour, poor educational achievement and recurrent victimisation (MacMillan *et al.* 2009; Rees *et al.* 2010). Rees and colleagues' study of adolescent neglect emphasises the vulnerability of adolescents and warns against the readiness to see adolescents as resilient primarily because they have survived into their teens (Rees *et al.* 2010; see Chapter 5 for an in-depth discussion of their findings). Recognition of these different stages is important to understanding what it is like to be a child living with neglect, its potential impact, and how it might reveal itself through the child's changing behaviour and responses.

Professional responses to child neglect as described in serious case reviews

In this chapter, learning about neglect, professional responses and the impact of neglect on the developing child are drawn from different subsamples from the total of more than 800 serious case reviews which took place over the eight-year period from 2003 to 2011. A mixed methods design was used in the analysis of each of the four original biennial studies, and in subsequent re-analyses. This combined a quantitative approach to examining and 'counting' large numbers of cases, with a qualitative approach to probing smaller numbers of cases in some depth. It is primarily the qualitative findings that are discussed in this chapter.

Some of these findings have been reported previously elsewhere: as a report for the National Society for the Prevention of Cruelty to Children (NSPCC) (Brandon *et al.* 2013); in a separate journal article (Brandon *et al.* 2014a); in a specific study of child development in SCRs (Brandon *et al.* 2011); and in a report on missed opportunities to recognise and respond to neglect for the Department for Education (Brandon *et al.* 2014b).

Figure 7.1 summarises the analysis of factors in a subsample of neglect cases primarily from 2010, and reveals the way that a number of consistent themes interact. These themes mostly concern professionals' behaviour and their responses to the families' multiple and complex needs, as well as to child neglect. A range of factors was apparent in professionals' understanding of the families and this had an impact on their behaviour. The end result in terms of professional response in these worst outcome cases tended to be that first, the changing developmental and other needs of the children were not seen; second, that (often severe) neglect was missed or downgraded, or masked other danger; and third that the handling of the case tended to drift, with a lack of any sense of urgency.

The way that the issues raised by these themes played out is considered below in relation to:

- six types or circumstances of neglect-related death and serious harm that we identified most frequently

- the child's development at different ages, and

- the professionals' responses.

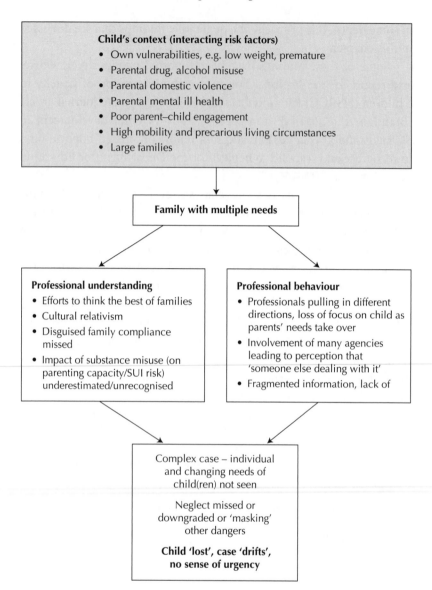

Figure 7.1 Common themes from a subsample of neglect serious case review cases

Unexpected and accidental death: The child's context

Infants who died suddenly and unexpectedly (sudden unexpected deaths of infants or SUDI cases) tended to be very young indeed and many died before the age of three months. SUDI cases make up over 15 per cent of all SCRs in England and the recurring finding about the very young age of death is in keeping with Blair and colleagues' study of SUDI in the wider community (2009). Cases where children died as a result of an accident (all of which had an element of forewarning) involved all age groups, although the focus here is on younger children. Most of the babies had particular vulnerabilities, for example being born prematurely or with a low birth weight and consequently with special feeding and/or care needs which placed higher demands on caregivers. Many parents struggled with alcohol misuse and/or drug misuse, but in these cases tended not to be honest with professionals about the extent of their alcohol or drug dependency, which was either underestimated or not known by the social worker. Some parents were young, under 20 years of age. Overall, we know that while approximately a quarter of the babies at the centre of an SCR had teenaged parents, by far the majority had older parents, with a significant minority being in their forties (Brandon *et al.* 2012).

A precarious and dangerous physical home environment

In many of the sudden unexplained infant deaths (SUDI) and accident cases, the child's home environment was dangerous, precarious or both; one review mentioned 'precarious living arrangements – homelessness, many moves'. In one of the most extreme cases, home conditions were so poor that there was a lack of the basic facilities of sanitation, electricity and running water. Conditions for babies and their siblings were often cramped and overcrowded, and housing tended to be described as 'inadequate', 'in a state of disrepair', 'sparsely furnished', 'unhygienic and unsafe' and with 'visible signs of rubbish'. At least two babies in such environments were seen by professionals to be very dirty and have ammonia burns from unchanged nappies when they were only weeks old. This type of child-toxic environment appeared to go beyond the result of poverty alone. Rather it was connected to the interaction of underlying problems such as addiction and mental ill health, not to a single cause.

A precarious emotional environment

Some of these babies and very young children were frequently left alone or unsupervised, or left with a succession of different carers. A feature of neglect is the inability of the parents to keep their child 'in mind' (see Chapter 1). This has damaging consequences for a child's long-term emotional wellbeing, but in these most dangerous cases of neglect of the youngest and most vulnerable babies, the inability to think about the child and keep them in mind could have immediate and life-threatening implications. For example, one baby with complex health needs was left unchecked by her parents for more than 12 hours. This was in spite of the fact that she had been unwell the day before she was found dead.

Professional responses to an unsafe physical and/or emotional environment

Professional concern in these cases tended to be dominated by practical needs and attempts to improve home conditions and the visible signs of physical neglect. However, even these somewhat narrow actions were not followed through with any sense of urgency or in a timescale that matched the extreme vulnerability of very young babies. The life-threatening nature of the neglect stemming from the combination of very poor home conditions (the physical environment) and parents not being attuned to their children's psychological needs (the emotional environment) was not recognised. This was the case in one family where 'the children were observed by police and children's social care to be unkempt, cold and dirty and the baby soaked in urine and very, very cold.' The major thrust of professionals' work in these dangerous environments was to inform each other of their concerns about the family, rather than taking urgent action to achieve change. Some professionals considered that they had discharged their duty by informing children's social care of the issues and took no responsibility for following up when action was not taken on that information.

The expression 'dirty but happy' was found in the health visitor's case recording of the family of one premature baby who died.

This revealed a professional tolerance of extremely poor, cramped and unsafe living conditions where the baby did not have a cot or sleeping space. The acceptance of this family's choice to live in this way, not as a matter of necessity but as a positive affirmation of their culture, reflected a sense of cultural relativism that endorsed dangerous conditions as an issue of cultural choice. As in many other SUDI cases, this was a large family with more than three children. In this and in other cases, all the children tended to be regarded by professionals as a single entity and not as individuals with differing needs and risks of harm (see Chapter 3).

The particular vulnerability of a low birth weight baby in these highly dangerous living circumstances was missed by professionals who should have been on high alert. Although there was a child protection plan for one infant in the category of neglect, professionals were falsely reassured about the baby's safety, not least because relationships between children and parents mostly appeared to be good:

> The GP and HV were aware of baby x's vulnerability due to prematurity. Records do not indicate that this was linked (by them) with other SUDI risk factors, which included parental smoking, parental substance misuse and co-sleeping, to identify the need for any specific intervention in that area.

In these circumstances an adequate emotional environment did not compensate for a dangerous physical environment and other risk factors for an infant's sudden unexpected death. In this and other cases, the children's welfare was thought to be 'good enough' and parents were considered to be 'just about' coping without there being any clear sense of what this meant in relation to the child's development or immediate safety: 'professionals did not focus sufficiently on the distinction between parents' motivation to change and factors that would indicate their capacity to do so'. In one case, a mother's keenness to stop drug taking meant that professionals minimised her continuing substance misuse and its actual impact on the children. In other cases, drug misuse was addressed narrowly without thinking of the pattern of drug use on a child's safety, for example:

> a tendency for professionals to concentrate on one feature of drug misuse (heroin), without an understanding of the more complex effects of chaotic or polydrug/alcohol misuse – a combination of

drugs that is likely to induce drowsiness/deep sleeping and impair parenting capacity.

Neglect combined with and masking violent assault/deliberate homicide

In cases where babies and pre-school-age children died as a result of assault, there were signs of neglect in the young child's delayed development and also, often, in the development of their siblings. Many of the children who had lived with neglect and died a violent death showed signs of faltering weight or serious weight loss. One toddler was described as 'thin and poorly nourished'. Another baby was 'seriously under-nourished and dehydrated', showing clear evidence of deprivation of food and water, with a weight fall from the 25th to the 2nd centile.

Parents' behaviour

Violent and volatile adult relationships tended to characterise the cases where the children lived with neglect and had a violent death, for example where there were concerns about both rough handling and weight loss. One young child who was thought to have died 'unexpectedly' was found at post-mortem to have fractures. The mother and her partner were said to be hostile and non-compliant with professionals and had not registered with a general medical practitioner (GP). The partner, who was known to be violent, often had sole care of siblings because the children's mother was not coping. In spite of being known to be struggling to cope, this mother was expected by professionals to supervise any contact her volatile partner had with their young child.

The child's home environment

The home environment of many of the neglected children who had a violent death was of a poor quality, with similar physical conditions to those children who died unexpectedly or through accidents. In other cases of assault on children, however, home conditions were good, or else chaotic and disorganised but not dirty or dilapidated. One household with four children was described as cluttered and untidy, with no signs of toys and not looking as though children lived there. Parents in these cases were, on the whole, hostile to professional contact and could control the parameters of their engagement, not least through engendering fear in professionals. In one example where the mother was very controlling, chaos in the house and illness were the only areas in which she would allow professionals to get involved. She made sure, for example, that they were not allowed to see the children alone.

Professional responses

Where professionals maintained a focus on the child rather than just on parental problems, this tended to be restricted to the child's physical health and development and not their emotional needs. Warning signs of problems from older siblings and their worsening behaviour in school were often missed. Other school-linked signs of neglect and harm in siblings included children always being hungry, or regularly arriving at school without a packed lunch and wearing poor or inappropriate or ill-fitting clothing.

Cases tended to be closed early because of poor or difficult engagement or on the false assumption of improvement: 'while the decision to close the case was made on the basis that the situation had improved, there was little evidence of this'. In one example, the mother said that the baby was feeding well, which was not so, and in another a father said that a Moses basket had been provided for the baby, but its existence was not checked as access to the bedroom was refused. In these cases there was little challenge of parents' insistence that they were complying with requests for change. Based on this, professional reassurance was not backed by supporting evidence of change.

An overriding sense of fear may have inhibited professionals from feeling safe enough to challenge parents and to 'be curious'. In a similar vein, little attention was paid to past family history. One assessment of 'low level neglect' was not changed after children's social care had received new information about a parent's previous offences against a younger child and a past pattern of dangerous behaviour with a new baby was missed.

Even when a child protection plan for neglect was in place, there was rarely a clear understanding of the harm that was stemming from the neglect itself, so that risks from both physical abuse and neglect were missed or downgraded. Professionals were sometimes said in the review to have been 'going through the motions' in carrying out the child protection process; for example, at the child protection conference, the severity of the neglect was played down. In these cases of death and serious injury there appeared to be a lack of skill, confidence and experience in dealing with the challenges that the case presented. Frequent turnover of staff tended to increase the proportion of new and newly qualified staff without experience of complex work, child protection or multiagency working.

Neglect and child disability

Particular issues prevented practitioners paying sufficient attention to the impact of neglect on disabled children's development, as follows:

* allowing the parents' voice to dominate (especially if they are volatile and difficult to confront)

* seeing the disability, not the child, and viewing a case essentially as supporting disability rather than supporting or protecting the child (including identifying and responding to signs and symptoms of harm)

* accepting a different and lower standard of parenting for a disabled child than would be tolerated for a non-disabled child.

One example of different expectations of care for a disabled rather than a non-disabled child is having an agreed strategy of locking a child in their bedroom at night. This was the case for a ten-year-old child whose disabilities were connected with a congenital neurological condition. Adam (not his real name) told his teachers about being locked in his bedroom each night and how he tried to get out. Trapped in his room, isolated and unable to get to the bathroom, he soiled and smeared faeces in his room, which was described as being 'in a terrible state'. The condition of his bare and filthy room contrasted with the rest of the house. Adam's parents spoke to the social worker and others in the multiagency team about locking their son in his room as a way of managing his sleep disturbance and sleep-walking problems and to stop him hurting himself. Despite many years of involvement, social workers had only seen Adam's bedroom four times. There is no evidence that any professional had considered the impact that spending a considerable amount of time isolated and locked away in this bare room was having on this child.

Parental behaviour

Adam's distressed behaviour (smearing) escalated frustration in his parents who, largely because of their own childhood experiences of rejection and abuse, had a heightened sensitivity to their child's behaviour and disability, which they interpreted as dependent, difficult and demanding. This triggered more coercive, rigid and insensitive care. In this example it was easy to see that the interaction of the vulnerabilities possessed by both child and parent played out to increase the risk of insensitive dangerous care and harm to the child (Howe 2006). The distressing outcome was that ten-year-old Adam died through hanging, although it was unclear whether the death was an accident or suicide.

Professional responses: Confusion over responsibility

In numerous cases, and often those where children had a disability, it was common for many agencies to be involved at the same time. But in spite of, or perhaps as a result of this, there could be no completed assessment and no coordinated multiagency response in place. Agencies could easily lose the thread with these complex cases: 'Children's social care became confused about the responsibility of different teams for different members of the family, and then closed the matter.' It is interesting to note the impersonal term 'matter' in relation to this child's case.

Adolescent neglect: Death by suicide or neglect

A significant minority of SCRs for older young people are prompted by a young person's suicide where there has been known maltreatment. When we studied seven suicides over one two-year period we discovered that all had experienced enduring and significant neglect. Loss, death of significant adult figures and rejection had been prominent in these young people's short lives. Some of these young people had long-standing mental health problems, which had been recognised during early school years when child and adolescent mental health services (CAMHS) became involved. At age five, professionals had serious concern about one child's emotional health, describing 'an angry, frightened little boy who would wait at school for his mother, but she would often not come, be late or be under the influence of alcohol or drugs'. One adolescent had been a carer for a sibling during childhood because of their mother's mental ill health and at one stage the house had been declared unfit for habitation. Poor weight gain and failure to thrive had been identified in this child from the age of two and continued throughout childhood. As an adolescent this young person talked of being hungry, with access to limited and poor quality food at home.

Neglect occurred during these young people's childhood and continued sporadically or continuously into adolescence, often combined with other types of maltreatment. As they grew up, these young people experienced an unpredictable or frightening family life. It was characterised by inconsistent bouts of parental mental ill health or violence towards them and their siblings, as well as between adults; bouts of parental alcohol and/or drug misuse; and two young people suffered sexual abuse from their mothers' partners. All these young people had experienced multiple types of maltreatment, multiple losses, separation and feelings of abandonment. They experienced multiple moves and a general lack of continuity. They had unresolved issues about abandonment – with one young person always seeking out his mother and wanting to be reunited with her, but experiencing repeated bouts of rejection. One child's mother warned him that she was going to die and he would have no one to look after him so he would be better off dead. Another child's father regularly issued threats to kill. The young people had limited sources of support and were isolated. To act preventively, it would have been important to know their early history to understand their development and their behaviour as older adolescents (see Chapters 1,3 and 5).

Professional responses

These young people who committed or attempted suicide tended to have long histories of involvement with a number of agencies (especially local government children's social care departments (CSC), CAMHS and youth offending teams). Child protection plans for either neglect or emotional abuse had been in place for most of the young people, often over extended time periods. Some had been in care for substantial periods of time and in all these cases CSC had responsibility for their protection and wellbeing.

Foster carers needed additional support to cope with one young person's behaviour, especially when he became 'threatening and dangerous', leading to another rejection. CSC sometimes closed the case at such points of heightened need; for example, they encouraged a 14-year-old to live with family friends. Serious offending led him into custody, but at the point of discharge from custody, CSC still maintained the decision that this 14-year-old was 'no longer a priority' for a service; he would not have received support had he lived long enough to be discharged.

One young person phoned children's social care asking to be accommodated at the age of 17 because she could no longer tolerate her mother's alcohol abuse and lack of food and care at home. The request for help was refused by CSC who thought this a lower-level case more appropriate for youth services or the youth offending service, and no service was offered. This young person experienced loss of protection as a child once she left school. There were no protected routes for her into adulthood, and no routes out of her neglectful situation at home and dangerous links to local gangs. No support was available in the transition to adulthood.

Some young people used school as a source of support and nurture (one young person had a 94% attendance record) and school could be a place of safety even during bouts of exclusion. There could be good engagement between the young people and both school and CAMHS workers: 'the CAMHS worker was in frequent and regular touch for the subsequent three years, developing a strong therapeutic relationship despite x's reputation for being difficult to engage'.

One young person's good intellectual development, and his capacity to make relationships and confide in professionals, showed that not all aspects of his development were negative. Yet it would be a substantial leap from here to say that he was resilient. Rees *et al.* (2010) have found that professionals can be prone to misinterpreting positive aspects of a young person's demeanour or development as resilience (or good development in adverse circumstances), and that this can blunt their capacity to appreciate the negative impact that maltreatment has on the young person's overall development and sense of self.

In one case the author of the overview (or summary) report within the SCR suggested that things might have been better for the young person if he had been assigned professionally 'inquisitive' social workers who wanted to know why his behaviour was so difficult at this point in his life, and who were also curious about the research behind neglect, attachment and child development.

It is important that social workers in particular work hard to develop a relationship with children and young people, getting to know and understand them as individuals. This includes taking notice of what they have to say, considering what it means – and where it meets with their best interests – and acting on what they have to say. The social worker should act as an advocate for young people who are being looked after or have child protection plans, or find them an independent advocate. They should make sure that specialist assessments are completed (in one case a full mental health assessment requested from CAMHS was never followed through). Clear plans for the future should be set out based on an understanding of the young person's developmental needs, and young people should be involved in these plans and understand them (see Chapter 5).

All of these activities are legitimately within the social worker's role and sphere of expertise. If the social worker is not able to carry out all aspects of this role, best practice demands that they make sure that someone else does. There are, of course, resource implications here, and budget savings in England have resulted in heavy cuts to all support services for young people, leaving many young people cast adrift.

Better responses by practitioners to children of all ages

Professional curiosity and analysis of the child's situation in context

We argued in our study of child development (Brandon et al. 2011, 2012) that practitioners need to be curious about the parents' early reactions to their child, and specifically that they need to observe and reflect on the child's responses to his or her caregivers. These parent–child interactions are the foundations of emotional development and of attachment behaviour. What happens during feeding, particularly, provides powerful clues to emotional development (see Chapters 1 and 2).

In most of the examples discussed in this chapter there has been an emphasis in the professional response on single issues: hostile parents, domestic violence, physical neglect and home conditions, heroin use, and with the babies and younger children, feeding and the mechanics of feeding. There was rarely any concerted attempt to try to understand the developing child in the context of their wider caregiving environment and to search for different possible explanations for the child's poor development.

Understanding the impact of parental care on the child's behaviour and development

For the older children it was clear that to obtain a good picture of their current developmental state, professionals needed to get a sense of their developmental pathway over time. Children who feel that their needs are repeatedly unrecognised, ignored or misunderstood are likely to become distressed, angry and desperate. Issues that prevented practitioners paying sufficient attention to the impact of maltreatment on children and young people's development were as follows:

- Not making a relationship or getting to know the child or young person.

- Not taking account of what the child or young person had to say to make sense of them as a person, and of the impact that their experiences (especially of poor care and nurture) had on their sense of themselves and on how they behaved.

- Not speaking to the child. In one case the only consistent efforts to gain the child's view were by staff at school (the child had disabilities and global developmental delay) but the child was not spoken to during a social work assessment.

- Pockets of good development in maltreated young people do not necessarily signal resilience.

The learning about emotional development and behavioural distress in all these children, including disabled children, suggests that there are linked questions that practitioners need to ask:

- What does each parent or parent figure bring, psychologically, to the relationship with their child?

- What does the child mean to the parent?

- What does the parent mean to the child?

Questioning the meaning of the child for the parent seems a good way for social workers and other professionals to make sense of the development of children of all ages, and of their care and nurture. Grappling with these questions can help the professional to understand the child in the context of the care they receive (the caregiving environment) or received at home before they left or became homeless. They can then build a clear plan for help, support and protection together with the child, the parent(s) and other professionals.

In many neglect-related SCRs there are examples of specific parental behaviour that is incongruent with the child's developmental needs. This potentially developmentally harmful parental behaviour included:

- not being emotionally available or attuned to the young child's needs (e.g. being constantly on the phone)

- not giving children adequate food or 'forgetting' to feed them

- locking children in their rooms for long periods or keeping them out of sight

- opting out of responsibility or giving up trying to control a pre-pubescent child

- expecting children to be carers for siblings and to protect siblings from harmful parental behaviour – for example, violence including domestic violence.

Considering the impact of such care on children's development emphasises the importance of puzzling over the meaning that each child has for his or her parents (or parent and step-parent) and the way each child makes their parent(s) feel. In some of these families one child is singled out for rejecting treatment; in others all the children in the family seem to be treated in a similar way. But even in families where the parenting seems to follow the same pattern for all children, each child's experiences will in reality be different.

As we have seen, a number of the children who were the subject of SCRs began their childhood in an environment where they experienced both unpredictable danger (e.g. being hit as infants, living with violence or in other frightening environments) and/or emotional abandonment experiences (not being tended to when distressed or ill, not being fed when hungry or not being held close when fed). These early patterns of experience repeated over time would be likely to set the scene for a developmentally damaging, disorganised attachment. There is evidence from the reviews that these children's carer or carers were likely to cause them distress and/or fear for much or part of the time during their early months and years. Their parents' behaviour seemed to fit into the typologies of parents who were hostile, helpless or intermittently hostile and helpless (Howe 2006; see also Chapter 1). These carers *frighten* their infants or behave in *frightened* way when they are faced with their child's basic needs for care and nurture. Howe describes how this plays out in the developing relationship between the parents and child: 'parent and child find themselves in a loop of catastrophic feedback, leading in each case to a state of emotional hyper-arousal and behaviour that becomes hopelessly out of control (hostile, helpless, or rapid switches between the two)' (Howe 2005, p.40).

Understanding the impact of parents' childhood experiences

The relationship histories of many of the carers in these SCRs revealed their own abuse, neglect, loss, rejection and trauma, increasing the likelihood that they would be emotionally and psychologically unavailable when their children needed them most. These parents were also living in a high-stress environment, where most had debt problems or faced eviction and struggled with mental ill health and substance misuse. Many parents were caught up in volatile relationships where there was domestic violence. These parents were highly likely to have felt overwhelmed by their own unresolved feelings of fear, abandonment and powerlessness. Studying these cases in retrospect, it is easier to recognise that some of these parents were finding ways to switch off from their children. There were examples of parents who did not feed babies or restricted their young child's intake of food, or made feeding a distressing experience. Other parents appeared to be too emotionally preoccupied and overwhelmed, or perhaps not intellectually able to keep in mind their child's need for regular food. Young children, especially babies, are wholly dependent on their carers for nurture and for survival, and by denying these children's most basic needs for survival, parents are in effect denying their child's existence. The child's demands appear to make these parents feel so distressed or angry that it feels better or safer not to connect with the child. Locking a child away each night for increasingly lengthy periods of time is a similar demonstration that the parent cannot bear to see or hear that child.

Understanding the impact of neglect at different developmental stages

The findings from SCRs reinforce the particular points of danger from neglect for children at different ages and developmental stages. The youngest babies are most vulnerable and the very young age of babies dying a 'sudden and unexpected' death (SUDI) highlight the life-threatening nature of poor conditions and poor or dangerous parental supervision. The parents' inability to keep these baby's needs in mind has long-term consequences for their emotional wellbeing, but at this very young age it also has consequences for their immediate survival.

Understanding the impact of a poor environment and /or poverty

As we have seen, the poor physical fabric of the household is in many cases a result of social and economic hardships not always wholly within parental control. On a societal level, heightened levels of poverty are likely to result in increasingly poor and precarious environments for children, which can in themselves present a threat to life for particularly vulnerable babies and children. Neglect and poverty can interact disastrously for children, and it takes a skilled and compassionate practitioner to understand the ways in which the two conditions need to be disentangled and not be seen as synonymous.

Conclusions

In dealing with interacting risks, the approach that comes most to the fore here is the need to ensure the child's safety in his or her environment, both emotionally and physically. Good relationships between parents and children are essential for emotional wellbeing, but good relationships cannot always protect against dangerous living conditions (e.g. fire hazards) nor against precarious parenting practices (e.g. dangerous co-sleeping), especially for the youngest innately vulnerable babies. In the same way, this chapter has shown that poor parent–child relationships, for instance rejection and changes of carer, can be disastrous even in the context of reasonable physical care.

Public health approaches which, when successful, reach whole populations, can potentially encourage professionals, families and communities to change their behaviour. The Marmot Report (2010) recommended primary prevention across six priority areas. These encompass ensuring a safe physical *and* emotional environment for children and their families, in order to:

- give every child the best start in life

- enable all children, young people and adults to maximise their capabilities and have control over their lives

- create fair employment and good work for all

- ensure a healthy standard of living for all

- create and develop healthy and sustainable places and communities

- strengthen the role and impact of ill-health prevention.

Public health approaches are important for preventing maltreatment for children of all ages. However, at a community level, these prevention strategies are at their most challenging in areas of high deprivation and vulnerability (Wood *et al.* 2012). Targeted support for families known to be vulnerable may help to prevent accidents (Reading *et al.* 2008). Specialist services like Safe Care, enhanced health visiting and Nurse Family Partnerships may also make a difference to the most serious neglect risks (Pecora *et al.* 2012; see also Chapter 9).

Adolescents, like younger children, need to be physically and emotionally healthy and to live in a safe and healthy environment. This means that practitioners need to be especially aware of the social ecology for vulnerable adolescents with a long history of neglect and rejection, which may also include care leavers (Finkelhor 2008).

These young people need a safe, supportive environment and cannot be expected to thrive living alone in isolated, poor quality accommodation (Rees *et al.* 2011).

Key learning points

The research on serious case reviews reported in this chapter offers two overarching learning points in relation to guarding against the most dangerous outcomes from child neglect:

– the need for children to be physically and emotionally healthy, and

– the need for children to have a safe and healthy living environment.

Questions for reflection

– How can you foster healthy physical and emotional environments for children?

– Are you curious about the interactions between parents and their children? For example, do you allow time to observe and reflect on the child's responses to his or her caregivers?

– What might assist you in doing more of these things?

References

Aldgate, J., Jones, D.P.H., Rose, W. and Jeffrey, C. (2006) *The Developing World of the Child.* London: Jessica Kingsley Publishers.

Blair, P., Sidebotham, P., Edmonds, M., Heckstall-Smith, E. and Fleming, P. (2009) 'Hazardous cosleeping environments and risk factors amenable to change: case-control study of SIDS in south west England.' *British Medical Journal.* DOI: 10.1136/bmj.b3666

Brandon, M., Bailey, S. and Belderson, P. (2010) *Building on the Learning from Serious Case Reviews: A Two-year Analysis of Serious Case Reviews 2007–2009.* Research Report DFE-RR040. London: Department for Education.

Brandon, M., Bailey, S., Belderson, P., Gardner, R., *et al.* (2009) *Understanding Serious Case Reviews and Their Impact: A Biennial Analysis of Serious Case Reviews 2005–7.* Research Report DCSF-RR129. London: Department for Children Schools and Families.

Brandon, M., Bailey, S., Belderson, P. and Larsson B. (2013) *Neglect and Serious Case Reviews.* Norwich: University of East Anglia/NSPCC.

Brandon, M., Bailey, S., Belderson, P. and Larsson, B. (2014a) 'The role of neglect in serious case reviews.' *Child Abuse Review 23,* 4, 235–245.

Brandon, M., Belderson, P., Warren, C., Gardner, R. *et al.* (2008) *Analysing Child Death and Serious Injury through Abuse and Neglect: What Can We Learn? A Biennial Analysis of Serious Case Reviews 2003–5.* Research Report DCSF-RR023. London: Department for Children, Schools and Families.

Brandon, M., Glaser, D., Maguire, S., McRory, E., Lushey, C. and Ward, H. (2014b) *Missed Opportunities: Indicators of Neglect – What is Ignored, Why and What Can Be Done.* DFE-RR404. Available at www.gov.uk/government/uploads/system/ uploads/attachment_data/file/379747/RR404_-_Indicators_of_neglect_missed_ opportunities.pdf, accessed on 23 May 2016.

Brandon, M., Sidebotham, P. Bailey, S., Belderson, P., Hawley, C., Ellis, C. and Megson, M. (2012) *New Learning from Serious Case Reviews.* Research Report DFE-RR226. London: Department for Education.

Brandon, M., Sidebotham, P., Ellis, C., Bailey, S. and Belderson, P. (2011) *Child and Family Practitioners' Understanding of Child Development: Lessons Learnt from a Small Sample of Serious Case Reviews.* DFE-RR110. London: Department for Education

Bronfrenbrenner, U. (1979) *The Ecology of Human Development.* Cambridge, MA: Harvard University Press.

Burgess, C., Daniel, B., Scott, J., Dobbin, H., Mulley, K., and Whitfield, E. (2014) *Preventing Child Neglect in the UK: An Annual Review by Action for Children in Partnership with the University of Stirling.* Watford: Action for Children.

Children Act 1989 c.41. London: The Stationery Office.

Cicchetti, D. and P.W. Howes (1991) 'Developmental psychopathology in the context of the family: illustrations from the study of child maltreatment.' *Canadian Journal of Behavioural Science 23,* 3, 257–281.

Cicchetti, D. and Valentino, K. (2005) 'An ecological–transactional perspective on child maltreatment: failure of the average expectable environment and its influence on child development.' *Developmental Psychopathology 3,* 129–201.

Community Care (2013) 'Social workers unlikely to act quickly on neglect cases.' *Community Care* 26 September 2012. Available at www.communitycare.co.uk/ articles/27/09/2012/118548/social-workers-unlikely-to-act-quickly-on-neglect-cases.htm 2012, accessed on 29 July 2014.

Connell-Carrick, K. (2003) 'A critical review of empirical literature: identifying correlates of child neglect.' *Child and Adolescent Social Work Journal 20,* 389–425.

Daniel, B., Taylor, J. and Scott, J. (2010) 'Recognition of neglect and early response: an overview of a systematic review of the literature.' *Child and Family Social Work 15,* 248–257.

Davies, C. and Ward, H. (2012) *Safeguarding Children Across Services: Messages from Research on Identifying and Responding to Child Maltreatment.* London: Department for Education.

Department for Education (2013) *Statistical First Release: Characteristics of Children in Need. Headlines.* London: Department for Education.

Dubowitz, H. (1999) *Neglected Children: Research Practice and Policy.* Thousand Oaks, CA: Sage.

European Court of Human Rights (1950) *European Convention on Human Rights.* Available at www.echr.coe.int/Documents/Convention_ENG.pdf, accessed on 23 May 2016.

Finkelhor, D. (1995) 'The victimization of children: a developmental perspective.' *American Journal of Orthopsychiatry 65,* 2, 177–193.

Finkelhor, D. (2008) *Childhood Victimisation: Violence, Crime and Abuse in the Lives of Young People.* New York: Oxford University Press.

Gardner, R. (2008) *Developing an effective response to neglect and emotional harm to children.* Norwich: University of East Anglia/NSPCC.

Gilbert, R., Widom, C.S., Brown, K., Fergusson, D., Webb, F. and Johnson, S. (2009) 'Burden and consequences of maltreatment in high income countries.' *Lancet 373*, 68–81.

Glisson, C. and Hemmelgarn, A. (1998) 'The effects of organizational climate and interorganizational coordination on the quality and outcomes of children's service systems.' *Child Abuse & Neglect 22*, 5, 401–421.

Goldson, E. (1998) 'Children with disabilities and child maltreatment.' *Child Abuse & Neglect 22*, 7, 663–667.

Harden, B.J. (2004) 'Safety and stability for foster children: a developmental perspective.' *Future of Children 14*, 1, 30–47.

HM Government (2015) *Working Together to Safeguard Children. A Guide to Inter-agency Working to Safeguard and Promote the Welfare of Children.* London: DfE. Available at www.gov.uk/government/publications/working-together-to-safeguard-children--2, accessed on 7 June 2016.

Hildyard, K.L. and Wolfe, D.A. (2002) 'Child neglect: developmental issues and outcomes.' *Child Abuse & Neglect 26*, 6–7, 679–695.

Horwath, J. (2007) *Child Neglect: Identification and Assessment.* Basingstoke: Palgrave.

Howe, D. (2005) *Child Abuse and Neglect: Attachment, Development and Intervention.* Houndmills: Palgrave Macmillan.

Howe, D. (2006) 'Disabled children, maltreatment and attachment.' *British Journal of Social Work 36*, 743–760.

Jay, A. (2014) *Independent Inquiry into Child Sexual Exploitation in Rotherham (1997–2013).* Rotherham Metropolitan Borough Council.

Macmillan, H.L., Wathen, C.N., Barlow, J., Fergusson, D.M., Leventhal, J.M. and Taussig, H.N. (2009) 'Interventions to prevent child maltreatment and associated impairment.' *Lancet 373*, 9659, 250–266.

Margolin, G. and Gordis, E. (2000) 'The effects of family and community violence on children.' *Annual Review of Psychology 51*, 445–479.

Marmot, M. (2010) *Fair Society, Healthy Lives: Strategic Review of Health Inequalities in England post-2010.* London: UCL Institute of health Equity. Available at www.instituteofhealthequity.org/projects/fair-society-healthy-lives-the-marmot-review, accessed on 23 May 2016.

Murray, M. and Osborne, C. (2009) *Safeguarding Disabled Children. Practice Guidance.* London: Department of Children, Schools and Families.

Ofsted (Office of Standards in Education, Children's Services and Skills) (2014) *In the Child's Time: Professional Responses to Neglect.* Manchester: Ofsted. Available at www.gov.uk/government/publications/professional-responses-to-neglect-in-the-childs-time, accessed on 23 May 2016.

Pecora, P., Sanders, D., Wilson, D., English, D., Puckett, A. and Rudlang-Perman, K. (2012) 'Addressing common forms of child maltreatment: evidence-informed interventions and gaps in current knowledge' *Child and Family Social Work.* DOI: 10.1111/cfs.12021

Reading, R., Jones, A., Haynes, R., Daras, K. and Edmond, A. (2008) 'Individual factors explain neighbourhood variations in accidents to children under 5 years of age.' *Social Science and Medicine 67*, 915–927.

Rees, G., Gorin, S., Jobe, A., Stein, M., Medforth, R. and Goswami, H. (2010) *Safeguarding Young People: Responding to Young People Aged 11 to 17 Who Are Maltreated.* London: The Children's Society.

Rees, G., Stein, M., Hicks, L. and Gorin, S. (2011) *Adolescent Neglect: Research, Policy and Practice.* London: Jessica Kingsley Publishers.

Sidebotham, P., Bailey, S., Belderson, P. and Brandon, M. (2011) 'Fatal child maltreatment in England 2005–2009.' *Child Abuse & Neglect 35*, 4, 299–306.

Stalker, K. and McArthur, K. (2012) 'Child abuse, child protection and disabled children: a review of recent research.' *Child Abuse Review 21*, 1, 24–40.

Sullivan, P.M. and Knutson, J.F. (2000) 'Maltreatment and disabilities: a population-based epidemiological study.' *Child Abuse & Neglect 24*, 10, 1257–1273.

Victorian Child Death Review Committee (2006) *Child Death Group Analysis: Effective Responses to Neglect.* Melbourne: Child Safety Commissioner.

Wood, A., Pasupathy, D., Pell, J., Fleming, M. and Smith, G. (2012) 'Trends in socioeconomic inequalities in risk of sudden infant death syndrome, other causes of infant mortality, and stillbirth in Scotland: population based study.' *BMJ 2012*, 344, e1552.

3

PREVENTING AND REVERSING CHILD NEGLECT

An international picture

8

'WHAT HAPPENS?' AND 'WHAT WORKS?' WITH SIGNS OF SAFETY AND NEGLECT

Amanda Bunn, Leigh Taylor, Dan
Koziolek and Andrew Turnell

Introduction

The Signs of Safety model is used in social care practice internationally in at least 12 different countries covering two hundred jurisdictions across Australasia, North America and Europe. Much interest has been generated about its potential and application in the field of child protection. This chapter introduces the Signs of Safety model and discusses findings from practice and research about how the approach is being used.

It is common, when researching social care and health interventions, to ask a 'what works?' question in order to determine which interventions are considered to be effective or appear to be working well. Many researchers and practitioners now stress the importance of also asking the question 'what happens?' in order to understand *how* effects may have come about, including when an intervention is used in different contexts and areas (Petticrew 2015).

It is important for practitioners or therapists to have an understanding of *both* what works *and* what happens when they use a particular approach. This will help them to understand mechanisms of change, including how particular techniques, tools or methods are having an impact on the client, both immediately and in the long term. Such information is vital for effective practice in order to know what the best course of action is in different presenting circumstances; more strategically, it helps to inform how interventions can be modified in order to improve their effectiveness or impact. With this in mind, this chapter aims to explore both what happens and what works when Signs of Safety is used in cases of child neglect.

The first part of the chapter introduces the Signs of Safety model, outlining some of the core principles, tools and techniques that are used. This is followed by a review of the current evidence about the model, in order to explore what research has revealed about 'what happens' when Signs of Safety is used with child protection cases. The thoughts and experiences of two experienced practitioners are presented, in order to explore in detail how the model is used in practice on the ground and some of the potential mechanisms of change and challenges involved in working with neglect. Dan Koziolek, Child and Family Manager, writes about his experiences and lessons learnt from widespread implementation of the Signs of Safety approach across Carver County, Minnesota USA and Leigh Taylor, a senior practitioner and licensed trainer of Signs of Safety writes about her experiences in Edinburgh, Scotland and more widely from her training across the UK. The chapter concludes with a discussion of these findings, and suggestions are made for further developments to take forward an understanding of the approach and its application to neglect.

Signs of Safety: The model

What is Signs of Safety?

Created in Western Australia during the 1990s by Andrew Turnell and Steve Edwards, Signs of Safety draws heavily from the brief therapy tradition and techniques from solution-focused brief therapy (SFBT). It aims to work collaboratively and in partnership with families and children to undertake risk assessments and produce action plans for increasing safety and reducing risk and danger for children by focusing on strengths, resources and networks that the family have. The model differs from SFBT practice in several ways: by integrating specific risk assessment procedures, by focusing on skilful use of statutory authority and by offering a suite of fit-for-purpose practice tools focused particularly on engaging children and building safety.

The Signs of Safety model has evolved since the 1990s and has been built on direct experiences and feedback about what works, from caseworkers adopting the approach in the field. In practice the model can be used from the first stages of gathering information about an allegation through to case closure and has broad applicability to child protection work. There is no set period of intervention and it can range from a number of brief sessions to long-term work with clients.

There are three core principles (Turnell and Murphy 2014) to the Signs of Safety approach. These are:

- establishing constructive working relationships and partnerships between professionals and family members, and between professionals themselves

- engaging in critical thinking and maintaining a position of inquiry, and

- staying grounded in the everyday work of child protection practitioners.

All of the three principles emphasise the need to move towards a constructive culture around child protection, rather than a hypothetically paternalistic model (where the professionals adopt the position that they know what is wrong and they also know specific solutions). Central to the Signs of Safety model is the principle of establishing constructive working relationships and partnerships between professionals and family members, and between professionals themselves. It is considered crucial to do everything possible to put children, parents and every person naturally connected to the children at the centre of the assessment and decision-making. This process involves giving them every opportunity to propose and try their own ideas to solve the maltreatment concerns, before the professionals and agency offer or impose theirs.

Assessment and planning framework (mapping)

In designing the Signs of Safety approach, a core aim was to develop an assessment method that adopts a comprehensive and participatory approach to risk. This means alongside forensic inquiry, also exploring rigorously everything that is going well, to then inform how to address issues and build safety (Turnell and Edwards 1999).

These aims are encapsulated in the Signs of Safety Assessment and Planning Framework. This process involves the use of a questioning approach to help the worker and family members to 'map' together or 'think themselves into and through' the case (known as mapping).

This is completed in a one-page document, which maps *harm, danger, complicating factors, strengths, existing safety* and *required safety*; and, where children have been maltreated or are vulnerable, includes a *safety judgement*. It is designed to be the action plan and central case record for use in organising interventions, from the beginning of a case through to its closure.

The Framework aims to address four domains:

1. What are we worried about? (past harm, future danger and complicating factors)

2. What's working well? (existing strengths and safety)

3. What needs to happen? (future safety and goals/next steps), and

4. Judgement: where are we on a scale of 0 to 10, where 10 means there is enough safety for the child protection authorities to close the case and 0 means it is certain the child will be re-abused? (0 also often indicates the situation is so dangerous the child will, at least temporarily, be moved).

The form and protocol can be viewed in Figure 8.1.

On the danger side of the equation, the Assessment and Planning Framework allows for past harm, future danger (also known as danger statements) and complicating factors to be named and explored (Turnell and Edwards 1999; Turnell and Murphy 2014). On the safety side existing strengths and safety are explored. As part of the process, examples and evidence of strengths and safety in the family are collected. The working definition of safety is regarded as 'strengths demonstrated as protection (in relation to the danger) over time' (Boffa and Podestra 2004, cited in Turnell and Essex 2006, p.114). Complicating factors such as mental health issues, drug and alcohol dependence, poverty, fear of children's services and other issues that may make the situation more difficult, are also explored.

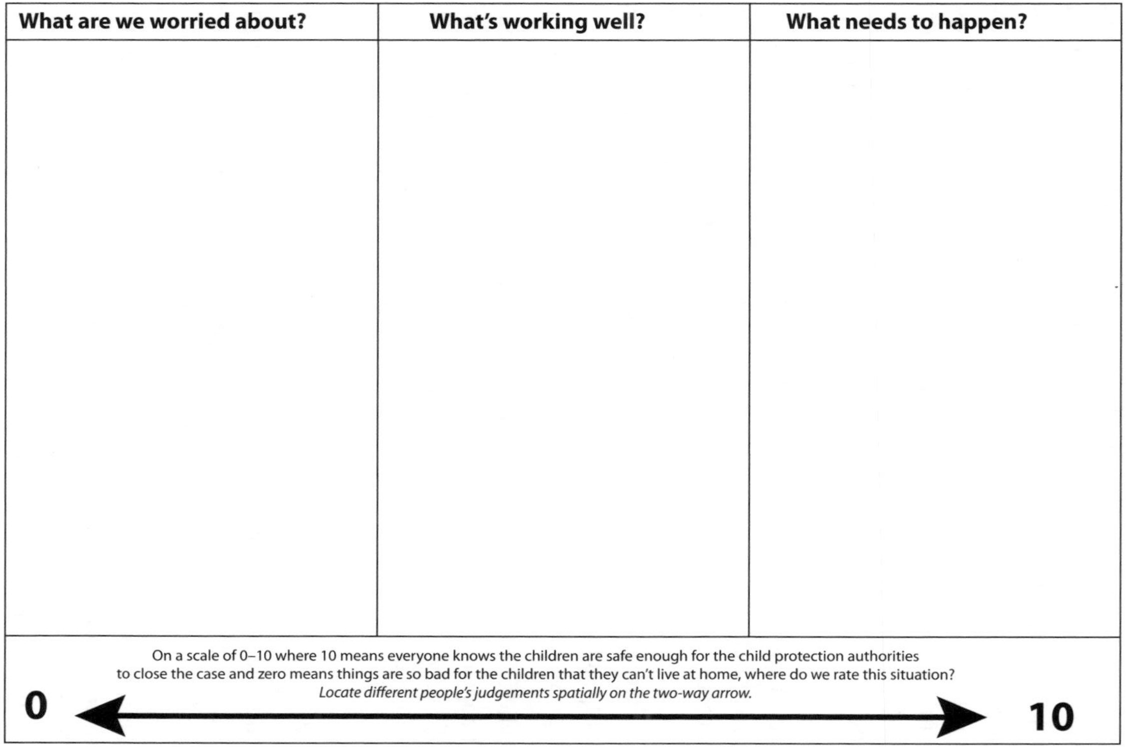

What are we worried about?	What's working well?	What needs to happen?

On a scale of 0–10 where 10 means everyone knows the children are safe enough for the child protection authorities to close the case and zero means things are so bad for the children that they can't live at home, where do we rate this situation?

Locate different people's judgements spatially on the two-way arrow.

0 ⟷ 10

Figure 8.1 Signs of Safety® Assessment and Planning Framework

As part of the Signs of Safety assessment process, the practitioner gathers and analyses the information from both the danger and safety sides of the equation, to best inform a judgement that is recorded in the form of a score on a scale (or continuum) of safety running from 0 to 10. This assessment work then lays the foundation to explore and develop the agency and family goals. These *safety goals* articulate what it is the agency needs to see happening that will satisfy them the child is safe, and what steps are needed to realise the goals. A *context scale* can also be used to quantify the overall seriousness of the case currently being assessed and planned for, in comparison to all other cases the agency is working with.

Practitioners use scaling questions with these assessment processes to frame the judgement and assessment within a *possibility of change*. This is intended to help move clients along the continuum from danger towards safety. All stakeholders, professional and family, are asked to offer their ratings in the scaling process. This is a straightforward way of assessing the perspective of the service recipient and how it might differ from the professionals involved in the case. An assessment using a scaling question made at regular intervals can also help to establish if change is occurring or perceived as a possibility. For example:

> where 10 means that you are certain this sort of incident won't happen again and your son is safe, and 0 means that you think there is every likelihood this will happen again, how would you rate the situation at the moment?' (Turnell and Edwards 1999, p.74)

Safety planning

During the risk assessment process and casework, *safety planning* is carried out to detail exactly how change will be achieved to increase the safety of the children concerned. A 'safety plan' is:

> [a] specific set of rules and arrangements created by the parents and support people that describe how the family will live its everyday life to show the children, the family's own network and the statutory authorities that the children will be safe in the future. (Turnell and Murphy 2014, p.35)

This plan is constructed collaboratively with all multiagency professionals and the case family, and utilises the support of wider family and friends (called the *safety network*) to detail action plans and set up procedures for ensuring they are being carried out. As part of this process, a straightforward and understandable description of the child protection concerns is included in a *danger statement*. *Harm statements* also detail what harm has happened to the child(ren), and they are based on observable behavioural evidence. This is then followed by an outline of clear behavioural safety goals about what is required and how the goals can be achieved.

Tools for children

Involving children is key to the Signs of Safety approach, and a number of special tools have been developed to achieve this aim and to help with safety planning and outcomes. Some of the tools are used to facilitate gathering information from the child's perspective and to explore their perception of events including current concerns (worries), things that are going well or help the child to cope (good things) and ideas about how the child would like things to change (wishes/dreams). These tools include the 'My Three Houses' tool and the 'Fairy and Wizard tool' and can be viewed in Figures 8.2 and 8.3.

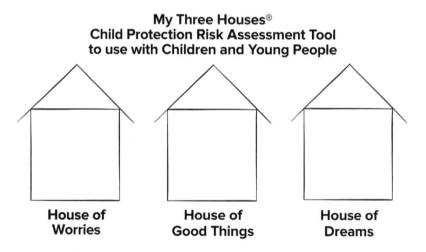

Figure 8.2 *'My Three Houses' tool*

Figure 8.3 Fairy and Wizard tool

Another tool called the 'Safety House' (Parker 2009) helps to represent and communicate how safe a child feels in their own home and what would be involved to improve this. In this tool a house is drawn and parts of the house are used to explore who lives in the house, who visits, the 'rules of the house' and any people the child feels unsafe with. This can be viewed in Figure 8.4.

There is evidence that children often have limited understanding of why children's services have got involved in their lives and a 'Words and Pictures' tool has been designed to help explain to the child what has happened that has led to professional intervention in their family (Turnell and Essex 2006) (see also Chapters 3 and 5). An easily understood account is created by the professionals together with the parents. This is presented to the children with the whole family and key support people (e.g. social worker or health visitor) present. The aim is to break the secrecy and shame that typically build up around child abuse problems, and to create a firm foundation on which to build the safety plan. The account and explanation create a way to talk to children with an age-appropriate story about what has happened. This prevents children from filling in the gaps of their knowledge and understanding with inaccurate information.

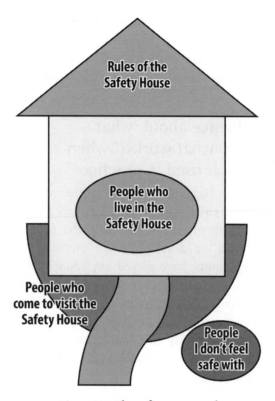

Figure 8.4 The Safety House tool

Appreciative inquiry and the evolution of Signs of Safety

The Signs of Safety model has evolved over the last 22 years, and during that period the methods and tools have been refined from practice experience. From the outset, a process of 'appreciative inquiry' based on practitioner experience has been used; the model is field-tested by workers in different locations around the world and evidence about best practice is shared between locations. During the 1990s, the approach built on the work of individual practitioners and by the late 1990s smaller jurisdictions began implementing it and learning about its successful practice. From the mid 2000s, larger jurisdictions undertook system-wide implementation, aligning the Signs of Safety principles and methods across practice, policy, supervision and leadership (Salveron *et al.* 2015). Based on this experience, five-year implementation plans are now underway in a number of jurisdictions setting out specific plans and procedures for system-wide development. Since 2000, a large number of practitioners have been trained as licensed trainers and consultants across Europe, the United Kingdom, North America, Japan, Australia and New Zealand.

Research evidence about 'what happens?' and 'what works?' when Signs of Safety is used in practice

To understand 'what happens' and 'what works' when Signs of Safety is used with cases of child neglect, we will explore the current evidence base and research about the use of the model for relevant findings and insights. Since the development of Signs of Safety, research and appreciative inquiry have played key roles in the development and evolution of its use in practice. Evidence ranges from internally produced qualitative work from practitioners of the model to externally commissioned evaluations and published articles. Studies have been completed or are underway in many countries including Western Australia, Canada, the USA, the Netherlands, Denmark, Finland, New Zealand and the UK.

The emergence of a research base about Signs of Safety

Early research studies about the impact of the model in the 1990s and 2000s were mainly carried out by agencies and practitioners involved in implementation. These studies investigated potential impact, outcomes and the array of active ingredients involved in creating change in families. Later studies have also involved independent evaluations from research groups or universities (see pp.255–262).

A strong and consistent finding in many of these studies was that using Signs of Safety appeared to result in improvements in practitioners' experiences, skills and job satisfaction. In the 1990s, Turnell and Edwards first measured these changes by tracking the views of 31 participants on their professional identity and job satisfaction on three occasions, that is, at the beginning and end of a six-month Signs of Safety development group, and 12 months after completion. Using a ten-point scale, it was found that an almost two-point increase on average occurred for workers' job satisfaction over the 18-month period (Turnell and Edwards 1999). Other studies have started to explore why these changes in perceptions and satisfaction occur. For instance, a survey carried out by Bureau Jeugdzorg Drenthe (BJZD, cited in Turnell and Murphy 2014), an agency that has been implementing Signs of Safety in the Netherlands, found workers reported positive changes in their satisfaction with practice – for example, more openness amongst practitioners about their practice, increased levels of support, faster work and greater pride and joy in their work with families. Focusing on good practice brought more energy and connection, better enabling practitioners to learn from each other. In Western Australia, the Department for Child Protection and Family Support (DCP 2010, 2012) found similar improvements in job satisfaction. Practitioners attributed change to better decision-making; practice being more open, transparent and honest; increases in collaborative working with partner agencies; useful tools; and the Signs of Safety Assessment and Planning Framework providing clarity and focus. As neglect is an area of acknowledged difficulty for practitioners (Action for Children 2014), this is an important finding.

Across research and evaluation studies from the past ten years there have been reports of improvements, both in family involvement in the child protection process and in the relationship between parents and practitioners. For example, as part of an independent evaluation undertaken by Wilder Research Group (Skrypek, Idzelis and Pecora 2012; Skrypek, Otteson and Owen 2010) 24 parents were followed up and interviewed about their experiences of Signs of Safety across five Minnesota counties (including Olmsted, Carver, Scott, St Louis and Yellow Medicine Counties). Of these parents as many as 83 per cent reported that their caseworker had been honest and 'straight up' with them about the case. Furthermore, about two-thirds felt their caseworker had taken the time to get to know them and their situation, and 71 per cent felt their caseworker had facilitated the identification of strengths and challenges during the 'safety planning' process.

An independent evaluation in Copenhagen, Denmark (Holmgård Sørensen 2013) involved interviewing 171 practitioners. Interviewees felt that using Signs of Safety resulted in increases in practitioner focus on family resources, including families' strategies and solutions, and thereby gave families more responsibility. Research in Western Australia by the Department for Child Protection (DCP 2011) found that using Signs of Safety was seen to improve collaboration between professionals and families. This was through its use in structured pre-hearing conferences in order to avoid full court hearings where possible.

Child protection case outcomes

Case outcomes have been an important focus of the research conducted about Signs of Safety to date. Internationally, a number of studies have been carried out to monitor changes in child protection objectives and outcomes, such as reductions in maltreatment incidents or the number of children taken into care. Some of the most extensive of these data sets involves work in the USA and Australia where outcome data has been gathered across large jurisdictions with widespread implementation of the model. An early study of this kind occurred across Olmsted County Child and Family Services (OCCFS) in Minnesota, USA where they began using the Signs of Safety model with casework in 2000 and started the first system-wide implementation in 2001 as part of a wider set of political reforms. Here a number of changes were reported, including the agency halving the number of children taken into care and halving the number of families taken to court. The county also recorded a recidivism rate (i.e. return to court) of less than 2 per cent in 2006, 2007 and 2008 measured through state and federal audit, compared to an expected federal standard in the USA of 6.7 per cent (Turnell and Murphy 2014).

Whilst these are promising trends, it has been important to consider them in the context of other organisational, structural or political changes occurring at the same time as the implementation of Signs of Safety. For example, with this data set and changes recorded by OCCFS in Minnesota, other radical changes to the structuring of teams, case conferences and court proceedings also occurred across these time periods, making it possible that these changes may have impacted on outcomes. However, it is worth considering that the reductions in Minnesota occurred despite increasing levels of child protection casework elsewhere across the country and rates tripling between 1994 and 2008.

In other countries and jurisdictions where Signs of Safety has been implemented, similar reports and improvements in monitored changes in child protection outcomes have occurred. Some of these studies have now included comparison and control groups, making it potentially more certain that change is attributable to Signs of Safety (see below for examples in Canada, the Netherlands and Denmark). These reductions in the proportion of children in care and families taken to court are also particularly significant in the context of global changes where most child protection agencies around the world have reported an increase (e.g. in the UK; McKeigue and Beckett 2004). Some of these reported trends are described below.

AREA AND OUTCOME DATA

Western Australia
The Department for Child Protection and Family Support (CPFS) is undertaking one of the largest system-wide implementations of Signs of Safety, which was adopted as the child protection framework in 2008. The annual increase in rates of children in care (2009–2013) was lower in comparison to increases across Australia nationally and previous increases within Western Australia. In this period, re-referral rates have declined slightly and child protection referrals following assessment to intensive family support have tripled. Child protection notifications doubled but the percentage of protection and care applications increased by only 16 per cent (Turnell and Murphy 2014). A 30 per cent reduction in child removals was recorded when Signs of Safety was used for pre-birth planning with pregnant women at high risk (DCP 2009).

British Colombia, Canada
Ktunaxa Kinbasket Child and Family Services (KKFCS) covers four areas of the Ktunaxa Nation within the Kootenay Region of British Colombia and delivers statutory child protection services to Aboriginal children and their families. Since implementation of Signs of Safety in 2008, there has been a substantial decrease in the number of children entering care, the number of contested court matters and fewer child protection re-notifications (Turnell and Murphy 2014).

Ontario, Canada
Since Toronto Children's Aid Society (TCAS) has used the Signs of Safety mapping process with families, case closure rates have increased in comparison both to other teams in the agency and to Ontario province averages. There were also reductions in

caseworker time and the number of investigations (Lwin *et al.* 2014).

Carver County, Minnesota, USA

In the past six years, removals during child protection assessments dropped from around 60 children before implementation of Signs of Safety to fewer than 30. Only four young people have remained in foster care over the last four years, in comparison to six to eight in each year prior to implementation. There has been a two-thirds reduction in the number of families needing ongoing casework, which has been attributed to the set-up of robust safety plans and networks (Turnell and Murphy 2014).

Sherburne County, Minnesota, USA

Between 2007 and 2009 the county halved the use of the courts in child protection cases. In 2009 the placement of children was reduced by 19 per cent (Turnell and Murphy 2014).

Sacramento, California, USA

Since 2006, Sacramento Country Child Protective Services (SCCPS) with Casey Family Programs saw a decrease in the rate of African American children entering foster care by 53 per cent in comparison to a statewide decrease of 5 per cent (Ellis *et al.* 2013).

The Netherlands

Bureau Jeugdzorg Drenthe (BJZD) has monitored a reduction in the percentage of children taken into care, the average length of involvement in long-term cases and number of cases directed to court since implementation in 2007. William Shrikker Groep (WSG) has initially analysed four pilot teams and found a 19 per cent rate of placements compared to 40 per cent of cases with a control group (Turnell and Murphy 2014).

Copenhagen, Denmark

A study by Holmgård-Sørensen (2013) examined a cohort of 66 cases and found safety planning work resulted in a 50 per cent reduction in the placement of children in comparison to equivalent cases where Signs of Safety had not been used.

City and County of Swansea, Wales, UK

Swansea Social Care Children and Family Services (SSCS) ·implemented Signs of Safety in late 2011 and by 2013 saw re-referral rates decline to 21 per cent, in comparison to 30 per cent in 2012. Assessments are more timely and the numbers of children taken into care and on the child protection register have reduced (SSCS 2014).

New research into Signs of Safety

The start of this complex process of unravelling and detailing mechanisms of change is currently underway, with international research projects around the world about the use of Signs of Safety. An extensive research programme at the University of South Australia has been set up to begin to establish a clear theory of change and results logic for Signs of Safety. This research has been commissioned by the Western Australian Department for Child Protection and Family Support (CPFS) to examine the system-wide implementation of Signs of Safety across Western Australia over the last five years. The project evaluates the impact of Signs of Safety on children, parents, families, carers, practitioners, partner agencies and key stakeholders. The results logic aims to identify how Signs of Safety may be working and creating change, and will present visual images to illustrate these assumptions and processes. Results from a quasi-experimental control over a three-year period in Western Australia are to be released in 2016 (Australian Centre for Child Protection, University of South Australia).

A Signs of Safety Fidelity Research Project led by Casey Family Programs (CFP) in America is currently underway to create a series of validated assessment tools that will enable agencies to evaluate the fidelity of Signs of Safety practice. This will involve tracking workers, supervisors, leadership and the supporting organisational climate. The aim is to standardise practice and to ensure tools and techniques are used consistently.

The Dutch National Government has provided funding for a two-year comparative research study to compare the outcomes of Signs of Safety in Bureau Jeugdzorg Drenthe and Bureau Jeugdzorg Groningen. In the UK, plans are currently being made to evaluate effective design and implementation of organisational procedures across ten local authorities (England Innovations Project, Social Care Workforce Research Unit, King's College London).

Mechanisms of change

Studies that seek to measure and understand case outcomes help to establish if an intervention appears to be effective and the difference a specific intervention makes. However, in order to understand 'what happens' and 'what works', and indeed how an intervention creates change, it is important to understand what individual aspects or elements of the intervention are influential in the change process, and their impacts on children, adults and families in the short and long term.

To date only one published study has reflected on how Signs of Safety may be having an impact with cases of neglect, based on the views of practitioners and managers. Gardner (2008) interviewed one hundred practitioners and managers across a range of professions to explore current challenges and achievements in working with child neglect and associated emotional harm. Here it was found that professionals who had used the Signs of Safety approach with cases of neglect felt it was useful because:

- parents say they are clearer about what is expected of them and receive more relevant support

- the approach is perceived as open and encourages transparent decision-making

- professionals had to be specific about their concerns for the child's safety

- this encouraged better presentation of evidence

- the degree of protective elements and of actual or apprehended risks could be set out visually on a scale, making the neglect easier for all to understand than lengthy narrative reports

- once set out, the risks did not have to continually be revisited but could be addressed and monitored

- the group could acknowledge strengths, and meetings could focus on how to build on them to achieve safety. (Gardner 2008, p.78)

Other studies, whilst not concentrating specifically on neglect, point to a number of elements that appear to be influential in the change process when using Signs of Safety with child protection cases generally. In one UK research study, 12 practitioners were asked about their experiences of using Signs of Safety methods and their views about how they might contribute to effective child protection. One of the key themes that emerged was that 'Signs of Safety helps to create partnerships and good working relationships with parents' (Bunn 2013, p.83). When asked to detail this process, interviewees explained that good working relationships with parents meant that they would be more likely to engage and cooperate, and there was less conflict and an increased willingness to take responsibility and work towards goals. Parents would be more likely to communicate openly about any difficulties they had with achieving goals and so steps could then be identified to overcome these with honest and transparent dialogue, reducing the possibility of disguised compliance. It was felt that parents were more willing to accept that risks were present if they had the chance to identify these issues themselves and take on board the views of their social network in the safety planning process. It was thought that all of these processes could lead to faster identification of problems, greater success in achieving goals and faster, more effective protection of children.

Keddell (2011a, 2011b), in a study of factors associated with successful reunification of children with their families after foster placement in New Zealand, also found that elements focusing on the relationship between client and worker were thought to be paramount. Important factors influencing change were thought to include:

- a lack of *culpability* in the construction of the problem (i.e. not blaming the parent but understanding why something has occurred)

- resisting *risk reactivity* (a worker's 'knee jerk' reaction to risk) while constantly monitoring (i.e. carrying out regular safety plans to evaluate any change and risk)

- the worker having a belief in *good enough parenting* (being realistic and negotiating criteria for the child's return wherever possible), and

- belief in the potential for change in parents (e.g. noticing when things do change and go well).

Factors identified by parents as rebuilding their parenting confidence included parenting courses, social work support availability, and an attitude of support and recognition of the changes that were made instead of criticism. Overall it was felt that many success factors were due to the negotiated nature of the partnership between parent and worker involving close collaborative working.

Specific features of the tools, techniques and measures involved in Signs of Safety assessment and intervention are also thought to be influential in change. In the interviews with 12 practitioners in the UK (Bunn 2013) many interviewees felt that the Assessment and Planning Framework with separate columns for risks, dangers and safety was a useful tool for ensuring all of these factors were analysed in detail. The visual presentation of information, with different factors being identified or categorised, was thought particularly helpful in facilitating analysis and prioritisation of the most pressing issues. The identification of risk and complicating factors allowed for analysis of the individual impact of each factor and necessary actions to address each one. Many practitioners also referred the value of targets that are SMART. This means running through the practicalities of goals or objectives and making sure they are specific; measurable – so it is known when they are achieved; achievable; realistic and timely – set to a timescale in order to achieve change and safety goals. The interviewees believed that by establishing who is doing what and by clear identifiable dates, actions would be more likely to happen. Regular reviews helped to see if goals are being achieved or if steps are being made in order to get closer to goals. This proactive approach was thought to encourage parental responsibility for actions and achieving change as well as preventing drift in case management, which is of special concern in cases of neglect (Farmer and Lutman 2010).

The techniques of Signs of Safety and the use of SMART goals were thought to help establish a clearer picture of child protection issues, risk and safety. Real examples of these matters are to be provided, as well as concrete evidence of change and meeting goals. The professional is asked to describe *actual behaviours and their frequency* (e.g. 'this child was left home alone twice this week') rather than apply global labels, such as 'the child has experienced "neglect" or "domestic abuse"'. It was thought to help practitioners think of families as unique rather than a family just having a generic problem. The need for clear, specific communication by practitioners working with neglect has been highlighted by the Office for Standards in Education, Children's Services and Skills (Ofsted) in England (Ofsted 2014).

The body of research discussed above has identified a number of important factors in Signs of Safety that are thought to influence outcomes and lead to change, but we do not yet have research about how these findings apply to different types of abuse and neglect. To explore in more detail how the model is used in practice with neglect and some of the potential mechanisms of change and challenges involved, the thoughts and experiences of two practitioners are detailed in the next section.

Signs of Safety in practice with child neglect

In order to find out about the real experiences of implementing and using Signs of Safety with cases of child neglect, interview questions were put to two experienced practitioners in different countries to explore 'what happens' and 'what works' in these circumstances.

City of Edinburgh Council, Scotland

Leigh Taylor is a senior practitioner working in a statutory children and families team for the City of Edinburgh in Scotland. She has been using Signs of Safety along with other colleagues since 2009 and has more recently become a licensed Signs of Safety trainer. Leigh explains her thoughts and experiences about the use of Signs of Safety with neglect.

How have you used Signs of Safety
with neglect where you work?

> My local authority is not undertaking full-scale implementation of Signs of Safety, but many individual practitioners use Signs of Safety or aspects of it such as the children's tools. I have been using Signs of Safety since 2009 within a statutory children and families team. This has included working with a number of families presenting with child protection concerns including child neglect. I start with mappings with family members and others involved; this includes danger statements, the My Three Houses tool, Fairy/Wizards tool, Words and Pictures and safety planning (see pp.241–2). Families are involved in the mapping from the initial point of contact and are full participants

in the mapping and safety planning process. Partner agencies are also invited to partake in these activities, planning alongside the family and their network to ensure good communication and transparency in multidisciplinary working. I also facilitate mappings for difficult cases and train colleagues in using Signs of Safety, both in my organisation and across the UK.

Children's worries, their wishes or dreams and good things about their life can be explored by using the Three Houses tool where children draw and write their thoughts. The example in Figure 8.5 draws upon different experiences of children who are chronically neglected. Here the pictures drawn by children are not included, but the chosen words have been collected.

Worries	Good things	Wishes
• How [...] feels when she sees her brothers and sisters getting hit from mum and dad	• I get to go out...golden times	• I want to see my brothers and sisters every week
• Worried uncle will stab dad	• My dog and my cat	• Want to go back to this school to see friends
• Don't like it when mum and dad drink because they fight with each other	• My skate board	• House to be tidy and clean
• The house is very dirty and get bullied sometimes at school for smelling bad		• Wants to go home but only if her mum and dad get rid of all her worries
• Worried mum has an eating problem because she only eats crackers		• To see mum and dad 1x a week

Figure 8.5 Example using the 'My Three Houses' tool

Practitioners can learn a lot about a child's day-to-day life from completing this exercise. It is most effective when, with the child's permission, the three houses are shared with the parents. Seeing the issues from their own child's perspective can be extremely powerful and emotional for parents. It is a very effective tool for helping parents shift from a state of denial about the neglect to talking about or accepting some of the worries as identified by their children.

What seems to be working well? What aspects of Signs of Safety do you think make a difference in working with neglect and why?

With Signs of Safety, 'harm statements' detail what harm has happened to the child(ren) and are based on evidence of observed behaviour, not simply on judgement-loaded statements. For example, stating 'Mary drinks a bottle of vodka per day' can be evidenced and is seen as less judgemental than writing 'Mary is an alcoholic', but both acknowledge the potential harm when the adult behaviour is linked to the impact upon the child. This creates an open forum for discussion because it is more difficult for the parents to deny the neglect when presented in this manner. By using straightforward language and avoiding professional jargon, the entire process becomes more accessible to families, who in turn are, in my experience, less defensive.

'Danger statements' help parents make the connections between current behaviours and the long-term likely outcomes for their children. We as professionals spend years studying the impact neglect can have on developing children and yet we somehow forget to explain this in layman's terms to the families we are working with. In my experience, parents describe neglectful home circumstances, as a 'bad phase' in their life but often they do not understand that this could affect their children negatively into adulthood or for the rest of their lives. Using danger statements to explain what we are worried about, why, and what might happen in the longer term has been extremely effective in helping parents understand the impact of neglect upon their children. I have found parents more likely to accept the worries of the professionals as a consequence. Very few parents I work with deliberately want to harm their children and if they understand and accept the worries they are more likely to work towards changing them. Danger statements also encourage the worker to draw upon their knowledge base of neglect to inform their assessment and judgement of the situation.

'Safety planning' requires a detailed plan of the child's home life and not just a list of services. In cases of physical neglect, safety planning helps guide the planning by asking what 'good enough' physical care looks like and what details are required for the family to understand this. Thresholds are openly discussed with the family and other professionals during safety planning, helping to reinforce partnership working.

In your role as a Signs of Safety trainer, what have other people told you about how Signs of Safety might work with neglect?

As a trainer, my experience of practitioners from across the UK is that they want to practise in the best possible way and to help people change. However, many workers feel overwhelmed by processes and often practice is led by an underlying fear of missing significant risks. Signs of Safety has given workers permission to refocus on their practice. For example, the use of language is one of the most common areas of feedback practitioners commonly reflect upon. Naming the neglect in straightforward language, and describing what we observe, helps to transform practice. Many practitioners report back that they like the use of language that is simple, factual, honest but not blaming. This is achieved through the development of good questions, which provide the information and basis for the assessment.

Many practitioners feel that asking the family and their network to *think about what they could do differently in terms of the harmful neglect* is refreshing, and removes the burden of practitioners always having to identify solutions. For example, asking them, 'Who can ensure the child attends all medical appointments?' or 'Who is the safest adult within the network to supervise the child?' Families often respond well to having their resources and ideas drawn on in this way.

'Words and Pictures' is a very popular tool. It helps practitioners to think about how complex situations and processes can be simplified and explained to children, to help them make sense of what is going on in their life at that specific moment.

If things are going well when working with neglect and Signs of Safety, what changes or signs would there be?

When starting the mapping process with family and agency goals, an immediate reduction in defensiveness and change in engagement can be seen. More often than not there are similarities between agency and family goals that can help shift the perceptions of the family. As the mapping continues, engagement is greatly improved by considering the strengths of a family in equal measure to dangers. One mum said to me, 'People like me know what we have done wrong, we are told often enough but we don't know what we are doing right!'

It can be awkward to talk to clients about personal/home hygiene but by using straightforward language with clients, I have seen parents make efforts to improve their personal and home hygiene, often stating no one had ever told them this before despite services being involved for a chronic situation of poor personal/home hygiene.

The key longer-term outcome is an improved working relationship. By working in this way, social workers are encouraged to be honest and open about child protection concerns, including neglect, and their actual and potential impact upon the children. Clearer planning with the families feels fairer, and arguably improves the likelihood of families buying into safety plans. A good working relationship is critical in evoking change. The legal routes become clearer for practitioners, especially in cases where the parents do not engage or the planned changes do not occur. Having used Signs of Safety with families, it is easier to demonstrate that the family have been well informed and involved in the entire mapping process and, despite this, the changes necessary to protect the children cannot be evidenced.

'Scaling' as a tool (see pp.248–250) can help improve outcomes by giving families something tangible with which to measure their progress. I have witnessed the scaling process transform working relationships, when social workers have evidence to scale the parent higher with more improvement than the parent expected. One parent cited this as the point at which her relationship with her social worker transformed. It provided those parents with a sense of hope, and some belief that they can perhaps achieve their goals (see also Chapter 10).

Have you experienced any difficulties? How have you overcome these?

Often practitioners in the UK are fearful of being over-optimistic in their assessments. This arguably stems from some of the previous paternalistic approaches employed by local authorities. As a consequence, practitioners in my experience then struggle with the strengths-based questions and sometimes miss really valuable information or existing safety within the family. Signs of Safety is a questioning approach and therefore requires practice in formulating good solid questions that help obtain the right information to contribute to robust assessments and plans. One suggestion would be that workers keep a shared database of questions to help less experienced workers get started.

Signs of Safety is a model that guides practitioners, but it does not replace the need for skilled workers with a solid knowledge and value base. In cases of neglect, understanding the outcomes for children living with neglect is crucial for undertaking assessments using the Signs of Safety approach. Often neglect is masked by other child protection issues that are perhaps easier to identify and define, such as sexual abuse or physical assault. This can result in practitioners shying away from the complexity of neglect issues and intervening with the more easily defined areas of abuse. Evidencing emotional neglect directly as an outcome of parental behaviours is particularly challenging; it requires a good knowledge base to help formulate and ask the right questions of families and professionals.

Identifying safe and reliable networks can also be very challenging. Often in cases of neglect there is a high degree of social isolation, and professionals have poor access to the home and the children. Drawing a genogram with the family is a good starting point for gathering information about potential network members.

Carver County Community Social Services, USA

Carver County Community Social Services (CCCSS) in Minnesota, USA have been implementing Signs of Safety across all of their statutory child protection services since 2005. CCCS provides child protection services within Carver County to a population of 88,000 on the outskirts of Minneapolis and St. Paul. Dan Koziolek, as the Child and Family Manager in Carver County has played a key role in implementation. As a result of continually striving for a better understanding of the Signs of Safety model and continual improvement in Carver's outcomes for children, Dan undertook a demonstration project on chronic neglect with Casey Family Programs and American Humane. The project incorporated the best available research and knowledge about neglect into Carver's developing Signs of Safety practice. Dan explains his thoughts below about 'what happens' with Signs of Safety and neglect.

How have you used Signs of Safety with neglect where you work?

Carver County began implementing the Signs of Safety approach in 2005. We use Signs of Safety in all of our child welfare work from intake through to case closure. We map all of our cases and we routinely use the Three Houses and Safety House tools to get the children's words. We are working toward quickly creating a short Words and Pictures story based on the harm and danger statements in our Signs of Safety maps in every case. These stories are now at the core of our work. The stories put the map into words and simple illustrations so that even young children in the family can understand. The social worker drafts a story using words from the family members, and negotiates any changes that are necessary to get the parents to accept the story, and by this time the social worker has developed a level of proof of a strong budding partnership with the parents around the children's safety. It is our hope that in providing children with a coherent story about their childhood trauma at our earliest opportunity, we can immediately set them on a path toward healing. We hope that the understanding that comes from this story will help the children experience fewer behaviour problems or mental health diagnoses, and other known effects of adverse experiences. We have had children take their story with them as they start therapy.

The social worker, parents, and other involved professionals have an understanding about the words they will use to talk to the children about what has, is, and will be happening. The parents have a story to use to explain the things that are going on for their family to relatives, friends or neighbours. When parents ask some of these people to help them ensure lasting safety for their children, the people being asked can get a clear idea from the story about what they are being asked to do. The story becomes the foundation for a strong and lasting safety plan. As the safety plan is developed it is often added to the Words and Pictures story using similar language and pictures, so the children know exactly what is being done to keep them safe in the future. When plans don't work as well as hoped, social workers help the family and network make adjustments and improvements to the plan until they are able to demonstrate lasting safety.

Although we always ask questions that will help us sort out what we can about the allegations that brought us into the family's life, our work is about understanding the entire family situation as well as possible. We try to uncover all past harm. We seek to understand all current dangers. We do our best to identify the times when the children are safe. We ask, 'What was different to enable the times when the children were cared for well?' In addition to identifying the sort of parenting the children receive when their parents are at their worst, we seek to understand, at least as well, the parenting that occurs when parents are at their best. We are always pleased to uncover family strengths. It's always easier to do just a little more of what's already working than to identify and start something completely new.

What seems to be working well? What aspect of Signs of Safety do you think make a difference in working with neglect and why?

Creating Signs of Safety maps, identifying all of the known harm and danger children have faced in neglect situations, has regularly humbled us. Traditionally we were so focused on the current report we simply didn't see the bigger picture of repeat reports of neglect. We didn't look at past reports or consider how much time had elapsed since the family was first reported to us. We were so frantic in our effort to protect children we didn't even recognise how much of our time went into protecting the same children again and again. As we began to challenge ourselves to figure out what it would take to consistently create lasting safety *from the first report*, we don't see as many children with long histories of neglect, and with fewer re-reports we aren't as frantic.

We started asking, 'What's in place *right now* that will keep the things that brought the family to our agency from happening again tonight?' Initially there were many unsatisfying answers. 'They know someone's watching.' 'They'll get arrested if they do it again.' 'They're afraid their children will be removed if it keeps happening.' 'They now know what they did isn't okay.' 'The parents have promised not to do it again.' Soon social workers were asking families and safety network members, 'What could they do differently to give us real confidence that the things we worry about won't happen in the future?' We learned to plan more effectively for safety, instead of only for services.

The shift from services to safety enabled us to survive repeated budget cuts during the economic recession. Learning to leave parents with the responsibility for their children's safety and wellbeing has dramatically improved our ability to partner with them. Professional dangerousness had been a particular challenge for us and for others in situations of neglect. It was easy to think we were making a difference when families cooperated. We had often been reluctant to have honest conversations or to define clear bottom lines, out of fear that doing so would destroy our relationships. We have learned instead that far stronger relationships are developed when firm and clear expectations are defined in a caring way. We now have many relationships continue informally long after the case is closed.

We have worked hard to reduce chronic maltreatment and repeat reporting during the past five years. We believe we have made significant inroads. The number of children in out-of-home placement is as low as at any point in the last 20 years, even as County population increased 60 per cent. This has been achieved in a context where available funding for services has been reduced by about 40 per cent as a result of budget cuts during the recession.

Have you experienced any difficulties? How have you overcome these?

Identifying neglect – that is, the instances when children were not attended to and the times when their needs were not adequately met – is still more challenging for us than discovering the times when something was done to children that hurt or harmed them. We still find it easier to describe the ways in which situations of sexual and physical abuse have harmed children than to describe neglect. Such harm is easier for safety network members to understand. It is easier to get family and network members engaged in effective safety planning when the dangers are clear to everyone.

Accordingly, reports of *severe* neglect and *clearly imminent* danger are also much easier for us to take seriously in the very beginning. We are able to use Signs of Safety very successfully in situations where children are failing to thrive or not getting clearly needed medical care. But the vast majority of our neglect reports don't initially strike us as being so serious. In 2014, of the 448 maltreatment allegations assessed in Carver County, 320 were allegations of neglect. Only one of these was identified as a life-threatening injury. Four were allegations of medical neglect. Most allegations were about lack of supervision, inadequate housing, lack of food and exposure to domestic violence. It may well be that we just see all of these things so often that we struggle to take them as seriously as the children's needs demand.

Slowing down to discuss the situation, or to look up research about the known effects of the specific behaviours we encounter or seek to encourage, helps us to communicate danger and safety better. By including this information in the harm, danger and goal statements we draft, we hope to help families and safety network members take initial neglect allegations more seriously.

We refer the more serious situations of neglect, where the assessment social worker has been unable to engage the family in effective safety planning, for ongoing casework. In situations of a second or subsequent assessment, we take responsibility for having failed to create a tight enough safety plan. When we fail to engage the family and their network around a tighter safety plan, and when we find ourselves involved in yet another assessment with the family, we know it's time to implement everything we have learned about chronic maltreatment and effective practice.

We turned to the professional literature to learn more about chronic neglect. We engaged in a demonstration project led by the late Caren Kaplan. We learned to make more frequent and shorter family contacts. We learned to get really clear about small next steps. We recognised that we need to get over the idea that years of alcohol or drug abuse, depression and anxiety can be overcome in a lasting way within months, and we need to get much better at developing strong enough leadership in the children's safety network to ensure the children's needs will continue to be well met over time. We came to recognise more clearly that when neglect continues, children are at much greater risk of being physically or sexually abused as well. We now talk about chronic maltreatment instead of chronic neglect.

Reflections on practitioner accounts

These two practice accounts provide insights into how practitioners are using Signs of Safety in cases of child neglect, and what they have learnt from their experiences. First, child neglect presents both practitioners with particularly complex challenges in comparison to the management of other types of maltreatment. Both practitioners talk about the inherent difficulties involved, for parents and safety networks of family and friends as for professionals, in identifying and acknowledging the seriousness of neglect. Ensuring safety for children whilst monitoring changes in the nature of neglect or the development of other types of abuse, are also important issues. In both jurisdictions, learning to better understand and cope with these complexities has been an important stage of practice.

Second, in line with previous research outlined above, the positive impact of Signs of Safety tools and techniques is confirmed. Both practitioners describe the benefits of the model for evidencing and analysing neglect, helping parents to understand the impact of this form of abuse and increasing their engagement and compliance. These findings are in line with change process research from solution focused brief therapy (SFBT) whereby scaling questions and 'solution talk' has been linked to establishing concrete steps for change and continuing and completing therapy (Estrada and Beyeback 2007; Shields, Sprenkle and Constantine 1991).

Third, both accounts strongly emphasise the importance of the client–practitioner relationship and the co-construction of issues and solutions, with all parties involved in the work to create content, using techniques such as scaling questions. This echoes findings from research about SFBT and psychotherapy that identifies critical factors in creating positive change as techniques, client optimism and the client–therapist relationship (McKeel 2012). A wealth of research in child protection has highlighted the importance of the relationship between workers and clients in cases of neglect and the value of gaining the perspective of the child (see, for example, Daniel, Taylor and Scott 2011). Finally, as with all types of intervention, training, required protocols with high standards, access to advanced skills and a knowledge base about what needs to happen with cases of neglect, were also considered to be vital to successful practice.

Future directions for understanding 'what happens' and 'what works' with Signs of Safety and neglect

Below are some potential research questions on features of child neglect as well as the skills and techniques required by practitioners to tackle it effectively. To explore them a variety of methods including quantitative, qualitative and participatory research will be needed.

- Can we better understand the course of neglect over time, 'what happens' and how tools, techniques and skills influence progression and case outcomes, 'what works'? This understanding is vital due to the complexity of chronic neglect and its link with other types of maltreatment. There may be both short-term indicators of successful practice and longer-term outcomes with the use of Signs of Safety and child neglect, and these may vary for parents and children.

- Can we understand how Signs of Safety tools may help to analyse and aid the management of co-existing or complicating factors such as parental mental health problems, substance misuse and life events that often accompany child neglect (Nair *et al.* 2003; Ondersma 2002)? Will the use of such tools provide greater clarity?

- Can problems in identifying and managing neglect be addressed, such as the 'misdirected gaze' (Akister 2009), whereby attention and focus is paid only to the immediate presenting problem?

- Can we understand the exact influence of the nature of the client–practitioner relationship and co-construction as casework progresses? Exactly what aspects make a difference to child neglect, at what junctures and how can this knowledge be harnessed in the future?

Conclusions

It is important to search for evidence about outcomes as shown in the research studies outlined in this chapter. It is also vital to explore the inner workings of what happens between 'A' (the intervention) and 'B' (the outcome in the child or family) and whether this process varies between different individuals or in different locations; accounts by expert practitioners can help us here. This type of evidence helps us to understand the process of change when working with child neglect, and provides useful detail for practitioners and programme designers. Investigating and establishing a culture of research based in practice depth of this nature will help to extend our knowledge of 'what happens' and 'what works' with Signs of Safety, and in the wider treatment of neglect.

Key learning points

- Complex interventions require in-depth research if we are to truly understand what is happening and their real impact on parents, children and families.

- Understanding *both* 'what happens' *and* 'what works' can provide valuable information about mechanisms of change, including the ways in which practitioners and programme designers can best harness their skills to create change.

– In order to tackle child neglect as well as other forms of abuse, research needs to explore practice depth about the mechanisms of change as well as concrete evidence about outcomes.

More information about Signs of Safety, including practice examples, can be found on the Signs of Safety website.[1]

Questions for reflection

– 'What happens' and 'what works' with your own practice or interventions with neglect?

– Does anything different or additional need to happen to tackle neglect in particular?

– How could research help to determine how mechanisms of change are working?

– How can research based in practice depth be developed, to complement research about outcomes?

References

Action for Children (2014) *Child Neglect: the Scandal That Never Breaks.* Watford: Action for Children. Available at www.actionforchildren.org.uk/resources-and-publications/reports/child-neglect-the-scandal-that-never-breaks, accessed on 23 October 2015.

Akister, J. (2009) 'Protecting children through supporting parents.' *Journal of Public Mental Health 8,* 4, 11–17.

Bunn, A. (2013) *Signs of Safety in England: An NSPCC Commissioned Report on the Signs of Safety Model in Child Protection.* London: NSPCC. Available at www.nspcc.org.uk/services-and-resources/research-and-resources/signs-of-safety-model-england, accessed on 31 July 2015.

Daniel, B., Taylor, J. and Scott, J. (2011) *Recognizing and Helping the Neglected Child: Evidence-based Practice for Assessment and Intervention.* London: Jessica Kingsley Publishers.

DCP (Department for Child Protection) (2009) *Project 32a – Interagency Early Intervention.* Final Evaluation Report. Perth, Western Australia. Available at www.signsofsafety.net/organisations/department-for-child-protection, accessed on 21 May 2016.

---

1   www.signsofsafety.net

DCP (Department for Child Protection and Family Support) (2010) *A Report on the Signs of Safety Survey 2010. Perth, Western Australia: Department for Child Protection.* Available at www.signsofsafety.net/organisations/department-for-child-protection, accessed on 29 July 2015.

DCP (Department for Child Protection and Family Support) (2011) *Pilot of Signs of Safety Lawyer-assisted Signs of Safety Conferences and Meetings.* Perth, Western Australia: Department for Child Protection. Available at www.signsofsafety.net/organisations/department-for-child-protection, accessed on 9 September 2015.

DCP (Department for Child Protection and Family Support) (2012) Signs of Safety Survey Results Report. Perth, Western Australia: Department for Child Protection. Available at www.signsofsafety.net/signs-of-safety-research, accessed on 30 July 2015.

Ellis, M.L., Eskenazi, S., Bonnell, R. and Pecora, P.J. (2013) *Taking a Closer Look at the Reduction in Entry Rates for Children in Sacramento County with an Emphasis on African American Children: A Spotlight on Practice.* Seattle: Casey Family Programs.

Estrada, B. and Beyeback, M. (2007) 'Solution-focused therapy with depressed deaf persons.' *Journal of Family Psychotherapy 18,* 45–63.

Farmer, E. and Lutman, E. (2010) *Case Management and Outcomes for Neglected Children Returned to Their Parents: A Five Year Follow-up Study.* Bristol: School for Policy Studies, University of Bristol.

Gardner, R. (2008) *Developing an Effective Response to Neglect and Emotional Harm to Children.* Norwich: UEA/NSPCC. Available at www.nspcc.org.uk/globalassets/documents/research-reports/developing-effective-response-neglect-emotional-harm-children.pdf, accessed on 27 July 2015.

Holmgård Sørensen, T. (2013) *Når forældre netværk skaber sikkerhed for barnet: en evaluering af 'sikkerhedsplaner' i arbejdet med udsatte børn familier I Københavns commune.* Socialforvaltningen: Københavns Kommune.

Keddell, E. (2011a) 'Going home: managing 'risk' through relationship in returning children from foster care to their families of origin.' *Qualitative Social Work 11,* 604–620.

Keddell, E. (2011b) 'Reasoning processes in child protection decision-making: negotiating moral minefields and risky relationships.' *British Journal of Social Work 41,* 1251–1270.

Lwin, K., Versanov, A., Cheung, C., Goodman, D. and Andrews, N. (2014) 'The use of mapping in child welfare investigations: a strength-based hybrid intervention.' *Child Care in Practice 20,* 1, 81–97.

McKeel, J. (2012) 'What Works in Solution-focused Brief Therapy: A Review of Change Process Research.' In C. Franklin, T. Trepper, W.J. Gingerich and E. McCollum (eds) *Solution-focused Brief Therapy: A Handbook of Evidence-based Practice.* New York: Oxford University Press.

McKeigue, B. and Beckett, C. (2004) 'Care proceedings under the 1989 Children Act: rhetoric and reality.' *British Journal of Social Work 34,* 6, 831–849.

Nair, P., Schuler, M.E., Black, M.M., Kettinger, L. and Harrington, D. (2003) 'Cumulative environmental risk in substance abusing women: early intervention, parenting stress, child abuse potential and child development.' *Child Abuse & Neglect 27,* 9, 997–1017.

Ofsted (Office for Standards in Education, Children's Services and Skills) (2014) *In the Child's Time: Professional Responses to Neglect.* Manchester: Ofsted.

Ondersma, S.J. (2002) 'Predictors of neglect within low SES families: the importance of substance abuse.' *American Journal of Orthopsychiatry 72,* 3, 383–391.

Parker, S. (2009) *The Safety House: A Tool for Including Children in Safety Planning.* Perth: Aspirations Consultancy. Available at www.aspirationsconsultancy.com, accessed on 28 July 2015.

Petticrew, M. (2015) 'Time to rethink the systematic review catechism? Moving from "what works" to "what happens".' *Systematic Reviews 4,* 1, 36. Available at www.systematicreviewsjournal.com/content/4/1/36, accessed on 28 July 2015.

Salveron, M., Bromfield, L., Kirika, C., Simmons, J. Murphy, T. and Turnell, A. (2015) '"Changing the way we do child protection": The implementation of Signs of Safety within the Western Australian Department for Child Protection and Family Support.' *Children and Youth Services Review 48,* 126–139.

Sheilds, C.G., Sprenkle, D.H and Constantine, J.A. (1991) 'Anatomy of an initial interview: the importance of joining and structuring skills.' *American Journal of Family Therapy 19,* 3–18.

Skrypek, M., Idzelis, M. and Pecora, P.J. (2012) *Signs of Safety in Minnesota: Parent Perceptions of a Signs of Safety Child Protection Experience.* St. Paul, MN: Wilder Research. Available at www.wilder.org/Wilder-Research/Publications/Studies/Forms/Study/docsethomepage.aspx?ID=925&RootFolder=%2FWilder-Research%2FPublications%2FStudies%2FSigns%20of%20Safety, accessed on 20 July 2015.

Skrypek, M., Otteson, C. and Owen, G. (2010) *Signs of Safety in Minnesota: Early Indicators of Successful Implementation in Child Protection Agencies.* St Paul, MN: Wilder Research. Available at www.wilder.org/Wilder-Research/Publications/Studies/Forms/Study/docsethomepage.aspx?ID=925&RootFolder=%2FWilder-Research%2FPublications%2FStudies%2FSigns%20of%20Safety, accessed on 20 July 2015.

SSCS (Swansea Social Care Children and Family Services) (2014) *Review of Implementing Signs of Safety: Solution and Safety Orientation Approach to Child Protection Case Work.* Swansea: City and County of Swansea. Available at www.signsofsafety.net/organisations/swansea-city-county-council, accessed on 22 July 2015.

Turnell, A. and Edwards, S. (1999) *Signs of Safety: A safety and Solution Oriented Approach to Child Protection Casework.* New York: W.W. Norton.

Turnell, A. and Essex S. (2006) *Working with 'Denied' Child Abuse: The Resolutions Approach.* Buckingham: Open University Press.

Turnell, A. and Murphy, T. (2014) *Signs of Safety Comprehensive Briefing Paper* (3rd edition). East Perth, WA: Resolutions Consultancy.

9

PRACTICES TARGETING CHILD NEGLECT

The use of SafeCare® to enhance parenting skills to reduce neglect

Whitney L. Rostad, John R. Lutzker and Katelyn M. Guastaferro, with a note on the UK evaluation of SafeCare® by Gillian Churchill

It is easier to build strong children than to repair broken men.

Frederick Douglass, abolitionist, 1855 (quoted by Kristof 2012)

Introduction

Child neglect comprises the majority of cases reported to child welfare systems in the United States. However, few interventions have been designed that focus on reducing neglect specifically; most focus on promoting positive parent–child interactions and discipline practices. A key aim here is to manage challenging child behaviours that may set the occasion for physical abuse. However, the consequences of child neglect are at least equivalent to, and perhaps more significant than, those associated with physical abuse.

Therefore, it is critical for prevention and intervention efforts to target the deficits in parental skills that can contribute to an increased risk for neglect. This chapter discusses various interventions and programmes, mostly designed to reduce the risk for and occurrence of child maltreatment. We also provide a detailed account of one home-visiting intervention, SafeCare, that explicitly focuses on helping parents with the skill deficits associated with child neglect.

To date, SafeCare has been implemented across 23 states in the US as well as in six other countries on three continents. It is one of the few interventions with independent and robust findings of effectiveness in reducing families' subsequent involvement with child welfare services. The chapter describes both the programme content and the implementation process for SafeCare. We argue that there is a good case for its wider implementation as well as for more extensive outcome research on the effectiveness of SafeCare to address the prevalence of child neglect.

Child maltreatment is a significant public health problem with substantial economic and personal consequences for its victims and for society. Therefore, prevention and intervention efforts are needed to reduce its prevalence (Fang *et al.* 2012; Sedlak *et al.* 2010). Considerable attention has been devoted to physical and sexual abuse, whether in terms of research, intervention and prevention efforts, policy and the media (see Chapter 4).

Child neglect, which arguably attracts less attention, in fact makes up the majority of cases referred to child welfare services in many countries, such as the United States (79.5%), the United Kingdom (44%), Canada (38%) and Australia (34%) (Australian Institute of Health and Welfare 2004; Gilbert *et al.* 2009a; Trocmé *et al.* 2003; US Department of Health & Human Services *et al.* 2015). Moreover, while recent decades have seen a decline in the rates of physical and sexual abuse, rates of child neglect have remained relatively stable (Finkelhor *et al.* 2013). For example, child neglect rose 1 per cent between 2012 and 2013. The reasons for this are not clear but may in part be due to a lack of tested interventions for child neglect.

The damaging outcomes associated with neglect are at least equivalent to those of physical and sexual abuse, and are perhaps even more severe, as evidenced by the fact that nearly a third of child maltreatment fatalities are due to child neglect (Hildyard and Wolfe 2002; Welch and Bonner 2013). Still, there continues to be a dearth of research on child neglect in comparison to physical and sexual abuse. Part of the 'neglect of neglect' (Wolock and Horowitz 1984) in research and intervention efforts may be due to inconsistent conceptualisations of neglect across and within disciplines (Hearn 2011; Welch and Bonner 2013). For instance, while some may focus on parental intrapersonal difficulties, others may focus on access to resources and external circumstances (e.g. poverty) that may put the caregiver at risk for such difficulties. Furthermore, definitions may vary within and across countries (Gilbert *et al.* 2009b). Accordingly, it is crucial for researchers and practitioners to reach a sufficient consensus in the definition of neglect so that effective interventions can be developed, rigorously tested and implemented. In order to facilitate research on child neglect specifically, it will also be important for researchers to measure neglect separately, perhaps utilising neglect-specific self-report measures, or administrative data on neglect reports that are independent of those for other types of maltreatment.

Given the ambiguity in defining child neglect, it is not surprising that few interventions target child neglect specifically. In general, most classify child neglect as 'inadequate care' and 'inadequate supervision' (Dubowitz 2007; Welch and Bonner 2013); however, it has been difficult to define 'inadequate supervision' in a consistent way, even though it contributes to the majority of child neglect fatalities (Welch and Bonner 2013). Not surprisingly, most interventions continue to focus on promoting positive parent–child interactions and teaching parents discipline strategies, to help them deal positively with challenging child behaviours rather than resort to physical abuse. Interventions rarely focus in depth on parental neglect of health and safety that can put children at risk for illness, injury or death.

This chapter argues that to remedy child neglect, parents need to develop the skills and confidence to *take proactive action* to address a range of age-appropriate developmental needs in their child, from play and discipline to health and environmental safety. Once there is visible and tangible improvement, albeit in small steps, parents are able to apply the process they have learned to overcome other challenges.

This chapter will begin with a brief overview of the determinants and consequences of child neglect, followed with a description of programmes that target child maltreatment and include at least some focus on the skill deficits associated with neglect. A description of a home visiting programme, SafeCare, and a demonstration of its utility in minimising neglectful parenting behaviours will follow. Finally, the implications of SafeCare for practice in child neglect will conclude the chapter.

Child neglect: Determinants and consequences

The inability to disentangle neglect from maltreatment more generally can impede a clear depiction of the burden of child neglect. Commonly, the determinants of neglect are conceptualised in an ecological framework, attributable to the seminal work of Bronfenbrenner (1979) and Belsky (1980). The ecological perspective depicts levels of influence on the occurrence of neglect (intrapersonal, interpersonal, social/community) and posits that these levels are interrelated and integrated (Gaudin 1993; Tanner and Turney 2003). Individual parental characteristics that contribute to neglect are comparable to the risk factors for maltreatment in general: young parental age, mental health issues, substance (drugs and/or alcohol) use or abuse, and a personal history of maltreatment and/or victimisation. At the interpersonal or familial level, the literature suggests that parenting characteristics most strongly predict neglect (Slack *et al.* 2004; Tanner and Turney 2003).

Specifically, attachment theory would suggest that those with a history of insecure attachment would be most at risk for perpetrating maltreatment; that is, a history of inconsistent, rejecting or frightening caregiving likely characterise individuals referred for suspected abuse or neglect (Zuravin *et al.* 1996). If parents do not have a good model of relationships because one was not provided as a child, it increases the difficulty of bonding with and providing one for one's own children. In the case of neglect, a parent's consistent unresponsiveness to the child's needs for protection, comfort and connection will eventually communicate to the child that he or she is unlovable and that attachment needs will go unmet. Some of these children will expect future relationship partners (and eventually their own children) to act the same. As a consequence, neglectful parenting practices can cross generations. Therefore, it is critical to intervene early with parents who themselves have experienced insensitive caregiving.

Despite the link between parenting characteristics and neglect, poverty (located at the social/community level) is the most commonly cited risk factor for, and predictor of, child neglect (Christoffersen and DePanfilis 2009; Jonson-Reid, Drake and Zhou 2012; Slack *et al.* 2004; Tanner and Turney 2003). Families living in poverty are over 40 times more likely to be referred to the child welfare system than their higher-income counterparts and income is, not surprisingly, the greatest predictor of child welfare entry (Boyer and Halbrook 2011; Drake and Pandey 1996). Though there is consensus that a strong correlation between poverty and neglect exists, the impact of this risk factor is not well understood (Slack et al. 2004). Although a family lives in poverty, a report for neglect is not inevitable; thus, the interrelated nature of the ecological perspective (see Chapters 4 and 7).

Slack and colleagues (2004) examined what aspects of poverty and parenting were strongly associated with neglect and found that in the United States, neglect reported to child welfare or child protective systems (hereafter referred to solely as child welfare systems) was associated with the parents' perceived financial situation and employment status. It was also positively associated with parental stress and corporal punishment, and inversely associated with parental warmth, thus demonstrating the interrelated levels of the ecological perspective. Aspects of poverty and parenting are recognised risk factors for neglect, but as Slack and colleagues (2004) suggest, these aspects must be analysed simultaneously to best understand how risk factors interact to influence neglect. In addition, racial disparities in poverty warrant an examination of the differences in types of and responses to neglect. Black children in the child welfare system had higher rates of neglect than White or Hispanic children and were more likely to be poor and live in economically disadvantaged communities (Jonson-Reid et al. 2012). If child welfare services are to be successful, then prevention and intervention efforts should employ the ecological perspective as a means of identifying and ameliorating disparities.

There have been challenges in identifying determinants or key factors specific to neglect, but research has been more successful in isolating the consequences of neglect on children as opposed to those of physical or sexual abuse. The effects of neglect are significant for infants, but also appear to be cumulative over time; indeed, neglect is often chronic in nature (Tanner and Turney 2003). The impacts of neglect are most evident in the behavioural, cognitive and emotional development of young children (Tyler, Allison and Winsler 2006). Cognitive and emotional development are contingent on and occur within the parent–child relationship, and thus, if the caregiver is neglectful and unresponsive, the child does not receive the necessary stimulation and interaction for healthy development.

Compared to those who have experienced physical abuse, children who have experienced neglect have higher rates of risky behaviour (e.g. young sexual initiation, teen pregnancy, substance use/abuse), delinquency and subsequent child maltreatment perpetration (Christoffersen and DePanfilis 2009; Jonson-Reid *et al.* 2012). Victims of neglect experience negative outcomes in multiple domains of their lives: poor health outcomes, social withdrawal, internalising and externalising disorders, lack of educational attainment and subsequent poor economic wellbeing, deficiencies in emotional and behavioural development, as well as poor family and social relationships (Christoffersen and DePanfilis 2009; Tanner and Turney 2003; Widom *et al.* 2012). Moreover, there may be racial variation in the sequelae experienced. Widom and colleagues (2012) reported White children to display poor mental health outcomes, Black children to display anxiety and chronic depression, and Hispanic children to display higher risk for alcohol problems.

The ultimate consequence, a child fatality, specifically attributable to neglect, is a relatively rare event. Often, disentangling the cause of death from physical abuse and neglect is a challenge for medical and forensic experts. In 2013, 71.4 per cent of child fatalities in the US were attributable to neglect alone or in combination with another maltreatment type (Child Welfare Information Gateway 2015). This is in large part due to under-reporting and inconsistent definitions of neglect and abuse; data at the state level is potentially more accurate given consistency in definition. In a review of 22 years of statewide data from Oklahoma, Welch and Bonner (2013) identified 372 deaths (49%) attributable to neglect out of a total of 754 fatalities linked to maltreatment. Of those 372 fatalities, 227 (61%) were a result of supervisory neglect specifically. Just one instance of death due to supervisory neglect speaks to the need for tested prevention and educational programmes at a number of levels. Although these cannot address all contributory stress factors that lead to child neglect, we believe that there is evidence to merit further testing the hypothesis that they have the potential to help the majority of parents to keep their children safer.

Child neglect: Prevention and intervention efforts

When a report of potential child maltreatment comes to the attention of child welfare services in the US, a caseworker is dispatched to determine whether any child from the family has in fact been abused or neglected, or in other words, to investigate whether a report should be substantiated. For a report to be substantiated or screened in, the actions of the parent or guardian must have resulted in harm or placed the child at serious risk for harm. Because the effects of neglect may not be directly observable, some cases of neglect that are harmful to the child may not be substantiated. Once a report has been substantiated, families are referred to services, with the goal of keeping the children in the home. These services typically include some form of supportive case management, service referrals, and education about parenting, child development and coping strategies. However, there is considerable variability in the delivery of services across and within states. Despite continued use, the standard services typically offered to families involved with child welfare systems have not demonstrated effectiveness in preventing placement of children outside the home or reducing recidivism (Schuerman, Rzepnicki and Littell 1994; Waldfogel 2009).

As noted above, child abuse and neglect are often considered (and addressed) collectively as child maltreatment, despite the fact that child neglect is much more prevalent than either physical or sexual abuse. To the detriment of child neglect research and intervention efforts, physical abuse and particularly sexual abuse have historically dominated public perceptions of child maltreatment (Chaffin 2006). While there are several programmes that address child maltreatment in general, there are few that have demonstrated effectiveness in addressing child neglect specifically. Abuse and neglect most commonly occur in the context of the caregiver–child relationship, and thus, many programmes target the parent to improve both child and parent outcomes. Though this approach is widely considered to be most effective and empirical evidence suggests this is so, community-directed interventions have also shown promise and attracted interest. The following sections give brief overviews of those programmes typically perceived as child maltreatment prevention that include more or less some degree of focus on neglectful behaviours, as well as the evidence to support each programme's utility. Programmes are discussed in the following order: community-targeted programmes, group-based programmes, and finally, home visiting programmes.

Positive Parenting Program (Triple P)

While most programmes focus on delivering services to parents or to children or in groups or parent–child dyads, the Positive Parenting Program (Triple P), originating in Australia, takes a public health approach to prevent child maltreatment by providing parent and family support at multiple levels of intervention (Prinz et al. 2009). Triple P has been implemented across the US and in 24 other countries. It is made up of five levels of intervention of increasing intensity and becoming more targeted (Sanders 1999). Level 1 (Universal Triple P) takes advantage of the family's social context by utilising the media and other communication strategies to convey the normality of stressful parenting experiences to parents generally. In doing this, the intention is to remove the stigma regarding help seeking, to provide information about parenting, and ultimately, to shift 'the community context for parenting' (Prinz et al. 2009, p.3). Level 2 (Selected Triple P) provides either large group-based parenting seminars or consultation to individual caregivers. Level 3 (Primary Care Triple P) builds on individual consultation by incorporating active skills training to help parents learn and implement parenting strategies with their children. Level 4 (Standard and Group Triple P) was designed for parents of children who may be manifesting behaviour problems, but do not yet have a diagnosable disorder, and involves the provision of child behaviour management strategies and practice applying them in a variety of situations, delivered in either a standard or group format. Finally, Level 5 (Enhanced Triple P) is much more intensive, involving a range of services directed towards parents' interpersonal communication, skills for coping with stress and strategies to manage emotions, as well as continuing to practise skills learned from previous levels. Triple P targets parents of children under the age of 12 years, although there is a modified programme for parents of teenagers up to 16 years old (i.e. Teen Triple P).

Triple P has been rigorously tested, with positive outcomes for families and their children, including child maltreatment. For example, in a randomised trial in which 18 counties in the US (i.e. a geographic sub-area of a state) were randomised to either Triple P or services as usual, those counties receiving Triple P had significantly fewer substantiated child maltreatment cases, out-of-home placements and injuries due to child maltreatment (including neglect) as measured by hospital and emergency room visits (Prinz *et al.* 2009). It should be noted, however, that in both the control counties and Triple P counties, identified child maltreatment increased over the duration of the study. Another study using a quasi-experimental design found that Triple P significantly reduced parent-reported child behaviour problems, parental depression, anxiety and stress as well as parental conflict, in comparison to a control group (Zubrick *et al.* 2005). Interestingly, this study also noted high rates of participation (86% at post test), especially from those at high risk of child maltreatment.

Incredible Years Parent Training Program

The only group-based programme to demonstrate a good degree of effectiveness in improving behavioural outcomes for children and parents is the Incredible Years (IY) Parent Training Program, which uses teachers in the classroom and peer support groups for parents in addition to parent education to prevent child maltreatment (Daro and McCurdy 2007; Webster-Stratton 1998). It has been widely implemented across the US and the world, and targets families with children up to 12 years old. The IY curriculum is comprised of interrelated evidence-based programmes intended primarily to target children's conduct problems. For example, one programme targets teachers' classroom management skills, while another uses video vignettes to stimulate parent conversation and reflection.

Randomised clinical trials and quasi-experimental studies have demonstrated that IY parents had reduced depressive symptoms, increased positive affect, and used less harsh discipline with their children (Letarte, Normandeau and Allard 2010; Webster-Stratton 1998). It is suggested that these improvements in the parenting experience as a result of programme participation translate into greater parental empathy and fewer dysfunctional interactions between parents and their children (Marcynyszyn, Maher and Corwin 2011). The IY programme was beneficial in minimising parents' neglectful behaviours as evidenced by their significant improvements in involvement with their children during free play (Hughes and Gottlieb 2004). Although the IY programme has had some success in preventing neglectful behaviours, its curriculum does not explicitly address the skill deficits associated with neglect and is much more focused on minimising children's challenging behaviours that may set the occasion for abuse.

Nurse-Family Partnership

The Nurse-Family Partnership (NFP) (Olds 2006) is the most widely used and empirically supported home visitation programme targeting child maltreatment and general parenting in the US, operating in 44 states. NFP focuses on enhancing first-time mothers' prenatal health behaviours, knowledge of child development, sensitive caregiving, and the mother's social environment in order to prevent abusive behaviours, unintentional injuries and promote positive parent–child relationships (Olds 2006, 2008). The programme recruits low-income, first-time expectant mothers – often teenage mothers – who are visited by a trained nurse until the child's second birthday; women who are not pregnant with their first child are not eligible for NFP services.

The home visits during pregnancy consist of the nurse providing information about prenatal nutrition, assessing the use of nicotine products, alcohol and illicit drugs, and offering strategies to reduce the use of substances. Following birth, nurses focus on improving the mother's provision of physical and emotional care of her baby, as well as a safe household. Mothers are taught to identify signs of illness, assess symptoms and determine when to seek professional care. Additionally, nurses promote positive parent–child interactions by helping mothers understand their children's cues and encouraging mothers' engagement in play with their children to facilitate emotional and cognitive development and bonding. Finally, nurses work with mothers to develop strategies to address problems that may hinder their education, employment and planning for future pregnancies.

Nurse-Family Partnership has demonstrated effectiveness in improving mothers' prenatal health behaviours (as measured by improved diets and fewer smoked cigarettes), healthier babies at delivery, more sensitive caregiving (e.g. less punishment and restrictive care), and safer home environments (as measured by observations of home hazards) than a control group (Olds 2008). In addition, NFP participants had nearly 80 per cent fewer substantiated cases of child abuse and neglect than their control counterparts, though this finding was only marginally significant ($p = 0.07$). Further, children in NFP had 35 per cent fewer emergency hospital visits, partly due to the reduction in visits because of injuries and harmful ingestions. While the programme's effect on emergency hospital visits and injuries was sustained two years after the programme ended, the difference between the groups in substantiated child abuse and neglect was no longer significant (Olds 2008; Olds, Henderson and Kitzman 1994). Finally, at the 15-year follow-up, mothers visited by nurses exhibited fewer subsequent pregnancies/births, greater spacing in between the first and second children's births, fewer months receiving welfare/food stamps and fewer problems due to substance abuse as compared to control mothers (Olds *et al.*1997). Notably, these effects are especially pronounced for unmarried teen mothers living in poverty.

Family Connections

Similar to NFP, Family Connections (FC) is a home visiting model; however, FC was specifically developed to prevent child neglect among children aged 5 to 11 years old from impoverished neighbourhoods (DePanfilis and Dubowitz 2005). Family Connections uses an ecological developmental framework to guide service provision given that various risk factors in the environment, the caregiver, family system and child contribute to the often chronic nature of child neglect. Accordingly, FC is a community-based programme that provides services to families in their homes and neighbourhoods to improve the ability of parents to meet their children's basic needs. Services personalised to the needs of each family are delivered by trained graduate students. Home visitors are trained to assess and assist with emergency concrete needs (e.g. food, utilities, eviction) before the programme commences, by linking families to existing community and monetary resources, and if those are not accessible or available, using resources provided by FC. Based on outcome assessments, service plans are designed to include specific goals and, as needed, link families with additional services. Finally, families are invited to local gatherings multiple times a year to enhance their social network.

Studies on Family Connections (FC) using pre-post designs, which assess participants before and after treatments or interventions to measure changes in outcomes, have demonstrated reductions in risk factors and increases in protective factors for child neglect, primarily with samples of low-income, largely Black caregivers (DePanfilis and

Dubowitz 2005; Lindsey, Hayward and DePanfilis 2010). In one study, parents using FC reported significant decreases in depressive symptoms, parenting stress and everyday life stress, as well as increases in empathy, sense of competence in parenting and perceived social support (DePanfilis and Dubowitz 2005). In addition, parents using FC provided safer households following programme completion, as evidenced by more adequate home furnishings, less overcrowding and more adequate home sanitation. The psychological care of children also improved, such that home visitor observations of the care of the child's mental health and parental stimulation of the child became significantly more adequate following programme completion. Parents also reported significant decreases in children's internalising and externalising behaviours following programme participation. A secondary analysis of these data revealed that boys may benefit to a greater extent from FC than girls, as boys exhibited greater decreases in internalising and externalising behaviours from baseline to programme completion (Lindsey et al. 2010). It was suggested that the social support provided to mothers by FC may have minimised behavioural problems for boys in particular since such problems tend to be more stable in males than females. Finally, the percentage of families with indicated or substantiated child abuse and neglect reports decreased from 38.3 per cent at baseline to 3.6 per cent at the six-month follow-up (DePanfilis and Dubowitz 2005).

Parents as Teachers

Parents as Teachers (PAT) is a less targeted, universal home visiting model with the goal of preventing child abuse and neglect, as well as improving children's readiness for school (Zigler, Pfannenstiel and Seitz 2008). It has been implemented widely across the US and in five other countries, and targets parents from conception to the child's fifth birthday. PAT focuses on teaching parents about child development, modelling developmentally appropriate activities and helping parents access needed resources. Like NFP, families enrol in the programme during pregnancy and can participate in the programme until the child is five years old. During home visits, the trained home visitor helps parents learn developmentally appropriate expectations for children. They also model and engage parents in activities with their children aimed at promoting learning and positive parent–child attachment.

Group meetings are a second component of PAT that provide parents the opportunity to share experiences and concerns with fellow parents. A third component involves teaching parents to observe and track their child's development so they can identify delays or difficulties early and solutions can be implemented as needed. Finally, as in many other home visiting models, PAT helps parents establish a resource and referral network for them to utilise in times of need.

In a study of nearly 6000 children, PAT parents were found to read to their children more often and be more likely to enrol their children in preschool, both of which in turn predict school readiness (e.g. enhanced communication, working with others and mathematical/physical knowledge) (Pfannenstiel, Seitz and Zigler 2002; Zigler *et al.* 2008). Participation in PAT also *directly* predicted children's school readiness, which has been shown to be the most powerful predictor of third-grade achievement (Zigler *et al.* 2008). Interestingly, children enrolled in schools in high poverty areas who had participated in PAT had similar scores to their low poverty counterparts who did not receive PAT or preschool (Pfannenstiel *et al.* 2002; Zigler *et al.* 2008). Finally, third-grade achievement is a significant predictor of high school graduation, suggesting that the benefits of PAT are potentially long lasting and attenuating of the influence of poverty (The Annie E. Casey Foundation 2012).

SafeCare: Targeting neglect

SafeCare is an evidence-based parent training programme for families with at least one child aged from birth to five years old who is at risk or reported for maltreatment (since the data reporting system is still being developed, information on the number of referrals for neglect specifically is unavailable). Home visitors provide parent training in modular form to address skill deficits in three core areas:

- first, parent–child or parent–infant interactions (module dependent on target child's age)

- second, child health, and

- third, home safety (Guastaferro *et al.* 2012; Lutzker and Chaffin 2012).

The in-home weekly visits by trained providers are an average of 60–90 minutes in duration over the course of the approximate 18 sessions of the programme (three modules with six sessions per module). The number and duration of sessions depends on the parents' improvement and mastery of the trained skills. To understand the significance of what SafeCare is able to achieve in reducing potential risk for child maltreatment, and neglect in particular, this section will describe the model's evolution, theoretical framework, and large-scale transportation and implementation efforts.

The origins of SafeCare

SafeCare originated in 1979 in rural southern Illinois as Project 12-Ways, an eco-behavioural, in-home parenting programme delivered by graduate students (Lutzker, Frame and Rice 1982). Delivered to the greatest risk and most concerning child welfare cases, Project 12-Ways trained parents in up to 12 skill sets: child basic living, parent–child interaction, health maintenance and nutrition, stress reduction, marital counselling, home safety, management of finances, job searching, alcoholism treatment, leisure time, self-control, and prenatal/postnatal services for single mothers (Guastaferro et al. 2012; Lutzker and Rice 1984). The comprehensive set of skills families acquired was indeed eco-behavioural, but notable changes in risk for maltreatment, specifically neglect, were observed in rates of recidivism. Families who received training in Project 12-ways were less likely to have repeat involvement with child welfare services than families that received services as usual (Dachman et al. 1984). The original 12-ways model has been continuously funded and implemented at Southern Illinois University at Carbondale in the US since 1979.

Despite the success of Project 12-Ways, its multiple components meant that the model was not easily disseminated, nor was it feasible to take the programme to scale. Thus, in 1994 a dissemination trial was funded in urban Los Angeles, California and the modules were condensed to the basic skills needed by all families and the three most frequently used by Project 12-Ways: parent–child/parent–infant interactions, home safety and child health (Guastaferro et al. 2012). Families in the San Fernando Valley of Los Angeles, having received the three modules only, still had improved rates of recidivism, and families who received SafeCare had statistically significant lower reports of maltreatment compared to families in standard family preservation services (Gershater-Molko, Lutzker and Wesch 2002). Thirty-six months post-intervention, 85 per cent of the SafeCare families had no child maltreatment reports compared to only 54 per cent of families receiving standard services.

Training, research, dissemination and implementation

In 2008, funding from the Doris Duke Charitable Trust allowed for the establishment of the National SafeCare Training and Research Center (NSTRC) in the School of Public Health at Georgia State University in Atlanta, USA. The NSTRC includes a staff of training specialists with experience as SafeCare home visitors and coaches, who travel to agencies and community-based organisations to train staff to be home visitors. Training utilises a train-the-trainer format. That is, a team or teams of local agency staff are trained as SafeCare practitioners (known as home visitors), from which one individual will then be trained to be a coach for the agency's home visitors (i.e. providing them with consultation and supervision). Eventually, it is possible for the coach to be trained as a trainer who can train others within the agency and the local child welfare system. This sort of built-in sustainability can help to eliminate some known implementation issues, such as staff turnover, and minimise the cost of multiple trainings by the programme purveyors (Fixsen *et al.* 2009). In its current form, SafeCare is implemented in 23 US states (with statewide rollouts in six of those states) and six other countries (Belarus, Spain, Israel, the UK, Australia and Canada).

Training theory

Like many other behavioural parenting programmes, the roots of SafeCare are firmly planted within applied behaviour analysis and social learning theory. The training paradigm, both for home visitor and parent, follows the following format: within a supportive relationship, behaviours are explained and modelled first, then practised through role-plays and scenarios, and finally, positive, corrective feedback is provided. The support structure is intended to give home visitors confidence as they build similar structure for families, challenging parents as well as celebrating their achievements. Each module consists of a baseline assessment, several training sessions, and an end-of-module assessment to evaluate skill acquisition as well as maintenance of newly learned skills. Assessments are completed through direct observation and the assessor evaluates the level of mastery of the trained skills using a checklist of criteria for each module.

Focus on neglect

The core modules of SafeCare (parent–child/parent–infant interaction, child health and home safety) specifically address aspects of child neglect. Like other behavioural parenting programmes, the parent–child or parent–infant interaction modules seek to improve interactions between parent and child and to prevent emotional neglect. SafeCare distinguishes the necessary parenting skills by the age of the child. Families with children who are not yet ambulatory receive the parent–infant interaction module whereas families with children who are ambulatory and who respond to simple verbal commands receive the parent–child interaction module. Parents learn to plan activities, to plan in advance, and to recognise developmentally appropriate behaviours and activities. The interaction modules are most closely related to preventing instances of supervisory neglect. The home safety module addresses hazards and filth in the home environment, with the goal of promoting a child-healthy environment and preventing environmental neglect. Finally, physical and medical neglect are prevented with the child health module by training parents to understand healthy child development, to identify symptoms and illnesses and to work through a checklist to determine the best course of treatment for their child. A range of visual and other tools are used to assist parents. Overall, SafeCare can instill a proactive approach to parenting and safe routines which are key to sustaining healthy child development. These routines can improve both the child's and the parents' wellbeing, and allow parents to engage in social and creative activity with their child.

Findings, outcomes, conclusions

SafeCare has been rigorously tested with multiple research designs, including single-case research studies, quasi-experimental studies and randomised clinical trials (Self-Brown *et al.* 2014). The outcomes used in each effectiveness study have included self-report measures of child abuse potential, home visitor observations of parental skills and child welfare administrative data. Thus, SafeCare has a broad range of outcomes to support its effectiveness and is not limited by only one type of outcome data. However, it should be noted that SafeCare has not been tested with child neglect cases and outcomes specifically, indicating a need for these outcomes to be tested in future research.

Comparisons with services as usual

Arguably the most supportive evidence for the effectiveness of SafeCare come from an independent statewide cluster randomised trial. This compared the effects on child welfare recidivism of SafeCare as against good quality, home-based services as usual (SAU; i.e. standard home-based case management and mental health services) in a sample of 2175 parents with substantiated maltreatment (Chaffin *et al.* 2012a). In this study, six agencies/regions were assigned to either SafeCare or SAU; assignment occurred so as to maximise similarities on baseline client demographics among agencies.

While child welfare recidivism was the outcome of most interest, parent reports of child abuse potential were also collected. Results detected significant reductions in recidivism of child maltreatment reports to child welfare at a seven-year follow-up for SafeCare compared to home-based SAU. Specifically, for every 1000 cases receiving home-based services, the implementation of SafeCare would prevent an estimated 64 to 104 re-reports to child welfare in the first year. The effects were even stronger for the subsample of parents who met SafeCare inclusion criteria (i.e. parents with at least one child 0 to 5 years old with no current untreated substance use disorder).

Another randomised clinical trial compared an augmented version of SafeCare to SAU on child welfare involvement and self-reports of parenting behaviours in a sample of high-risk rural families (Silovsky *et al.* 2011). The augmented version of SafeCare used in this trial incorporated Motivational Interviewing (Miller and Rollnick 2004) and home visitors trained in identifying and responding to child maltreatment and other risk factors, such as substance use, depression and interpersonal violence. The following findings are of interest, and although short of statistical significance, suggest that research with a larger sample size would be worthwhile. Compared to families receiving services as usual (SAU), those in the augmented SafeCare condition were less likely to have subsequent involvement with child welfare and those that did lasted longer before their first report to child welfare (Silovsky *et al.* 2011). Among those with referrals for neglect specifically, the number of days until a first report to child welfare was over twice as long (200 versus 90 days) for those receiving SafeCare than those receiving SAU.

Engaging Families

While no statistically significant findings were detected for child welfare and parent outcomes, significant differences between augmented SafeCare and SAU *were* detected for engagement and satisfaction with services (Silovsky *et al.* 2011). Those assigned to SafeCare were significantly more likely to complete an intake as well as receive more hours of service than those in SAU care. Further, participants in the SafeCare condition reported greater satisfaction with services, perceived the programme as more helpful and reported greater progress on SafeCare goals (e.g. knowledge of child health and care, hazards to children, and better parent–child relationships). Finally, SafeCare home visitors were considerably more likely to link their families with additional services than SAU providers.

Strategies to reduce attrition

Families cannot benefit from programmes they do not receive, and engagement/participation and attrition are considerable barriers to programme impact, particularly with families living in poverty who are most likely to be referred to child welfare systems (Boyer and Halbrook 2011; McCurdy and Daro 2001). Therefore, it is crucial for interventions to utilise innovative strategies to help minimise these barriers; the use of technology provides one potential strategy to enhance family engagement, and consequently, retention and programme effectiveness. In another augmentation of SafeCare, handheld smart phones were utilised in delivering the home safety module to examine whether the use of cellphones would enhance family engagement, minimise face-to-face contact with home visitors and reduce the number of hazards in the home (Jabaley *et al.* 2011). Three families were given iPhones to be used for training, filming household hazards for data collection and communication with the home visitors (e.g. praise and feedback). Data from these families demonstrated that the iPhone augmentation did appear to assist in a reduction of household hazards, the number of training sessions and the time needed for data collection. These findings suggest that technology may be an important mechanism in reducing the costs associated with delivering and receiving services.

SafeCare with diverse populations

Differences among families may impact programme effectiveness, and it is important to examine programme benefit across diverse child welfare populations. Using a subsample (n = 354) of the statewide cluster randomised trial reported above (Chaffin *et al.* 2012a), Chaffin and colleagues examined whether findings for the larger sample were comparable for a subsample of American Indians (Chaffin *et al.* 2012b). While recidivism reduction was not observed for the entire subsample, among those families meeting traditional SafeCare inclusion criteria (i.e. at least one child 0–5 years old and no current untreated substance use disorder), the reduction in recidivism was nearly equivalent to that found for the full sample. A common concern with highly structured, manualised interventions is that they may be culturally insensitive; however, American Indian families reported that SafeCare was *more* appreciative of cultural differences and compatible with their cultural traditions and beliefs, and they perceived SafeCare as being *more* helpful than SAU. These results highlight the potential of SafeCare delivery in diverse settings across cultures, but also suggest that practitioners should not implement the programme with families for whom the programme was not intended. The 'fit' of programmes to particular groups and populations of parents is another vital area for new research.

A significant proportion of parents involved with child welfare systems have an intellectual disability (ID) and these parents may come to the attention of child welfare because of suspected neglect (Gaskin *et al.* 2012). SafeCare structured modules are particularly well-suited to addressing the skill deficits – similar to those found in typical child welfare populations – that may render parents with ID susceptible to neglecting their children.

In order to assist parents with ID, the SafeCare parent–infant interaction (PII) module incorporated a digital picture frame and adapted training materials with more pictorial information and rudimentary phrasing for use with one mother with ID. The use of technology has been particularly helpful for skill acquisition in individuals with ID. The digital picture frame was used to facilitate self-modelling, by displaying pictures of the mother herself showing mastery of parent–infant interaction (PII) skills performance criteria with her infant. Thus, the mother acted as her own model. Photos were uploaded at the end of each session. There was a considerable increase in the mother's display of both non-physical (e.g. smiling, positive verbalising) and physical (e.g. holding, touching) skills, and the improvement in her physical skills was even more substantial (83% versus 33.3% increase). Since scores decreased slightly at the one- and two-month follow-ups, booster sessions were implemented that helped recover skills to post-test levels. The mother indicated overall satisfaction with the adapted module, although she reported some discomfort having her picture taken. Overall, these results suggest that SafeCare modules, when modified with sensitivity, can be adapted for use with parents of varying cognitive capacity.

Another population over-represented in child welfare cases is that of parents with a history of a substance use disorder, who are at significant risk for child neglect specifically (Strong et al. 2014). SafeCare currently excludes parents who do not agree to treatment of their substance misuse. A multiple-baseline single-case research design with two mothers in a residential recovery facility was used to examine the effectiveness of the SafeCare health module in improving the mothers' ability to identify children's symptoms and illness, as well as decide on a suitable course of action. Both mothers demonstrated improvements in skill acquisition, with both mothers exhibiting 100 per cent skill mastery for all three health scenarios (i.e. call the doctor, treat the child at home, take the child to emergency room) at the end of the programme. This study offers an initial indication that the health module can be beneficial for those at high-risk of neglect, and medical neglect in particular, and merits replication on a larger scale.

As mentioned before, SafeCare has been implemented in several countries, with the UK being one of the few contexts where SafeCare is currently being evaluated outside its original setting (Gardner et al. 2014). Instead of examining the effectiveness of SafeCare in the UK specifically, researchers are analysing the application of the programme to the UK with regard to outcomes, programme participation and attrition. This project will provide a guide for evaluation efforts in other countries implementing SafeCare, which are much needed in order to analyse the translation of SafeCare (and its impact on child neglect) to settings outside the US.

Table 9.1 Interventions for child maltreatment

Intervention	Target	Primary focus	Explicit focus on neglect?	Research references
Positive Parenting Program (Triple P)	Community, parent	Community and family perceptions of and strategies for parenting	No	Prinz *et al.* (2009) Zubrick *et al.* (2005)
Incredible Years Parent Training Program	Teachers, parents	Child conduct problems	No	Letarte *et al.* (2010) Marcynyszyn *et al.* (2011)
Nurse-Family Partnership	First-time mothers	General parenting skills	No	Olds, D.L. (2008) Olds *et al.* (1994)
Family Connections	Families from impoverished neighbourhoods	Concrete needs and personalised service plans	Yes	DePanfilis and Dubowitz (2005) Lindsey *et al.* (2010)
Parents as Teachers	Parents	School readiness	No	Pfannenstiel *et al.* (2002) Zigler *et al.* (2008)
SafeCare	Parents	Skill deficits associated with neglect and abuse	Yes	Chaffin *et al.* (2012a) Strong *et al.* (2014)

Implications for research, policy and practice
The need to test SafeCare as an intervention to prevent child neglect

Results from multiple studies using various designs have supported the use of SafeCare to reduce the risk of child maltreatment. SafeCare has demonstrated effectiveness in reducing hazards in the home, promoting appropriate responses to children's medical needs and reducing recidivism to child welfare systems. However, much of this work has examined child maltreatment cases and outcomes more generally, without examining the influence of SafeCare on child neglect specifically. Future research on the ability of SafeCare to reduce recidivism for child neglect reports would help support its claim as a neglect prevention programme. Further, modifications or augmentations of SafeCare have yet to be rigorously tested outside small sample designs and case studies; research with larger samples will help remedy this situation.

Historically, child maltreatment has been synonymous with sexual or physical abuse (Chaffin 2006). The landscape concerning child maltreatment is shifting, yet child neglect still falls under the shadow of other types of child abuse, partly because of high-profile and celebrity cases that attract considerable media attention. Therefore, it is imperative for practitioners and policymakers to understand and acknowledge that a majority of cases reported to child welfare systems are attributable to child neglect and that the consequences of neglect are at least as damaging as those of child abuse. Such acknowledgement is important to garner support for policies and funding for research and interventions specific to neglect.

There are multiple prevention and intervention efforts with the goal of preventing child maltreatment, all with more or less evidence to support their use; as we state above, many of the programmes target the parental behaviours typically associated with risk of physical child abuse (e.g. discipline and behaviour management strategies). Moreover, many programmes that are evidence based experience problems in sustainability when disseminated outside the setting in which the programme was developed. Thus, the implications of SafeCare for practices targeting child neglect are twofold. First, SafeCare provides a rare example of a skills-based behavioural parenting programme that is demonstrably effective in reducing both neglectful parenting behaviours and repeated involvement with child welfare systems, with clear implications for cost saving in both human and economic terms. Second, the dissemination and implementation model used by SafeCare – the train-the-trainer model – demonstrates how prevention efforts can be taken to large scale with built-in sustainability. Again, the initial outlay is efficient in terms of sustaining valuable expertise.

Supplementing interventions with SafeCare

SafeCare offers a potential resource for programmes that focus on maltreatment more generally given its unique focus on the skill deficits commonly associated with child neglect (i.e. skills in proactive parenting, home safety and child health). For example, programmes that focus primarily on promoting more positive and stimulating parent–child interactions to enhance the child's school readiness and reduce the risk of child maltreatment could incorporate in their curriculum a component that explicitly targets parents' wider skill deficits and neglectful parenting behaviours.

Efforts are currently underway to examine the effectiveness of such endeavours. Recently, in three states in the US, the programme Parents As Teachers (PAT) was systematically braided (i.e. combined) with SafeCare to explore the effect of a braided programme on parenting behaviours, child development and school readiness, and overall risk for maltreatment. The traditional PAT parent educator is trained in the braided curriculum, known as Parents as Teachers and SafeCare at Home (PATSCH), and sessions occur in the home on a weekly or bi-weekly basis. PATSCH offers families already enrolled in PAT services an intensive, yet brief, skill-based embedded curriculum which addresses parental skill deficits not addressed in standard PAT implementation. PAT focuses on parent–child interaction in a similar way to SafeCare; however, PATSCH adds the home safety and child health modules of SafeCare, which have historically not been present in the PAT curriculum.

A cluster randomised trial is currently underway (PI: Lutzker, Annie E. Casey Foundation Grant No. 211.0003) testing the effectiveness of the braided curriculum; therefore, it is not yet known whether the combination of programmes is effective in minimising neglectful parenting behaviours and improving parental skills. However, anecdotal and informal feedback from families and providers is that the SafeCare safety and health modules are much needed and well received. Interim data analysis supports this qualitative feedback. Among interim baseline data alone, a modest correlation (r = 0.23; p <.05) was found between the number of hazards counted in the home and the potential for abuse (Walsh 2014). This example demonstrates the potential utility of incorporating SafeCare modules, and an explicit focus on neglectful parenting behaviours, within the

PAT curriculum that is primarily intended to minimise parents' risk for physical abuse.

Resource efficiency

It is well known that many of the families in child welfare systems do not receive evidence-based programmes, but instead receive services as usual or family preservation services, which have little to no evidence of effectiveness (Barth *et al.* 2005). Some of the primary reasons are that evidence-based practices can be costly and difficult to sustain. SafeCare has proven cost-beneficial as evidenced by a study demonstrating a $14.65 benefit to cost ratio (Lee *et al.* 2012). (In the UK, the Investing in Children project at the Social Research Unit at Dartington has adapted the economic model used by the Washington State Institute for Public Policy (WSIPP) to estimate the benefit–cost ratio of interventions. They give a 'cautious estimate' of 2.2:1 as the benefit–cost ratio for SafeCare, with a 10% return on investment.)

We would argue that the train-the-trainer model utilised by SafeCare helps minimise the costs associated with the need for multiple trainings by the purveyor, which helps ensure the programme becomes part of an agency's regular practice. Because trained home visitors can become coaches, and eventually trainers who can train others within their agency and local service system in the SafeCare model, staff turnover is less of a concern as new staff can be trained without the need for additional, costly trainings from the programme's purveyor. In addition, when programmes are implemented in settings outside of the one in which it was developed, the programme may not be delivered as intended. SafeCare, on the other hand, involves ongoing quality monitoring by regularly assessing home visitor fidelity, and thus ensuring that the programme is continually delivered with integrity. This model significantly contributes to the sustainability of SafeCare and provides a guide for other programmes that suffer from common implementation issues.

THE UK EVALUATION OF SAFECARE

Gillian Churchill, Senior Evaluation Officer, NSPCC, UK

Between 2011 and 2015, SafeCare was implemented and evaluated in six sites in England by the National Society for the Prevention of Cruelty to Children (NSPCC), a large children's charity in the UK. This work contributes to the international body of evidence on the effectiveness of SafeCare, the focus of the NSPCC evaluation being on the transferability of SafeCare to a UK context and on what, if any, adaptions are required to enhance its effectiveness in the UK. The evaluation also looks at outcomes for parents and whether SafeCare provides benefits for practitioners in terms of their knowledge, skills and learning for practice more widely.

The NSPCC has stayed close to the original SafeCare model in order to learn about its effectiveness in a new setting. However, the NSPCC's home visitors were usually qualified social workers and children were accepted onto the programme up to their sixth birthday.

Evaluation design

The evaluation adopted a mixed methods approach, incorporating quantitative and qualitative methods. Interviews were conducted with practitioners and with parents who completed the programme to identify the facilitators and barriers to service users achieving positive outcomes and to understand their experience of the programme. Outcomes were measured using a pre-post intervention design to consider the extent to which the programme's intended outcomes for parents were achieved, based on SafeCare in-built module assessments and two independent measures – the North Carolina Family Assessment Scale for General Services and the Parent Child Neglect Scale. An online survey gathered referrers' views of the outcomes achieved for families that they referred to the programme and their perceptions of SafeCare in general, including any changes that they thought might be required to increase its acceptability and effectiveness in the context of the child protection system in England. Finally, analysis of 12 case records generated learning around the causes of attrition.

Key findings

The NSPCC evaluation supports existing evidence about the effectiveness of SafeCare. There do not appear to be any significant barriers to SafeCare having an impact within a UK context for parents who engage with the programme, evidence from module assessments, practitioner assessments, parent self-ratings and the survey of referrers all suggesting improvements in outcomes and a reduction in neglectful behaviours in particular. Analysis of practitioners' ratings of family functioning suggest a range of positive outcomes for families taking part in the programme in the areas of neglect, parental capabilities, family interactions, environment, family safety, child wellbeing and self-sufficiency. However, the largest improvement was in the area of neglect. At the start of the programme, 32 families were assessed by practitioners to be presenting difficulties significant enough to warrant a statutory intervention for neglect. By the end of the programme, 21 (66%) of those families had improved to a point where statutory intervention was no longer considered necessary (Churchill 2015a).

The parents interviewed for the evaluation had engaged fully with SafeCare and credited the programme with effecting positive improvements in their parenting knowledge, skills and behaviours. The establishment of a trusting relationship between parents and the home visitor and the perceived partnership approach to working played a vital role in parents' engagement with SafeCare and the success of the programme. Other strengths of the programme included home-based delivery, which enabled parents to practise their skills in a 'safe' place; the use of a variety of practical modes of delivery, which enhanced their enjoyment; and the provision of positive feedback, which built parents' confidence in their parenting abilities (Churchill 2015b).

Despite the positive findings, families referred to SafeCare (in common with many other social care programmes) exhibited high rates of programme attrition (Churchill 2015a). Although attrition commonly has negative connotations, the case review revealed a range of positive outcomes related to the programme that were achieved by families who exited the programme prior to completion. Moreover, for the majority of these families there were no outstanding safeguarding concerns at the point of closure. In over half of the cases reviewed, parents' success in accessing appropriate long-term sources of support to meet their family's needs featured in the decision to exit the programme prior to completion, including support from both child and adult mental health services, paediatrics and education. For other parents the support was more informal such as help from extended family members. This underlines the need for research that looks beyond the usual demographic and parental risk variables to a broader range of influences and a more in-depth understanding of reasons for engagement and attrition.

In addition to the analysis presented in this report, the evaluation design for SafeCare also included interviews with practitioners to identify the facilitators and barriers to service users achieving positive outcomes, to understand their experience of delivering/receiving the programme and to consider the transportability of the programme to the UK context. This will be reported within a separate report in 2016.

Key learning points

- Child neglect constitutes the majority of cases referred to child welfare systems, yet few programmes exist that target neglect specifically; most focus – either implicitly or explicitly – on preventing child maltreatment more generally, or on physical abuse.

- SafeCare is arguably one of very few programmes that explicitly targets the parental skill deficits associated with child neglect (e.g. health, home safety and parent–child interaction) with a substantial evidence base to support its effectiveness in reducing neglectful parenting and subsequent involvement with child welfare services; its effectiveness should be further tested in this area.

- The train-the-trainer implementation model used by SafeCare is a useful and efficient strategy to take evidence-based programmes to scale, and provides a guide for other programmes that struggle in implementation, and sustainability in particular.

- SafeCare modules are being used to supplement other programmes that focus solely – either explicitly or implicitly – on minimising risk for physical abuse and to pick up comorbidity of child neglect, and this combined approach is being researched. Such efforts are needed to combat the appallingly high rates of neglect and its subsequent costs to children, families and societies across the world.

Questions for reflection

– How could practices with supporting evidence for effectiveness in reducing child maltreatment incorporate a focus on neglect specifically?

– In order to facilitate the development of interventions that target neglectful parenting behaviours, how can researchers design studies that disentangle neglect from child maltreatment and examine neglect determinants and outcomes specifically?

– Does the implementation and sustainment model utilised by SafeCare (i.e. the train-the-trainer model, see p.292) have potential as an effective strategy for implementing and sustaining other models that target child maltreatment more broadly?

References

Australian Institute of Health and Welfare (2004) *Australia's Health.* Canberra: AIHW.

Barth, R.P., Landsverk, J., Chamberlain, P., Reid, J.B., Rolls, J.A. and Kohl, P.L. (2005) 'Parent-training programs in child welfare services: planning for a more evidence-based approach to serving biological parents.' *Research on Social Work Practice 15,* 5, 353–371.

Belsky, J. (1980) 'Child maltreatment: an ecological integration.' *American Psychologist 35,* 4, 320–335.

Boyer, B.A. and Halbrook, A.E. (2011) 'Advocating for children in care in a climate of economic recession: the relationship between poverty and child maltreatment.' *Journal of Law and Social Policy 6,* 2, 300–317.

Bronfenbrenner, U. (1979) *The Ecology of Human Development: Experiments by Nature and Design.* Cambridge, MA: Harvard University Press.

Chaffin, M. (2006) 'The changing focus of child maltreatment research and practice within psychology.' *Journal of Social Issues 62,* 4, 663–684.

Chaffin, M., Hecht, D., Bard, D., Silovsky, J.F. and Beasley, H.W. (2012a) 'A statewide trial of the SafeCare home-based services model with parents in child protective services.' *Pediatrics 129,* 3, 509–515.

Chaffin, M., Bard, D., Bigfoot, S. D., and Maher, E.J. (2012 (b)) Is a structured, manualized, evidence-based treatment protocol culturally competent and equivalently effective among American Indian parents in child welfare? *Child Maltreatment 17,* 3, 242–252.

Child Welfare Information Gateway (2015) *Child Abuse and Neglect Fatalities 2013: Statstics and Interventions.* Washington, DC: US Department of Health and Human Services, Children's Bureau. Available at www.childwelfare.gov/pubPDFs/fatality.pdf, accessed on 4 February 2015.

Christoffersen, M.N. and DePanfilis, D. (2009) 'Prevention of child abuse and neglect and improvements in child development.' *Child Abuse Review 18,* 24–40.

Churchill, G. (2015a) *SafeCare: Evidence from a Home Based Parenting Programme for Neglect.* London: NSPCC.

Churchill, G. (2015b) *SafeCare: Parents' Perspectives on a Home-based Parenting Programme for Neglect.* London: NSPCC.

Dachman, R.S., Halasz, M.M., Bickett, A.D. and Lutzker, J.R. (1984) 'A home-based eco-behavioral parent-training and generalization package with a neglectful mother.' *Education and Treatment of Children 7*, 183–200.

Daro, D. and McCurdy, K. (2007) 'Intervention to Prevent Maltreatment.' In L. Doll, S. Bonzo, D. Sleet, J. Mercy and E.N. Haas (eds) *The Handbook of Injury and Violence Prevention.* New York: Springer.

DePanfilis, D. and Dubowitz, H. (2005) 'Family connections: a program for preventing child neglect.' *Child Maltreatment 10*, 2, 108–123.

Drake, B. and Pandey, S. (1996) 'Understanding the relationship between neighborhood poverty and specific types of child maltreatment.' *Child Abuse & Neglect 20*, 11, 1003–1018.

Dubowitz, H. (2007) 'Understanding and addressing the "neglect of neglect": digging into the molehill.' *Child Abuse & Neglect 31*, 6, 603–606.

Fang, Z., Brown, D.S., Florence, C.S. and Mercy, J.A. (2012) 'The economic burden of child maltreatment in the United States and implications for prevention.' *Child Abuse & Neglect 36*, 156–165.

Finkelhor, D., Jones, L., Shattuck, A. and Saito, K. (2013) *Updated Trends in Child Maltreatment, 2012.* Durham, NH: Crimes against Children Research Center (CV203).

Fixsen, D.L., Blasé, K.A., Naoom, S.F. and Wallace, F. (2009) 'Core implementation components.' *Research on Social Work Practice 19*, 5, 531–540.

Gardner, R., Hodson, D., Churchill, G. and Cotmore, R. (2014) 'Transporting and implementing the SafeCare® home-based programme for parents, designed to reduce and mitigate the effects of child neglect: an initial progress report.' *Child Abuse Review 23*, 297–303.

Gaskin, E.H., Lutzker, J.R., Crimmins, D.B. and Robinson, L. (2012) 'Using a digital frame and pictorial information to enhance the SafeCare® parent-infant interactions module with a mother with intellectual disabilities: results of a pilot study.' *Journal of Mental Health Research in Intellectual Disabilities 5*, 187–202.

Gaudin, J.M. (1993) *Child Neglect: A Guide for Intervention.* US Department of Health and Human Services. Washington, DC: US Government Printing Office.

Gershater-Molko, R.M., Lutzker, J.R. and Wesch, D. (2002) 'Using recidivism data to evaluate Project SafeCare: teaching bonding, safety, and health care skills to parents.' *Child Maltreatment 7*, 277–285.

Gilbert, R., Kemp, A., Thoburn, J., Sidebotham, P., Radford, L. and MacMillan, H.L. (2009b) 'Recognising and responding to child maltreatment.' *The Lancet 373*, 9658, 167–180.

Gilbert, R., Widom, C.S., Browne, K., Fergusson, D., Webb, E. and Janson, S. (2009a) 'Burden and consequences of child maltreatment in high-income countries.' *The Lancet 373*, 9657, 68–81.

Guastaferro, K.M., Lutzker, J.R., Graham, M.L., Shanley, J.R. and Whitaker, D.J. (2012) 'SafeCare®: historical perspective and dynamic development of an evidence-based scaled-up model for the prevention of child maltreatment.' *Psychosocial Intervention 21*, 2, 171–180.

Hearn, J. (2011) 'Unmet needs in addressing child neglect: should we go back to the drawing board?' *Children and Youth Services Review 33*, 715–722.

Hildyard, K.L. and Wolfe, D.A. (2002) 'Child neglect: developmental issues and outcomes.' *Child Abuse & Neglect 26*, 679–695.

Hughes, J.R. and Gottlieb, L.N. (2004) 'The effects of the Webster-Stratton parenting program on maltreating families: fostering strengths.' *Child Abuse & Neglect 28*, 10, 1081–1097.

Jabaley, J.J., Lutzker, J.R., Whitaker, D.J. and Self-Brown, S. (2011) 'Using iPhones to enhance and reduce face-to-face home safety sessions within SafeCare®: an evidence-based child maltreatment prevention program.' *Journal of Family Violence 26*, 5, 377–385.

Jonson-Reid, M., Drake, B. and Zhou, P. (2012) 'Neglect subtypes, race, and poverty: individual, family, and service characteristics.' *Child Maltreatment 18*, 1, 30–41.

Kristof, N. (2012) 'A Poverty Solution That Starts with a Hug.' *The New York Times*, Sunday Review, 7 January 2012. Available at www.nytimes.com/2012/01/08/opinion/sunday/kristof-a-poverty-solution-that-starts-with-a-hug.html?_r=0, accessed on 4 February 2015.

Lee, S., Aos, S., Drake, E., Pennucci, A., Miller, M. and Anderson, L. (2012) *Return on Investment: Evidence-based Options to Improve Statewide Outcomes, April 2012 Update.* (Document No. 12-04-1201.) Olympia: Washington State Institute for Public Policy.

Letarte, M.J., Normandeau, S. and Allard, J. (2010) 'Effectiveness of a parent training program "Incredible Years" in a child protection service.' *Child Abuse & Neglect 34*, 4, 253–261.

Lindsey, M.A., Hayward, R.A. and DePanfilis, D. (2010) 'Gender differences in behavioral outcomes among children at risk of neglect: findings from a family-focused prevention intervention.' *Research on Social Work Practice 20*, 6, 572–581.

Lutzker, J.R. and Chaffin, M. (2012) 'SafeCare®: An Evidence-based Constantly Dynamic Model to Prevent Child Maltreatment.' In H. Dubowitz (ed.) *World Perspectives on Child Abuse.* (10th ed.). Canberra, Australia: The International Society for the Prevention of Child Abuse and Neglect.

Lutzker, J.R. and Rice, J.M. (1984) 'Project 12-Ways: measuring outcome of a large in-home service for treatment and prevention of child abuse and neglect.' *Child Abuse & Neglect 8*, 519–524.

Lutzker, J.R., Frame, R.E. and Rice, J.M. (1982) 'Project 12-Ways: an ecobehavioral approach to the treatment and prevention of child abuse and neglect.' *Education and Treatment of Children 5*, 141–155.

Marcynyszyn, L.A., Maher, E.J. and Corwin, T.W. (2011) 'Getting with the (evidence-based) program: an evaluation of the Incredible Years parenting training program in child welfare.' *Children and Youth Services Review 33*, 5, 747–757.

McCurdy, K. and Daro, D. (2001) 'Parent involvement in family support programs: an integrated theory.' *Family Relations 50*, 113–121.

Miller, W.R. and Rollnick, S. (2004) 'Talking oneself into change: motivational interviewing, stages of change, and therapeutic process.' *Journal of Cognitive Psychotherapy 18*, 299–308.

Olds, D.L. (2006) 'The Nurse–Family Partnership: an evidence-based preventive intervention.' *Infant Mental Health Journal 27*, 1, 5–25.

Olds, D.L. (2008) 'Preventing child maltreatment and crime with prenatal and infancy support of parents: the Nurse-Family Partnership.' *Journal of Scandinavian Studies in Criminology and Crime Prevention 9*, 2–24.

Olds, D.L., Eckenrode, J., Henderson, C.R., Jr., Kitzman, H., *et al.* (1997) 'Long-term effects of home visitation on maternal life course and child abuse and neglect: fifteen-year follow-up of a randomized trial.' *Journal of the American Medical Association 278*, 637–643.

Olds, D.L., Henderson, C.R. and Kitzman, H. (1994) 'Does prenatal and infancy nurse home visitation have enduring effects on qualities of parental caregiving and child health at 25 to 50 months of life?' *Pediatrics 93*, 1, 89–98.

Pfannenstiel, J.C., Seitz, V. and Zigler, E. (2002) 'Promoting school readiness: the role of the Parents as Teachers program.' *NHSA Dialog 6*, 71–86.

Prinz, R.J., Sanders, M.R., Shapiro, C.J., Whitaker, D.W. and Lutzker, J.R. (2009) 'Population-based prevention of child maltreatment: the US Triple P system population trial.' *Prevention Science 10*, 1, 1–12.

Sanders, M.R. (1999) 'Triple P-Positive Parenting Program: towards an empirically validated multilevel parenting and family support strategy for the prevention of behavior and emotional problems in children.' *Clinical Child and Family Psychology Review 2*, 71–90.

Schuerman, J.R., Rzepnicki, T.L. and Littell, J.H. (1994) *Putting Families First: An Experiment in Family Preservation.* Hawthorne, NY: Aldine de Gruyter.

Sedlak, A.J., Mettenburg, J., Basena, M., Peta, I., McPherson, K. and Greene, A. (2010) *Fourth National Incidence Study of Child Abuse and Neglect (NIS-4).* Washington, DC: US Department of Health and Human Services. Available at www.acf.hhs.gov/sites/default/files/opre/nis4_report_congress_full_pdf_jan2010.pdf, accessed on 9 July 2010.

Self-Brown, S., McFry, E., Montesanti, A., Edwards-Guara, A., *et al.* (2014) '"SafeCare": A Prevention and Intervention Program for Child Neglect and Physical Abuse.' In R.M. Reece, R.F. Hanson, and J. Sargent (eds) *Treatment of Child Abuse: Common Ground for Mental Health, Medical, and Legal Practitioners* (2nd edition). Baltimore, MD: Johns Hopkins University Press.

Silovsky, J.F., Bard, D., Chaffin, M., Hecht, D., *et al.* (2011) 'Prevention of child maltreatment in high-risk rural families: a randomized clinical trial with child welfare outcomes.' *Children and Youth Services Review 33*, 1435–1444.

Slack, K.S., Holl, J.L., McDaniel, M., Yoo, J. and Bolger, K. (2004) 'Understanding the risks of child neglect: an exploration of poverty and parenting characteristics.' *Child Maltreatment 9*, 4, 395–408.

Strong, L.E.A., Lutzker, J.R., Jabaley, J.J., Shanley, J.R., Self-Brown, S. and Guastaferro, K.M. (2014) 'Training mothers recovering from substance abuse to identify and treat their children's illnesses.' *International Journal of Child Health and Human Development 7*, 2, 157–166.

Tanner, K. and Turney, D. (2003) 'What do we know about child neglect? A critical review of the literature and its application to social work practice.' *Child and Family Social Work 8*, 1, 25–34.

The Annie E. Casey Foundation (2012) *Double Jeopardy: How Third Grade Reading Skills and Poverty Influence High School Graduation.* Baltimore, MD: Donald J. Hernandez. Available at www.aecf.org/resources/double-jeopardy, accessed on 4 February 2015.

Trocmé, N., MacMillan, H., Fallon, B. and De Marco, R. (2003) 'Nature and severity of physical harm caused by child abuse and neglect: results from the Canadian Incidence Study.' *Canadian Medical Association Journal 169*, 9, 911–915.

Tyler, S., Allison, K. and Winsler, A. (2006) 'Child neglect: developmental consequences, intervention and policy implications.' *Child and Youth Care Forum 35*, 1, 1–20.

US Department of Health & Human Services, Administration for Children and Families, Administration on Children, Youth and Families and Children's Bureau (2015) *Child Maltreatment 2013.* Available from www.acf.hhs.gov/programs/cb/research-data-technology/statistics-research/child-maltreatment, accessed on 20 July 2016.

Waldfogel, J. (2009) 'Prevention and the child protection system.' *The Future of Children* *19*, 2, 195–210.

Walsh, J. (2014) 'A Preliminary Analysis of the Relationship between Hazards in the Home and the Potential for Abuse with Families At-Risk.' Thesis, Georgia State University. Available at http://scholarworks.gsu.edu/iph_theses/320, accessed on 4 February 2015.

Webster-Stratton, C. (1998) 'Preventing conduct problems in head start children: strengthening parenting competencies.' *Journal of Consulting and Clinical Psychology* *66*, 5, 715–730.

Welch, G.L. and Bonner, B.L. (2013) 'Fatal child neglect: characteristics, causation, and strategies for prevention.' *Child Abuse & Neglect 37*, 10, 745–752.

Widom, C.S., Czaja, S., Wilson, H.W., Allwood, M. and Chauhan, P. (2012) 'Do the long-term consequences of neglect differ for children of different races and ethnic backgrounds?' *Child Maltreatment 18*, 1, 42–55.

Wolock, I. and Horowitz, B. (1984) 'Child maltreatment as a social problem: the neglect of neglect.' *American Journal of Orthopsychiatry 54*, 4, 530–543.

Zigler, E., Pfannenstiel, J.C. and Seitz, V. (2008) 'The Parents as Teachers program and school success: a replication and extension.' *Journal of Primary Prevention 29*, 103–120.

Zubrick, S.R., Ward, K.A., Silburn, S.R., Lawrence, D., *et al.* (2005) 'Prevention of child behavior problems through universal implementation of a group behavioral family intervention.' *Prevention Science 6*, 4, 287–304.

Zuravin, S., McMillen, C., DePanfilis, D. and Risley-Curtiss, C. (1996) 'The intergenerational cycle of child maltreatment: continuity versus discontinuity.' *Journal of Interpersonal Violence 11*, 3, 315–334.

10

VIDEO INTERACTION GUIDANCE

Providing an effective response for neglected children

Hilary Kennedy, Maeve Macdonald and Paul Whalley

Introduction

This chapter explains how the relationship-based intervention, Video Interaction Guidance (VIG) works (Kennedy, Landor and Todd 2011). It discusses why VIG should work and provides new data from the National Society for the Prevention of Cruelty to Children (NSPCC) which shows that VIG has potential as an effective intervention for noticing and helping neglected children. It seems that it goes much further: while VIG notices, nurtures and helps neglectful and neglected parents, they start to find the strength to love and enjoy their children.

Interestingly, results from the NSPCC project show a marked increase in parents' behavioural management strategies. This spin-off from the VIG intervention, which focuses on the parent–child relationship, makes sense. Although the parents were not taught behavioural management strategies, they discovered that once they had restored a loving relationship with their child by listening to her or him, they could effectively set limits. In turn, the child starts listening to the parent so their behaviour improves.

What is Video Interaction Guidance and how does it work?

Values and beliefs behind VIG

Video Interaction Guidance is a compassionate approach where hope is maintained and trust is built through the construction of a respectful and appreciative therapeutic relationship. VIG practitioners demonstrate their values and beliefs (see Fig 10.1) through all their interactions with their clients, from the first meeting. These values and beliefs underpin the VIG method.

AViGuk VALUES AND BELIEFS
Our Values[1]
Respect Trust Hope Compassion Co-operation Appreciation Connections Empathy
Our beliefs[2]
▪ Everybody is doing the best they can at the time ▪ All people, even in adverse situations, have the capacity to change ▪ People have an innate desire to connect with others ▪ People must be actively involved in their own change process ▪ Affirmation and appreciation of strengths is the key to supporting change ▪ Recognition and empathetic regard for what people are managing builds trust

1 The size of the words in rows "Values and Beliefs ..., Respect... Trust ... Hope" signifies the ranking of 52 AViGuk Supervisors with respect to their views of the importance of short-listed VIG-VERP values in January 2014.

2 The beliefs statements have been adapted from SPIN (The Netherlands) 1990 originals. They were debated by AViGuk Supervisors in meetings and by discussion forum over the Autumn of 2013.

Figure 10.1 Values and beliefs (Kennedy, Landor and Todd 2015, p.20)

Video Interaction Guidance in a nutshell

VIG starts by engaging parents in a possible change process and helps them form questions to explore how they can improve their relationship with their child. A filming session is carefully set up aiming to capture the best possible interactions achievable at that time. The VIG practitioner then takes five to ten minutes of video of the parent interacting with their child. The aim is to capture moments of 'better than usual' interaction on video, if necessary by prompting or encouraging. It is interesting that despite a history of considerable difficulties, the vast majority of families show at least fleeting moments of the principles of attuned (or sensitive and responsive) interactions (see Chapter 1) when they are supported during the filming by the VIG practitioner.

The VIG practitioner then edits the video, selecting a few very short clips of successful interaction that link to the parent's goals for change. These are very likely to be exceptions to the usual pattern and exemplify various principles of attuned contact, especially the parent's reception of their child's initiatives.

In the shared review session that follows, the parent and VIG practitioner study the selected micro-moments very carefully, working out together what the parent is doing that helps to build an attuned relationship with her child and the parent moves towards her own goal.

Through seeing their own attuned responses to their children, parents can start to observe and then to understand how important these experiences are for their children. The parents are active in their own learning process, first describing what they see themselves and their children doing, then exploring their thoughts, feelings and developmental needs. They lead their own 'learning journey' by identifying their own strengths and setting new goals at each reflective session. At the same time they are experiencing an attuned interaction with the VIG practitioner who follows their initiatives.

The steps in VIG unpacked

The aim of VIG is to support the parents and their children to move from 'no' to 'yes' cycle interaction patterns, as illustrated in Figure 10.2 (Kennedy, Landor and Todd 2011).

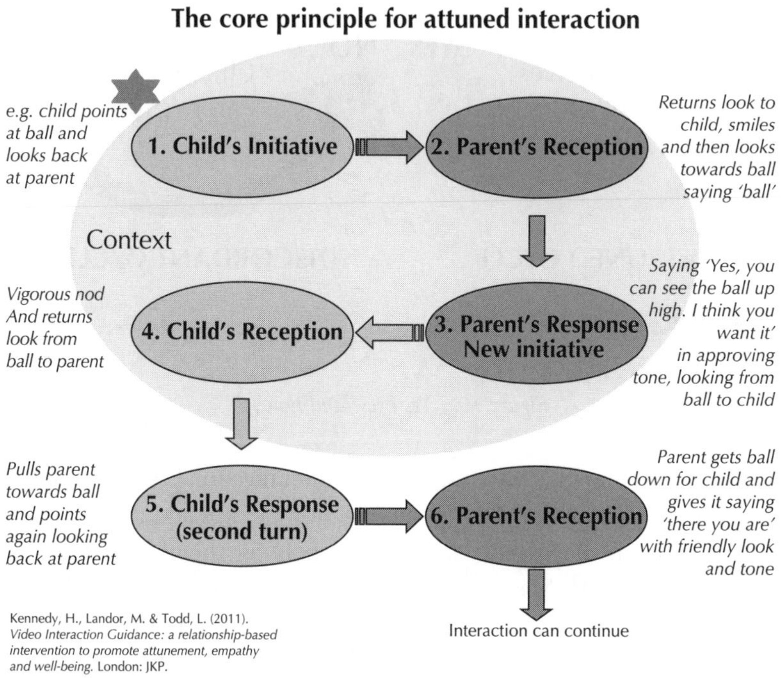

The core principle for attuned interaction

e.g. child points at ball and looks back at parent

1. Child's Initiative → **2. Parent's Reception**

Returns look to child, smiles and then looks towards ball saying 'ball'

Context

Vigorous nod And returns look from ball to parent

4. Child's Reception ← **3. Parent's Response New initiative**

Saying 'Yes, you can see the ball up high. I think you want it' in approving tone, looking from ball to child

Pulls parent towards ball and points again looking back at parent

5. Child's Response (second turn) → **6. Parent's Reception**

Parent gets ball down for child and gives it saying 'there you are' with friendly look and tone

Kennedy, H., Landor, M. & Todd, L. (2011). *Video Interaction Guidance: a relationship-based intervention to promote attunement, empathy and well-being.* London: JKP.

Interaction can continue

Figure 10.2 Core principles for attuned interaction

Where neglect has been identified as a concern, the parent will often ignore most of their children's initiatives (signals), and respond in a discordant way to those signals that are noticed (e.g. a child's loud demands or protests). Video Interaction Guidance can immediately focus on the heart of the problem and support the parent first to notice the child's initiatives more consistently and then to respond in a sensitive, attuned way, as shown in Figure 10.2. It is important to convey the importance of emotional (often non-verbal) responses, such as looking towards the child with interest, (returning eye contact, smiling) as well as more cognitive (verbal) responses by the parent.

DOES PARENT RECEIVE CHILD'S INITIATIVE?

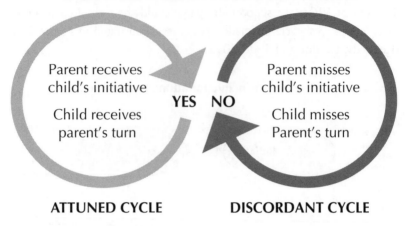

Figure 10.3 Yes cycle and no cycle

The VIG building blocks for improved communication (see Figure 10.4) support the VIG practitioner in the selection of clips and they can also be shared with the parents as a way of helping them to understand their child's needs. Many children who have been neglected do not make attuned initiatives to their parents. The two bottom steps in Figure 10.3 are the starting point for the VIG work. Video clips of the parents, first being attentive to their child and then encouraging their children to make initiatives, are captured, edited and then explored with the parents. These video clips will include examples of them watching carefully, smiling towards their child, leaving space and saying what they see their child doing, and perhaps what they sense that the child may be thinking or feeling.

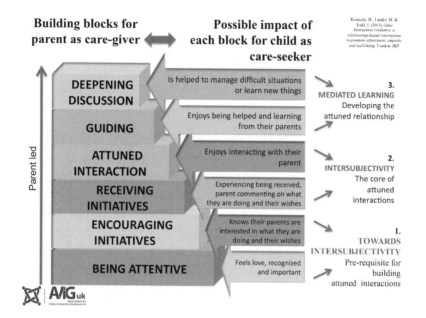

Figure 10.4 Building blocks to attuned interaction

The shared review

In the shared review, the parents are not taught how to interact better with their children in a didactic way, but rather to learn experientially, by seeing themselves being attentive to their children's signals and then seeing the impact on their children of returning an attuned response. Skilled use of video clips and still images is part of the art of using VIG. There are few definite rules; one is that the VIG practitioner and the parent stop the video clip when they want to discuss something. The VIG practitioner looks attentively for the parent's initiative to discuss a certain moment in the clip, or to review and study the micro-moment again together.

This combination, of parents seeing themselves attuning to their children and experiencing the VIG practitioner attuning to them may be the key to the restored interest and affection reported and observed in so many parents. The VIG practitioner also observes the pleasure on parents' faces as they see themselves succeeding in responding to their child and how their child enjoys the interaction. This is the first step in restoring a sense of pride in themselves as parents, turning away from the feelings of shame that have predominated.

Before the end of the shared review, parents express their thoughts about what they are proud of and what they would like to improve further, and a new cycle of video recording and shared review begins. The cycles are repeated until the client's desired pattern of interaction is established. In practice, this usually takes three to four cycles.

Training Video Interaction Guidance practitioners

The delivery of VIG is a therapeutic art. Skills are developed through an intense supervision process over 18 months, after the two-day initial training course. Trainee VIG practitioners bring a video of their client for micro-analysis of moments of attunement between parent and child, and later a video of themselves in interaction with their clients. The fidelity of both training and delivery of the VIG method is quality assured and monitored by the Association for Video Interaction Guidance UK (AVIGuk). The whole process of training is learner-led, mirroring the process with the families, where the VIG practitioner places the parent(s) in the driving seat of their own change.

The attunement of the VIG supervisor to the trainee VIG practitioner during the training process is essential and is underpinned by values based on hope, trust and appreciation (see Figure 10.1). The trainee experiences the VIG method themselves through interactions with their supervisor during their supervision sessions. This leads to enhanced wellbeing for the practitioner, the parent and then for the child, and of course for the VIG supervisor.

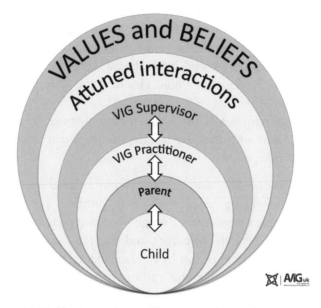

Figure 10.5 Video Interaction Guidance: Nested intersubjectivity

Does VIG support change?

At its fundamental core, VIG is based on a cooperative inter-subjective model where the interaction in the space between people is the main focus (Trevarthen and Aitken 2001). This means that VIG considers that in every interaction there are two (or more) equally important people.

Maria Doria (Doria *et al.* 2013) explored the reasons why VIG was working by completing a content analysis of 15 therapeutic sessions as well as interviews and focus groups about VIG intervention with five families where neglect was a central issue. The results suggested that VIG improves family happiness, parental self-esteem and self-efficacy, and attitude or behaviour change. There are four key methodological components of VIG:

1. the professional's reception and support

2. the videoed interaction

3. the success-focused approach, and

4. the video as a proof of success and change.

There appear to be two key underlying mechanisms of VIG success: first the metacognitive (reflective) processes and second the shared construction of a new reality. For an in-depth discussion of the reasons why VIG works, the reader is referred to Cross and Kennedy (2011) and the 2014 VIG International Conference presentation by Jane Barlow, Professor of Public Health at the University of Warwick (Barlow 2014).

For the purposes of this chapter, three theories are proposed that are congruent with the new research findings that are reported later in this chapter.

- *'Broaden-and-build' theory of positive emotions (Fredrickson 2001):* The theory emphasises that positive emotions broaden people's momentary thought–action repertoires, which in turn build personal resources, and that the capacity to experience these emotions may be fundamental to human flourishing. In VIG the parents and children experience positive emotions during the videoing session and then again when they relive the experience in the shared review. This opens up the parent and child to consider change.

- *Reflective function/mentalization (Fonagy, Gergely and Target 2007):* The parent learns to reflect not only to their and their child's behaviour, but to their own and their child's mental states and intentions. In turn, the child who is understood in this way will learn to understand others. Peter Fonagy has produced evidence for an association between the quality of attachment relationship and reflective function in the parent and the child (ibid. 2007). In VIG, the shared review process provides an opportunity for the parent to develop reflective function about themselves, their child and their relationship.

- *Cognitive dissonance theory (Festinger 1957):* The recognition of an inconsistency between two or more cognitions, or between cognition and behaviour, would place a person in an uncomfortable state of psychological tension or dissonance that people are fundamentally motivated to reduce. In VIG, the confrontation or dissonance is between the prior negative beliefs of parents seeking help (e.g. 'I'm a terrible mother';

'my children never listen to me') and the new evidence of positive behaviour (demonstrated by viewing the edited video clip). This tension triggers the metacognitive insight process that ultimately results in an attitude and behavioural change to fit the observed and successful parent–child interaction pattern (Doria *et al.* 2013).

There is a growing evidence base from an international perspective on the effectiveness of relatively short, sensitivity-focused interventions with parents and professionals who use video feedback in an attuned way as described above. Evidence sources can be found in meta-analyses of researchers from the Netherlands such as Fukkink (2008) and Bakermans-Kranenburg *et al.* (2003). (Fukkink, Kennedy and Todd have summarised the research to 2011 in Kennedy *et al.* (2011)).

More recently, impressive results have been reported worldwide in populations vulnerable to child neglect. These findings come from several international sources; from Leiden, on video-feedback interventions to promote positive parenting and sensitive discipline (VIPP-SD) (Yagmur *et al.* 2014); from Quebec, on a video-based attachment intervention for one- to five-year-olds experiencing maltreatment or neglect (Moss *et al.* 2011, 2014); from Norway, on video feedback for parents and children under two years old with interaction difficulties in a multi-site project (Høivik *et al.* 2015); and from New York, on paediatric primary health, (Berluke *et al.* 2014; Mendelsohn *et al.* 2011).

All these studies show significant short- and long-term effects on parent–child interaction, and the results from Norway and New York also show a significant decrease in depressive symptoms of the mother and enhanced development of the child.

At the 2015 Society for Research in Child Development (SRCD) conference in Philadelphia, several presentations described new evidence on the effectiveness of video-feedback interventions in the field of maltreatment and neglect. These included the work of a team from the University of Leiden, on a new meta-analysis of what works in preventing or reducing maltreatment (Alink *et al.* 2015). This research showed that few interventions achieve these goals, with the exception of methods using video feedback and focusing on sensitivity (such as VIG), which consistently showed a significant effect size. Results were also presented from the Université du Québec à Montréal on a randomised control study of a video-feedback, attachment-based intervention (similar to VIG) alongside a psycho-educational intervention and a control group. The research was undertaken with 106 families of children aged 0–5 where maltreatment, predominantly neglect, was the concern (Cyr *et al.* 2015). The results indicated that the video-feedback intervention enhanced the sensitivity and reciprocity of the parent–child interaction, diminished the children's externalising behaviour and significantly enhanced attachment patterns post-test, compared to the psycho-educational intervention and the control group. Similar earlier results have been published by the same team at the Université du Québec à Montréal (Moss *et al.* 2011, 2014).

Another result presented by Chantal Cyr concerned professionals' ability to predict accurately parents' capacity to care for their children. Following these interventions, all the groups assessed that children of parents with greater capacity were less likely to be placed out of the family home. However, one year on only the predictions of those professionals using the video attachment-based intervention were realised. This is an important and interesting finding, showing that those using video-feedback interventions can develop an accurate ability to predict and identify those families *not* showing capacity to change.

Because of the accumulating research evidence, VIG is recommended as an evidence-based intervention in the National Institute for Clinical Excellence (NICE) guidelines; Children's Attachment: attachment in children and young people who are adopted from care, in care, or at high risk of going into care NICE guidelines (NICE 2015); Social and Emotional Wellbeing – Early years (NICE 2012). The All Party Parliamentary Group for Conception to Age 2 (2015) and Public Health England (2015) have both selected VIG, with other video-feedback interventions, as recommended evidence-based methods.

Qualitative evaluation of the NSPCC's VIG intervention

Preparing to deliver VIG

The ambitious plan to train 23 NSPCC practitioners from seven centres in the use of VIG began in July 2011, and the focus for the VIG intervention was families where there was concern about neglect.

This involved the staff attending the official Association for Video Interaction Guidance (AVIGuk) introductory two-day courses at various locations and receiving monthly supervision for two years at their centres. A team of eight AVIGuk supervisors carried out this supervision and worked together to ensure fidelity of VIG across the UK. The official AVIGuk transition and accreditation meetings took place every six to eight months, timed to suit individuals' pace of learning and their access to suitable families. Once practitioners had completed Stage 1, they took part in the NSPCC evaluation led by Paul Whalley, the preliminary results of which form part of this chapter.

This is the first time VIG has been implemented and evaluated at multiple sites within a single organisation across a wide geographic area. After addressing challenges about implementing an intervention with a substantial technological component, the implementation went smoothly. As soon as practitioners experienced the power of VIG to change the relationships in families from the first visit, they became most enthusiastic and took a full and active part in the VIG training process.

How parents in Belfast experienced the VIG intervention

Note: All names have been changed and some information omitted to protect the families' identities.

Parents' experience of VIG is introduced in this section by quoting a research interview undertaken by Maeve Macdonald with Barbara, a mother diagnosed with bipolar disorder and who has had seven of her nine children removed into care. She agreed to the VIG intervention (delivered by the NSPCC) to help with her relationship with her two remaining children. Reflecting on the start of the intervention, she said, 'I was quite sceptical because other stuff hadn't worked', then explained how VIG was different:

> from the minute she [the VIG practitioner] came out, you know, 'I'm not here to judge you, I'm not here about things from your past. I'm here to help you with what's going on now'…she never judged anything that happened…I never felt uncomfortable around her.

By the end of the VIG intervention, her relationships with her children had improved. Barbara knows that these relationships are still hard for her, but she is determined to persevere; she knows why she is doing so, and has tools to help her:

> I'm frightened, but the VIG practitioner gave me the confidence from letting me see the videos...there's obviously gonna be bad days with good, but that doesn't mean I'm not doing a good job. Because I've seen that I can get it right...and just keepin' that in my mind, you know that, yes, fair enough I've had this help, but there's no reason I can't do this by myself.

This section will explain and show how parents like Barbara, who have never before engaged successfully in changing their neglectful behaviour, are encouraged and inspired by the VIG practitioner to start noticing and responding to their children.

Maeve Macdonald, as a trainee educational psychologist at Queen's University Belfast, set out to explore the perceived efficacy of using VIG as a tool to improve parent–child relationships in families in which children's needs were being neglected, such as where the parents ignored their children most of the time and then responded inappropriately to their children's emotional needs – for instance, by shouting at a child who was evidently frustrated by his difficulties or upset about an experience. Four parent–child dyads were recruited from families involved in the NSPCC's VIG intervention to address child neglect and who were already participating (with consent) in an ongoing large-scale evaluation.

One part of this doctoral study (Macdonald 2014) used a qualitative methodology to explore parents' experiences of completing a VIG programme, as reported and discussed below. Limitations of the study included the fact that such a small number of participants were involved, and so the ability to generalise findings is limited. Furthermore, it was only possible to analyse short clips from the recordings, and so full interactions were not observed.

Descriptions of participants

Rachael, a VIG trainee practitioner at stage two of her training, delivered the VIG intervention with all four parents included in the study. She was trained and supervised by an AVIGuk supervisor throughout the

VIG work. The parents were all single mothers aged 29–37 years. A short description of each of the families is included below.

- *Family one:* Anne had two children, Ethan and Harry. Both had been removed from Anne's care approximately two years earlier and were living in separate foster placements. Anne had weekly contact with her boys and she had been referred to the NSPCC for VIG by her social worker. She reported to Rachael that she most wanted help with having conversations with Ethan, particularly about difficult issues such as their living arrangements and their father, who no longer had contact with Anne or her children. Anne had suffered from depression in the past.

- *Family two:* Barbara had nine children, seven of whom were no longer in her care. Two children remained in Barbara's care, Joseph and Conor. Barbara was referred to the NSPCC for VIG by her social worker. She reported to Rachael that she most wanted help in dealing with Joseph's challenging behaviour. Barbara had a diagnosis of bipolar disorder.

- *Family three:* Clare had two children, Mark and Patrick, and was pregnant with her third child. Clare had social services involvement, but had been referred to the NSPCC for VIG by an educational welfare officer as she was not bringing Mark to school. Clare reported to Rachel that she most wanted help with improving the bond between Mark and herself. Clare suffered from depression.

- *Family four:* Diane had three children, two of whom, Alice and Rory, were no longer in her care, having been placed with their father a number of years earlier, and one, Stephen, who lived with her. Diane had weekly contact with Alice and Rory. She was referred to the NSPCC for VIG by her social worker. Diane reported to Rachael that she most wanted help with improving the relationship between Rory and herself. Diane suffered from a personality disorder.

Methodology

Once the parents had finished their VIG interventions with Rachael, they were provided with information about the research and asked to give their permission for a selection of the video clips to be analysed. The parents were also asked if they would be happy to participate in a semi-structured interview regarding their experience of the VIG intervention. The first four parents who were asked to be involved in the research were happy to give their permission. The interviews were semi-structured in that a core set of pre-defined questions was asked; however, each interview was steered by issues raised by the parents.

Interviews with the parents were carried out within two weeks of their completing the intervention. The level of openness and honesty demonstrated by the parents was instrumental in producing rich data that provided a valuable insight into how the parents experienced the VIG intervention.

Transcripts of the interviews were analysed using thematic analysis to categorise the findings (Braun and Clarke 2006). Five overarching categories from the parents' responses emerged from the data: 1) Parents' experience prior to VIG; 2) Changes identified; 3) Impact of changes; 4) Why does VIG work? and 5) Reflections on VIG. Within each category, a number of superordinate themes were identified. Table 10.3 provides a list of these categories or themes, along with a corresponding quote from a parent.

Table 10.3 Quotes illustrating superordinate themes

Superordinate theme	Quotation
1. Prior to VIG	
Sense of self as a parent	'it wasn't that I didn't…you know…like, neglect him in any way, but I just felt, or that I didn't put their needs first, I just didn't put them a hundred per cent first… I think sometimes I was getting distracted with other stuff, so their needs weren't being met fully a hundred per cent.' (Barbara)
Presentation (of parent/child)	'at the start I was just really at my wits' end. I was just crying, going "it has to stop… I don't know how much more of this I can take".' (Barbara)
Parent–child relationship	'thinking I'd no relationship with [Rory], and because I thought that, I was kinda keeping my distance from him… and I know he's my child and this is terrible saying that, but I was putting a barrier up against him.' (Diane)
Motivation to participate	'I would do whatever it takes…' (Anne)
Initial feelings towards participation	'I was quite sceptical because other stuff hadn't worked…' (Barbara)
2. Changes identified	
Communication	'I know he can sit down and talk to me more. He never used to sit down and talk to me…and tell me what's wrong with him.' (Clare)
Parents' behaviours	'They're still, you know at the stage where they're not sure, they're like "I'm angry" and I'll say "well, you know, are you sure you're angry, or are you maybe just a bit cross, are you maybe a bit sad?" and they're like still trying to distinguish the difference of it…' (Anne)

Superordinate theme	Quotation
Parent–child relationship	'I think it opened my eyes that, you know, you can't just expect as a God-given to get respect for your children if you don't give a wee bit back...' (Barbara)
Increased awareness	'I'll do that with the boys because it is all about, like reading in to how they're actually feeling, rather than just guessing it...' (Anne)
Taking responsibility	'it's hard as a parent to admit you could improve habits. Like not getting wound up so quick, or not allowing that viciousness because it's easier to argue with your child than to sit, or, you know, it's easier to go "Get to your room!" than solve the problem.' (Barbara)
Roles within family	'My [Alice] used to take the mummy role all the time... whereas now she'll take a back seat...' (Diane)
Timing of change	'In the very first review I started to see, you know, the changes...' (Anne)
3. Impact of changes	
Thoughts/feelings	'It feels...amazing. Just seeing his wee face light up...it feels nice for me, but it's nicer to know that he's obviously enjoying it...' (Anne)
Sense of self as parent	'it was then I was thinking "aw that should've been recorded", because, I suppose, again, that was maybe me sorta wanting to boast about, you know, "I dealt with that well"...' (Anne)
Impact on children	'he's warming to me a lot more... I've noticed, you know, he's now just coming up and sitting on my knee and cuddling into me...' (Anne)
Parent–child relationship	'And if I was smiling, then you'd see him starting to smile, you know, he was feeding off me.'(Diane)

Influence on services	'that proved to them that the bond was there…' (Diane)

4. Why does VIG work?

Practical aspects	'I thought me and [Rory] didn't have a relationship, but by going by the video clips and stuff, it's there…' (Diane) 'it's just easy habits to fall into and until you see it, I think until you actually see it, not be told it, you actually see it for yourself, that's when you're like "Oh… right. You know, it's not all [Joseph]'s fault. I need to take responsibility for my part in that." And I think that's why it's good.' (Barbara)
Interpersonal aspects (Guider)	'She wasn't telling you, she gives you a chance to figure it out… I thought that was helpful.' (Diane) 'Hearing you're doing everything wrong all the time, it's not good on your confidence. Whereas if someone's pointing out "look, you're doing this right" and "what do you think you're doing there?" you know. It gives you the confidence… Coming into somebody's life when they're vulnerable and not good themselves, it's not good. But if you can go in and show them "Here, there is positives here, you know, you just need to add more work on them", you know?' (Diane)

5. Reflections on VIG

Overcoming initial concerns	'I honestly didn't expect to get out of it what I did. I honestly thought "this is just gonna be another thing, and by the end of it, things are probably still going to be no better, and then I'll just get pushed on to the next person… I was actually shocked it went as well as it did!' (Barbara)
Motivation	'seeing the benefits of it made me continue…' (Anne)
Attitudes about participation	'I think she came in just at the right time… Because I think if she hadn't have come in when she did, I probably would've let him go to his dad…' (Barbara)

Superordinate theme	Quotation
Attitudes about programme	'It's a fantastic service, and whoever thought it up was, got the right idea in mind, definitely…' (Diane)
Comparisons with other services	'a lot of the stuff was just for (Joseph) and I think it was because it was for us…we weren't being split off where I spoke to one person and he spoke to someone else. I think that needed to happen, to get me and [Joseph] together' (Barbara)
Suggested improvements	'sessions that other parents can meet each other and go "well, you know, I had VIG out and I thought they were fantastic"…' (Barbara)
Moving on from VIG	'I'm frightened, but she's give me the confidence from letting me see the videos to go "d'you know what, there's obviously gonna be bad days with good, but that doesn't mean I'm not doing a good job". Because I've seen that I can get it right…and just keepin' that in my mind, you know that, yes, fair enough I've had this help, but there's no reason I can't do this by myself.' (Barbara)

Findings

Parents' experience prior to VIG

Prior to the VIG intervention, the parents had an extremely low sense of self-worth, both as individuals and as parents. In many ways, they had lost hope for both their current and their future relationships with their children. The parents seemed to have been able to accept little or no positive feedback from within themselves, from external agencies or, in some cases, from their own children. The relationships between the parents and children typically involved conflict and distress, with inappropriate interactions in the form of shouting and ignoring, for example.

The candid way in which the parents spoke of their situations before the VIG intervention was admirable and very much appreciated. The fact that the parents felt able to discuss their difficult circumstances in such a way was considered to be a reflection of their awareness of, and indeed pride in, how far they had come by the end of the intervention. What was also admirable was the fact that, despite the many reasons they reported for not wanting to participate initially, they still had the motivation to engage with the VIG intervention. Immediately after beginning the intervention, the clear evidence that it was making a difference became a crucial motivating force.

Changes identified by parents

Video Interaction Guidance is an intervention aimed at improving effective communication, so it is perhaps not surprising that all parents reported improvement in their communication with their children, even in cases as extreme as there being previously 'no communication at all' (Barbara). Parents also thought they had gained a better understanding of what communication entails, in that it is not simply about conversation: 'it's not even so much about what you're saying, it's contact as well' (Barbara) and that 'it's all different things: body languages, facial expressions, stuff like that' (Diane).

Another change that parents identified was an improved ability to engage in thinking about their own behaviour, and their child's behaviour, thoughts and feeling (mentalisation). Their increasing interest and skill in this area were demonstrated during interviews and shared reviews. It was also apparent that, as a result of the parents modelling this approach, their children's ability to reflect upon the underlying causes of their own behaviour was also enhanced.

For example, parents reported that their children became more able to indicate that they were embarrassed, or that work was too difficult, rather than simply getting angry and lashing out.

Impact of changes

Findings from the study suggested that in these parents' view, VIG was successful in enhancing the thoughts and feelings of the parents and improving their sense of self as parents (for the role of positive emotions). They said it had impacted positively on their children's emotional states and behaviours and enhanced the parent–child relationship. One parent, Barbara, described her son as 'aggressive' and 'violent' prior to VIG, and a situation so hopeless that she was going to let him live with his father. By the end of the intervention she had progressed to referring to her relationship with him as 'probably not any worse than any other parent's getting with their seven year old'. The impact on the re-establishment of a bond between parent and child could perhaps not be described more powerfully than it was by Anne, who commented that 'it's kind of like getting your wee boy back'.

Why does Video Interaction Guidance work?

Analysis of the interviews demonstrated that both practical and interpersonal aspects of VIG were of key importance to these parents. The main practical aspect behind VIG's success was considered to be the *use of video*. All parents made reference to the value of watching their recorded interactions with their children, especially being able to see the interaction 'from the outside'. They referred to how being *told* they were doing something positive would not have made them believe it, but that actually *seeing* the evidence was crucial.

The interpersonal aspect of the VIG intervention that was most influential for the parents was the role of the VIG practitioner's underlying values and beliefs (see Figure 10.1). This was evident in the parents' reflections on Rachael's manner towards them. Despite the concerns of many parents about involvement with social services and the NSPCC, the social worker delivering this programme was able to use her role as the VIG practitioner to build a trusting and respectful relationship with these parents.

Another interpersonal aspect identified by the parents as crucial to VIG's success was that of its positive approach. It is because of this approach that VIG is particularly appropriate for use with vulnerable families, such as those included in the study, as the VIG practitioner 'looks for strengths and exceptions to the family's normal patterns of communication and interaction' (Doria, Strathie and Strathie 2011, p.122).

Parents' reflections on Video Interaction Guidance

The parents who were interviewed in Belfast engaged in candid and personal reflections about the VIG intervention and were all extremely positive about their experiences. They were able to identify many positive aspects of the VIG intervention, as well as a number of suggestions for improvements, such as longer duration of the intervention and the establishment of a network of parents who have participated in VIG.

From interviewing the parents and analysing the shared reviews, it became evident that, over the course of the VIG intervention, the parents had become more reflective about themselves, their children and the relationships between them. In later shared reviews, Rachael no longer needed to provide the parents with substantial prompts and encouragement to engage in reflections, as she had done at the beginning. Parents became more able to generate reflections and identify positive interactions independently. Furthermore, analysis of the parent–child recordings demonstrated that, as the intervention progressed, the parents developed an ability to make reflections about their own and their children's behaviours during sessions with their children on the video recordings.

Summary messages from Belfast qualitative data (Macdonald 2014)

- VIG was perceived as successful in improving the parent–child relationships in all four families in which the children's needs were being neglected.

- Parents reported that they appreciated the attuned support from the VIG practitioner. This enabled them to find their own way to improve their relationships with their children, to respond to their communications with greater timeliness and to manage their behaviour safely.

Quantitative results from the NSPCC evaluation of VIG

Aims of the intervention

Video Interaction Guidance (VIG) has been offered to parents where child neglect is a possible concern, as part of an NSPCC service in the UK called 'Improving Parenting Improving Practice'. The Common Assessment Framework (CAF) or an equivalent assessment has established that this is a child in need, that is,'a child who is unlikely to achieve or maintain a satisfactory level of health or development, or their health and development will be significantly impaired, without the provision of services' (Children Act 1989 England and Wales, section 17).

Children in need include a distinct group of children assessed as suffering 'significant harm', which is defined as 'ill treatment including sexual or physical abuse, or the impairment of physical or mental health, and physical, intellectual, emotional, social or behavioural development' (Children Act 1989, section 31(9)). The Common Assessment Framework (CAF) is a tool and process used across England to conduct an assessment of a child's needs, and to help practitioners to decide how those needs should be met. The equivalent equivalent processes exist in Scotland and Northern Ireland and a range of tools is being used in the assessment of child neglect.

The particular focus in this NSPCC service is parents with a child aged 2 to12 years for whom parental neglect or unavailability are active concerns, likely to result in emotional harm and/or behavioural difficulties. The theory of change is that the provision of the parenting programme will lead to the parent having a clearer view of what is required of them in their parenting task – for instance, being more sensitive to the needs of their child; showing a change in their commitment and engagement with their child; and showing change in their parenting capability and behaviour by managing the behaviour of their child better. It is hypothesised that these changes will in turn potentially lead to the child's needs, both physical and emotional, being better met, and the risk of child's behavioural problems and emotional harm reducing.

The NSPCC's evaluation of VIG has been the largest study of its use in the UK to date and has assessed both the outcomes and the process of the intervention. Data from seven sites across England,

Scotland and Northern Ireland have been analysed. The data have been obtained using standardised measures (detailed below) with informed consent from parents using VIG. They were asked to opt into the evaluation research if they wished and could also decide to withdraw their consent at any time (whether they continued with the intervention or not).

Methodology

Three standardised evaluation measures at the start of the VIG work (T1) and at the end of the work (T2). The paired data range is from two months to ten months, with two thirds of the VIG work taking between three months to seven months and four months being the most common time period for the intervention.

The three measures used in the evaluation are the Parenting Scale, the Strengths and Difficulties Questionnaire (SDQ) and the Parent–Child Relationship Inventory (PCRI). The findings from each measure are set out below.

Limitations to the evaluation

Selective attrition can reduce the amount of data at the start and end of the intervention, as well as reducing the amount of data assessing maintenance of changes after the programme has ceased. Attrition could also mean that the data we have to analyse on parents are not representative of all the parents receiving the programme. There has not been a contemporaneous process collecting comparison data from a similar group of parents who did not receive the VIG service at the same time, so improvements could be due to other factors, such as the maturation of children or other learning by the parents over the same time period. Finally, the data is obtained by means of self-report by the parents and not the result of observation or objective assessments by practitioners.

Findings using the Parenting Scale

PARENTING SCALE

The Parenting Scale (or PS; Arnold *et al*. 1993) is a measure of dysfunctional discipline practices in parents of young children. Three stable factors of dysfunctional discipline style have been identified which are included in the scale: laxness, which is permissive discipline, characterised by avoiding the use of control, giving in and allowing rules to go unenforced; over-reactivity, which is an authoritarian style of parenting that includes harsh or punitive responses, anger, meanness and irritability; and verbosity, which describes where parents become involved in long, wordy and ineffective responses which provide positive reinforcement for negative behaviour.

The Parenting Scale looks at specific aspects of parental discipline practice rather than providing a global measure of all attitudes and beliefs. It is typically used in conjunction with other measures to assess the success or otherwise of parenting strategies and practices in parenting programmes such as Incredible Years and Triple P (see Chapter (9)).

The PS has good internal consistency on the laxness (0.83) and over-reactivity (0.82) subscales and fair consistency for the verbosity subscale (0.63). This is measured by splitting the responses by the same parent and then comparing the two sets of response for consistency. Test and retest reliability is measured by asking the parent to complete the measure on two separate occasions about two weeks apart, when no intervention or major change has taken place between the two administrations. The responses of the parent are then compared for consistency, with correlations over 0.8 considered highly positive. The scores for the subscales are reported as +0.83 for laxness, +0.82 for over-reactivity and +0.79 for verbosity, meaning they are all considered highly reliable measures of these concepts in parenting (Arnold *et al*. 1993).

Results

The results of the NSPCC evaluation of VIG using the Parenting Scale are encouraging. They yield evidence to suggest that the use of VIG by parents for whom there is concern about possible child neglect has resulted in their adopting more effective parenting strategies.

Table 10.4 Parenting scale data-analysis (n = 52 paired cases)

Parenting scale subscale	T1 mean (standard deviation)	T2 mean (standard deviation)	Wilcoxon signed ranks test score (p)
Over-reactivity	2.67 (0.98)	2.47 (1.02)	-1.6 (0.116)
Laxness	2.87 (0.09)	2.54 (0.96)	-3.1 (0.002)**
Verbosity	3.63 (1.14)	3.30 (1.08)	-3.02 (0.003)**
Overall parenting score	3.12 (0.78)	2.82 (0.84)	-3.22 (0.001)***

* p<=0.05; **p<=0.01; *** p<=0.001

Table 10.4 shows reductions in the mean average scores for dysfunctional discipline practices, from T1 to T2 for all the PS subscales and the overall parenting score. This suggests (allowing for the limitations above) that VIG is effective in the short term in raising the effectiveness of parenting strategies.

The next step was to test the nature of the change from T1 to T2 for statistical significance, as seen in Table 10.4. As the subscale data at both time points are not normally distributed, it was decided to carry out the more conservative Wilcoxon signed ranks test, which is a non-parametric test.[1]

There were indications of statistically significant change between T1 to T2 in the scores for laxness and verbosity. The degree of change in these two subscales means that there was highly significant change in the overall parenting score. The results suggest that parents are reporting greater consistency in their parenting after VIG and engaging less in long verbal exchanges. Harsh discipline or irritability, though less often reported by parents, was not so much reduced.

In terms of service goals, these results indicate that parents are reporting a better understanding of the needs of their children, and are clearer as to what is expected of their children. The greater consistency in their parenting strategies is seen as a pre-requisite for a reduction in child neglect and greater child safety.

---

1   The Wilcoxon signed ranks test is used when comparing two repeated measurements from the same subject and is used as an alternative to the t-test for matched pairs, when the population cannot be assumed to be normally distributed or the data is generated from a rating scale that does not have equal interval data. The data for VIG is slightly positively skewed so the analysis is using the Wilcoxon signed ranks test.

Findings from the Strengths and Difficulties Questionnaire

STRENGTHS AND DIFFICULTIES QUESTIONNAIRE

The Strengths and Difficulties Questionnaire (SDQ; Goodman 1997) is a brief behavioural screening questionnaire that can be completed on children aged from 2–17 years, to meet the needs of parents, practitioners and researchers, and is available in many different languages (Goodman 1997). In the current study the SDQ has been completed by one or both parents. There are versions for parents, a child self-report and a version for a teacher or other adult to complete. The SDQ reports on five subscales, each in the form of five items or questions on the scale. The five subscales are as follows;

- *emotional symptoms*, e.g.headaches, worries, feeling down-hearted or nervous

- *conduct problems*, e.g. feeling angry, being disobedient, fighting with other children, lying, cheating and stealing

- *hyperactivity*, e.g. being restless, fidgeting, being easily distracted, thinking things out before acting, seeing tasks through to the end

- *peer problems*, e.g. being solitary, at least having one good friend, generally liked by other children, picked on or bullied by other children, and

- *prosocial scale*, positive strengths recorded such as being considerate of others, sharing, being helpful, kind.

Parents complete the SDQ and the four 'difficulties' subscales are combined into a total 'overall difficulties' score, and the 'prosocial' scale is the 'strength' subscale (see Table 10.5). The table shows the results of the differences between T1 and T2 with the more conservative Wilcoxon signed ranks test. Scores that are above the clinical cut-off are considered to be in the clinical range for the difficulties scale and below the clinical cut-off for the strength scale (pro-social).

Table 10.5 SDQ data analysis (n = 50 paired cases)

SDQ subscales	Clinical cut-off	T1 mean (standard deviation)	T2 mean (standard deviation)	Wilcoxon signed ranks test score (p)
Conduct problems	> 4	5.22 (2.80)	4.00 (2.47)	-3.68 (0.000)***
Emotional symptoms	> 5	4.62 (2.70)	3.64 (2.62)	-2.62 (0.009)**
Hyperactivity	>7	7.14 (2.34)	6.64 (2.72)	-1.79 (0.073)
Peer problems	> 4	3.86 (2.31)	3.56 (2.30)	-1.426 (0.154)
Overall difficulties	> 17	20.84 (6.44)	17.84 (7.40)	-2.27 (0.023)*
Pro-social	< 4	5.98 (2.27)	6.88 (2.28)	-3.55 (0.000)***

* $p<=0.05$; **$p<=0.01$; *** $p< =0.001$ scores above clinical cut-off

Results

There were indications of statistically significant positive change in the SDQ scores for conduct problems, emotional symptoms and overall difficulties. In addition, there was a statistically significant increase on the pro-social or strengths subscale of the SDQ. There was no statistically significant change reported in hyperactivity or peer problems.

The changes in scores for parenting strategies and consistency, together with reported reductions in behavioural and emotional problems, suggest that, after the VIG intervention, parents are meeting their child's unmet physical and emotional needs better. The theory of change here is that children are less likely to experience neglect in these circumstances. If children's behaviour is being managed more effectively, the theory of change for the NSPCC is that as a result they are more likely to enjoy greater safety.

Findings using the Parent Child Relationship Inventory (PCRI)

PARENT CHILD RELATIONSHIP INVENTORY

The Parent Child Relationship Inventory (PCRI; Gerard 1994) reports on how parents view the task of parenting and how they feel about their children. Its 78 items cover domains such as parental support, satisfaction with parenting and involvement. It has six subscales and can be completed in about 15 minutes as seen in Table 10.6.

The subscales are:

- *parental support*: the practical help and emotional support that the parent feels they receive, so items on financial strain or lack of others to help are included

- *satisfaction with parenting*: the level of enjoyment that the parent derives from being a parent or if the parent sees their parenting role positively

- *involvement*: the parent's likelihood of seeking out their child and showing interest in their activities

- *communication*: the parent's awareness of how well they communicate with their child in different situations

- *limit setting*: the effectiveness of the parent's discipline techniques, ensuring that children know what is required of them and can tell if they exceed these boundaries, and

- *autonomy*: the willingness of the parent to promote their child's independence which is associated with greater maturity in children and young people.

Table 10.6 Parent–child relationship inventory
data analysis (n = 45 paired cases)

Parent–child relationship inventory subscales	Low cut-off (1SD below mean)	T1 mean (standard deviation)	T2 mean (standard deviation)	Wilcoxon signed ranks test score (p)
Parental support	<18	23.3 (4.65)	24.8 (4.40)	-2.39 (0.017)*
Satisfaction with parenting	<27	33.6 (5.00)	34.2 (3.97)	-0.49 (0.627)
Involvement	<43	39.2 (4.87)	42.3 (5.34)	-3.12 (0.002)**
Communication	<27	26.2 (3.35)	27.9 (3.61)	-3.42 (0.001)***
Limit setting	<25	29.5 (5.34)	33.1 (5.23)	-3.66 (0.000)***
Autonomy	<22	25.0 (3.95)	24.9 (3.74)	-0.44 (0.661)

*p<=0.05; **p<=0.01; *** p< =0.001 Emboldened numbers below cut-off at 1SD below

Results

At the start of the VIG intervention (T1), scores on this measure suggested that at least one quarter of parents achieved low scores on the PCRI. Particularly high levels of parenting difficulty were reported with regard to 'lack of involvement with their child' (51%) and 'struggles with setting limits' (33%). Of all the PCRI subscales at T1, the lowest is the mean score for 'parental involvement', within the low score range, suggesting that parents had a lower than average interest in their child's activities (at school or elsewhere), or in spending time with them. For example, many parents in this position report not having a photograph of their child, or say that they do not really know their child.

After the use of VIG (T2), the same measure indicated fewer, around one fifth, of cases being high levels of parenting difficulty. The percentage of reports concerning 'lack of parental involvement' falls to 29 per cent and 'struggles with limit setting' to 13 per cent.

There were indications of statistically significant change in the scores for the subscales concerning 'communication', 'limit setting' and 'involvement' and, to a lesser extent, those for 'parental support'. There was no statistically significant change reported in 'satisfaction with parenting' or 'autonomy'.

Parents' reports of significantly greater involvement with their child's life is a major part of the wider change sought by the VIG service, including greater engagement, sensitivity and commitment to their child. The significant improvement in communication between parent and child is also an indicator of greater change towards acquiring this better understanding of the needs of their children and potentially towards a reduction in neglectful behaviours. The significant increase in the score for limit setting is consistent with the improvement in the 'laxness' subscore of the Parenting Scale, indicating more consistent application of discipline.

The lack of significant change in the subscale for 'autonomy' may reflect the age range of the children in the evaluation. Most were aged between five and nine years old and still somewhat dependent. Additionally, the focus of VIG was to increase parental involvement when a child is neglected. For these reasons, increased autonomy of the child at T2 might be an unlikely finding.

Reflections on NSPCC findings (quantitative results)

The data from 50 parents who received VIG from the NSPCC indicate promising levels of change in both the greater effectiveness of their parenting strategies, and the behavioural and emotional problems of their children, as perceived by their parents.

The results of the Parent–Child Relationship Inventory show clearly that initial problems presented by parents concerned relationships, specifically their involvement and communication with their child. Since neglect constituted the reason they were referred for help, it is unsurprising that scores at T1 for these scales were in the clinical cut-off range, but this confirms the relationship difficulties being experienced by the parents. It is encouraging that there was a significant improvement in parents' reported involvement and communication. Similarly, the significant improvement in measures on the 'pro-social' scale (i.e. in the way the parents see their children relate to others, such as 'considerate of other people's feelings', and the significant decrease in perceived 'emotional symptoms' in the child) is what would be hoped for from a relationship-based intervention such as VIG and is important for the child's social development.

The highly significant improvement in parents' perceptions of their own behavioural management and management of their children's behaviour is more unexpected, because these changes are not the immediate aims of the VIG intervention. This is shown in the significant change for the better on the 'limit-setting' scale in the PCRI, the conduct problems in the SDQ and the overall Parenting Scale score that measures dysfunctional discipline. The findings suggest that if greater parent–child attunement is being achieved, it may be linked to changes in the way parents relate to their children in several key areas around the parents managing their children's behaviour.

Two summary messages from the quantitative NSPCC data

- The use of VIG increased parents' perceived sensitivity, communication and involvement with children in the context of possible and actual child neglect.

- Using VIG resulted in improvements in perceived parental confidence and parenting strategies as well as children's reported behaviour.

Discussion of findings

Research in Belfast (see p.321) indicates that VIG improved parent–child relationships in four families in which the children's needs were being neglected and parents were coping with significant life problems (Macdonald 2014).

This is an impressive result as it should not be taken for granted that people, particularly those in chaotic, stressful situations, know what they are 'doing right'. To acknowledge positives in oneself demands confidence that vulnerable parents often lack. Until such confidence is present, the VIG practitioner must make use of video to point out evidence of good communication for the parent.

As a result, Anne identified a change in her perception of her own parenting capacity: 'things I'm doing well at I don't...well, I suppose I did need help with 'coz I didn't know I was always doing them well, you know, I didn't trust myself.' One parent who was experiencing difficulty in identifying the attuned behaviours she was demonstrating in a recording, commented, 'it's just what you do, you know…'coz when you're a mother, it's just instinct'. This mother, perhaps like countless others, appeared to hold the belief that when a parent and child love each other, the parent instinctively knows what to do with the child. Reflecting on the findings in the study, it is suggested that the reverse may be true for parents such as those we have worked with, that when you know how to interact with your child, you and your child can develop a loving, attuned relationship. The VIG practitioner delivering the intervention was not an expert in the sense of imparting knowledge to the parents, but through practical and interpersonal means supported them in growing and using skills they had within themselves to develop loving, attuned relationships with their children.

As professionals working to help neglected children and their families, we should perhaps take time to reflect upon the poignant comment made by Anne about re-establishing a bond with her son that 'it's kind of like getting my wee boy back'. For Anne to feel like she 'got him back' indicates that she was experiencing a sense of loss during the period in which she was identified as being neglectful. For some parents in situations similar to Anne's, there is the emotional loss of a relationship with their children; moreover, for some there is physical loss of their children into the care system. Whatever the case, the vast majority of these parents, if not all, will be grieving.

The professional response, therefore, should demonstrate an appreciation of the vulnerable state of these parents by providing them with positive support rather than negative criticism, and this may be one reason for parents' positive engagement with VIG. Those working to help neglected children and their families are urged to remember Diane's words:

> Hearing you're doing everything wrong all the time, it's not good on your confidence. Whereas if someone's pointing out 'Look, you're doing this right' and 'what do you think that you're doing there?' you know. It gives you the confidence… Coming into somebody's life when they're vulnerable and not good themselves, it's not good. But if you can go in and show them – 'here, there is positives here, you know, you just need to add more work on them', you know?

The results from the NSPCC research above are perhaps surprising to the extent that VIG, an intervention that focuses primarily on enhancing parents' sensitivity to their child, is also seen to have an impressive effect on parents' perceived ability to set limits as well as on their children's ability to follow instructions and conform to those limits.

At the same time as this NSPCC data was being analysed, very similar results were received from Cornwall on VIG and parents' reported improvement behaviour management with their children (Lowry *et al.* 2014). Evaluators there were using the Tool to Measure Parental Self-Efficacy (TOPSE) (Kendall and Bloomfield 2005), developed by the University of Hertfordshire as part of their evaluation of the first eight families receiving VIG in the Cornwall project because of neglect and other child protection concerns. The results indicate that, overall, seven out of the eight parents who took part in the VIG intervention reported an improvement in their parenting self-efficacy. On average, post-VIG intervention TOPSE scores increased by over a sixth across the eight cases analysed, with the greatest impact in the TOPSE scores seen in 'empathy and understanding', and 'discipline and boundaries', and 'play and enjoyment' achieving the next highest score (Lowry *et al.* 2014).

Clare Lowry explains these findings with the following points:

• The principles of attuned interaction are a hierarchical set of behaviours (see Figure 10.4) and attitudes used to describe interaction between the client and child. It would seem that embedding basic skills (the first two steps in Figure 10.4), such as being attentive and encouraging the child's initiatives, leads to more attuned parent–child interaction, fostering cooperation rather than conflict.

• VIG develops parental confidence by focusing on strengths and, with increased confidence, they are more able to be consistent and calmer when needing to apply boundaries.

• The parents' reflective functioning increases through VIG, leading to clients having a better understanding of the child and the underlying reasons for particular behaviours (Lowry *et al.* 2014, p.15).

This spin-off from the VIG intervention makes sense. Although the parents were not taught behavioural management strategies, they discovered that, once they had restored a loving relationship with their child, they could effectively set limits. VIG moves between the encouragement of attuned interaction and attuned guidance (supportive limit-setting and teaching) in a flexible way.

Key learning points

We propose that the evidence set out in this chapter, and which is continuing to accumulate, shows that Video Interaction Guidance can rise to the challenge posed here, and that VIG is an effective intervention for noticing and helping neglected children. It is an easily understood method that can nevertheless be skilfully applied in complex families and systems. It can support the family in and beyond the child protection system and works from the basis of what the child needs and what the adults around the child have to do to start noticing, appreciating and nurturing the child.

Most importantly, VIG simultaneously notices, appreciates and nurtures the adults who have been missing their child's needs and signals. So often, parents who neglect their children were, and are still, neglected themselves. In our view, parents must feel valued by hopeful, helping professionals before they can start to engage in changing their neglectful behaviour. VIG carefully supports professionals to grow these attributes.

VIG appears to help parents and professionals to grow, or to re-grow, attuned interactions between the parent and child, encouraging a more loving, mutually pleasing and less neglectful relationship.

Questions for reflection

- What evidence is there here of VIG helping parents whose children are at risk of neglect? What other research would you like to see undertaken and why?

- How might a parent's increased attentiveness to their interaction with a child help to prevent neglect?

- How does the use of video contribute? Would you consider its use in working with parents and children? What are the pros and cons in your view?

References

Alink, L., Euser, S., Stoltenborgh, M., Bakermans-Kranenburg M.J. and Van Ijzendoorn, M.H. (2015) 'Are Interventions Effective in Preventing or Reducing Maltreatment? Meta-anlyses of Randomised Controlled Trials.' Conference presentation at SRCD Biennial Meeting, March, Philadelphia.

All Party Parliamentary Group for Conception to Age 2 (2015) *Building Great Britons.* Available at www.wavetrust.org/sites/default/files/reports/Building_Great_Britons_Report-APPG_Conception_to_Age_2-Wednesday_25th_February_2015. pdf, accessed on 29 October 2015.

Arnold, D.S., O'Leary, S.G., Wolff, L.S. and Acker, M.M. (1993) 'The parenting scale: A measure of dysfunctional parenting and discipline situations.' *Psychological Assessment 5*, 137–144.

Bakermans-Kranenburg, M.J., van Ijzendoorn, M.H. and Juffer, F. (2003) 'Less is more: Meta-analyses of sensitivity and attachment interventions in early childhood.' *Psychological Bulletin 129*, 2, 195–215.

Barlow, J. (2014) 'Why VIG?' Keynote address, VIG International Conference, Manchester, October 2014. Available at http://tinyurl.com/barlow2014, accessed on 29 October 2015.

Berluke, S.B., Cates, C.B., Dreyer, B.P., Huberman, H.S. *et al.* (2014) 'Reducing maternal depressive symptoms through promotion of parenting in pediatric primary care.' *Clinical Pediatrics 53*, 5, 460–469.

Braun, V. and Clarke, V. (2006) 'Using thematic analysis in psychology.' *Qualitative Research in Psychology 3*, 2, 77–101.

Cross, J. and Kennedy, H. (2011) *Video Interaction Guidance: Why does it work? In Video Interaction Guidance: A Relationship-based Intervention to Promote Attunement, Empathy and Well-being* (eds H. Kennedy, M. Landor and L. Todd). London: Jessica Kingsley Publishers.

Cyr, C., Paquette, D., Dubois-Comtois, K. and Lopez, L. (2015) 'An attachment-based intervention protocol for the assessment of parenting capacities in child welfare cases.' Presentation at SRCD Biennial Meeting, Philadelphia.

Doria, M., Kennedy, H., Strathie, C. and Strathie, S. (2014) 'Explanations for the success of video interaction guidance (VIG): an emerging method in family psychotherapy.' *Family Journal.*

Doria, M., Strathie, C. and Strathie, S. (2011) 'Supporting Vulnerable Families to Change.' In H. Kennedy, M. Landor and L. Todd (eds) *Video Interaction Guidance: A Relationship-based Intervention to Promote Attunement, Empathy and Well-being.* London: Jessica Kingsley Publishers.

Festinger, L. (1957). *A theory of cognitive dissonance.* Stanford, CA: Stanford University Press.

Fonagy, P., Gergely, G. and Target, M. (2007) 'The parent–infant dyad and the construction of the subjective self.' *Journal of Child Psychology and Psychiatry 48*, 3/4, 288–328.

Fredrickson, B. (2001) 'The role of positive emotions in positive psychology: the broaden-and-build theory of positive emotions.' *American Psychologist 56*, 3, 218–226.

Fukkink, R.G. (2008) 'Video feedback in the widescreen: a meta-analysis of family programs.' *Clinical Psychology Review 28*, 6, 904–916.

Fukkink, R., Kennedy, H. and Todd, L. (2011) 'Video Interaction Guidance: Does It Work?' In H. Kennedy, M. Landor and L. Todd (eds) *Video Interaction Guidance: A Relationship-based Intervention to Promote Attunement, Empathy and Well-being.* London: Jessica Kingsley Publishers.

Gerard, A.B. (1994) *Parent–Child Relationship Inventory (PCRI) Manual.* Los Angeles, CA: WPS.

Goodman, R. (1997) 'The Strengths and Difficulties Questionnaire: a research note.' *Journal of Child Psychology and Psychiatry 38,* 581–586.

Høivik, M., Lydersen, S., Drugli, M., Onsøien, R., Hansen, M. and Berg-Neilson, T. (2015) 'Video feedback compared to treatment as usual in families with parent–child interactions problems: a randomized controlled trial.' *Child and Adolescent Psychiatry and Mental Health 9,* 3.

Kendall, S. and Bloomfield, L. (2005) 'Developing and validating a tool to measure parenting self-efficacy.' *Journal of Advanced Nursing 51,* 2, 174–181.

Kennedy, H., Landor, M. and Todd, L. (eds) (2011) *Video Interaction Guidance: A Relationship-based Intervention to Promote Attunement, Empathy and Wellbeing.* London: Jessica Kingsley Publishers.

Kennedy, H., Landor, M. and Todd, L. (eds) (2015) *Video Enhanced Reflective Practice: Professional Development through Attuned Interactions.* London: Jessica Kingsley Publishers.

Lowry, C., O'Neill, K., Stephens, Z. and Auguarde, S. (2014) Video Interaction Guidance Service Cornwall, Interim Evaluation Report.

Macdonald, M. (2014) '"Like getting your wee boy back": Video Interaction Guidance and Child Neglect.' Doctoral dissertation, Queen's University Belfast.

Mendelsohn, A., Huberman, H.S., Berkule, S.B., Brockmeyer, C.A., Morrow, L.M. and Dreyer, B.P. (2011) 'Primary care strategies for promoting parent-child interactions and school readiness in at-risk families.' *Archives of Pediatric Adolescent Medicine 165,* 1, 33–41. DOI: 10.1001/archpediatrics

Moss, E., Dubois-Comtois, K., Cyr, C., Tarabulsy, G.M., St-Laurent, D. and Bernier, A. (2011) 'Efficacy of a home-visiting intervention aimed at improving maternal sensitivity, child attachment, and behavioral outcomes for maltreated children: A randomized control trial.' *Development and Psychopathology 23,* 195–210.

Moss E., Tarabulsy, G.M., St-Georges, R., Dubois-Comtois, K. *et al.* (2014) 'Video-feedback intervention with maltreating parents and their children: program implementation and case study.' *Attachment and Human Development 16,* 4, 329–342. DOI: 10.1080/14616734.2014.912486

NICE (2012) *NICE Guidelines: Social and Emotional Wellbeing.* Available at www.nice.org.uk/guidance/PH40, accessed on 29 October 2015.

NICE (2015) *NICE Guidelines: Children's attachment: attachment in children and young people who are adopted from care, in care or at high risk of going into care,* available at www.nice.org.uk/guidance/ng26, accessed 3 July 2016.

Public Health England (2015) *Rapid Review to Update Evidence for the Healthy Child Programme 0–5.* Available at www.gov.uk/government/publications/healthy-child-programme-rapid-review-to-update-evidence accessed on 29 October 2015.

Trevarthen, C. and Aitken, K.J. (2001) 'Infant intersubjectivity: research, theory, and clinical application.' *Journal of Child Psychology and Psychiatry 42,* 1, 3–48.

Whalley, P. and Williams, M. (2015) *Child Neglect and Video Interaction Guidance: An Evaluation of an NSPCC Service Offered to Parents Where Initial Concerns of Neglect Have Been Noted.* London: NSPCC. Available at www.nspcc.org.uk/globalassets/documents/research-reports/video-interactive-guidance-vig-evaluation-report.pdf, accessed on 8 June 2016.

Yagmur, S., Mesman, M., Malda, M., Bakermans-Kranenburg, M.J. and Ekmekci, H. (2014) 'Video-feedback intervention increases sensitive parenting in ethnic minority mothers: a randomized control trial.' *Attachment and Human Development 16,* 4, 371–386, DOI: 10.1080/14616734.2014.912489

CONCLUSION
The needs of parents
Ruth Gardner

In this concluding section, I propose that there are three sets of essential resources that parents need in order to bring up children successfully: physical or material resources; emotional or relational resources; and learning resources (see Figure 11.1 for examples of component elements of each of these). These are then explored in a discussion of themes from the book.

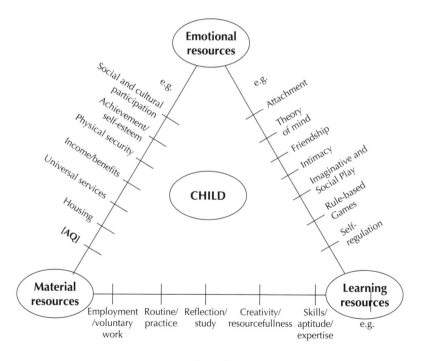

Figure 11.1 An outline of parenting resources

Most parents have sufficient resources to draw on with their family and network, to survive life-events and periods of family stress. If we consider these three sets of 'parenting assets' as, at least in part, interdependent, then if one set is depleted, there is pressure on the others to compensate. If all are depleted, the family faces massive stress and ultimately there is a risk that parents may abandon a child or children, whether physically or emotionally. This risk underlies concerns about serious child neglect.

In many cases, as we have seen in preceding chapters, these resources can be discovered and grown with skilful assistance, can reinforce one another and can divert or even reverse the accumulated damage of neglect. Depending on the level and the cause of depletion, some can be recovered over a relatively short timescale and others need much longer. Resiliency or vulnerability to child neglect can be considered in relation to the type and level of resources available to a particular family at a particular time, and also the degree of flexibility with which they can be deployed. Shonkoff and Garner (2012 p.236–7) set out evidence that the chronic stress associated with childhood neglect, if not addressed, can adversely affect a child's cognitive development and adaptability to new experiences.

Crittenden says (2015, p.243), 'many (though not all) deep seated problems will respond to 'good assessment, good formulation and good therapeutic relationships'; with the caveat that there is no 'silver bullet' and that 'sometimes the damage will take longer than the children can wait… possibly this is an opportunity for compassion' (p.246). De Panfilis (2006, quoted in Steib and Blome 2009) describes diverse activities to achieve a positive outcome with neglect; they include addressing concrete needs such as housing, child care and transportation; building trust and instilling hope; addressing social isolation and skills deficits; and providing (remedial) services to children. If these three sets of resources are essential to effective parenting then it makes strategic sense to look across outcomes in all three areas in order to achieve the greatest and the most lasting impact. We should be intent on improving the learning environment, as well as the emotional and physical environment, for whole families. Solutions that simply focus on a single area of investment, without considering its impact on the others, will only partially succeed. We now try to make schools both physically and emotionally supportive of learning for children; why do we not think of their home life, so crucial to learning outcomes, in the same way? Some of the interventions described in this book work in this way, usually (though not exclusively) with mothers and children, but a wider 'whole family', community based approach is needed to share resources.

Physical resources

Rostad et al. (Chapter 9) point out that 'families living in poverty are over 40 times more likely to be referred to the child welfare system than their higher income counterparts and income is, not surprisingly, the greatest predictor of child welfare entry'.

While no direct causal link has been established between poverty and maltreatment, poverty, like poor housing, heightens stress, which is in itself a risk factor, so that both the effects and causes of material deficits in individual families have to be addressed. Slack et al. (2004) compared parents in poverty who were reported for child neglect with those who were not reported, and found that neglect had stronger associations with unemployment, perceived financial status, stress, use of corporal punishment and emotional coldness, than it had with actual income. They concluded that aspects of parenting and poverty must be analysed together to understand interactions relating to child neglect. Hooper et al. (2007) undertook such a study. They concluded that poverty is an equalities issue and as such ways of addressing it should be required training for practitioners at all levels (including child protection) who work with families; that health, education and community services should all be regularly updated on how to help or obtain support for families in hardship; and they end with a call for more positive, directed efforts to 'counter stigma' and ensure the take-up of benefits and early intervention services for parents and their children. Physical resources include all public provision currently under huge pressure including safe communities, healthcare, housing and cultural and social activities.

Emotional resources

Discussing possible links between between poverty and maltreatment, Hooper et al. (2007) say that 'since living in poverty involves multiple threats to well-being and high levels of insecurity...attachment is also highly relevant to how people manage it'. As in the descriptions of practice in this book (Part 3), they say that families ascribed importance 'to support that is openly available and allows for a sense of reliability and trust, reflecting the attachment concept of a "secure base"'. The need for an honest yet trustworthy relationship (a metaphorical 'secure base') is also the primary message from young people in the research described by Gorin (Chapter 5). There is perhaps a lesson here about discovering what (who and where) makes children and parents feel secure before we start to add to their stress by asking them to make changes. As we have seen in earlier chapters (Chapters 1 and 9) parents who were themselves neglected often lack a sense of efficacy, making new learning a potentially stressful or even threatening experience.

Depending on whether they are supportive or negative, partners, family and social networks can either buffer or compound existing emotional insecurity in parents. These are powerful stressors when combined with ill health or a life crisis, and they may be one link between material hardship and child neglect, with neglect of a child being partly (like drugs or alcohol using other mechanisms) a last-resort way of switching off or avoiding demands that seem impossible to meet. The importance of partner relationships is often ignored in working with neglect, unless the partner is seen as another source of risk; we still know too little about attachment relationships and fatherhood, or the supportive and protective role that fathers or father-figures can play. As Crittenden (2015, p.36) says, 'men are such important members of families that, if they are overlooked, the services given to mothers may not take hold'. As we have seen in earlier chapters (Chapters 1 and 9) parents who were themselves neglected often lack a sense of efficacy, making new learning a potentially stressful or even threatening experience.

Bowlby, writing in 1953, asked, 'why do families fail?' and his first answer was 'neglect'. He quoted a review by practitioners who pointed to parents' (particularly mothers') poor mental and physical health as the main contributory factor. This was more important, they thought, than family income or size – except in so far as this affected health, or housing or the parents working arrangements. In some of the most difficult and chaotic situations, child neglect seemed related to parents' poor relationships, 'inability...to learn', and difficulties in engaging with help. Bowlby (p.94) recommended research into parents' early experiences, but noted that taking case histories was difficult because 'many had led unsettled lives...(and) appeared to have been either neglected or cruelly treated as children'.

The effects of adverse childhood experiences

Many studies of family support and protection services still find parents to have critical levels of past adversity and current stress, including serious and often lasting mental and health issues, often chronic yet not fully addressed (Aldgate and Tunstill 2000; Gardner 2005; Ghate and Hazel 2002; Hooper *et al.* 2007). Chapter 6 sheds light on these findings as we hear from general medical practitioners trying to maintain often fragile links with mothers suffering poor mental and physical health. Yet, as Woodman points out, health and social care or community-based services for children are often disconnected.

Bowlby drew attention to the crucial role of the child's primary carer and the interactive parent–child relationship in all areas of a child's healthy development, and described the damage caused by 'maternal deprivation'. Rutter (1973) challenged the limitations of this term and deconstructed it, identifying a number of mechanisms, such as privation, disruption and distortion of aspects of parental care, each of which has different effects. Crittenden (2015) more recently developed typologies of neglectful parenting, involving distorted representations of the child, for example parents who cannot consistently prioritise their child's signals and are 'marginally maltreating' them (perhaps throughout their childhood), through to parents whose own preoccupations take absolute precedence or who simply 'fail to recognise the child's need for protection and comfort' (ibid. p.171). Possible causes are their own poor care as children, drug use, mental ill health, trauma or violence. For the child 'in some cases, the psychological consequences of not being crucial in parents' lives (nor anyone else's) can become as extreme as forming the basis for suicidal thoughts and actions' (see Chapter 7) for a discussion of adolescent suicide and neglect).

Rutter (1979) went on to study the 'multiplication effect' of risks or adverse childhood experiences (ACEs) including maltreatment or neglect, and subsequently it has been found that 'past a certain number of risk factors...the outcomes worsen dramatically' (Jones *et al.* 2002; see also Chapter 4). There is now evidence that extreme stress (including maltreatment) has the potential to affect learning, decision-making and memory functions later in life (Shonkoff and Garner 2012) but it is also hypothesised that inherited adversities lead to poor outcomes in adulthood such as mental ill health and substance misuse, which in turn mean multiple service use. Spratt (2012) argues that (p.13) new types of assessment and intervention are needed, to help children in families facing multiple adversities, not reached by current service configurations.

If this is the way forward, clearly the quality and timeliness of assessment of neglect is crucial. In terms of earlier intervention and a public health approach to neglect, there is a very strong cost-effectiveness argument to be made for investing in high-quality, evidence-based assessment of child neglect. This is in order, first to bring families' own strengths and collaborative creativity to bear at the first opportunity; second, to identify and plan accurately for the help and resources individual family members need; third, to combine levels of support to whole families more effectively; and finally to measure progress and modify the approach accordingly. Too often the assessment of neglect is largely an administrative task, collecting large amounts of data but without any account of the child's experience or a purposeful analysis. The Office of Standards in Education, Children's Services and Skills (Ofsted 2014), inspecting children's services for neglect in England, found that some children are left in situations of neglect for too long (p.4) but that 'the use of evidence-based methodologies to address neglect was valued by professionals and was making a positive difference' (p.36). In complex cases, the assessment of child neglect is far from straightforward, and Crittenden (2015) gives detailed examples of assessment in these contexts.

If we are to combine light touch and therapeutic help we need a 'balanced' model of service delivery that combines different levels and numbers of services, depending on each family's unique set of needs (e.g. intensive help with substance misuse alongside light-touch parenting support) is most acceptable and efficient. Gascoigne (2015) writes that a sound commissioning model covers *all* relevant systems and sectors, that is, supporting families, communities and professional groups to address the issue. She sets out a 'Balanced System®' (p.33) and suggests that universal, targeted and specialist support to families should be deployed in as systematic and mutually reinforcing way as is possible; that overall, provision should be flexible enough to meet each individual child's needs promptly and effectively, in a planned and timely way; and that the quality of assessment is key to success. While this report relates to services supporting children's speech, language and communication, it is equally valid in relation to a wider spectrum of services for neglected children and their families.

Learning resources

There is now evidence that early stress, including neglect, can interfere with a child's learning capacity in many ways – socially and emotionally, as well as cognitively – and that a damaged parenting relationship can also affect a child's emotional development. As Crittenden writes (2015, p.184):

> The brain expects certain kinds of input and uses the input to stimulate further maturation. When that input is absent, the maturation fails to occur. In cases of child neglect, normal parental caregiving and protection fail to occur. When nothing the child does makes any difference, learning cannot occur.

Parents who have themselves experienced neglect or a lack of parent–child interactions, may struggle to explore and play with their own children and sometimes cannot believe that their child feels affection for them. We also know that this is not an inevitable outcome. If more attention is paid to research on adult learning preferences and styles we may be able to engage and retain their involvement in interventions, generating creativity and enjoyment in the process.

We have seen that a trusting yet honest relationship with the practitioner or therapist is a bridge to effective learning and change – the practitioner has to share the learning process. Crittenden points out that particularly vulnerable parents may require a 'transitional attachment figure' (2015, pp.281–2) and managing these relationships requires special training or support. However, all the interventions discussed in the book have examples of parents grasping opportunities for positive change. The methods of delivery should support the relationship, offer new insights and skills (practical, observational, behavioural) and also encourage other supports to flourish so that families can sustain the dialogue and the positive change. To end with the words of a parent: 'I've seen that I can get it right…and just keepin' that in my mind, you know – that yes, fair enough, I've had this help, but there's no reason I can't do this myself' (Chapter 10).

References

Bowlby, J. (1953) *Child Care and the Growth of Love.* London: Penguin Books.

Crittenden, P.M. (2015) *Raising Parents: Attachment, Repair and Treatment.* London and New York: Routledge.

DePanfilis, D. (2006) *Child Neglect: A Guide for Prevention, Assessment, and Intervention.* Washington, DC: US Department of Health and Human Services.

Gardner, R. (2005, 2003) *Supporting Families: Child Protection in the Community.* Chichester: Wiley.

Gascoigne, M.T. (2015) *Commissioning for Speech, Language and Communication needs (SLCN): Using the Evidence from the Better Communication Research Programme.* Harpenden: Better Communication.

Ghate, D. and Hazel, N. (2002) *Parenting in Poor Environments: Stress, Support and Coping.* London: Jessica Kingsley Publishers.

Hooper, C., Gorin, S., Cabral, C. and Dyson, C. (2007) *Living With Hardship 24/7: The Diverse Experiences of Families in Poverty in England.* London: The Frank Buttle Trust.

Jones, D., Forehand, R., Brody, G. and Arminstead, L. (2002) 'Psychosocial adjustment of African American children in single-mother families: a test of three risk models.' *Journal of Marriage and Family 64,* 105–115.

Ofsted (Office of Standards in Education, Children's Services and Skills) (2014) *In the Child's Time: Professional Responses to Neglect.* Manchester: Ofsted. Available at https://www.gov.uk/government/publications/professional-responses-to-neglect-in-the-childs-time, accessed 16 May 2016.

Rutter, M. (1973) *Maternal Deprivation Re-assessed.* Harmondsworth: Penguin Education.

Rutter, M. (1979) 'Protective Factors in Children's Response to Stress and Disadvantage.' In M.W. Kent and J.E. Rolf (eds) *Primary Prevention of Psychopathology Vol 3: Social Competence in Children.* Hanover, NH: University of New England Press.

Shonkoff, J.P. and Garner, A.S. (2012) 'The lifelong effects of early childhood adversity and stress.' *Paediatrics 129,* 1, 232–245. Available at http://pediatrics.aappublications.org/content/pediatrics/early/2011/12/21/peds.2011-2663.full.pdf, accessed 16 May 2016.

Slack, K.S., Holl, J.L., McDaniel, M., Yoo, J. and Bolger, K. (2004) 'Understanding the risks of child neglect: an exploration of poverty and parenting characteristics.' *Child Maltreatment 9,* 4, 395–408.

Spratt, T. (2012) 'Why multiples matter: reconceptualising the population referred to child and family social workers.' *British Journal of Social Work 42,* 8, 1574–1591.

Steib, S. and Blome, W.W. (2009) 'How can neglected organizations serve neglected children?' *Protecting Children 24,* 1, 9–19.

Tunstill, J. and Aldgate, J. (2000) *Services for Children in Need.* London: The Stationery Office.

SUBJECT INDEX

AUTHOR INDEX